The Workfc
of the
Royal Gunpowder Mills
1787 - 1841

Derek Armes

Sandra Taylor

ROYAL
GUNPOWDER
MILLS
Waltham Abbey

An Archive project of the Royal Gunpowder Mills

First Edition 2013

© Copyright 2013 Royal Gunpowder Mills

ISBN: 978-1492365822

Published by

Royal Gunpowder Mills
Beaulieu Drive, Waltham Abbey, Essex, EN9 1JY
Registered Charity No. 1062968
www.royalgunpowdermills.com

Cover Illustrations

Top: Watercolour (RGM Archive WAI-1248-01) by Peter Jackson based on the 1735 engraving of the Waltham Abbey Mills published by J. Farmer (RGM Archive WAI-0093-01).
Left side: The Waltham Uniform. (The Navy and Army Illustrated, article by Frederick G. Engelbach, 14 October 1899) (RGM Archive WAI -0102-06).
Right side top: The Turnhams at the Mills. (RGM Archive WAI-0321-01).
Right side bottom: Checking for Matches. (Strand Magazine, Volume 9, 1895) (RGM Archive WAI-0101-01).

The Workforce of the Royal Gunpowder Mills 1787 - 1841

By Derek Armes and Sandra Taylor

Edited by Sandra Taylor

"As when a spark lights up a heap of nitrous powder, laid
Fit for the tun, some magazine to store,
Against a rumoured war, the smutty grain
With sudden blaze diffused, inflames the air"
(John Milton, Paradise Lost)

This book documents the personnel employed at the Mills during the period from 1787 to 1841. Its production was initiated by Les Tucker, the Archivist at the Waltham Abbey Royal Gunpowder Mills, and is based on the considerable volume of Personnel Records held in the National Archives and documents within the Archive of the Waltham Abbey Royal Gunpowder Mills. The Waltham Abbey Historical Society generously provided numerous copies of the documents which were employed by the late Raymond Cassidy for his PhD study of the Poor of Waltham Abbey.

Table of Contents

Acknowledgements

Chip Bragg, U.S.A., for information on Frederick Wright in America. Richard Venn for his papers on Charles Wilks.

Mrs. Valerie Day of Nazeing, Dr. Ridpath, David Bishop, Sally Thorn, Sally Wilkes and Simon Malone.

D. F. Harding for information on treatise *A Memoir on Gunpowder* by John Braddock.

Peter Huggins for his publications on the Wright family and Waltham Abbey Gunpowder People.

Les Tucker for his proofreading and expert knowledge of the manufacturing process of Gunpowder.

The Waltham Abbey Historical Society for making available copies of their documents.

Ian MacFarlane for his layout and design.

The Royal Gunpowder Mills acknowledge the generosity of the Gunpowder and Explosives History Group in sponsoring this booklet. The group was established in 1985 as the Gunpowder Mills Study Group to investigate all aspects of the manufacture of gunpowder. Later its interests expanded to include more modern explosives. In 2009 it became an e-group and donated its remaining funds to furthering the study of the explosives industry through supporting publications by the Royal Gunpowder Mills, where many successful meetings had been held. Back issues of the group's newsletters may be found at:

http://www.royalgunpowdermills.com/history-and-heritage/gehg/

Foreword

The Royal Gunpowder Mills at Waltham Abbey form a major chapter in the history of explosives in England. They were among the earliest powder manufactories in the country, and continued existing as an explosives factory for some three hundred years.

The early history of the factory is obscure, most writers on the subject having drawn extensively on the first attempt at a comprehensive account of its origins and growth from William Winters' *Centenary Memorial* which was printed in 1887.

Winters was an interesting character. His father died when he was young, and his widowed mother, Mary Ann, subsequently married William Perry in 1839. Perry worked on the land before he was employed at the Gunpowder Mills. Winters became a bookseller, and was the Pastor at the Ebenezer Particular Baptist Chapel, as well as being an author of a number of books on local and religious subjects. His work on the early history of the Mills, however, needs to be treated with caution because his transcription of the original documents was sometimes inaccurate. Nevertheless, he had access to the Ordnance Board's documentation from 1787 onwards, following its purchase of the Mills from Mr. John Walton, and the authors have made extensive use of his research within this publication.

Besides factual information on the Mills' operations, Winters included details of the working conditions and treatment of the workforce with the manufactory. He made it clear that the Board of Ordnance was a progressive employer, appreciating that the Mills were a dangerous workplace by providing suitable clothing and footwear for the employees in order to reduce the risk of explosions. Safe working practices were also introduced and enforced to further reduce the number of explosions.

Furthermore, medical facilities were provided for both the workforce and their families. In the event of a fatality during the production of gunpowder, the widow received a pension for life unless she remarried, and an allowance was also given for her children until they were of working age. Numerous examples of the safety and welfare measures instigated by the Board at the Mills are contained within the notes of some 950 people listed in this publication. Many of these employees started work at the Mills as 10 or 11-year-old Apprentices, and continued to work there well into their seventies.

It is clear that the Royal Gunpowder Mills at Waltham Abbey constituted an institution which cared for its employees and probably held a unique place in the memories of those who worked there.

Derek Armes

Introduction

A Brief History of the Workforce

His Majesty's Government purchased the Powder Mills and premises at Waltham Abbey and Barking Creek from John Walton for some £13,628. The Mills at Waltham Abbey consisted of three powder mills, "wrought by three wheels", a dwelling house and outbuildings and several outhouse and buildings associated with the manufacture of gunpowder. Various members of the Walton family had been manufacturing gunpowder there since the early 1700s.

The Board of Ordnance clearly anticipated that the transfer of the Powder Mills would be completed by the end of September 1787, since Major William Congreve of the Artillery and the Deputy Comptroller of the Royal Laboratory at Woolwich, wrote to David Cornish at Waltham Abbey as follows:

"I am directed by his Grace the Duke of Richmond to desire you will immediately hire the best of the millmen and labourers who lately worked at Mr. Walton's Powder Mills. They will be paid nine shillings per week for a month certain, and for every week they may be continued in these Powder Mills if they should be purchased by the Government; and they will be allowed every advantage that has been hitherto given to the millmen and labourers who work in the Royal Powder Mills at Faversham.

(Signed) W. Congreve, Major of Artillery, Waltham Abbey, 21st September, 1787.

Mr. Cornish, you will be paid fifteen shillings a week from the date hereof for one month certain.

(Signed) W. Congreve"

A comment by Winters on page 116 of his book *Centenary of the Royal Gunpowder Mills at Waltham Abbey*, noted that New Mill was "ready to begin working on gunpowder, 17th Oct., 1787, the time of taking possession", which confirms the Board's expectations of the completion date.

Cornish appeared to have a good knowledge of the local labour pool, for a Return for October 1787 showed that he had recruited twelve artificers such as Millwrights and Carpenters, as well as 31 Labourers and an acting Overseer. The descendents of some of the men engaged by Cornish such as the Guinns, the Palletts and the Turnhams, etc., were working at the Mills in 1841. It was apparent that the Mills and their surrounds had been neglected, since on the 7th November 1787, J. Bullock, the Acting Overseer, recorded, "Four Labourers employed for several nights to pump water out of the ditches leading from the Powder Mills. Unless this service is performed, the men will be obliged to stop working for several hours in the day." The repairs and renovations continued throughout November, and Major Congreve visited Waltham Abbey to select men to send to the Royal Gunpowder Mills at Faversham, where they were to learn how to make "powder for the service at Waltham Abbey", presumably in accordance with the Ordnance Board's current practice. James Wright from the Faversham Mills was appointed as the Storekeeper at Waltham Abbey on the 6th November 1787, and soon after his appointment, three other men were transferred from Faversham to Waltham, including John Goodfellow as the Master Mixer.

The manufacture of gunpowder was a dangerous occupation, and the Board's practice was to retain the services of a local surgeon, and Waltham Surgeon, W. Marchant, was appointed to this position in 1787. Sometime later, Artificers and Labourers paid the Surgeon sixpence per month for medicines and treatment for themselves and their families.

Extensive alterations and repairs continued, and in December 1787, new facilities such as a Mixing House and Saltpetre Mills were ordered, new Gloom Stoves (for drying gunpowder) were being cast by Packetts & Co., and in January 1788, two fire-engines similar to those kept at the Royal Laboratory, were delivered to Waltham Abbey. By the 10th February 1788, six Mills had been commissioned, but the initial optimism regarding the start of regular production proved flawed, since it was found that the available water supply would not be adequate to power the expanded production facilities. In order to rectify this, on Congreve's recommendation the Board purchased the Cheshunt and Waltham Abbey Mills' water only (the Board did not purchase Waltham Abbey Corn Mill buildings until June 1809) and regular production commenced on the 9th February 1789. By the end of 1789, approximately £5,663 had been spent on the new facilities, renovations, security fencing and improving waterways and ditches, and by the turn of the century some £35000 had been spent – approximately two and a half times the original purchase price.

With the onset of the Anglo-French wars in 1793, on the 27th December, Sunday working was introduced at the Mills, and at the same time, Major Congreve, the driving force behind the modernisation of the Mills, was ordered to Flanders to command a force of Artillery. By 1801 the Royal Engineers were responsible for all building maintenance works within the manufactory. They were based within a compound in Powder Mill Lane with their own Establishment of civilian labour which was supplemented as required with casual labour.

The workforce at the Mills expanded during the Anglo-French wars, peaking in 1812 along with wages, which included a "cost of living allowance" granted in August of that year. With the defeat of Napoleon at the Battle of Waterloo in 1815 and a reduced requirement for gunpowder, the workforce and wages were cut in 1816, and again in 1818 and 1820. Wherever possible, the Storekeeper recommended that the long-service employees were discharged with a pension on the grounds of ill-health and injuries received in, "this dangerous manufactory"; long service alone was not a qualification under a directive issued by the Board on the 2nd April 1816, but the Storekeeper's recommendations were generally accepted. Wages were also reduced by a directive issued by the Board on the 19th April 1816 which read, "Considerable reduction has been made in the prices of the Necessaries of Life, that the advance of Six-pence per Day authorised by His Lordship's and the Board's Order of the 10th August 1812 be discontinued."

In May 1816, the Board had approved the reworking or regenerating of gunpowder which had been brought back from the battle fields or from warships returning from long tours, and a considerable quantity was regenerated in the 1820's as opposed to the manufacture of new gunpowder. This trend continued throughout the 1830's; the workforce remained static, although manufacture and regeneration fluctuated, as can be seen by the statistics included on the following page.

The Engineers' Department remained in Powder Mill Lane maintaining the Royal Gunpowder Mills as well as the Royal Ordnance Small Arms Manufactory at Enfield.

Labour and Production Statistics

The following table shows the number of Artificers and Labourers employed at the Mills, together with the amount of powder manufactured or regenerated in selected years.

Year	Number Employed in the Mills	Number Employed in the Engineers Dept	Barrels Manufactured	Barrels Regenerated
1787	48			
1790	67		5410 +	
Jul 1795	92			
May 1801	104			
Jun 1807	205			
Jun 1810	222		18484	
Aug 1812	279	68	21033	
1816		36	3918 ++	
Jun 1818	105	32	1127	
Sep 1820	82	31	1007	
Apr 1823	49	29	208	1589
Apr 1826	47	32	519	3055
Apr 1830	47	32	2070	1988
Oct 1834	48	-	1077	254
+ Half year January to June ++ January to March				

Glossary of Trades

Barrel Markers - These men used stencils to mark the end of the barrels, listing the quantity in the barrel, giving the place of manufacture, description of the powder, date of stoving, number of barrels in the stoving, number of the barrel, number of the lot and the tare of the barrel.

Charcoal and Brimstone Millmen - As the names imply, Charcoal and Brimstone Millmen ground the raw materials used to make gunpowder to the correct consistency required before they were mixed together. Saltpetre was ground until c.1860.

Clerk of the Cheque - This man was responsible for the general administration and discipline within the manufactory; he was the equivalent of the adjutant in an army regiment.

Collar Maker - Horses were used to power some of the mills and their collars were made and maintained by the Collar Maker, even though the horses were owned by a contractor.

Coopers - The Coopers made the wooden barrels which held 100lb of gunpowder. In 1825 Coopers were making cement casks for gunpowder and were used to take the gunpowder to Harwich. For some reasons unknown, Coopers were not allowed to 'watch'.

Coppersmiths - In order to prevent sparks, fittings and fixtures, etc. were made of copper wherever practical and maintained by a Coppersmith employed by the Manufactory. Other trades, such as the Millwrights – who maintained the millstones – were employed by the Engineers' Department.

Corning Men - Corning House Men transformed the press cake into grains of gunpowder. Corning or granulating produced uniform grains in a range of sizes essential for controlled operation and predictability of firing.

Cylindermen - Prior to 1795, the Clerk of the Cheque spent much time scouring Essex for suitable supplies of Alder wood, said to be the best for making charcoal, although Black Birch and Poplar were also used. Up to 1795 there are numerous references to Labourers from the Mills spending the summer months in the country cutting and bagging Alder wood for "charring" or "charring wood". Charring was the term used for manufacturing charcoal, although no evidence was found to show that this process was carried out at the Waltham Abbey Manufactory until 1831. In 1795 the Comptroller decreed that charcoal for Waltham was to be produced at Fernhurst and Fisher Street in West Sussex, using the new slip cylinder method which was being installed there. James Wright, the Waltham Abbey Storekeeper, was directed by Major Congreve to supervise painstaking experiments and field trials in the charcoal production, which eventually wore him out. In the meantime, the Clerk of the Cheque, Robert Coleman, spent a considerable amount of his time scouring the adjacent counties for charcoal wood and travelling to Sussex to ensure that the cylinders were producing charcoal to the required specification (Winters, *op.cit.* p.48). The men who worked the cylinders were known as Cylindermen. Charcoal was shipped from West Sussex to Waltham Abbey by barges which, presumably, returned to West Sussex with loads of charring wood. The Board sold Fernhurst (WO44/481a) although charcoal was still produced at Fisher Street until c.1831. Four men employed at Faversham were transferred in July 1831 to Waltham Abbey to work the new slip cylinders recently established there.

Dusting or Reeling House Men - These men removed the dust particles from the grains in dusting reels, the action of dusting removing grain imperfections, corners and protrusions, which would form further dust. The process also created a spherical shape which gave the best performance. Dust removal also reduced the absorption of moisture, which improved transportation and storage qualities.

Glazing Men - Operated glazing barrels in which grains were tumbled. In the case of larger grains, graphite was added. Glazing imparted a hard finish which improved performance, increased robustness, lessened moisture absorption and slightly retarded ignition, thereby avoiding damage to the gun.

Hoop Maker or Hoop Bender - These were men who made the copper rings the Cooper fixed round the outside of the wooden barrels filled with gunpowder.

Incorporating Millmen - These men were employed to grind the charge under edge runners in the incorporating mills to obtain the closest mix possible into a more even form to produce "mill cake". Mill cake was then pressed by manually operated screw presses to form "press cake" prior to the next operation, "corning". The majority of the major accidents within the mills occurred during this operation. One of the reasons for this was that the amount of mix milled at any one time was 40lb, but it appears that the Millmen often exceeded this weight and numerous explosions followed. Even when the official quantity was reduced to 38lb, explosions occurred at regular intervals.

Magazine Foreman - He was responsible for the storage of the gunpowder barrels within the magazines which were surrounded by traverses.

Master Worker - The Master Worker was in charge of the labour force within the manufactory. Normally, this man would have held a senior foreman's position such as the Master Mixer, before being promoted to the position of Master Worker

Mixing House Men - Working under the Mixing House Foreman, these men weighed and mixed the basic ingredients together in standard proportions to form what was known as a "green charge".

Office Keeper - This man was the general factotum and messenger to the clerical staff.

Proof House Man - This man was the quality controller at the Mills who carried out tests to ensure that the gunpowder met the standard tests laid down by the Comptroller at Woolwich. The principal test was that a standard shot, fired from an eight-inch mortar using a two or four ounce charge, had to reach a set distance.

Puntmen - In reality, these were boatmen. All gunpowder, etc. was transported within the Mills by small, purpose-built boats.

Refiners - Gunpowder was made from three main ingredients, i.e., saltpetre, brimstone (sulphur) and charcoal. Labourers refined the first two constituents in the Refineries located in West or High Bridge Street and at the northern end of Lower Island respectively.

Rounders - These men were generally foremen or assistant foremen who checked that the watchmen were at their posts and performing their duties correctly at night. Generally, they were on duty every third night, for which they received 1/6d. Before the watch was set, the Rounder was given a form by the Master Worker which read, "Sir, I visited each station twice during the night at uncertain hours, viz. between ....and....o'clock, and found the watchmen doing their duty and everything regular. I also visited the steam stove at ....o'clock, and found all correct. I visited the Incorporating Mills and found the Millmen doing their duty. No.1 Watch:- Patrolled from Payne's (Pain's) Island to the Long Walk Gate: No. 2 Watch:- Patrolled from Long Walk Gate to end of Powder Mill Lane; No. 3 Watch:- Patrolled the Refinery, Town Mead, Storehouse Yard and Lower Island to the end of Powder Mill Lane. The Superintendent, Royal Gunpowder Factory, etc. (Signed)... Rounder"

Sieve Puncher - This man's job entailed punching holes in copper sheets to form sieves for the Corning Houses. The occupant of this position often acted as the Proof House Man.

Storekeeper - The modern equivalent of this position would be the Chief Executive of a Company. At the Royal Gunpowder Mills, the Storekeeper's main responsibility was to implement the general directions issued by the Comptroller of the Royal Laboratory based at Woolwich. This position was eventually replaced by a military man who was known as the Superintendent, with the Storekeeper becoming his deputy.

Storemen - As opposed to the Storekeeper, these men worked in the Stores.

Stovemen - The final moisture was removed from the gunpowder by 'stoving' or drying in rooms heated by gloom stoves. This took place within a building consisting of two rooms, one with drying racks and trays, and the other with a fire transmitting radiant heat to the drying room via a cast iron fireback (gloom). There were two gloom stoves, one at the northern end of Horse Mill Island and the second at the northern end of Little Hoppit; this was obviously a dangerous operation since both were protected by traverse or protective banks. In July 1795 the

Comptroller, Major Congreve, gave directions for a new steam stove of the type recently designed and built by James Watt, to be installed at Waltham Abbey, and trials were undertaken to determine if it was suitable for drying the powder. The experiment was a success since the steam stove - located at Edmonsey Mead - was shown on Drayson's and subsequent maps and a new trade of **Steam Stovemen** appeared in the records. All Stovemen were paid an extra 1/-d per night when on duty.

Watchmen - The majority of the labour force at the manufactory was allowed to "watch in turn" which, on average was every fifth night, for which they were usually paid 1/-d. Two separate watches were set each night, one at Pain's Island in Edmonsey, and a second within the Saltpetre Refinery in High Bridge Street. A third operated on a Sunday night at the Grand Watch Tower. Each watch was divided into three shifts of approximately three hours; each watch had to strike the bells on his beat every hour during his watch. Beds were provided in the watch houses, as were sheets, fuel, oil lamps, tinder boxes and brimstone matches. The "watch" practice ceased in 1860 when it was undertaken by the Ordnance Police.

Warders - These men acted as gatekeepers or porters and usually lived in Ordnance-owned lodges at the entrance to the manufactory, or outlying facilities, such as the Refinery.

The Workforce

A

George Abraham worked as a casual Labourer in the Engineers' Department during September 1812, and was paid 2/8d per day for a six-day week (WO54/512).

George Adams (1) was born circa 1778/1780. He trained as a Brazier before starting work as a Labourer in the Corning House on the 1st September 1804 (Supply 5/232). In January 1806, he was working as a Puntman earning 2/-d per day (Supply 5/224). He continued to work on the punts with the same pay until 1810, but was then allowed to watch in turn (Supply 5/227). In 1810 he became a Millman with his pay increased to a daily rate of 2/3d, and an additional 1/6d per night if it was his turn to watch (Supply 5/228). He continued to work as a Millman with his wage increased to 3/-d per day and an extra 6d if he had to work a night shift (Supply 5/230). The end of the Napoleonic wars saw a reduction in the manufacture and regeneration of gunpowder, and as a consequence, the workforce and their wages were reduced. However, a List of Employees to be retained at the Mills between the 3rd September and the 31st December 1818 included George Adams (Supply 5/231 dated the 28th August 1818).

An Order of the Board dated the 4th September 1818, verified George was to be retained as a Brimstone Refiner with his pay reduced to 2/4d daily (Supply 5/232) but he was still allowed to watch in turn, although he now only received 1/-d each time (Supply 5/231). He continued to refine Brimstone, with his position confirmed by a second Board Order dated the 4th October 1819 (Supply 5/232) but by the 13th September 1820, he was refining Saltpetre with similar pay and conditions (Supply 5/232). He was still a Refiner in February 1822, when his total annual income including allowances amounted to £41.14.4d (Supply 5/232). The same document recorded that he was a 41-year-old married man with 3 children, living in Waltham Abbey.

In the spring of 1822, the Ordnance Board reduced the production and regeneration of gunpowder still further and the Establishment was cut again. Empsom Middleton and James Wright drew up a list of people who were to leave (Supply 5/232 dated the 21st March 1822) and the men were subsequently dismissed on the 1st June. This time, George Adams was on the list. Several requests were submitted by the men asking for financial assistance; many were long-service employees in their middle-age and they pointed out they had little hope of finding employment once the corn harvest had been gathered. The Storekeeper was sympathetic and forwarded their petitions to the Board for consideration. George was one of four men who signed a second petition (with a cross) on the 12th July 1822, saying that he had been away looking for work – unsuccessfully. He was consequently awarded two weeks' pay to ease his financial burden. The 1841 Census showed that he and his wife, Phoebe, both born in Essex, were living in Green Yard, and that he was then working as a Labourer.

George Adams (2) commenced work as a temporary Labourer in the Engineers' Department in June 1825. He was a married man with 4 children and was paid 2/2d per day, but was due to be discharged at the end of October 1825 (WO54/550).

John Adams (1) was employed as a Saltpetre Refiner in 1804, with pay of 2/-d per day. All Refiners received an additional allowance of 1/-d per night when it was their turn to watch, which, on average, was every fifth night (Supply 5/222). His name did not appear in the records again until 1812, so it is assumed that he had, perhaps, left the Ordnance Board's employment, returning by August of 1812 as a Collar Maker (horse collars). He earned 3/6d a day, with an additional 2/-d when he was allowed to watch - every third night (Supply 5/229). He continued to work on the same pay and allowances until at least February 1814, according to Supply 5/230.

John Adams (2) started work as a General Labourer on the 1st December 1837 and was paid £39.0.0d per annum, which included an allowance to watch in turn (WO54/632). He was born circa 1813, and the 1841 Census recorded that he was still a Labourer who lived in Romeland with his wife Sarah, who was possibly the daughter of Benjamin Guinn (see entry for Benjamin Guinn (1) – Supply 5/238 dated September 1840).

Richard Adams received £10 for meritorious conduct on the 13th April 1843 when some 40 barrels of gunpowder exploded in the Corning House, together with another 20 in the Press House. Seven men were killed and much damage was done to the town (Winters' *Centenary Memorial*, p.107).

Robert Adams was born circa 1781, and spent most of his working life as a Labourer with the Engineers' Department, commencing on the 21st May 1804 (WO54/542). The early records relating to the Engineers' Department are sparse, but in February 1816 (WO54/512) it was recorded that he was employed as a casual Labourer at 2/8d per day; he was then a 34-year-old married man living in Waltham Abbey with 3 children.

By February 1817, his daily pay had been reduced to 2/1d (WO54/520) and according to this Return, he had 4 children. He worked "occasionally as required" in 1818, and was then paid 2/4d daily (WO54/527). Robert, together with others in the Engineers' Department, suffered another pay cut in 1823, reducing his income to 2/2d per day. This equated to £33.18.2d annually, on which he then had to provide for 5 children (WO54/542). A Return of Persons belonging to the Civil

Establishment of the Ordnance and Small Arms Manufactories at Waltham Abbey, Faversham and Enfield, recorded that Robert was one of 15 Labourers to be employed at Waltham Abbey Gunpowder Mills and Enfield Small Arms Factory. He was still paid 2/2d per day and engaged to undertake different services as a Labourer in the Manufactories where "steadiness and sobriety are particularly required" (WO54/575). He was still a Labourer in April 1839 on the same rate of pay, according to WO54/623 dated the 1st April that year. The 1841 Census stated that he was a widower living in Green Yard, Waltham Abbey, with Thomas Parker and his family. At that time he was still working as a Labourer, and was born in the County.

William Adams (1) was a Master Carpenter set to work by Daniel Cornish in October 1787, renovating the Mills following their purchase from Mr Walton by the Government (Winters, *op.cit.* p.28).

William Adams (2) was born circa 1789, and commenced work as a Labourer on the 26th March 1805 (WO54/632). After some 6 months' service he was employed as a Puntman earning 2/-d per day (Supply 5/224). By June 1807 he had changed his occupation again, and was employed in the Corning House at 2/2d daily as well as being allowed to watch in turn (Supply 5/226). By August 1812, he was working as a Bargeman (Supply 5/229) and in 1814, his wages peaked at 3/10d per day (Supply 5/230). A Return for May 1818, recorded that he was a single man living in Waltham Abbey (Supply 5/231).

In 1818 it was proposed to reduce the numbers on the Establishment, and a list drawn up on the 28th August showed that William was to be retained as a Saltpetre Refiner between the 3rd September and 31st December 1818 at 2/11d per day (Supply 5/231). However, a few days later, a letter from Waltham Abbey to the Board stated, "We respectfully beg leave to add to the names and stations of those persons it will be necessary to discharge in consequence of this arrangement" (reduction of the workforce) and William Adams, "Bargeman" was then to be discharged (Supply 5/231). Nevertheless, he was retained by an Order of the Board dated the 4th September 1818, and was appointed a Saltpetre Refiner at a daily rate of 2/4d. He was also allowed to watch in turn, for which he received 1/-d per night. The Board confirmed his appointment on the 4th October 1819, and his annual earnings, including his watch allowance, amounted to £41.15.4d (Supply 5/232).

A List of Employees dated the 13th September 1820 recorded that William was then a 31-year-old married man living in Waltham Abbey (Supply 5/232) and that by the end of December 1821 (Supply 5/232) he had one child. The workforce was reduced again in March 1822, but William retained his position as a Refiner. According to Supply 5/233, in October 1822 he had 3 children.

Wages continued to be reduced, and in 1825 William's total annual remuneration was £39.0.0d (WO54/550). His pay remained the same until 1827, when he became a Corning House Man with a basic income of £42.18.0d per annum, and since he was still allowed to watch, his total annual remuneration was £48.2.0d (WO54/558). This document confirmed that he had 3 children. On the 6th April 1829, Benjamin Guinn moved from his cottage in the old Tanyard on the south side of High Bridge Street, to a tenement on the opposite side of the road (Supply 5/237), and from a List of Properties dated the 28th May 1840 (WO54/133) it seems probable that Guinn's old home was then occupied by William. The property in question was Plot No. 52 on the Town Map in Appendix 1. On the 22nd September 1837, he was promoted to Second Foreman of the Corning House and made a Rounder, with his pay and allowances increased to £59.2.8d per annum (WO54/632). The 1841 Census stated that

William and his wife, Mary, lived on the south side of High Bridge Street with 6 children, Richard (15) Samuel (12) Mary (8) William (6) Sarah (5) and Ruth (3).

On the 13th April 1843 there was a huge explosion in the Corning House, details of which are recorded in the notes of Richard Adams, who was possibly William's son. William was awarded £5 for his meritorious conduct that day (Winters, *op.cit.* p.106). Among the people killed was Thomas Sadd, the Master Worker, and on the 13th August that year, it was recommended that William Adams should be put into Sadd's place, and his appointment in that capacity took effect on the 11th October 1843 (Winters, *op.cit.* p.107). William died on the 9th March 1855 (Winters, *op.cit.* p.111).

William Adams (3) was born circa 1770, and was first employed as a casual Labourer within the Engineers' Department on the 27th March 1806 (WO54/520). Between the 15th and 21st July 1809 he worked in the Manufactory, for which he was paid 17/-d (Supply 5/228).

He was still employed as a casual Labourer in February 1816, paid 2/8d per day for a six-day week (WO54/512) and the same document revealed that he was a 46-year-old married man with 6 children, living in Waltham Abbey. He was still working in the Engineers' Department on the 28th February 1817, but by then his pay had been reduced to 2/4d daily. It would appear that William (3) left the Gunpowder Mills shortly after this date, since there are no further entries in the records.

William Akers worked as a Saltpetre Refiner in August 1812 (Supply 5/229) to February 1814 (Supply 5/230), after which there are no further entries. During this period he was paid 2/8d per day, and in addition, Saltpetre Refiners "when not working extra were allowed to watch in turn", for which they received 1/-d.

William Alexander was employed on the 21st May 1815 as a casual Labourer within the Engineers' Department, and was paid 2/8d per day. In February 1816, he was a 37-year-old bachelor living in Waltham Abbey (WO54/512). There are no further entries for this man after that date.

Francis Bell Allison was a 26-year-old bachelor when he started work on the 1st December 1837 as a General Labourer at the Mills. His annual remuneration, including an allowance to watch in turn, was £39.0.0d (WO54/632).

Daniel Allsup Snr. was the son of William and Mary Allsup, and was baptised at Waltham Abbey on the 2nd July 1760 (Huggins, *Waltham Abbey Gunpowder People,* p.134). He was the first of the Allsup family to work at the Royal Powder Mills, and in addition, three of his four sons followed in his footsteps for short spells.

Daniel started work as a Dusting House Man in 1805 earning 2/1d per day (Supply 5/224). He continued to work in the Dusting House, and by 1807, was allowed an extra 1/-d to watch in turn (Supply 5/226). In 1808 his daily rate of pay had increased to 2/3d (Supply 5/227). Further pay increases followed, and by August 1812 he earned 3/-d daily, with his watch money raised to 1/6d per night (Supply 5/229). He was still employed by the Board in 1814 (Supply 5/230) but by 1817 his name had disappeared from the Establishment Lists. On the 16th June 1808 the Board purchased two tenements from a Miss Jones on the north side of High Bridge Street, and the sketch map attached to the document clearly shows that they formed part of High Bank or Bank Cottages. The two tenants then in occupation were "Alsop and Aylin" (WO44/681a).

A Statement dated the 4th April 1822 of "monies to which the public are entitled to receive credit" recorded that Daniel had been living in a house later purchased by the Board of Ordnance, and that under an Order dated the 4th May 1821, the property had been leased to Daniel for an annual rent of £8.9.0d (Supply 5/232). The same information is given on a similar Return made the following year. The tenement has been identified as that at the western end of 5 cottages known as Bank Cottages, on the north side of High Bridge Street, shown as Plot No. 48 on the Town Map in Appendix 1. A Return of Domestic Properties dated the 28th May 1840 (WO44/133) recorded that sometime prior to that date, the property had been occupied by "D Alsup labr, discharged" and that it was "now occupied by T Baldock", which confirmed that Daniel was living in the cottage when the Board purchased it. Daniel died in December 1840 at the age of 80, and was buried at Waltham Abbey on the 3rd January 1841 (Huggins, *op.cit.* p.134) .

The 1841 Census showed that Susanna, his wife, had moved to the opposite side of High Bridge Street, and was looking after 2 of her grandsons. She died at the age of 77, and on the 16th April 1848, was also buried at Waltham (Huggins, *op.cit.* p.134).

Daniel Allsup, Jnr. was the eldest son of Daniel and Susanna, and was baptised at Waltham Abbey on the 9th February 1794. He married Ann, and they had 3 children, James, Sophia and William, all of whom were baptised at Waltham Abbey (Huggins, *op.cit.* p.134). Daniel was working as a Saltpetre Refiner in August 1812 (Supply 5/229) through to at least February 1814 (Supply 5/230). During this period he was paid 2/8d per day, and, in addition, Saltpetre Refiners when not working extra were allowed to watch in turn, for which they received 1/-d. He had left the Ordnance by 1817, and the 1841 Census showed that Daniel was then working as a Calico Printer and was living in Romeland with his family.

James Allsup was the brother of Daniel Allsup, Snr. and a Postmaster. Although he never worked at the Royal Gunpowder Mills, he leased property from the Ordnance Board in High Bridge Street for £10.8.0d annually, from which he ran the town's Post Office. This was the eastern part of Plot 49, shown on the Town Map in Appendix 1. For further information on the Allsup family see Huggins, *op. cit.* pp.132-140.

Samuel Allsup was the fourth and youngest son of Daniel and Susanna, and was baptised at Waltham Abbey on the 20th March 1803 (Huggins, *op.cit.* p.134). He joined the Engineers' Department as a Labourer on the 16th August 1823 (WO54/550). In April 1825 he was a 22-year-old bachelor living in Waltham Abbey earning 2/2d per day, which gave him an annual income of £33.18.2d (WO54/550). The last record for Samuel is dated the 1st April 1828 (WO54/562) and confirmed he was receiving the same pay as before. He married Ann, and their 2 children, Samuel and Mary, were baptised at Waltham Abbey on the 14th October 1838 (Huggins, *op.cit.* p.134).

William Allsup was the second son of Daniel and Susanna, and was baptised at Waltham Abbey on the 19th February 1797 (Huggins, *op.cit.* p.134). He began an Apprenticeship of seven years at the Powder Mills on the 26th March 1808 under the Master Mixer of Composition, George Pittendrigh (Supply 5/232). His remuneration was 6/-d per week, with his Master receiving the same sum (Supply 5/227). A document dated the 30th September 1808 (Supply 5/220) indicated that he was illiterate. During his seven-year Apprenticeship his pay rose steadily to 6/8d per week by February 1814, while Pittendrigh's allowance for teaching him the different aspects of making gunpowder was then 8/-d per week (Supply 5/230). With his Apprenticeship completed, William started work as a casual Labourer in the Engineers' Department on the 4th August 1815, and was still labouring in February 1816 for 2/8d per day

(WO51/512). The same document recorded that he was an 18-year-old bachelor living in Waltham Abbey.

Together with another Apprentice, Robert Perkis, William was one of the casualties of the reduction in the workforce in 1818. They petitioned the Board stating that they were Articled Apprentices who paid three pounds when first Articled, and that they had served seven years, continuing two years after the term of Apprenticeship had expired, after which they were discharged upon the reduction. Having gone into the Works at an early age, they were now unable to earn a livelihood in any other employment. They further stated that they had "…made themselves proficient in their several Departments" and hoped that "…their Lordships would take into their benign consideration their disagreeable case, and replace them again into their former situation in the Works, in which case your humble Petitioners will as in duty bound to you for ever pray" (Supply 5/231).

The Board required more information from the Storekeeper at Waltham Abbey but he appeared to have been unsympathetic to their plea, giving preference to family men employed at the Mills. In a letter to the Board dated the 7th April 1818 (also Supply 5/231) the Storekeeper replied "In obedience to the Honourable Board's commands contained in your letter of the 1st instant desiring us to report upon the enclosed Petition of Robert Perkis and William Allsup praying that they may be restored to their situations in the Royal Powder Mills, having served their Apprenticeship in the Department from which they were discharged on account of the reduction. We beg leave respectfully to represent that Robert Perkis and William Allsup were taken as Apprentices, the one as Apprentice to the Assistant Master Worker, the other as Apprentice to the Master of Composition, [and] after serving their Apprenticeship they were employed as Labourers in the Manufactory." Further, "In forming an arrangement to comply with the Honourable Board's commands of the 22nd December last that a reduction should take place at the Royal Gunpowder Manufactory at Waltham abbey, the beforementioned Robert Perkis and William Allsup were selected, amongst others, as junior labourers to be discharged, for if a preference had to be given to them to be retained, other Labourers with families who had been longer in the service than themselves who are single young men [would feel the same]. We are therefore humbly of opinion that they do not have cause for complaint." Nevertheless, in a letter dated the 10th April 1818 (Supply 5/202) the Board ordered that the two should be "re-entered when any augmentation be required."

Shortly after this, William was reinstated as a Saltpetre Refiner by an Order of the Board dated the 4th September 1818, which was confirmed by a second Board Order on the 4th October 1819 (Supply 5/232). He was paid 2/4d per day with an additional 1/6d when it was his turn to watch. In September 1820, William, now 23 and still a bachelor living in Waltham Abbey, was paid £41.14.4d annually as a Saltpetre Refiner (Supply 5/232). In the spring of 1822 the Board reduced the production and regeneration of gunpowder, and the Establishment was decreased again. Accordingly Empson Middleton and James Wright drew up a list of people to be discharged on the 1st June (Supply 5/232). The men asking for financial assistance submitted several Petitions; many were long-service employees in their middle age, who pointed out that they had little hope of finding employment after the hay and corn harvest had been gathered. This time the Storekeeper was sympathetic, forwarding their Petition to the Board, and William was one of those awarded two weeks' pay to ease his financial burden (Supply 5/203).

After he left the Royal Gunpowder Mills, William married Esther (Ester) and by the time their son, also William, was baptised at Waltham Abbey on the 10th January 1830 (Huggins, *op.cit.*

31

p.134) he was working as a Miller. According to a list of property owned by the Board at that date and prepared by the Royal Engineers' Office in May 1840, William Alsop, Miller, was living in a cottage previously occupied by Benjamin Guinn (WO44/133). This would have been part of Plot 62 shown on the Town Map in Appendix 1. Nevertheless, he must have moved shortly after this, since the 1841 Census confirmed that he was still a Miller and that the family were living in Romeland. William died at the age of 71, and was buried on the 20th June 1868 in Waltham Abbey (Huggins, *op.cit.* p.134).

Thomas Anderson was employed as a Labourer in the Engineers' Department in May 1804. He earned 1/6d per day, with "one day extra allowed per week, agreeable to the Board's Order dated the 12th March, 1801" (Supply 5/222).

William Anderson was employed as a Charcoal Millman in the spring of 1805, earning 2/-d per day (Supply 5/224). Although still a Charcoal and Brimstone Millman on the same rate of pay in June 1807 (Supply 5/226) and August 1808 (Supply 5/227) he was then allowed to watch in turn, for which he received 1/-d.

Thomas Andrews was born circa 1809 and joined the Engineers' Department as a Labourer on the 9th June 1837 at 2/2d per day. WO54/623 dated the 1st April 1839 recorded that he was then a 30-year-old bachelor living in Waltham Abbey. The 1841 Census recorded that he was still employed as a Labourer, and lived in Paradise Row with an Elizabeth Biss.

Benjamin Archer was born circa 1760, and spent practically his entire working life at the Waltham Abbey Powder Mills, which the Royal Ordnance purchased from John Walton in 1787. Benjamin was taken on to the Ordnance Establishment on the 27th March 1788 (WO54/558) and a Report on Employees dated the 27th November 1788, noted that he was "promised to be

continued because he had lately been employed by Mr Walton"
(Winters, *op.cit.* pp.31-32). A Return dated the 21st March 1789
recorded that he was paid 1/6d per day (Supply 5/212). Benjamin
was also paid 2/-d on the 26th February 1802 for "catching eight
moles" according to Winters, (*op.cit.* p.61).

Initially Benjamin was employed as a General Labourer "cutting
and planting willow trees, cutting canal at the new Corning
House, removing earth to store, unloading barges of coal and
charring wood" (Supply 5/213). In 1789 he was 29 and employed
"attending the stoves" (Supply 5/214) which would have been the
newly installed Gloom stoves.

From March 1790 until 1806 he worked in the Stores, initially as
a Labourer but then re-classified as a Storeman (Supply 5/214
and Supply 5/215). His pay remained at 1/6d per day with an
additional 6d for night work. However, by the 8th May 1806, he
earned 2/-d per day and received an additional allowance of 1/-d
per night when it was his turn to watch - on average every fifth
night (Supply 5/222).

In common with most of the workmen, he enlisted as a Private in
the Military Volunteer Company on the 7th May 1794 (Supply
5/219). A Petition relating to pay and conditions dated the 2nd
February 1800 revealed that he was illiterate (Supply 5/220).
Another Return for 1801 recorded that he was a married man
with one child (Supply 5/221) and the same document stated that
in November of 1801 he would be employed in "cleaning and
deepening the river, canals and ditches and other necessary
works."

By the 30th January 1806 Benjamin's occupation had changed to
that of a Warder, but he was in receipt of the same pay and
allowances as before (Supply 5/227). As the Napoleonic War
peaked so did his wages, and by 1812 he was receiving 2/8d per
day and had been promoted to a Rounder, carrying out his rounds

every third night and being paid 2/-d for this duty (Supply 5/229). With the cessation of the war the Ordnance Board reduced the Establishment and cut wages; by the 25th June 1818, Benjamin's pay had been reduced to 2/4d per day and he was no longer a Rounder but instead was allowed to watch in turn, for which he received 1/-d (Supply 5/231). The same document recorded that he was then a widower aged 58, with one child. A List of Employees dated the 28th August 1818 (Supply 5/231) showed the names of people to be retained between the 3rd September and 31st December 1818. Benjamin Archer was retained with his pay unchanged, and it was also recorded that he was the Warder at the "Refining House Gate." Subsequent Returns by the Royal Engineers show that he lived in a cottage which was owned by the Board in High Bridge Street on the opposite side of the Refinery in the Storehouse Yard (WO44/133), and marked as Plot No. 21 on the Town Map shown in Appendix 1. By December of 1821 wages were being recorded annually, and, including his watch allowance, he received £41.14.4d per annum (Supply 5/232).

In the spring of 1822 the Ordnance Board decided to reduce the production and regeneration of gunpowder still further and the Establishment was to be cut accordingly. Empson Middleton and James Wright drew up a list of people to be dismissed on the 1st June 1822 (Supply 5/232). Benjamin Archer's name was included, yet a List of Employees dated the 1st October 1822, (Supply 5/233) indicated that he had been retained and was still living in a porter's lodge as a Labourer. A Return dated the 1st April 1823 confirmed that he was then classified as "a Labourer for general purposes to be sent to all parts of the Manufactory wherever his services may be requested" (WO54/542). Another document of the same reference noted that his annual pay was to be reduced by £2.10.0d, and, with his allowance for watching, his 'take-home' pay was £39.0.0d per annum.

By the 1st October 1824, Benjamin, then aged 65, had worked for the Ordnance Board for nearly 37 years (WO54/546). He continued working as a General Labourer on the same pay and allowances until the 1st April 1834, when his basic pay was cut to £28.5.6d per annum; however, he was still allowed to watch, so his total pay for the year amounted to £33.9.6d (WO54/593). He had remained a widower and still lived in the Porter's Lodge at the entrance to the Refinery. However, by December 1834 he had retired, since a Return made by the Royal Engineers' Office on the 20th of that month revealing how it was proposed to allocate vacant houses and cottages owned by the Board, recorded that Benjamin had been superannuated, and that his cottage was to be let to "G. Redpath, Storehouseman" (Supply 5/237). It would appear, however, that Charles Claydon occupied the cottage instead, since a List of Domestic Properties attached to the Royal Powder Mills at Waltham Abbey dated the 28th May 1840 (WO44/133) recorded that Benjamin had died, and confirmed that Charles Clayden then occupied the cottage in question.

Edward Archer was set to work as a Labourer in October 1787 by Daniel Cornish, possibly renovating the Mills following their purchase by the Government from Mr. Walton (Winters, *op.cit.* p.29). However, he does not appear to have been retained.

William Archer was born circa 1795 and started work as a casual Labourer in the Engineers' Department on the 25th July 1812, when he was paid 2/8d per day (WO54/512 and WO54/516). He was still in the same position in February 1817, but on a reduced daily rate of 2/4d (WO54/520) and appears to have left the Mills soon after. However, he rejoined the Engineers' Department on a temporary basis on the 19th September 1828 (no reference given). A Return of Employees dated the 1st April 1829 (WO54/566) recorded that he was a 33-year-old married man with 4 children living in Waltham Abbey, with pay amounting to £33.18.2d annually. In January 1831, he was one of 15 Labourers retained to work at Waltham Abbey and Enfield (WO54/575) – see the notes on Robert Adams - and he continued to work in the Engineers' Department on the same pay and conditions.

According to the 1841 Census, he and his wife, Mary, were living in Silver Street with 7 children - sons William (20) George (15) Charles (8) and James (4) and daughters Martha (10) Helen (4) and Emma (1).

Isaac Argent was employed as a Millman in 1805. By the 30th January 1806, he had been working in that capacity for some 6 months and was earning 2/3d per day (Supply 5/224). There were no further entries for this man.

John Arnold was born circa 1796 and worked as a Labourer in the Storehouse between 1820 and 1821, for which he was paid 2/4d per day. He was a bachelor living in Waltham Abbey (Supply 5/1232).

R. Ashford started work as a Labourer in the Corning House in the summer of 1805, and earned 2/2d per day (Supply 5/224). His name does not appear in the records after January 1806.

John Ashton was employed as a Carpenter (Second Class) by the Engineers' Department. Between the 15th and 21st July 1809 he was paid £1.8.4d for work carried out within the Manufactory (Supply 5/228).

John Ashwood was born circa 1762, and was originally employed in 1787 to mark barrels (Supply 5/212 dated the 21st March 1789). He served in the Artillery from the 1st April 1771 until the 1st May 1784 (Supply 5/217) and became a Sergeant in the Volunteer Company on the 7th May 1794 (Supply 5/219).

Winters, (*op.cit.* p.29) recorded that on the 29th December 1787 "Glooms of great weight in course of preparation" and on the 4th January 1788 "Glooms introduced and set up." On the 1st January 1788, about the time Gloom stoves (for drying gunpowder) were being installed at Waltham Abbey, John was seconded to Faversham for training as a Labourer "attending the stoves" (Supply 5/70) and, presumably, it was intended that he should operate the new stoves at Waltham. However, he did not return to Waltham Abbey until the 1st February 1789 (Supply 5/217) and by the 21st March 1789 he was "weighing powder in the Corning House and marking barrels" - not attending the stoves (Supply 5/212).

In common with the majority of the workforce In April 1789, he was carrying out essential works around the Manufactory (see notes on Benjamin Archer) for which he was paid 1/6d per day (Supply 5/213). In September 1789, he was again "marking powder barrels" (Supply 5/213) and the same document recorded that he was aged 27 (See also Supply 5/215 of the 16th April 1791 and September 1792, as well as Supply 5/216 of the 28th February 1793). He continued to weigh powder and mark barrels until the 28th February 1793, when he was promoted to the position of Foreman of Labour from the 1st March 1793 (footnote to Supply 5/216). In June of 1793 he became Master Mixer (Supply 5/217 dated the 24th June, 1793).

An anonymous letter sent to "His Majesties Honble. Board of Ordnance" in January 1791 (Supply 5/190) made serious allegations against three employees, viz., John Goodfellow, John Ashwood and John White. The charge against Ashwood was that he "...often made complaints and finding fault without cause with those men which he has no business with and whose business he knows nothing of." The matter was referred to Major Congreve who was to "cause enquiry to be made and report the result to the Board." The letter did not succeed since no action was taken against Ashwood, and he was still working at the Mills in 1793. Winters (*op.cit.* pp.34-35) also referred to this incident, saying that the report was an anonymous letter complaining about several Millmen, i.e., John Ashwood, John Goodfellow and John White, and recorded also, "the complaints were without foundation." The Storekeeper received a second letter of complaint against John Ashwood in August 1795. Full details are not known, but "two men discharged, (William) Fulham and Mason, the charge being non-proven" according to Winters (*op.cit.* p.52).

A signed document relating to a Petition on Pay (Supply 5/220 of the 2nd February 1800) showed that Ashwood was literate; another Report of the 8th May 1801 (also 5/220) confirmed that Ashwood was the Master Mixer and that he earned 3/-d per day. This document also indicated that he was married and had 4 children. Supply 5/221 of the 3rd November 1801, showed that he was superintending the Millmen and Labourers, "…cleansing and deepening the river." By March of 1805, he was shown as the Master Mixer of Composition on a weekly wage of £1.6.0d (Supply 5/223) as he was at the end of that year, but by then his wage had been increased to 5/-d per day (Supply 5/224 dated December, 1805). A List of Foreman Artificers and Labourers dated the 30th January 1806 (also Supply 5/224) described him as a Master Refiner of Composition, and that at that date he had been with the Ordnance for 18 years. In June 1807, he was still in the same position with the same wage, but in the 'Remarks Column' of Supply 5/226 dated the 18th June 1807, it was specified that he was provided with a house and entitled to an Apprentice. Further promotion followed, since an entry on Supply 5/227 dated the 23rd August 1808 described Mr. Ashwood as Assistant to the Master Worker, although his rate of pay remained the same; he was still entitled to a house and 6/-d weekly to train an Apprentice, who in 1808 was Robert Perkis, Jnr. (Supply 5/227).

A Return dated the 1st September 1810 confirmed that he was still the Assistant to the Master Worker (Supply 5/228) but by August 1812, George Pittendrigh had taken this position, and John's name no longer appeared in the records (Supply 5/229). A list of "persons to whom pensions or charitable allowances had been granted by the Honourable Board as widows, orphans or relations who have lost their lives in the Manufactory, etc." recorded that among the recipients was Elizabeth Ashwood, the widow of John Ashwood. Elizabeth had been in receipt of 3/6d per week but died on the 7th March 1818 (Supply 5/231). This document did not record when or how her husband died, but, bearing in mind the information recorded in Supply 5/228 and the fact that Pittendrigh had taken over Ashwood's position, it would have been sometime between 1810 and 1812.

Thomas Ashwood was possibly the son of John Ashwood. He was Apprenticed in 1804 to the Master Mixer, who, in that year, was John Ashwood. He was paid 1/4d per day and in addition "one day extra [was] allowed per week, agreeable to the Board's Order of 12th March, 1801" (Supply 5/222). Supply 5/223 confirmed his Apprenticeship in 1805, as does Supply 5/224 dated January 1806. The last entry for Thomas was in June 1807; he was still an Apprentice serving under the Master Mixer, and according to Supply 5/226 of that date, he was then earning 1/6d per day.

Nathaniel Attridge was employed as a Labourer in the Engineers' Department at 1/6d per day. In August and September 1790, he worked in the Manufactory with his wages submitted by William Spry, Colonel Commanding the Royal Engineers, for payment by the Storekeeper, James Wright, at which time he signed for his pay with a cross, "his mark" (WASC 1382). Between April 1791 and January 1792, he was "grinding salt petre, charcoal and brimstone" with a wage of 1/6d per day (Supply 5/215). According to Supply 5/216 dated September

1792, from July to September of that year, he was working in the Corning Houses.

James Austen was born circa 1797/1798, and although there appears to be little doubt that he started work as an Apprentice Millwright at the Royal Gunpowder Mills at Waltham Abbey on the 9th April 1814 (WO54/512) where he had trained is unknown. If he followed the usual trend, he would have signed his Articles of Indenture at the age of 11, i.e. circa 1808, for a period of seven years, becoming a fully qualified artisan by 1815.

Details in the early records appear inconsistent as regards his age, trade and marital status, but a Return dated the 19th February 1816 (WO54/550) recorded that he was an 18-year-old bachelor living in Waltham Abbey, who was then working as a casual Labourer in the Engineers' Department at 2/8d per day. The following year he was recorded as working as a Millwright "occasionally as the Service Required" and was paid the rate for a fully qualified tradesman - 5/2d per day (WO54/520). His position and wage remained the same until December 1821 (WO54/536) after which, his name was not recorded at Waltham Abbey until he was appointed on the 15th June 1822 as a Millwright on the Establishment, with pay of £80.17.2d annually (WO54/542). Since there was no break in his service with the Ordnance Board, it is assumed he had been working at one of their other Manufactories. This same Return stated that he was a married man, and W054/550 dated April of 1925, indicated that a second child had been born to him by then. It would appear, however, that both mother and child died soon afterwards because the Return dated October 1827 (WO54/558) mentioned that he was a widower, and stated that he had only one child. James seems to have left the Mills (and possibly the town) thereafter, because there were no further entries for him after October 1827.

It is also possible that James and Thomas Austen were related (see following entry). Both came to Waltham Abbey in 1814, and both were Millwrights. However, no positive evidence has come to light linking the two.

Thomas Austen was born circa 1786 at Challock to the south of Faversham, according to the 1851 Census, and was married to Mary of Faversham. He started work with the Ordnance Board on the 1st January 1804 (WO54/512).

Returns dated the 1st October 1834 (WO54/593) and 1st October 1839 (WO54/632) summarised his career with the Board. He became a Millwright on the 31st August 1807, and by the 12th January 1814, was appointed Superintendent of Machinery at Waltham Abbey (WO54/632). The Ordnance Board had purchased the Waltham Abbey Corn Mill in 1808 in order to have better control over the waters of the River Lea, which were then used to drive most of the machinery within the Manufactory. Promotion to Superintendent of the Corn Mill and Millwrights came on the 5th June 1818, and was confirmed by a Return in 1833 (WO54/587). Finally, he became a Second-class Clerk of the Works on the 24th December 1827 (WO54/587).

Where Thomas trained or worked prior to his appointment in 1814 at Waltham Abbey is unknown. His eldest daughter Mary was born circa 1810 at Faversham (Huggins, *op.cit.* p.122), yet Thomas does not appear in the Faversham records *(FGPR)* listing Apprentices and Millwrights who trained or worked there; it is possible, therefore, that he was instead trained at one of the nearby Government Establishments, such as Purfleet or Sheerness. A Return dated February 1816 (WO54/516) recorded that he was a Millwright on the Establishment, that he was a 31-year-old married man with 4 children, and that he was trained as a Millwright and Engineer. He was allowed a house and was paid 5/8d per day, with an additional allowance of 2/10d per day for an unspecified reason. It is likely that the additional payment was a housing allowance, because the amount in question ceased when he moved into a rent-free house owned by the Board in 1818. His family expanded at regular intervals, and a daughter - Sarah Ann - was baptised at Waltham Abbey on the 16th March 1816 (Huggins, *op.cit.* p.122).

He was still recorded as a Millwright in February 1817, but in common with the rest of the workforce, his rate of pay had been reduced and he then received only 5/2d per day. However, he was still entitled to a house and was in receipt of his additional allowance (WO54/520).

A Statement dated the 31st December 1820 "of monies to which the public was entitled to receive credit..." (Supply 5/232) showed that Thomas had been living rent-free in a Board of Ordnance property since the 21st October 1818. The property was Plot No. 65 on the Town Map in Appendix 1, located on the north side of High Bridge Street adjacent to the church, and then known as the Miller's House. Proposals were made in August 1818 to reduce the Establishment at Waltham Abbey, but a list of people to be retained between September and December 1818, indicated that Thomas was to become the "Superintendent for cutting materials for the Cooperage" and paid 4/-d per day (Supply 5/231). However, he retained his position at the Corn Mill on the same pay, but he then had an annual allowance of £12.10.0d for coal and candles for his rent-free house in High Bridge Street.

A Return dated the 2nd April 1821 (WO54/536) recorded that Thomas was then aged 37, that he had 6 children, and that his pay and allowances were unchanged at £164.5.0d per annum. A footnote to this Return stated that "The Superintendent of the Cornmill, Thos. Austen is paid from the receipts of a Water Corn Mill, which he has improved, the working of which he superintends. The profit received by the Board from the Concern exceeds £450 for the year." For the next six years he continued to run the Corn Mill on the same terms until his job description was changed on the 24th December 1827 (WO54/587) to that of "Superintendent of the Cornmills and Machinery, and Second-Class Clerk of Works." His basic pay was increased to 12/6d per day, which equated, with allowances, to £228.2.6d annually. At that time his family had grown to 8 children.

A Return dated the 31st January 1831 of Persons belonging to the Civil Establishment of the Ordnance at the Gunpowder and Small Arms Manufactories at Waltham Abbey, Faversham and Enfield (WO54/587) recorded that "Thomas Austen was to be paid £228.2.6d per annum and provided with a house. His presence was required constantly, and he was to have a practical knowledge of mechanics connected with Gunpowder and Small Arms Manufactories and Flour Mills." The Return also stated, "he had to have honesty and attention to his accounts, since all the money for the work at the Grist Mill was to pass through his hands." He was still in the same position and receiving the same pay and allowances in 1839 (WO54/632) and he and his wife, Mary, then had 9 children. A Return of Domestic Properties prepared by the Royal Engineers on the 28th May 1840 (WO44/133) showed that Mr Austen, "superintendent of machinery was living in house No. 65 on the General Plan...previously occupied by the Rev Mr Picthall." The property number was the same as that used by Drayson on his 1830 map, and confirmed its location as being adjacent to the church.

The 1841 Census recorded that Thomas, listed as an Engineer in the Gunpowder Mills, and Mary, were living in High Bridge Street north with 6 of their children, Mary (30) Sarah (25) twins James and Caroline (20) William (12) and Henry (6). Thomas continued to live in the Miller's House, but on the 4th December 1848 it was recorded that the Board was "recommending that Mr

Austen, superintendent of machinery, to be dispensed with" (Winters, *op.cit.* p.110). However, the 1851 Census showed that he was still employed with the Board as an Engineer and was still residing in High Bridge Street with his wife, Mary, and his unmarried children Mary, Sarah and William, although a list of persons employed in the Government Works in 1855 did not record his name (Winters, *op.cit.* p.113).

Another record dated the 28th August 1855, noted, "£150 per annum rent had been offered for the Corn Mill" (Winters, *op.cit.* p.111) which clearly indicated that the Board had ceased, or were about to cease, operations at the Corn Mill. Thomas apparently left the Mills and possibly Waltham Abbey, since his name does not appear in the 1861 Census, and a Thomas Webb had been appointed as the Chief Foreman of Machinery on the 1st April 1861 according to Winters (*op.cit.* p.131). Thomas died on the 13th July 1863, aged 77; Mary died on the 29th January 1872, aged 84, and both are buried at Waltham Abbey (Huggins, *op.cit.* p.124).

William George Austen signed his Indentures as an Apprentice on the 4th July 1840 (Supply 5/238) although details of his trade are unknown.

John Avis was working as a Saltpetre Refiner in August 1812 earning 2/8d per day, and in addition, Refiners when not working extra, were allowed to watch in turn. (Supply 5/229). The same information applied in February 1814 (Supply 5/230).

William Aylett's initial work was "in the punts and setting and drawing stoves etc." earning 1/6d per day (Supply 5/215). A Return of Employees dated the 16th April 1791, recorded that William was then employed as a Millman at 2/-d per day, and this was confirmed by a further Return dated August of that year (also Supply 5/215). He continued working as a Millman throughout 1791 and into 1792.

A letter to the Board from the Storekeeper, James Wright, and John Clowdersly dated the 26th July 1791, noted, "at half past 1 o'clock the Lower Queens Mead Mill blew up. W. Aylett the Millman had just laid on Green Charges and drawn the water gate just sufficient to move the runners and going to the Mill to liquor the Charge when it went off." William was uninjured and the Mill was working again that evening (WASC 0475).

Henry Aylin was employed as a Puntman for a short time in 1807, earning 2/-d per day (Supply 5/226).

Jeremiah Aylin was born circa 1786/87 and commenced work as a "Labourer employed in refining Salt Petre & other parts of the manufactory" at the Mills on the 1st March 1804. He earned 2/-d per day and was allowed to watch in turn - on average every 5th night - for which he received 1/-d (Supply 5/222). By the 30th January 1806, Jeremiah was described as "an extra Bargeman" and was still earning 2/-d per day (Supply 5/224). He continued working on the barges with frequent increases in his daily rate of pay, which, by August 1808 (Supply 5/227) had risen to 3/-d, and this was confirmed in September 1810 in Supply 5/228. By August 1812, his pay had risen again to 3/10d per day (Supply 5/230) and remained so until May 1818, when he was described as a Master Bargeman or Bargemaster earning 4/2d per day (Supply 5/231). The same document revealed that he was a married man with 4 children, living in Waltham Abbey. Aylin survived the redundancies made at Waltham in the spring of 1818 (Supply 5/231) continuing his employment as a Bargemaster.

On the 16th June 1808, the Board purchased two tenements from a Miss Jones on the north side of High Bridge Street, and the sketch map attached to the document clearly shows that they formed part of High Bank or Bank Cottages. The two tenants then in occupation were "Alsop and Aylin" (WO44/681a). A statement "of monies to which the public were entitled to receive credit" recorded that he was living in a house later owned by the Board, and on the 4th May 1821, the Board leased this house to him at an annual rent of £8.9.0d (Supply 5/232). The tenement has been identified as that at the western end of five cottages on the north side of High Bridge Street known as Bank Cottages, and shown as Plot No. 48 on the Town Map in Appendix 1.

Although he was still in the same position in December 1821 (Supply 5/232) it was proposed to reduce production and regeneration of gunpowder still further in 1822; Jeremiah's name was on the redundancy list and he was dismissed on the 1st June that year (Supply 5/232). An arguable assumption can be made that after redundancy, Jeremiah remained in Waltham Abbey as a Publican in Sun Street; the rounded-down age of Aylin is correct in the 1841 Census, but the surname is given as Ayliss.

B

John Bailey signed a Petition relating to pay and conditions at the Royal Gunpowder Mills at Waltham Abbey on the 2nd February 1800 with a cross (Supply 5/220). The same document recorded that he worked as a general Labourer in the Corning House and was paid 1/6d per day.

On the 18th April 1801, there was a huge explosion at the Mills. Reporting the event to the Board of Ordnance in London the following day, the Storekeeper, James Wright, who witnessed the event, said that the new Corning House on Horse Mill Island blew up the day before with a tremendous explosion at "1/4 past 3 o'clock." Nine men were in the building and all were killed, including John Bailey, and 4 horses also perished (Supply 5/220). "The mangled bodies of the poor men were buried without a memorial stone in a high heap in the yard, near the path leading to Mr King's House and in front of the Wollard tombs" (Winters, *Centenary Memorial,* p.59). (Mr King was a Market Gardener at the Abbey Gardens). John Bailey's wife, Sarah, together with the other widows and two mothers of the deceased, sent a petition to the Board via the Storekeeper on the 24th April requesting "...relief in their distress..." (Supply 5/194). In a Report dated the 29th April regarding the ages of the children and the circumstances of the widows and children, the Storekeeper stated "Sarah was aged 37 and had no children from her husband, Labourer, but has reason to believe she is with child." Sarah was indeed pregnant and gave birth to a son in October (Winters, *op.cit.* p.57). At this date the Board agreed that the pension awarded to Mrs Bailey should be 5/3d per week (Supply 5/220). In May, the Storekeeper in another document suggested to the Board that the dependant's pension should be modified, and recommended that Sarah Baillee (Bailey) should receive half of her husband's weekly pay of 10/6d, plus 1/6d "on account of the severity of the times." However, the Board decreed that the widows' pensions should be based on their husbands' basic pay and should not include the extra "due to the severity of the times" (Supply 5/194).

Sarah was still in receipt of her pension in 1818 (Supply 5/231). In 1821, a note appended to the List of Pensioners stated that her superannuation should continue at £27.6.0d per annum (Supply 5/232). A letter dated the 21st July 1826 (Supply 5/205) recorded that Sarah had died, and that any pension due to her could be paid to her legal representative.

William Bailey was employed in August 1808 as a Labourer "setting and drawing stoves, etc." for which he was paid 2/-d per day, and was allowed to watch in turn (Supply 5/227). He was undertaking the same work in September 1810 for the same money (Supply 5/228) as well as in February 1814, but by then his wage had increased to 2/8d per day (Supply 5/230).

Charles Baker was working as a Saltpetre Refiner at the Powder Mills on the 29th August 1812 at 2/8d per day, and was allowed to "watch in turn when not working extra" (Supply 5/229). He was still in the same position on the 13th February 1814 (Supply 5/230).

David B. Baker commenced work as a Labourer in the Corning House on the 11th September 1794, earning 1/6d per day (Supply 5/217). He was still a Corning House Labourer in July 1795 (Supply 5/217).

Isaac Baker was born circa 1791, and joined the Ordnance Board as an Apprentice Bricklayer in the Engineers' Department on the 11th June 1804 (WO54/516). By September 1812, he was employed as a casual Bricklayer earning 4/7d per day for a six-day week (WO54/512) as he was in February 1816 (WO54/516). In common with the rest of the workforce, his wage was reduced in 1818 when he worked "occasionally as required" at 4/1d per day (WO54/524). This equated to £63.18.1d annually for 313 working days in the year.

A List of Personnel working in the Engineers' Department dated the 1st April 1823, recorded that Isaac was a 32-year-old married man, with 1 child (WO54/542). Another child was born in 1825/26 (WO54/554) and a third had arrived by April 1827 (WO54/558). Another list of persons belonging to the "Civil Establishment of the Ordnance at the Gunpowder and Small Arms Manufactories at Waltham Abbey, Faversham and Enfield" recorded that Isaac was the only Bricklayer to be employed at the Waltham Abbey Powder Mills and the Small Arms Manufactory at Enfield, where he was required to "undertake general services as a bricklayer in the manufactory where care, attention, sobriety are indispensably necessary." Isaac and his wife had had a fourth child by 1831 (WO54/575). In 1839 he was still being paid £63.18.1d (WO54/623).

James Baker was born circa 1791; he was listed as an Apprentice on the 4th May 1804, and paid 9d per day with "one day extra allowed for week agreeable to the Board's Order – 12th March 1801." although no details of his Apprenticeship were given (Supply 5/222). The next document relating to James was dated the 13th September 1820, and recorded that he was a Bricklayer employed "occasionally as the service required" at 4/1d per day, that he was a 29-year-old married man with 2 children and that he lived in Waltham Abbey WO54/532).

John Baker was born circa 1756, and was employed as a Labourer and Refiner at the Royal Laboratory from the 25th November 1779 until the 13th April 1789, when he joined the Royal Gunpowder Mills at Waltham Abbey as the "Master Refiner of Salt Petre" at 2/6d per day (Supply 5/213). He was 33 years of age in September 1789 (Supply 5/214) and his daily wage had increased to 3/-d by January 1794 (Supply 5/216).

A Return of Pay and Allowances for Artificers and Labourers dated the 3rd July 1795 confirmed that his pay remained at 3/-d per day, and in addition, he had an annual allowance of £4.4.0d for coal and candles (Supply 5/217). In September 1798, he joined the Waltham Military Volunteer Company and held the rank of Sergeant (Supply 5/219).

A letter to the Board dated the 3rd December 1798 signed by James Wright and Robert Coleman, stated that John Baker had died, and that he had left 4 orphaned children, a girl of 12 and 3 boys aged 11, 8 and 7. The eldest boy, Thomas, had been Apprenticed to his father to clean bags at the Refining House and received 3/6d per week. Wright and Coleman requested that the Board employ the other two boys cleaning "Salt Petre sacks at 9d per day, increasing to 1/-d per day as soon as they had grown useful." They also stated that Baker's brother-in-law worked as a Labourer in the Refining House, but having a family of his own, he could not look after these "poor orphans" (WO13/202). The Board's findings and decision are not recorded.

John W. Baker trained as a Carpenter and Builder, and was engaged on the 10th September 1830 as the Foreman Carpenter in the Engineers' Department. Promotion followed quickly since he was appointed Foreman of Works on the 29th September 1833, and on the 27th July 1836, he was made a Fourth-Class Clerk of the Works. In 1839 his annual salary was £137.5.0d and he was provided with a house attached to the Engineers' office in Powder Mill Lane (WO44/133 and WO54/623) being Plot No. 73 on the Town Map in Appendix 1. The 1841 Census recorded that neither John nor his wife, Mary, were born in Essex, and that their rounded-down ages were 40 and 35 years respectively. They were still living in Powder Mill Lane with their children Sophia

(15) Mary (12) Richard (6) Henry (4) Charles (2) and Alfred (1), and hey had a live-in servant, Ann Boston, who was 15 years of age.

March Baker started an Apprenticeship on the 1st June 1804 under the Master Saltpetre Refiner, Samuel Knowler, Snr., and was paid 1/4d per day (Supply 5/223). On the 5th August 1808 his recorded rate of pay 1/6d per week, while Knowler received 7/-d for teaching his Apprentice the arts of refining Saltpetre (Supply 5/227). A second document of the same date showed that March Baker was literate (Supply 5/227). Towards the end of his Apprenticeship, March's weekly pay was recorded as 7/-d (which was probably a clerical error) while his Master received 9/-d (Supply 5/228).

A List of Employees dated the 29th August 1812, recorded that he was employed as a Saltpetre Refiner at 2/8d per day, and in addition, "when not working extra [was] allowed to watch in turn" (Supply 5/229). This was also the case in February 1814 (Supply 5/230).

Robert Baker started an Apprenticeship as a Refiner on the 1st October 1789 when he was 10 years' old, and was paid 1/-d per day (Supply 5/213). He was still serving his time in July 1795 (Supply 5/217) but did not appear to have completed his Apprenticeship, so it must be assumed that he left the Mills.

Thomas Baker, the son of Master Refiner John Baker, was born circa 1787, and started an Apprenticeship as a Saltpetre Refiner on the1st February 1797, at 3/6d per week. He served as a Private in the Military Volunteer Company (Supply 5/219). His father died either in late November or early December 1798, leaving Thomas and his 3 siblings orphans. Thomas continued to live in Waltham Abbey and work at the Powder Mills. In May 1804, he worked as a Saltpetre Refiner earning 1/6d per day, and was allowed, "one day extra per week agreeable to the Board's Order – 12th March 1801" (Supply 5/222). The last record relating to him is dated the 30th January 1806, when he was still working in the Saltpetre Refinery earning 2/-d per day (Supply 5/224).

Edward Baldock was born circa 1794 and started work as a casual Labourer in the Engineers' Department on the 30th July 1815, earning 2/8d per day. In February 1816, it was recorded that he was a 21-year-old married man with 1 child, living in Waltham Abbey (WO54/516).

George Baldock was born circa 1773 (Supply 5/231) and commenced work in the Corning House on the 21st July 1793 at 1/6d per day (Supply 5/216). He enlisted as a Private in the Military Volunteer Company on the 7th May 1794 (Winters, *op.cit.* p.42). In July 1795, George was working as a Refiner (Supply 5/217) and by September of the same year he was employed as a Millman with a daily wage of 2/-d, and was still serving in the Militia (Supply 5/219). In February 1800, he 'signed' the document relating to pay and conditions with a cross (Supply 5/220). A Return in 1801 showing the marital status of the employees, noted that he was a married man with 5 children (Supply 5/221). Sometime after this he left the Ordnance Board; however, a Return of Employees dated the 31st December 1821 (Supply 5/232) recorded that he had 16 years' service, which indicated that he rejoined the Board in 1805. It is not known where he worked in the interim period.

He had returned to the Waltham Abbey Mills by June 1813, being employed as a Brimstone and Saltpetre Millman (Winters, *op.cit.* p.76). This information was confirmed in a List of Employees dated February 1814 (Supply 5/230), which document also recorded that he was earning 2/8d per day as well as being allowed to watch in turn, for which he received 1/6d per night. In June 1818, George was reclassified as a Saltpetre Refiner, with his pay and watch monies reduced to 2/4d and 1/-d respectively (Supply 5/231 and WO54/524).

Peace in Europe saw a reduction in the manufacture and regeneration of gunpowder, and as a consequence, the Board required the Establishment at the Royal Powder Mills to be cut back and expenditure reduced. A list sent from Waltham Abbey to the Board on the 28th August 1818, indicated the names of the people the Storekeeper proposed to retain between the 3rd September and the 31st December 1818 to meet the new production and financial requirements. George's name was included, but he had lost his entitlement to watch (Supply 5/231). However, a few days later, a letter from the Mills to the Board stated "We respectfully beg leave to add the names and stations of those people whom it will be necessary to discharge in consequence of this arrangement." George Baldock, "Salt Petre Refiner" was on that list (Supply 5/231). An Order of the Board dated the 4th September 1818, nevertheless rescinded this second proposal, and George continued to be employed as a Saltpetre Refiner at 2/4d per day. He was still allowed to watch in turn, for which he received 1/-d (Supply 5/232).

His position as a Saltpetre Refiner was reconfirmed by an Order of the Board in October 1819, and his wage, including his watch allowance, was then £41.14.4d annually (Supply 5/232). This Return also showed that he was 46 years' old, lived in Waltham Abbey and now had 9 children. However, he did lose his job in 1822 when further cuts were made to the Establishment at the Waltham Abbey Mills (see the notes on George Adams). George Baldock was dismissed on the 1st June, and was awarded two weeks' wages to ease his financial burden.

John Baldock was born circa 1752, and started work as a Labourer in the Corning House on the 1st April 1792 (Supply 5/216). Between 1792 and 1803 he worked as a general Labourer in various parts of the Manufactory, and in 1794 he was described as "setting and drawing stoves and in the punts" (Supply 5/216). In 1801 he was "cleaning and deepening the river, canals and performing necessary work" and during this period he was paid 1/6d per day (Supply 5/221). In 1794 he joined the Military Volunteer Company as a Private (Winters, *op.cit.* p.49) and a Petition on Pay and Conditions presented to the Board in 1800 showed that he was illiterate (Supply 5/220). A Return on the marital status of the employees in 1801, recorded that John was a married man with 1 child (Supply 5/221).

In May 1804, he was working as a Saltpetre Refiner earning 2/-d per day. In common with all other Refiners he was allowed to watch in turn, which was, on average, every fifth night, for which he received 1/-d (Supply 5/222). He continued to refine either Saltpetre or Brimstone until March 1816, and during this period his daily rate of pay rose to 2/8d and he was still allowed to watch (Supply 5/230). In a footnote to this Return was a comment that Baldock and others should be superannuated "because of the hurts they have received in this dangerous Manufactory." It went on to say that Baldock "has been twice severely hurt in the right hand in the discharge of his duty, has become very feeble and incapable of exerting himself at work." The Storekeeper recommended that his superannuation should be 2/8d per day. The Board awarded John Baldock a pension of 12/-d a week commencing on the 1st April 1816 (Supply 5/200). In spite of being described as being "very feeble" John was still receiving his annual pension of £31.4.0d in 1826, ten years after his retirement (Winters, *op.cit.* p.96).

Thomas Baldock was born circa 1779/1780 and Apprenticed in the general manufacture of gunpowder on the 1st February 1793 (Supply 5/216). Initially he was paid 1/-d per day, which rose to 1/6d on completion of his Apprenticeship on the 11th April 1800. In 1798, he was working in the Corning House and served in the

Military Volunteer Company as a Private (Supply 5/219). A Petition relating to pay and conditions at the Powder Mills was 'signed' by the employees in 1800, and showed that Thomas was illiterate. It also recorded that he was still a Corning House Man (Supply 5/220) and was still a bachelor (Supply 5/221).

Robert Coleman, the Clerk of the Cheque, recorded in his Minute Book on the 20th October 1801 that Baldock was one of 24 men who were required to work at Faversham or be discharged. Thomas agreed to go (Winters, op.cit. p.60). However, his name did not appear in the Faversham records, nor did the subsequent Waltham Returns show that he had a break in his service record. Therefore, it must be assumed that he remained at the Abbey, continuing to work in the Corning House. In 1806 he was earning 2/2d per day and allowed to watch in turn, for which he received an extra 1/-d per shift (Supply 5/224).

By the 23rd August 1808 Thomas was the Reeling House Foreman, earning 2/10d per day and still allowed to watch in turn, for which he received 1/-d (Supply 5/227) but by the 29th August 1812, he was the Corning House Foreman with his daily rate of pay increased to 4/-d. He was also a Rounder, which earned him an extra 2/-d every third night (Supply 5/229 and Supply 5/230). In June 1818 he was a married man with 3 children (Supply 5/231). Thomas escaped the redundancies made in 1818, and was retained on the 4th September as the Dusting House Foreman, but although he lost his position as a Rounder, he was still allowed to watch in turn (Supply 5/232). His pay was subsequently reduced to 3/4d per day with an additional 1/6d when it was his turn to watch. Further economies were made in March 1822, and by an Order of the Board dated the 22nd May 1822, Thomas was demoted to being a Corning House Man (Supply 5/232). A Return dated the 1st April 1823 (WO54/542) recorded that his annual pay as a Corning House man was £48.2.0d, which included his watch monies. This remained his rate of pay until 1828, when on the 1st April that year, he was promoted to Junior Corning House Foreman working under Henry Coreham, and his pay was increased to £52.0.0d annually, which included his allowances (WO54/558).

On the 18th July 1831, the Board agreed to pay Thomas Baldock, described then as the Foreman of the Corning House, 2 days' pay "in consequence of the hurt he received in the performance of his duties." Details of his injuries, however, were not recorded (Supply 5/207).

Thomas lived in a cottage owned by the Board previously occupied by Daniel Allsup, and in February 1832, he applied for a reduction in his rent from 3/3d to 2/-d per week (Supply 5/207). His application was successful, since his annual rent was reduced to £5.4.0d with effect from the 15th February 1832 (Supply 5/237). The cottage was at the western end of Bank Cottages on the north side of High Bridge Street, being part of Plot No. 48 on the Town Map in Appendix 1. A Return of Employees dated the 10th October 1839 (WO54/623) revealed that he had been reinstated as a Rounder and that he now received £64.16.0d per annum. The 1841 census confirmed that he and his wife, Mary, lived on the north side of High Bridge Street. Living with them was James Robinson, a Labourer at the Mills, and his wife, Mary, and it appeared that none of the occupants were born in Essex.

William Baldock filled one of 7 vacancies which were available for Labourers at the Waltham Abbey Mills on the 15th August 1793 (Winters, *op.cit.* p.40). His name was not recorded on the list of men who joined the Military Volunteer Company on the 7th May 1794 (Winters, *op.cit.* p.42) and since no mention of his name was made in the records again until 1804, it can only be supposed that his was a casual post, or that he had quit the Powder Mills. On the 8th May 1804, however, records show he was working as a Refiner earning 2/-d per day, with an additional allowance of 1/-d a night when it was his turn to watch (Supply 5/222). In January 1806 he was working in the Corning House (Supply 5/224) as he was in June 1807 (Supply 5/227) and during that period, he was paid 2/2d per day and still allowed to watch in turn.

Promotion soon followed; by August 1808 he was the "Foreman of the Reeling Houses" receiving a daily wage of 2/10d (Supply 5/227) which rose to 3/10d by August 1812, and he was then acting as a Rounder earning an additional 1/6d every third night (Supply 5/229). He was still in the same position with the same pay and allowances in February 1814 (Supply 5/230) after which, his name does not appear in the Powder Mill records.

Robert Bale worked at the Royal Powder Mills on the 8th May 1804 as a Refiner, earning 2/-d per day. Like all other Refiners he was allowed to watch in turn, on average every fifth night, for which he received 1/-d (Supply 5/222).

Thomas Barby worked as a Labourer in the Corning House on the 31st July 1792, earning 1/6d per day (Supply 5/216).

John Bardle (Bardell) was working as a Millman on the 18th June 1807, earning 2/3d per day with an extra 3d per shift when on night duty (Supply 5/226). By August of the following year he was employed in the Dusting House on the same rate of pay, and was allowed to watch in turn, for which he received 1/-d (Supply 5/227). He continued on the same pay in the Dusting House until at least September 1810, but his watch money had increased to 1/6d per night (Supply 5/228).

Thomas Bardle (Bardell) worked in the Mixing House from at least August 1812 (Supply 5/229) to February 1814 (Supply 5/230). During that period he was paid 3/-d daily and allowed to watch in turn, for which he received 1/6d per night.

William Bardle (Bardell) was the son of Thomas Bardle. He was born circa 1811, and died in 1834 at the age of 23, leaving a young widow, Ann, who was pregnant (Information from Sally Thorn). Their son, also William, started work in the Cylinder House in 1854 (Winters, *op.cit.* p.131) and was working as a 2nd class Labourer at the Mills in 1855 (Winters, *op.cit.* p.113). At that date he was allowed to watch in turn – on average every third night - for which he would have received 1/6d (Winters, *op.cit.* p.128). William was eventually promoted as the Senior Foreman of the Cylinder Houses making Charcoal (Winters, *op.cit.*, p.131). Ann remarried circa 1839 – see notes on Thomas Hilton.

Joseph Barfoot was born circa 1797, and worked as a Cooper between 1814 and 1821. His pay in 1814 was 1/9d per day, possibly soon after he had completed an Apprenticeship (Supply 5/229) and this rose to 2/4d by February 1814 (Supply 5/230). His services were retained when the workforce was reduced in 1818, when he was paid 3/6d per day (Supply 5/231). A List of Employees dated the 9th April 1821 recorded that he was a 23-year-old bachelor living in Waltham Abbey, and indicated that he was then only paid a daily wage of 3/-d. Like all other Coopers, he was not allowed to watch in turn (Supply 5/232).

Valentine Barford was working as a Puntman on the 13th February 1814, earning 2/8d per day. He was also allowed to watch in turn (Supply 5/230).

James Barker had first been employed as a Puntman circa March 1805, for which he was paid 1/6d per day (Supply 5/224). By June 1807, he had become a Millman with his daily wage increased to 2/3d, plus an additional 3d when working at night (Supply 5/226). James was still in the same trade in August 1808, but at that date, his night shift allowance had been increased to 6d (Supply 5/227). His wages peaked to 3/-d per day in 1812 (Supply 5/229) and remained at this level until February 1814

(Supply 5/230) after which, his name does not appear in the records.

Samuel Barker was working as a Labourer in the Engineers' Department on the 8th May 1804, and paid 1/6d per day with "one day extra allowed per week, agreeable with the Board's Order dated the 12th March 1801" (Supply 5/222).

Thomas Barker was a Millman who worked at the Powder Mills from at least August 1812 (Supply 5/229) until February 1814 (Supply 5/230). During that time he was paid 3/-d per day, plus an extra 6d if he had to work at night.

W Barker was mixing composition at the Waltham Abbey Powder Mills in July 1792 at 1/6d per day (Supply 5/216). He transferred to the Corning House in August 1792 with his daily wage increased to 2/-d (Supply 5/216) and was still working there on the 31st January 1794 (Supply 5/216).

John Barnard was a Sawyer who worked for the Engineers' Department between the 15th and 21st July 1809, and was paid £1.9.9d for work carried out within the Manufactory (Supply 5/228).

George Barnes (1) born circa 1763, trained as a Bricklayer and Builder, and joined the Ordnance Board on the 3rd October 1786. By the 10th January 1791 he was a Master Bricklayer, but at which manufactory is unknown (WO54/516). He was appointed to the Establishment on the 19th January 1792 (WO51/512) and again, where he was working is unknown. Barnes was appointed the Overseer of the Works in the Engineers' Department at Waltham Abbey on the 31st July 1809 (WO54/512) and his immediate superior was the Clerk of the Works, William Drayson, who had been the Overseer of the Works at the Royal Gunpowder Mills at Faversham. A George Barnes was working as the Foreman Bricklayer at the Faversham Mills in 1795

(*FGPR. op.cit.* p.12) and there is little doubt that he was the George Barnes who came to Waltham Abbey.

In 1812, Barnes was paid 7/-d per day and provided with a house. The location of his accommodation was revealed in a statement "of monies to which the public were entitled to receive credit between the 1st January and 31st December 1821, showing the amounts received by the storekeeper" (Supply 5/232). This document stated, "George Barnes, Overseer of the Works, by an Order of the Board dated the 29th September 1809 was provided with a Board of Ordnance house rent free." The house was in Powder Mill Lane at the entrance to the Engineers' yard, being Plot 92 on the Waltham Abbey Town Map in Appendix 1.

In 1816 George was still paid 7/-d daily, and receiving a coal and candle allowance of £8.0.0d per annum for his rent-free house (WO54/516). The same document recorded that he was then a 52-year-old widower with 4 married and 2 unmarried children. He continued to be employed as the Overseer of the Works, and by 1820 he had remarried and was being paid a daily wage of 10/-d (WO54/532). A Return dated the 31st December 1821, recorded that George and his new wife had an addition to the family (WO51/536) but a footnote to this document read, "The appointment of Overseer (George Barnes) is abolished from this day 31st December 1821."

Finally, an entry in the Faversham Records (*RGPR op.cit.* p.12) showed that George Barnes was awarded a pension on the 30th March 1822, and that in 1825 it was to be £44.14.3d per annum (Supply 5/116).

George Barnes (2) was employed as a casual Millwright in the Engineers' Department during September 1812, earning 5/2d per day (WO54/512).

C W Barnham was a 22-year-old bachelor living in Loughton when he was appointed on the 15ᵗʰ November 1815 as an Assistant Clerk at Waltham Abbey. He was not on the Establishment, and his pay was £70 per annum with a gratuity of £20 (Supply 5/231). In May 1819, he was living in Waltham Abbey (Supply 5/231) and the following year had moved to Enfield (Supply 5/232). He was still living in Enfield in April 1821, but his gratuity had been consolidated with his pay, and he was then allowed "£20 house rent, coals and candles" (Supply 5/232). However, by the Board's Order dated the 29ᵗʰ December 1821, Barnham's post was to be discontinued, and he was dismissed two days later (WO54/536).

Thomas Bates, born circa 1765/66, started work as a Labourer at the Royal Faversham Gunpowder Manufactory on the 1ˢᵗ November 1787 (Supply 5/217). He was one of 7 men transferred to the Waltham Abbey Mills, but quit the service on the 4ᵗʰ January 1788 "on account of the smallness of their Wages and the great difficulty they found to get any one to lodge them except Publicans; because they were so black and dirty by being engaged in Manufacturing Gunpowder. viz. (among seven) Thos. Bates (signed)" (Supply 5/113). However, it would appear that Bates did not "quit" the Ordnance, since a Return dated the 24ᵗʰ June 1789 recorded that he eventually started work at Waltham on the 1ˢᵗ February 1788 (Supply 5/217). This was confirmed on the 30ᵗʰ January 1806, when it was recorded that he had 18 years' service with the Board (Supply 5/224).

At Waltham he carried out a variety of tasks for a daily rate of pay of 1/6d. In March 1789, he was grinding "salt petre and charcoal etc." (Supply 5/212) a task he was to undertake at other times. In April 1789, Thomas was "cutting and planting willow trees, cutting of canal at the new Corning House, removing earth to the Store, unloading barges of coals and charring wood" (Supply 5/213). He also worked in the Corning House (Supply

5/215) and the Mixing House (Supply 5/215) but from the summer of 1792 onwards, he alternated with others from being in the country "cutting charring wood", returning to the Mills in the winter months, where he usually worked on the punts (Supply 5/216).

In July 1795 he was described as a Charcoal Burner who was still paid 1/6d per day (Supply 5/217). Thomas was designated a Cylinder man (i.e., he made charcoal by the slip-cylinder method) at Waltham Abbey on the 1st November 1797, before being transferred to Fisher Street in West Sussex on the 14th January 1798. As a Cylinder man he was paid 2/-d per day (Supply 5/219) and a Return made in 1801 recorded that Bates was a single man (Supply 5/221). Another Return of Artificers and Labourers for November 1801, stated that "since cylinders had been out for repair Bates had been employed in stacking timber in the yards and levelling and preparing the ground where the cylinders were to be re-sited." (Supply 5/221). Thomas remained in West Sussex making charcoal until at least August 1812 (Supply 5/221 and Supply 5/228) after which, his name no longer appeared in the records.

Timothy Bates was born circa 1777 (Supply 5/231) and started work as a General Labourer on the 27th March 1797. By September 1798, his work was described as "setting and drawing stoves and clearing willow plantation" (Supply 5/219). He served with the Waltham Military Volunteer Company as a Private (Supply 2/219). The Petition relating to pay and conditions 'signed' by most of the workforce in February 1800 showed that he was illiterate, and also confirmed his position as a Labourer (Supply 5/220). A further Report dated 1801 recorded that he was a bachelor (Supply 5/221).

On the 16th June 1801, Timothy, with others, was repairing the Corning House when it caught fire following an explosion. The fire was caused "from a blow of a copper hammer on a pit wheel" (Winters, *op.cit.* p.57). The Storekeeper sent a letter dated the 23rd June to the Board listing the names of the men who had suffered terrible burns seeking permission to support the casualties, and Timothy's name was included. The letter went on to state, "we beg to represent the situation of the poor men who were burnt when the Corning House took fire on the 16th instant when under repair." It continued, "...these men are burnt in a dreadful manner. Their pain is very great...." and "Our surgeon has represented the necessity of the men most burnt having immediate assistance in wine, as a considerable suppuration is come on their constitutions. They cannot support it without wine, and we have directed wine to be immediately provided to them, we request your permission for our continuing to support these poor men with such wine or other proper support as their surgeon may think their respective situations require" (Supply 5/195).

The Board responded immediately, for, replying the same day, the writer said he had "the Board's commands to transmit to you on the other side hereof a list of the men who have been burnt and otherwise hurt by the fire which lately destroyed the Corning House at Waltham Abbey; and I am to desire the Storekeeper will pay the men all their pay until they are recovered" (Supply 5/195).

Another letter to the Board dated the 29th July 1801 (Supply 5/221) stated that the men who had been burnt at the Corning House requested that they be reimbursed for the loss of clothing. The list included Mr Bates whose claim amounted to £2.13.6d in all – for a hat (6/-d), handkerchiefs (4/6d), stockings (4/6d), shirt (5/6d), waistcoat (5/-d), breeches (12/-d) and sheets (16/-d). The letter went on to say that Mr Bates, amongst others, "suffered so much that he wished for death to release him from his torture, and that it is a matter of surprise that he is recovering." The constant attention the men needed meant that their wives could not undertake seasonal work (haymaking) at which they could earn sufficient to pay the rent. It was requested that financial allowances were made, but no record of the Board's response has come to light.

Timothy Bates did recover from his terrible burns because in January 1806, he was working as a Saltpetre Refiner earning 2/-d per day (Supply 5/224). This was also the case in June 1807 when, in addition, he was allowed to "watch in turn" for which he received 1/-d. His daily rate of pay as a Refiner peaked at 2/8d in 1812 and remained at this level until after the Napoleonic wars had ceased, and he was still allowed "to watch in turn when not working extra" (Supply 5/229).

Bates survived the redundancies made in 1818; he lost his job as a Refiner but was retained as a Warder. His pay was reduced to 2/4d daily but he was still allowed to watch in turn for which he received 1/-d a night (Supply 5/231). The same document records that he was a 41-year-old married man with 3 children, living in Waltham Abbey. Another document dated August 1818 (also Supply 5/231) recorded that Timothy and his family lived in a cottage (described as a Porter's Lodge) on Stove Island (Horse Mill Island) and this remained their home for many years. A Return of Domestic Properties made in 1840 (WO144/133) indicated that the family had occupied the Watch House on Horse Mill Island since it had been built. The house is Plot No. 98 on the Town Map in Appendix 1.

Timothy retained his position as a Warder; his pay was slightly reduced in 1823, and for the rest of his working life his pay and allowances amounted to £39.0.0d annually. Although in most Returns he was described as a Warder, in reality Timothy was most probably a Water Warden since he is described as such in a letter written to the Board dated the 20th June 1835 by James Wright, the Deputy Storekeeper (Supply 5/238). In this letter he recorded that Timothy Bates, Water Warden, caught James Turnham and one other poaching [for fish] on the Board's water at Lower Island. Turnham had been convicted for poaching previously, and Wright asked, therefore, if they should be prosecuted. Another incident recorded was that on the 16th April 1836, explosions occurred when "No. 125 mill was shut up." Bates, Water Warden, was called before Lt. Col. Moody as a witness (Winters, *op.cit.* p.103).

The 1841 Census indicated that Timothy and his wife, Elizabeth, were both in their sixties and had been born in Essex, that he was still working as a Water Warden, and that they lived in Waltham Marsh off High Bridge Street South (Horse Mill Island).

William Bave was born circa 1800 and started work as a Labourer in the Engineers' Department on the 26th May 1828. In October 1829, he was paid 2/2d per hour which equated to £33.18.2d annually, and at the time he was a 29-year-old married man with 3 children (WO54/587). William continued to work as a Labourer and a Return dated October 1830 (WO54/570) recorded that he was one of 15 Labourers to be employed at Waltham Abbey Powder Mills and the Enfield Small Arms Manufactory where they were "to undertake different services as labourers in the manufactories where steadiness and sobriety are required."

On the 15th July 1833, William transferred from the Engineers' Department to the Manufactory, replacing Charles Clayden as a General Labourer. He was then allowed to watch in turn which increased his annual pay to £39.0.0d (WO54/587). The same document recorded that he was a married man with 5 children. A Return of Domestic Properties owned by the Board showed that he lived in a cottage on the corner of Powder Mill Lane and High Bridge Street (WO44/133). His wages were cut in 1834 to

£33.9.6d (WO54/593) and his employment with the Ordnance ceased some time after October 1834.

Nathaniel Beckwith worked as a Puntman in August 1808. He was paid 2/-d per day and was allowed to watch in turn (Supply 5/227).

Abraham Bell was born circa 1770, and started work at Waltham Abbey as a Labourer on the 19th September 1805 (WO54/536). By January 1806, he was working as a Saltpetre Refiner earning 2/-d per day (Supply 5/224). Abraham continued to work in the Refinery, with his daily wage peaking at 2/8d in 1812, and in addition, if he wasn't working extra (overtime), he was allowed to watch in turn, for which he received 1/-d. (Supply 5/228).

On the 30th June 1813, Abraham was promoted to a Storehouse Man (WO54/554) and a Return of Employees dated February 1814 recorded that he was being paid 3/10d per day (Supply 5/230). Another Return in June 1818, noted that he was a 50-year-old married man with 3 children (Supply 5/231). He retained his position in the Stores when the Establishment was reduced in numbers in September 1818, although his daily rate of pay was reduced to 3/4d (Supply 5/231). His position and rate of pay were confirmed in May 1819 and, in addition, he was now a Rounder, for which he received an extra 1/6d every third night (WO54/528). In 1820 his basic pay remained unchanged, but his allowance as a Rounder had increased to 2/-d, and his annual monies now amounted to £64.6.8d (WO54/536).

On the 25th May 1825, Abraham became the Master Mixer, replacing Hugh Jones, and was then paid £91.5.10d per annum (WO54/550). He continued to be the Master Mixer on the same pay until he retired on the 26th November 1834, and was still in receipt of his pension in 1837 (Supply 5/237).

Edward Bellchambers was first employed as a Casual Millwright on the 1st October 1815 by the Engineers' Department. In February 1816 he was paid 5/8d per day, "occasionally as the service required." At that time Edward was a 25-year-old bachelor living in Waltham Abbey (WO54/516).

Thomas Belsham started work in the Corning House in the summer of 1805 (Supply 5/224) and continued to do so until the 27th November 1811, when he died in an horrific explosion (Supply 5/229). Initially he was paid 2/2d per day, which had risen to 2/6d by 1811 (Supply 5/217). Thomas was also allowed to watch in turn, for which he was paid 1/6d each night.

At 11.15 a.m. on the 27th November 1811, there was a huge explosion at No. 4 Press House and the ensuing fire engulfed the Corning House, together with the Reel House which also exploded. There was much damage to the town with many windows shattered and reports in the press recorded that the explosion was heard as far away as Hackney, Blackwall and Marylebone (Winters, *op.cit.* p.72). Among those killed was Thomas Belsham, who left a widow, Ann, 2 sons - Benjamin (18) and Thomas (14) and a daughter - Louisa (16) - (Supply 5/229). These 3 children were in service, but he also had 5 other children at home – William (13) Joshua (4) John (2) Mary (8) and Ann (6). Ann was awarded a weekly pension of 17/6d commencing the 28th November that year (Supply 5/231) which she was still receiving in 1837, although it was then recorded as £45.10.0d per annum (Supply 5/237).

William Belsham was a Cooper employed at Waltham Abbey in August 1812, receiving a daily wage of 1/9d (Supply 5/229). For a Cooper at the height of the Napoleonic Wars this was a low rate of pay and it is possible that he had only just completed his training, and had not yet reached the output expected of a

Cooper. He was still a Cooper in February 1814, but was then paid 2/4d per day (Supply 5/230).

Job Bendall was born circa 1777 and worked as a Labourer in the Saltpetre Refinery in May 1804 (Supply 5/222) where he was earning 2/- per day. He also received an additional allowance of 1/-d per night when it was his turn to watch which was, on average, every fifth night. Over the ensuing twelve years he was continually changing jobs within the Manufactory.

From January 1806 until at least August 1808, he was a Millman earning 2/3d per day with an extra 3d per night when on duty (Supply 5/224). In August 1810, he was working as a Brimstone Refiner earning 2/3d per day, with an extra 1/-d when he was on watch (Supply 5/227). By the 1st September 1810 he was working in the Dusting House on the same rate of pay, and was still allowed to watch in turn (Supply 5/228). From 1812 onwards until he was superannuated in 1816, he was employed as a Warder and was paid 2/8d daily (Supply 5/230).

In a Return of Employees dated the 2nd March 1816 (Supply 5/230) it was recorded that Job had been employed by the Ordnance for 12 years, that he was aged 38, and that it was recommended that he should received a daily superannuation of 2/8d. In the notes attached to this Return was a comment that Bendall and others should be superannuated because of "the hurts they have received in this dangerous manufactory." The notes went on to say "before he was admitted into these works, [he] had been a soldier for several years in a Regiment of the Line, was severely wounded in the West Indies and has no pension, and was severely burnt by a fall in the Brimestone Refining House in the execution of his duty." In addition it also stated "…he has been changed about in various parts of the Manufactory to afford him a very fair chance of recovery, but he is now so debilitated as to be incapable of any exertion whatever." By a letter dated the

6th March 1816, Bendall was awarded a pension of 2/-d per day by the Board commencing on the 1st April, and at the same time they desired that "The office of Ordnance cause Job Bendall to be examined by the Ordnance Surgeon, and a Report made of his present state of health" (Supply 5/230).

It appears that at some stage his pension was reduced to 8/-d per week, or £20.16.0d annually (Supply 5/232). Job died late in 1826, and the Board authorised payment of his outstanding pension of £1.9.8d to his legal representative (Supply 5/205).

Thomas Benfield was the Master of the barge "The Andrew Lighter" operating out of the Waltham Abbey Manufactory in 1805 (Winters, *op.cit.* p.56).

Bartholomew Bennett was born circa 1720, and was appointed Overseer of Works at the Faversham Powder Mills on the 25th April 1772. On the 18th October 1787, Bartholomew, together with Mr. Cowell, John Goodfellow and William Easton, was "…to go immediately to Mr. Walton's Mills at Waltham Abbey." (Supply 5/66).

It would appear that this was on the order of his Grace, the Master General (of Ordnance), the Duke of Richmond (Supply 5/113). At Waltham he supervised William Sutton, acting Overseer (also from Faversham), and the Artificers and Labourers, etc., employed on the renovation of Mr. Walton's Mills (Winters, *op.cit.*p.28). During this period, "…he took a very active interest in, and gave much good sound technical advice on, improvements to the Waltham Abbey Powder Mills after the Government bought them in 1787." (W. H. Simmonds, *A Short History of the Royal Gunpowder Factory)*. By January 1789 he had returned to Faversham, although Sutton remained at Waltham Abbey until at least November of that year, possibly to supervise the repairs, etc., and was paid 3/-d per day as a

Millwright (Winters, *op.cit*.p.32). For more information on Bartholomew Bennett, see the *Faversham Gunpowder Personnel Register*: 1573-1840, p.13).

James Bennett was a Labourer set to work by Daniel Cornish in October 1787 at 9/-d per week, following the purchase of the Mills by the Government from John Walton (Winters, *op.cit.* p.28). A Return dated the 27th January 1789, recorded that James was to be tried as a Millman (Supply 5/212). However, it appears that he was unsuccessful, since in March 1789 he was employed as a Labourer setting and drawing stoves, for which he received 1/6d daily (also Supply 5/212).

On the 12th September 1789, J. Wright and J. Clowdersly wrote to Major Congreve saying, "We beg leave to report that last night at 6 O'clock the 2nd of No. Head Mills blew up. The charge had not been upon the bed more than five minutes and the Mill did not receive any injury; it was set to work this day at 10 O'clock. The Master Worker has removed James Bennett and Stephen Cock out of the Mills as he found them incapable of doing their business; we therefore desire to know if you would have them discharged." (WASC 1392). Nevertheless, it appears that Bennett was not discharged, since a Petition dated February 1800 relating to pay and conditions at the Mills, showed that he was one of the few Labourers who were literate (Supply 5/220).

Mathew Bennett, born circa 1764, was working as a Brimstone and Saltpetre Refiner on the 29th August 1812. He was paid 2/8d per day and, in addition, he was allowed to watch in turn, for which he earned 1/6d per night (Supply 5/229). He was still in the same position with the same pay and conditions in 1814 (Supply 5/230). However, a Return of Employees dated the 2nd March 1816 recorded that he was then a Dusting House Man earning 3/-d per day, that he was 51 years' old and that he had 21 years' service with the Board, although it is not known where he worked before coming to Waltham Abbey. A footnote to this Return commented that Bennett and others should be superannuated because "of the hurts they have received in this dangerous manufactory." It went on to recommend that Bennett should receive a daily superannuation of 3/-d since he "is become so feeble as to be totally unfit to exert himself at work" (Supply 5/200). The Board awarded him a pension of 2/6d per day for a six-day week, which started on the 1st April 1816 (Supply 5/200).

Nathaniel Bennett started work as a Sulphur Millman on the 8th July 1797 (Supply 5/219). The same document shows that he had joined the Military Volunteer Company as a Private. A Report dated May 1801 giving the marital status of the employees indicated that he was a married man with no children (Supply 5/221). A Return of Artificers and Labourers dated the 3rd November 1801 (Supply 5/221) indicated that although he was employed as a Labourer refining Saltpetre, at that time he was engaged "in cleaning and deepening the river, canals ditches and other work necessary to be performed," for which he was paid 1/6d per day. Nathaniel continued to work as a Saltpetre Millman until at least September 1810 (Supply 5228). During this time he was paid 2/-d a day (Supply 5/224) and had an allowance of 1/-d to "watch in turn" which was, on average, every fifth night (Supply 5/226).

William Benson commenced work on the 20th May 1820 as a casual Labourer in the Engineers' Department where he was paid 2/4d a day. In February 1816 he was a 25-year-old bachelor living in Waltham Abbey (WO54/516).

William Bettles, born circa 1776 and trained as a Millwright, was employed by the Engineers' Department "occasionally as the service required." In February 1817 he was paid 5/2d per day (WO54/520). The same document noted that he was a married man without children who lived in Waltham Abbey.

Jeremiah Betts was born circa 1770 and trained as a Wool Comber before starting work at the Royal Powder Mills as a Saltpetre Refiner on the 6th September 1805 (Supply 5/232). In January 1806, he was paid 2/2d per day (Supply 5/224). The Saltpetre Refinery was to be his work place for the next seventeen years. During this period Jeremiah and his wife, Mary, had 3 children (Supply 5/231). His daily wage peaked during the Napoleonic wars at 2/8d (Supply 5/229) and he was allowed to watch in turn. He survived the reduction to Waltham Abbey Establishment in 1818, and his position as a Saltpetre Refiner was confirmed by Orders of the Board dated the 4th September 1818 and the 4th October 1819 (Supply 5/232). His annual wage then, including his allowance to watch, was £41.14.4d.

A statement "of monies to which the public were entitled to receive credit between the 1st January and the 31st December, 1821" - see notes on George Barnes (1) – stated that by an Order of the Board dated the 6th May 1812, Jeremiah was able to rent a house owned by the Board for an annual fee of £5.4.0d, but he location of the property is not mentioned (Supply 5/232). However, Jeremiah did not survive the review of the Establishment in 1822 – see notes on George Adams for more details on the economies made – and he was dismissed on the 1st June that year with two weeks' extra pay to "ease his financial burden."

Nevertheless, Jeremiah returned to the Powder Mills a year later when he joined the Engineers' Department as a Labourer on the 16th June 1823, and he was then paid £33.18.2d annually (WO54/550). A Return dated the 31st January 1831, recorded that he was one of 15 Labourers employed at the Waltham Abbey Gunpowder Mills and the Enfield Small Arms Manufactory "where steadiness and sobriety are particularly required" (WO54/ 570), and he was still paid £33.18.2d.

On the 14th October 1834, Jeremiah, then aged 64, was appointed as the Office Keeper and Messenger to the Engineers' Department; he was still classified as a Labourer and received £33.18.2d per annum, as he did in 1838. A Return of Domestic Properties date the 28th May 1840, indicated that "J Betts labourer" was living in a cottage formerly occupied by "Mr. C Newton, son of a former master worker" (WO/44/133). Newton's house was on Horse Mill Island and had been converted into two dwellings by 1828. The Tenement is Plot No. 98 on the Town Map in Appendix 1. Jeremiah retired soon after May 1840, and he and his wife, Mary, moved to High Bridge Street south, opposite Powder Mill Lane (1841 Census). His cottage, previously occupied by J. Davy, was one of 3 tenements formed out of a dwelling house in the Tanyard, purchased from a Mr Cannopp in 1816.

Thomas Betts was a Labourer and a single man according to a Return of the Marital Status of the Employees at Waltham Abbey in 1801. Thomas, together with others, was repairing the Old Corning House on the 16th June 1801 when it caught fire following an explosion, and was badly burnt. Full details of the event are recorded under the notes on Timothy Bates. A Return of Artificers and Labourers dated the 3rd November 1801 noted that Thomas was so severely burnt in the Old Corning House that it would have been dangerous to expose him with the other men repairing the river banks at the time, but that "he could perform trifling jobs as they occurred" (Supply 5/221). Betts appears to have fully recovered, since he was working as a Refiner in May 1804 at 2/-d per day and also allowed to watch in turn, for which he received 1/-d (Supply 5/222).

Thomas Bilton started work as a Labourer on the 13th April1791 "setting and drawing stoves and in the punts" earning 1/6d per day (Supply 5/215), and by July 1792, he was working in the Corning House on the same rate of pay (Supply 5/216). He was chequered (fined) one day's pay on the 16th March 1793 for not having obeyed orders to ensure that his shoes were free of gravel when he entered the Corning House, and, together with others, was chequered one day's pay in the following July "for having gone across the Hoppit contrary to repeated orders" (Winters, *op.cit.* p.39). He enlisted as a Private in the Military Volunteer Company on the 7th May 1794 (Winters, *op.cit.* p.42) and he signed a Petition relating to pay and conditions in February 1800 with a cross (Supply 5/220).

Thomas was working in the new Corning House on the 19th April 1801 when it blew up with a tremendous explosion, and was one of nine men killed that day, along with four horses (Supply 5/220). Full details of the explosion can be found under John Bailey's notes. A Petition dated the 24th April was signed by his widow, Ann, along with the other widows and mothers of the deceased, requesting "relief in their distress" (Supply 5/194). A Report was forwarded to the Board on the 29th April giving the ages of the children and the circumstances of the widows (Supply 5/220). The Report stated that Ann was aged 32, and had suffered an accident three or four years previously, which prevented her "doing for herself." She had several children, of which, a boy of 12 years' old and a girl of 3 survived. She was also believed to be with child, and on the 23rd March 1802, the Board decided that Ann's pension should be 10/-d per week (Supply 5/195).

Thomas Bird was working in the Dusting House in June 1807, earning 2/1d per day (Supply 5/226). He continued to do so until at least August 1808, when his pay rose to 2/3d daily (Supply 5/227) and he was allowed to watch in turn, for which he received 1/-d. By September 1810, Thomas had transferred to the Corning House and was earning 2/6d per day, with an increased allowance to watch of 1/6d per night (Supply 5/228). He remained in the Corning House until at least February 1814, when his pay had increased to 3/3d daily but his allowance to watch was unchanged (Supply 5/230). This is the last reference to Thomas Bird working in the manufactory.

Nevertheless, Thomas possibly returned to work as a temporary Labourer in the Engineers' Department, because a temporary Labourer of the same name was working there in June 1825 earning 2/2d per day, although he was due to be discharged in October 1825. He was a 49-year-old married man with 6 children (WO54/550).

John Blackbee was employed as a Millman in 1807 earning 2/3d per day (Supply 5/226). This was also the case in August 1808 when he was earning the same daily wage, but also "allowed 6d per night when on duty" (Supply 5/227).

On the 6th October 1808, John was spreading a green charge when No. 6 Horse Mill exploded at 11.15 p.m. He received burns to his face, which, although not severe, caused him to be on the sick list from that date until the 24th November. There was little damage to the Mill, although one horse had its mane singed. No blame, however, was attached to Blackbee (Supply 5/227) and he returned to work after he had recovered, He continued working as a Millman and was then paid 3/-d per day, plus 6d when he was on a night shift. This was also the case in 1812 (Supply 5/229) and in February 1814 (Supply 5/230). John appears to have left the Mills at the end of the Napoleonic wars.

George Blackford worked as a Millman at the Powder Mills from September 1810 (Supply 5/228) until at least February 1814 (Supply 5/230). During this period his rate of pay increased from 2/-d to 3/-d a day with an extra 6d when on night duty.

Donald Blackmore signed his Indentures as an Apprentice on the 4th July 1840 (Supply 5/238). The 1841 Census recorded that he was a 13-year-old Apprentice Saltpetre Refiner lodging in High Bridge Street with the Master Saltpetre Refiner.

William Blenkings was born circa 1785, and started work in the Engineers' Department as a casual Labourer "occasionally as the service requires" on the 5th October 1809 (WO54/516). In September 1812 he was employed as a casual Bricklayer earning 2/8d per day for a six-day week (WO54/512). By February 1816, as a 31-year-old bachelor living in Waltham Abbey, he had reverted to being a casual Labourer within the Engineers' Department and still earned 2/8d per day (WO54/516).

George Bloomfield was born circa 1781 and was engaged as a Corning House Man on the 29th November 1804 (Supply 5/232). He was to work in the Corning House for the next 21 years, surviving the reductions made to the Establishment at Waltham Abbey in 1818 and 1822. When he started work in 1804 he was paid 2/2d a day (Supply 5/224), which peaked at 3/3d at the height of the Napoleonic wars (Supply 5/229) but had decreased to 2/11d per day by May 1819 (Supply 5/231). As a Corning House Man he was allowed to watch in turn, and, like his daily rate of pay, this varied between 1/-d and 1/6d per night.

With his basic pay and allowances his annual income in 1821 was £50.16.11d, on which, he and his wife, Mary, provided for 7 children (Supply 5/232). Life appeared to have become harder when a Board Order dated the 27th December 1822 reduced his basic wage by £2.12.0d per annum, giving George an estimated income of £48.2.0d. Under a further Board Order dated the 15th January 1823, his wage was cut again to £33.16.0d per annum, which, with an allowance to watch, equated to £39.0.0d annually. Furthermore, it would appear that he had been demoted to being a general Labourer, since Corning House men were still paid a basic wage of £42.18.0d (WO54/542).

A Return dated the 1st April 1825, confirmed that George was then a general purpose Labourer (WO54/550) and in October of the same year, he was "drawing stoves" (Winters, *op.cit.* p.94). For the next 6 years he was a general Labourer working within the Manufactory on the same pay, but by an Order of the Board dated the 31st May 1831, he then replaced John Simpson as a Millman. George was then paid a basic wage of £39.0.0d, which, with an allowance to watch in turn, gave him an annual income of £46.16.0d (WO54/581). He was still a Millman in October 1839 earning the same monies (WO54/623). Sometime between 1835 and 1840, George moved into a cottage in Powder Mill Lane previously occupied by John Lockyer (WO44/133) being Plot No. 63 on the Town Map in Appendix 1. The 1841 Census confirmed the location, listing George, together with his wife, Mary, and daughter, Eliza, as the occupants.

John Bond started work as a casual Labourer in the Engineers' Department on the 2nd September 1815. In February 1816, as a 20-year-old bachelor, he earned 2/8d per day (WO54/516).

William Bond was working as a Labourer "in the punts and drawing stoves etc." between July and September 1792, for which he received 1/6d per day. In September that year, he replaced Edward Reyley "mixing composition" and continued in that capacity for the next 12 months (Supply 5/216).

On the night of Sunday, the 17th February 1793, Robert Coleman, the Clerk of the Cheque, reported that William was not on his watch but finally arrived at 10.00 p.m. – drunk. He was chequered (fined) one day's pay and "ordered off watch for present" (Winters, *op.cit.* p.37). From January to August 1794, he was "drawing and setting stoves & in the punts" and enlisted as a Private in the Military Volunteer Company on the 7th May 1794. From December 1794 until July 1795 he was working in the Corning House (Supply 5/219).

David Bonner was a Labourer in March 1789 at 1/6d per day "grinding salt petre and charcoal etc." (Supply 5/212).

J. W. Bordwin was appointed Clerk of the Works on the 25th May 1805, in place of Charles Wilks. He was paid 10/-d per day and allowed £20 per annum for house rent, coal and candles (Winters, *op.cit*.p.63).

Thomas Boreham was working as a Millman in August 1812 (Supply 5/229) as he was in February 1814 (Supply 5/230). His daily wage during this period was 3/-d, with an additional 6d when on night duty.

William Boreham was born circa 1784 and started work as a Millman in the summer of 1805, and by January 1806, he was earning 2/3d per day (Supply 5/224). In June 1807 his basic wage remained unchanged, but he was allowed an extra 3d for a night shift, which, by August 1808, had been increased to 6d per shift (Supply 5/227). In August 1812 his pay had been increased to 3/-d daily with the same premium for night work (Supply 5/229) and it remained at this level during 1814 (Supply 5/230).

Sometime after this he became a Warder, because a letter dated the 10th December 1817 from the "Office of Ordnance" to the Board (Supply 5/201) stated that a small tenement which was to be vacated by John Braddock should be continued to be let at the same rent of 2/- per week to William Boreham, who was the Warder at the Magazine Watch House. A list of Employees dated the 25th June 1818 stated that William was still a Warder, that he was a married man with 4 children and earned 2/4d per day, and that he was also allowed to watch in turn, for which he received 1/- a night (Supply 5/231). He was retained as a Warder between September 1818 and the 31st December 1818, but his pay had been reduced to 2/4d a day (Supply 5/231). It would appear he left the Board's employment after this, since there was no further reference to him.

George Boswell (1) was working as a Refiner at Waltham Abbey in May 1804. He was paid 2/- per day and allowed to watch in turn, on average every fifth night, for which he received 1/-d (Supply 5/222).

George Boswell (2) was born circa 1755 and started work as a casual Labourer in the Engineers' Department on the 29th March 1806 (WO54/516). In September 1812, he was paid 2/8d per day for a six-day week (WO54/512) and in 1816, it was recorded that he was a 60-year-old married man with 3 children, two of whom were married (WO54/516). George continued to be employed in the Engineers' Department as a casual Labourer but had become a widower by May 1819 (WO54/528). In April 1823, he had 17 years' service, and at that date was paid £33.18.2d annually (WO54/542).

George Boswell (3) was working as a Bargeman in September 1818, but was under notice to be discharged (Supply 5/231).

James Boswell was born circa 1787 and commenced work as a Labourer on the 1st January 1804 (Supply 5/232). In May of that year he was working in the Corning House earning 2/-d per day (Supply 5/222). By January 1806, he had been transferred to the Mixing House on the same pay (Supply 5/224) and was still in the Mixing House in June 1807, when he was also allowed to watch in turn, for which he received 1/-d. Sometime between 1807 and 1812 he returned to the Corning House as an Artificer, whereas before he had been a Labourer there. He then earned 3/3d a day, with an additional 1/6d when it was his turn to watch (Supply 5/229). He was still a Corning House Man in February 1814 on the same pay and conditions (Supply 5/230).

A List of Employees dated the 25th June 1818 (Supply 5/231) stated that James Boswell was then a Bargeman who was paid 3/-d per day. He was a married man, aged 30, with 3 children, and lived in Waltham Abbey. A Return for May 1819, however, showed that James had become a widower (Supply 5/231) and from subsequent records it would appear that he did not remarry. A statement dated the 4th April 1822 "of monies to which the public were entitled to receive credit" recorded that James was one of several employees "having occupied their present residences previous to the Hon. Board purchasing the same, sanction will be asked for their future residing in them." Under an Order of the Board dated the 4th May 1821, the property had been leased to him for an annual rent of £8.9.0d (Supply 5/231) – see notes on Jeremiah Betts for details. The house was on the north side of High Bridge Street, at the western end of a row of tenements known as Bank Cottages, being part of Plot No. 48 on the Town Map in Appendix 1. His rent was reduced to £5.4.0d annually from the 6th April 1829 (Supply 5/237).

James continued his employment as a Bargeman, and in December 1821, his annual wage was £46.19.0d (Supply 5/232). This was the case until April 1834, when his income was reduced to £39.3.0d annually (WO54/593). During 1826, a Return of Employees stated that he was "employed with the barges transporting gunpowder and stores" (WO54/554). James was away from work through sickness between the 7th and 30th September 1832, and the Board agreed to pay him 30 days' sick pay at 3/-d per day (Supply 5/207).

John Nigh, the Master Bargeman at the Mills, died on the 20th August 1837, and the Ordnance Office at Waltham recommended that James Boswell should replace him (Supply 5/237). In October 1839, Boswell as the Master Bargeman, was earning £65.4.2d per annum navigating barges between Waltham Abbey and the Thames (WO54/623). This is confirmed in a letter from the Deputy Storekeeper dated the 12th March 1841, informing the Board that James Boswell, Master Bargeman, "was to be at the West India Docks in four days' time." The 1841 Census indicated that James, a Bargeman, was then living in Silver Street with a Mary Saunders, aged 25.

Richard Boswell was working as a Millwright in the Engineers' Department in May 1801. He was paid 3/-d a day and was a single man (Supply 5/221).

William Boswell (1) worked as a Labourer in the Mixing House in September 1798 at 1/6d per day, and was also a Private in the Military Volunteer Company (Supply 5/219). A Return of the Marital Status of the Employees made in May 1801, showed that William was married and had 3 children (Supply 5/221). In October 1801, Robert Coleman, the Clerk of the Cheque, noted in his Minute Book that 24 men were required to work at Faversham or face discharge, and William agreed to go (Winters, *op.cit.* p.66). However, William's name did not appear in the Faversham records and the Waltham records do not show a break in his service years, so it can only be assumed that he was retained.

On the 8th May 1804, he was still working as a Labourer, paid 2/1d per day and allowed to watch in turn, which, on average, was every fifth night, for which he received a shilling (Supply 5/222). In January 1806, he was a Millman with daily pay of 2/6d (Supply 5/224) and the same document stated that he had 9 years' service with the Ordnance Board. In 1808, William was back in the Dusting House earning only 2/3d per day. Dusting House Men "in addition to their pay…were allowed to watch in turn, for which they received one shilling" (Supply 5/227).

By August 1812, William had changed his work place yet again, and was now in the Saltpetre Refinery earning 2/8d per day. In addition, when not working extra, he was allowed to watch in turn (Supply 5/229). He remained a Saltpetre Refiner until September 1818, when his services were no longer required by the Ordnance Board (Supply 5/231).

William Boswell (2) born circa 1765, was employed as a Labourer in the Engineers' Department in June 1825, earning 2/2d daily. His employment was on a temporary basis, and he was due to be discharged at the end of October 1825 (WO54/550). William was a 60-year-old married man with 6 children.

Peter Bowie was a 15-year-old Waltham Abbey lad when he started an Apprenticeship under the Master Carpenter on the 5th January 1815 (WO54/516). Initially he was paid 6/-d per week increasing to 6/8d by May 1819 (WO54/528) and to 7/-d by September 1820 (WO54/532). It is not known if he completed his Apprenticeship.

William Bowles was born circa 1762 and started work as a Labourer in the Saltpetre Refinery on the 7th April 1789, being paid 1 /6d per day (Supply 5/213). By March 1790, he was employed as a Millman earning 2/-d daily (Supply 5/214). the western end of a row of tenements known as "Bank Cottages." His rent was reduced to £5.4.0d annually from the 6th April 1829 (Supply 5/237).

Richard Boxall was a married man with 4 children working as a Labourer in May 1801, earning 1/6d per day in the Charcoal Cylinders at Fisher Street, West Sussex. (Supply 5/221). The cylinders were under repair in November 1801, so instead Richard was employed "stacking timber in the yards and levelling and preparing the ground where the cylinders were to be re-sited", but he was also under notice to leave (Supply 5/221).

However, he rejoined the Ordnance Board and was working as a Cylinder man earning 2/-d per day in January 1806. A Labour Return (Supply 5/224) showed that he had two years' service. Richard continued to work at Sussex producing charcoal for the Waltham Abbey Mills until at least February 1814, and was paid 2/8d per day (Supply 5/230).

William Boxall, a bachelor, worked as a Labourer in the Cylinder House in Sussex in May 1801 earning 1/6d per day (Supply 5/221). A Return of Artificers and Labourers dated the 3rd November 1801 (Supply 5/221) showed that he was still employed as a Labourer in the Cylinder House. This document also said that "since the cylinders have been out of repair, Boxall has been employed stacking timber in the yards and levelling and preparing the ground where the cylinders were to be re-sited" and that he had been "given notice to leave".

Nevertheless, In January 1806, William is described as a Cylinder Man in Sussex earning 2/-d a day and that he had two years' service, indicating that he had been re-engaged (Supply 5/224). He continued to work in the Cylinder House with his pay increased to 2/8d per day by August 1812 (Supply 5/229). This was also the case in February 1814 (Supply 5/230).

William Boyd was a Bargemaster working out of the Mills in 1796 (Winters, *op.cit.* p.55).

Samuel Brace was born circa 1766 and commenced work in the Engineer' Department as a casual Labourer earning 2/8d per day on the 2nd December 1815. He was a married man without issue living in Enfield (WO54/51).

John Braddock Snr. was born circa 1762, and married his wife, Sarah, in 1793. They had two children, John, jnr. born in 1794 who was baptised at St. Martin in the Fields, and Sarah, born in

1803. He started work as a Barrel Marker at 2/-d a day on the 20th December 1804 (Supply 5/224). Prior to starting at the Mills he had been trained as a Silk Throwster (Supply 5/231). John continued to work as a Barrel Marker and in January 1810, his daily pay was 2/6d (Supply 5/199). He was also allowed to watch in turn for which he received 1/6d per night (Supply 5/228). By August 1812 his pay had increased to 3/3d per day, and he was also a Rounder, for which he received 2/-d every third night (Supply 5/229). On the 11th January 1813, he was appointed as the Foreman of Magazines (5/230) and paid 5/2d per day, as well as still being a Rounder with the same allowance.

In a letter to the Board dated the 10th December 1817 (Supply 5/201) it was stated that the dwelling house formerly occupied by James Allsup "will be ready to let in two distinct tenements on the 31st instant" and continued "…those tenements should be let at 3/-d per week each to John Braddock, Foreman of Magazines, and Michael Summers, Millman." The letter revealed that John was then living in a small tenement which, when vacated, would be let at the same rent of 2/-d per week to William Boreham (see notes on Boreham). A statement "of monies to which the public were entitled to receive credit" for the year 1821 (Supply 5/232) revealed that an Order of the Board dated the 10th December 1817, authorised John to live in his new accommodation. This property has been identified as one of the cottages on the south side of High Bridge Street almost opposite Powder Mill Lane, and shown as Plot No. 56 on the Town Map in Appendix 1.

Following the defeat of Napoleon, wages at the Powder Mills were cut. A List of Employees dated the 29th June 1818 showed that John's pay had been reduced to 4/2d per day and his Rounder's allowance to 1/6d every fifth night (Supply 5/231). The same Return noted that John was a married man with 2 children, one of whom, John Jnr., wrote the influential treatise *A Memoir on Gunpowder* (WASC 0677)/ He continued to be employed as the Magazines' Foreman with his basic rate of pay unchanged, but by April 1821, he was acting as a Rounder every third night with his allowance reverting to 2/-d (Supply 5/232).

A list of persons who were to form an Establishment at Waltham Abbey to regenerate 2,000 barrels of gunpowder as well as to make 100 or 200 barrels of gunpowder annually (Supply 5/232 dated March, 1822), indicated that John Braddock, Foreman of Magazines and Stoves, was to be retained and he continued in this position, receiving the same pay and allowances (WO54/542). The position of Master Saltpetre Refiner became vacant in 1825 and Braddock wrote to Board on the 25th February soliciting the post (Winters, *op.cit.* p.92). He was appointed as the Master Saltpetre Refiner on the 11th March 1825 (Winters, *op.cit.* p.93). At the same time Hugh Jones, the Master Mixer, who was living in a house associated with the Saltpetre Refinery in High Bridge Street, was promoted to Master Worker following the death of William Newton. Braddock correctly assumed that Jones would move to the Master Worker's house on Horse Mill Island, so applied for Jones' house in High Bridge Street. However, Jones did not move to Horse Mill Island, but relocated to Powder Mill Lane sometime during 1825, and this enabled John to move into the house within the Saltpetre Refinery, and is shown as Plot No. 39 on the Town Map in Appendix 1. His pay was then £118.3.7d per annum, and he was entitled to a rent-free house and an allowance to teach an Apprentice (WO54/550). His pay and conditions remained unchanged for the rest of his working life at the Mills.

Sarah, John's wife, died in 1834, aged 70. On the 27th June 1836, John, then aged 74, was "desirous of his pension in order to proceed to Graham's Town, Cape of Good Hope" (Winters, *op.cit.* p.104), and he was granted a pension from the 30th December 1836 (Supply 5/237). A letter to the Board dated the 28th March 1840 stated that John Braddock had died on the 26th of that month, and that his pension was worth £35.12.0d annually (Supply 5/237). The two days' difference in dates between his death and the letter would indicate that he was not living in South Africa, which was confirmed by the fact that he was buried close to the south wall of Waltham Abbey Church.

John Braddock, Jnr., son of John Braddock, the Master Refiner of Saltpetre (1762-1840) was baptised at St. Martin in the Fields on the 30th April 1794 (WASC 2229). He was trained as a Powder Maker, and by August 1812 was working as a Labourer "drawing and setting stoves and in the willow plantation" at 2/8d per day as well as being allowed to watch in turn, for which he received 1/6d per night (Supply 5/229). He was then engaged by the East India Company on a five-year contract as an "expert in making gunpowder" at 10/d per day, sailing for India on the ship *Hugh Inglis,* arriving at Madras on the 9th August 1813. In Madras he married Elizabeth Stephenson at St. Mary's Church in January 1819.

According to D. F. Harding, author of "Small Arms of the East India Company: 1600-1856, Vol.III – Ammunition and Performance, 1999 (p.38), John Braddock, Jnr. wrote *A Memoir on Gunpowder* (WASC 0677) on the theory and practice of the manufacture and proof of gunpowder, which was originally published in Madras for the East India Company, and reprinted in London in 1832 by Braddock's father. He apparently spent extra time among the workmen to master every part of the process and to pick up opinions, after which he was recruited by the East India Company and sent out to India in 1813 as one of "Captain Thomas Fraser's team of specialists in the various branches of powder-making." (WASC 2229)

On page 80 of the same book, Harding said that *A Memoir on Gunpowder* filled a gap on the subject of gunpowder in English Scholarship, and in the 1840's it was often quoted in the

Company's records as the best authority on gunpowder. It also "received high praise from the gunmaker and author, Henry Wilkinson, is frequently quoted by later authors on gunpowder, and was even summarised in French." (WASC 2229). John died in Madras on the 9th September 1840. More information on his life in India can be found in an article in *Powder Master* written by one of his descendants, Sylvia Murphy (WASC 2229).

George Brand was a casual Labourer in the Engineers' Department in September 1812, earning 2/8d per day for a six-day week (WO54/512).

Steven Brand was a Labourer set to work by Daniel Cornish in October 1787 renovating the Waltham Abbey Powder Mills following their purchase from Mr. Walton, and according to Winters (*op.cit.* p.29) he was paid 9/-d per week.

James Brass was a casual Labourer in the Engineers' Department in September 1812. He was paid 2/8d per day for a six-day week (WO54/512).

Joseph Bray was born circa 1778 and joined the Engineers' Department on the 2nd May 1815 as a casual Labourer. He was paid 2/8d per day, and was then a 36-year-old married man with a family of 7 children who lived in Cheshunt, and had previously trained as a Baker (WO4/516). He continued to work within the Engineers' Department "occasionally as required," with his daily wage reduced to 2/4d in 1817 (WO54/520), and was still on the same rate of pay in April 1821 (WO54/536).

William Breeze was born circa 1768 and appointed to the Ordnance Board as a Junior Clerk at Sheerness on the 26 May 1878. He rose to the position of First Clerk at Sheerness before being transferred to the Royal Gunpowder Mills at Waltham Abbey on the 6th February 1805 as the Clerk of the Cheque

(Supply 5/223). At Waltham Abbey his income was £150.0.0d per annum, plus a service gratuity of £50.0.0d; in addition, he was allowed £26.0.0d per annum for lodging allowance, and £12.10.0d annually for coal and candles (Supply 5/229). By June 1809 he was provided with a rent-free house, retaining his allowance for heat and light, but where his house was located at the time is unknown. His gratuity, based on his length of service with the Ordnance Board, was now £65.0.0d (Supply 5/226).

On the 26th February 1812, Breeze was promoted to the Clerk of the Survey, and this position ranked as number two in the Manufactory, directly under the Storekeeper. His salary was £200.0.0d per annum, and he was still entitled to a rent-free house and the allowances which went with it (Supply 5/229). An Order of the Board dated the 12th September 1814, authorised him to live without paying rent in a property owned by the Ordnance (Supply 5/232). A perquisite, which does not appear in the records until 1821, was that he was provided with a Labourer, possibly to tend his garden, etc. Board Orders dated the 2nd March 1812 and the 20th January 1819 authorised him to rent 14 acres of Lammas or half-year land within the Manufactory grounds at £1.1.0d per acre (Supply 5/232). The land he rented from 1819 was described in a note set against his pay details for 1821 and read, "The Clerk of the Survey had 7 acres of grass amongst the Willow plantation cutting, the same at his expense, the supposed value £15" (Supply 5/232 dated the 6th February 1822).

William continued to work as the Clerk of the Survey, and various Returns, such as Supply 5/231, record that he was a married man with 4 children. Over the years his salary remained at £200.0.0d, but his service gratuity increased annually. His total income for 1821 was £476.6.0d, consisting of his salary of £200.0.0d, his service gratuity of £250.0.0d, his coal and candle allowance of £12.10.0d, and a further £13.16.0d in lieu of a

Labourer from the 1st July to the 31st December 1821 (Supply 5/232). However, a very faint note set against his pay details stated that by the Master General and Board's Order dated the 1st August 1821, the position of the Clerk of the Survey was to be abolished on the 31st December that year.

A List of Employees dated February 1822 (WO54/524) did not record Breeze's name, so the Order in question must have been enforced, and William died soon after he was made redundant, because an analysis of the Land Records and Returns, the 1825 Rateable Value of properties owned by the Board clearly indicated that a G. Lovell was occupying a house in High Bridge Street, being Plot No. 51 on the Town Map in Appendix 1. Lovell is also recorded as occupying the same area of Lammas Land, being Parcel No. 386 in Edmonsea Mead; this was Lammas Land of the same area that Breeze had rented in 1812 and 1819. In addition, a Return of Domestic Properties dated the 28th May 1840 (WO44/133) recorded that William Breeze was deceased and that "the property he had lived in was occupied by G Lovell, Esq."

John Brett, a single man, was working for the Engineers' Department as a Foreman in charge of Labourers in May 1801 and was paid 1/9d per day (Supply 5/221). By May 1804, he a Labourer in the "Engineers' Department Established" with his pay reduced to 1/6d a day (Supply 5/222). Sometime during 1804 he transferred to the Manufactory where he was employed in the Corning House. In January 1806, he was earning 2/2d per day (Supply 5/224) and the following year he was allowed to watch in turn (Supply 5/226). His daily wage and watch allowance peaked in 1812 to 3/3d and 1/6d respectively (Supply 5/229) and the last record of John working at the Royal Gunpowder Mills was dated February 1814, when he was still working in the Corning House (Supply 5/230).

Richard Brett, born circa 1797, joined the Engineers' Department as a casual Labourer on the 22nd October 1815, and was paid 2/4d per day. He was an 18-year-old bachelor living in Waltham Abbey (WO54/516).

William Bride was born circa 1759 and started work as a general Labourer in the Corning House on the 21st April 1794, earning 1/6d per day (Supply 5/216) but had transferred to the Dusting House by December 1784 (Supply 5/216). He served in the Military Volunteer Company as a Private in 1794 (Supply 5/219) and in 1800 had signed a Petition on pay and conditions in the Gunpowder Manufactory with a cross (Supply 5/220). A Return listing the marital status of the Employees at the Mills in 1801 recorded that he was a married man with 2 children (Supply 5/221).

The Dusting House continued to be his work place until April 1816 when he was "superannuated" (Supply 5/200) although in May 1801, in common with most of the workforce, he was employed as a Labourer "cleaning and deepening the river, canals etc., performing necessary work" (Supply 5/221). During this period he was allowed to watch in turn and both his daily pay and watch allowance peaked at 3/-d and 1/6d respectively in 1812 (Supply 5/229).

On the 2nd March 1816 the Storekeeper at Waltham Abbey recommended that William Bride, a Dusting House man then aged 56 with 22 years' service, should be superannuated at 3/-d a day (Supply 5/230). A footnote to this document sent to the Board said that Bride should be "superannuated because of the hurts he had received in this dangerous Manufactory" and went on to say "being very severely ruptured, is quite unfit for any exertion." A letter from the Board dated the 6th March 1816 awarded Bride a pension of 2/6d per day for a six-day week commencing the 1st April 1816 (Supply 5/200). A document in

1818 recorded that he was receiving 15/-d per week (Supply 5/231) and in 1821 his pension is given as £39.0.0d per annum (Supply 5/232). He was still alive and in receipt of his pension in 1826 (Winters, *op.cit.* p.96).

Samuel Britton, born circa 1770, first worked for the Ordnance Board as a Millwright on the 26th March 1806, but where is unknown (WO54/516). The first record that he worked at the Waltham Abbey Powder Mills is when the Engineers' Department carried out works within the Manufactory in 1809, when Samuel was paid £1.9.9d for tasks undertaken between the 15th and 21st July of that year (Supply 5/228). Samuel continued to work in the Engineers' Department as a casual Millwright, and his daily rate of pay in 1812 was 5/2d (WO54/512) as it was in 1816 (WO54/516). The last document recorded that he was a 44-year-old man living in Waltham Abbey with 2 children, one of whom was married.

A Statement dated the 4th April 1822, "of monies to which the public were entitled to receive credit" recorded that Samuel was one of several employees "having occupied their present residences previous to the Hon. Board purchasing the same, sanction will be asked for their future residing in them." He was to live in this cottage with a large garden as from the date of the Board's Order (4th May 1821) when the amount under his lease was set at £16.0.0d per annum (Supply 5/232). The property has been identified as being on the north side of High Bridge Street to the west of a row of tenements known as Bank Cottages, forming part of Plot 44 on the Waltham Abbey Town Map in Appendix 1. Another List of Properties dated 1834, confirmed that he had occupied the cottage by the Board's Order dated the 4th May 1821 (Supply 5/237).

A Return of Personnel Employed in the Engineers' Department in April 1823 indicated that Samuel was on the Establishment, since he was then paid 5/2d as a Millwright for 313 days, giving him an income of £81.17.2d for the year (WO54/542). Confirmation of this was given in a Return of Persons belonging to the Civil Establishment of the Ordnance at the Gunpowder and Small Arms Manufactories at Waltham Abbey, Faversham and Enfield, which recorded that Samuel Britton was one of 3 Millwrights to be employed at Waltham Abbey (WO54/570). Samuel was still working as a Millwright in April 1834; he was then nearly 64 years' old, and still earned £80.17.2d per annum (WO54/593). A Return of Domestic Properties made by the Royal Engineers' dated the 20th May 1840 noted that Samuel had died, and that his cottage in High Bridge Street was then occupied by J. O'Brien (WO44/133).

William Brodstock (Broadstock) was born circa 1789 and started work as a Labourer in the Corning House in the summer of 1805, earning 2/2d per day (Supply 5/224). William continued to work in the Corning House on the same pay, but by June 1807 he was "allowed to watch in turn" for which he received 1/-d (Supply 5/226). By August 1808, his daily pay had risen to 2/6d (Supply 5/227).

A List of Employees dated September 1810, recorded that Brodstock was now employed as a Saltpetre Refiner earning 2/-d per day, and that he was still allowed to "watch in turn when not working extra" (Supply 5/228). His pay in August 1812 had been increased to 2/8d per day (Supply 5/229) and remained so in 1814 (Supply 5/230).

A Return dated the 25th June 1818 showed that William was then employed as a Bargeman earning 3/-d per day. The same document stated that he was a 28-year-old married man with 3 children living in Enfield. When the Establishment at the Powder Mills was cut a couple of months later, William was made redundant (Supply 5/231).

Mr. Brookland was a Millman at Waltham Abbey. On the 11th August 1793, Robert Coleman, the Clerk of the Cheque, noted in his Minute Book "Brookland Mill stopt" and on the 14th August, "Brookland has set his Mill to work" (Winters, *op.cit.* pp.39-40). Note: it was common for a Mill to be known after its Millman.

Horace Broom was employed in the Corning House in 1805 at 2/2d per day (Supply 5/224).

Matthew Broom was employed as a Corning House Man between 1807 (Supply 5/226) and 1814 (Supply 5/230). His initial rate of pay was 2/2d per day, rising to 3/3d in 1812. Matthew was also allowed to watch in turn, for which he received 1/-d in June 1807, rising to 1/6d per night by 1812 (Supply 5/229).

Edward Brown was employed as a Millman in the spring of 1805 at 2/3d per day (Supply 5/224). He continued to work as a Millman during 1807 (Supply 5/226) and August 1808 (Supply 5/227) on the same rate of pay, but with an additional 6d if he had to work at night.

Henry Brown, born circa 1762, was employed as a Labourer on the 12th November 1804 (WO54/536). In January 1806, he was recorded as being employed as a Millman who was paid 2/3d per day (Supply 5/224) and this was to be Henry's trade for the rest of his working life. His daily wage peaked at 3/-d in 1812, coupled with an additional 6d when he was on a night shift (Supply 5/229). In June 1818, a List of Employees stated that Henry was a 56-year-old married man with 8 children, living in Waltham Abbey (Supply 5/231).

He retained his position as a Millman when the Establishment at the Mills was reduced in numbers in 1818, and again in 1822. Although his wages were cut, he was then allowed to watch in turn. In April 1823 he was earning £44.4.0d per annum, which included his watch allowance (WO54/542). The following October Henry was stated to be a widower (WO54/546).

On the 13th March 1826, Henry was injured in an explosion (Winters, *op.cit.* p.95) but no further details were given. However, on the 31st January 1828, The Director General of the Ordnance Medical Department wrote to the Mills at Waltham agreeing that Henry Brown should be provided with a truss to "prevent him incurring further injury" (Supply 5/205). In 1827 the Board agreed that he could occupy the cottage in Powder Mill Lane which had previously been occupied by William Davis, and the rent was set at £5.4.0d per annum (Supply 5/205). The cottage formed part of Plot No. 63 on the Town Map in Appendix 1.

A Return of Employees dated the 1st October 1829 noted that Henry was still a widower (WO54/566). A year later, a similar Return had a footnote that John Fleming had been appointed a Labourer "in the room (in place of) of Henry Brown on the 12th May 1830." The Board agreed by letter in July 1831 that Henry Brown should be superannuated at the rate of £10 per annum (Supply 5/205) but a Schedule of Pensions Paid dated 1837, clearly stated that his pension commenced on the 23rd April 1833 (Supply 5/237). The 1840 Census described Henry as an Ordnance Pensioner, with his 'rounded down' age as 80, and noted that he was still living in Powder Mill Lane with a Henry Brown (aged 30) and his family.

John Brown (1) was born circa 1776, and started work on the 11th December 1792 as a Labourer, melting and refining Saltpetre, for which he was paid 1/6d per day (Supply 5/216 ad Supply 5/217). Between 1793 and 1796, Robert Coleman, the Clerk of the Cheque, kept a Minute Book on the way things were conducted within the Manufactory. On July 29th 1793, he recorded that John Brown, together with others, "having gone across the Hoppit contrary to repeated orders, chequered (fined) them one day each for the same". Why the men were not allowed was not explained, but it is possible that the Hoppit may have been a short cut to West Street (High Bridge Street) thereby avoiding the main entrance to the Mills. On the 7th May 1794, a Military Volunteer Company was formed from the men employed at the Mills, but John was one of the few men who did not enlist (Winters, *op.cit.* p.42).

By July 1795 John had been promoted to the position of a Millman, replacing R. Jameson, and he then earned 2/-d per day (Supply 5/217). The work of a Millman was hazardous; on February 13th 1796, John was working at the Upper 15 Head Mill when it blew up at 4 o'clock in the afternoon. Although his clothes caught fire, he was uninjured (Winters, *op.cit.* p.52). A Petition was submitted by the employees to the Board of Ordnance on the 2nd February 1800 relating to pay and conditions at the Mills, and John was one of the few signatories who were literate (Supply 5/220).

A Return of Employees dated the May 8th 1801, recorded that John was still a Millman on the same pay, and that he had 4 children (Supply 5/221). Towards the end of 1801, gunpowder production virtually stopped, and Coleman noted in his Minute Book on October 23rd that 24 men were required to work at the Royal Gunpowder Factory at Faversham, or be discharged. John Brown refused to go, but he was not discharged immediately, since a Return of the 3rd November showed that nearly the whole work force was engaged in "cleaning and deepening the river, canals and performing necessary work" (Supply 5/221). Brown's name does not appear in the Faversham records or in subsequent records for Waltham such as Supply 5/222 for May 1804, so he may by then have left his employment with the Royal Ordnance. With the onset of the Napoleonic and Peninsular wars, the Establishment at the Royal Gunpowder Mills was expanded and

John was re-engaged at Waltham Abbey as a Labourer on the 1st March 1805. He was soon promoted as one of 3 working foremen in the Corning Houses, and paid 2/6d per day; in addition to his daily pay, he was allowed 1/6d every third night as a Rounder (Supply 5/225). During the war his wages and Rounder's allowance peaked in 1812 to 4/-d and 2/-d respectively (Supply 5/230) with his daily wage reducing to 3/6d by 1818 (Supply 5/231).

A Return of "monies to which the public were entitled to receive credit between the 1st January and the 31st December 1821" showed that John and his family had been living rent-free in an Ordnance Board cottage from December 1810 (Supply 5/232) and were still in occupation in the autumn of 1832 (WO54/581) but in return for free accommodation, his family had "to look after the waters". A List of Domestic Properties dated the 20th December 1834, stated that John Brown and John Goats were living in a pair of cottages on Aqueduct Island, with a rentable value of £5.4.0d (Supply 5/237).

With the cessation of war, the Ordnance Board reduced the Establishment in their gunpowder mills; but John was retained as the sole Corning House Foreman on the 4th September 1818 (Supply 5/231). The Establishment was reviewed again in 1822, and John retained his position and still acted as a Rounder (Supply 5/232). By then his salary was recorded as £52.3.4d per annum with an additional £12.3.4d per annum for being a Rounder, giving him an annual income of £64.6.8d. On the 25th May 1825, John replaced John Braddock as the Foreman of Stoves and Magazines and he was still allowed to act as a Rounder, making his total income £77.7.6d per annum (WO54/554). He continued to be employed in the same capacity with the same pay and allowances in 1834 (WO54/593). On the 16th April 1836 two mills exploded "when shut up and not at work;" and John, as the Rounder on duty, was called before Lt. Col. Moody as a witness (Winters, *op.cit.* p.103).

A Return of Domestic Properties dated May 1840, confirmed that he was still the Foreman of the Stoves and that he and his wife were living on Aqueduct Island, where "his wife is a kind of Watch on bargemen taking more water than is necessary" (WO44/133).

John Brown (2) was working as a Labourer at the Powder Mills on the 8th May 1801. He was a married man with one child (Supply 5/221).

Joseph Brown, born circa 1771, started his life-long employment at the Royal Gunpowder Mills at Waltham Abbey as a Millman on the 6th February 1790 (Supply 5/232) and in March 1790, he was paid 2/-d per day (Supply 5/214). In July 1792 he was described as a Labourer working in the Corning House, with his pay reduced to 1/6d per day (Supply 5/216) but by January 1794, he had returned to being a Millman "grinding Salt Petre, Charcoal and Brimstone" on the same rate of pay (Supply 5/216). He enlisted as a Private in the Military Volunteer Company on the 7th May 1794 (Supply 5/219). In June 1794, he was designated as a Charcoal Millman still earning 1/6d per day (Supply 5/219).

A Petition raised by the employees in 1800 on the conditions and rates of pay within the Manufactory was signed by Joseph with a cross (Supply 5/220) and a Return of the Marital Status of the Employees dated 1801 showed that he was then a married man without children (Supply 5/221). Further records showed that the couple were to remain childless. In May 1804, Joseph was working in the Saltpetre Refinery earning 2/-d per day. All the Refiners were allowed to watch in turn, on average every fifth night, for which they received 1/-d per night (Supply 5/222). By

September 1810 he had changed his occupation again, and had became a Bargeman, with a daily rate of pay of 3/-d (Supply 5/228) which rose to 3/10d by August 1814 (Supply 5/230) but fell back to 3/-d by June 1818 (Supply 5/231).

When the Establishment was reduced in numbers in September 1818, Joseph Brown was retained, not as a Bargeman, but as the Office Keeper. In this position he was paid 2/-d per day, but was allowed to watch in turn for which he received 1/-d (Supply 5/231). He continued to be the Office Keeper for the rest of his working life. His daily wage had been increased to 2/11d by May 1819, but his allowance to Watch remained the same (Supply 5/221). This gave him an annual income of £50.14.0d, which remained unchanged for the next 4 years.

An Order of the Board dated the 4th May 1821 authorised Joseph to live in a cottage owned by the Ordnance, paying a rent of £5.4.0d annually (Supply 5/232) – see notes on Samuel Britton for details. The tenement was listed as No.40 in the Return, but its location is uncertain. A Return of Domestic Properties prepared by the Engineers' Office on the 20th December 1834, showed that Joseph Brown was occupying a tenement in Powder Mill Lane with the same rent as before (Supply 5/237). A similar Return for 1840 showed that he was living in a cottage originally built as a surgery in 1814 for £249 (Winters, *op.cit*.p.79) which would locate it at the entrance to the Engineers' Yard (WO44/133) being Plot 92 on the Town Map in Appendix 1.

Joseph was retained as the Office Keeper (variously described as the Office Keeper and Messenger) when the Establishment was reduced still further in 1822 (Supply 5/232) but his pay was reduced by £2.12.0d per annum in accordance with Orders of the Board dated the 27th December 1822 and the 15th January 1823. His annual pay, including his watch allowance, was £48.2.0d (WO54/546). In 1825 his basic wage was still £42.18.0d but he was now a Rounder, which gave him on average an extra 2/-d per week, so his annual take-home pay was £55.1.4d (WO54/550) and remained at this level until at least 1834 (WO54/593). Sometime during his employment, Joseph suffered an injury, possibly while he was a Bargeman, since the Director General of the Ordnance Medical Department in his letter dated the 31st January 1828 to the Ordnance at Waltham Abbey, agreed that Joseph should be supplied with a "spring truss to prevent him incurring further injury" (Supply 5/205).

In the 1841 Census Joseph, described as a Labourer, and his wife, Phillis, were still living in the same cottage in Powder Mill Lane. Neither was born in Essex, and both had the rounded-down age of 70 years.

Samuel Brown was born circa 1814, and started work as a general Labourer on the 6th May 1835. In October 1839 he was a 20-year-old bachelor with annual pay, including an allowance to watch in turn, of £39.0.0d (WO54/623). The 1841 Census did not record him as living in Waltham Abbey. On the 13th April 1843, some 40 barrels of gunpowder exploded in the Corning House, together with another 20 in the Press House; 7 men were killed and a great deal of damage was caused to the town. Among those killed was Samuel Brown (Winters, *op.cit.* p.106).

William Brown was born circa 1766, and trained as a Cabinet Maker before being appointed as the Foreman Carpenter in the Engineers' Department on the 1st August 1806 (WO54/512 and WO54/520). Between the 15th and 21st July 1809, he was paid £1.15.0d as a Master Carpenter for work carried out in the Manufactory (WO54/228).

In 1812, his wage was set at 6/4d per day for 6 days' work and one and a half days' pay for working on a Sunday. In addition, he was also entitled to 6/-d per week to train an Apprentice

(WO54/512). A Return of Employees made in February 1816 recorded that he was then a 49-year-old widower without children, and that he was still paid 6/4d per day (WO54/516). In common with the rest of the workforce at Waltham Abbey, his wage was reduced in 1817 with his daily pay only 5/10d, but his entitlement to train an Apprentice was unchanged (WO54/528).

In 1821, he was listed as the Master Carpenter and paid 5/10d per day for 313 days in a year, or, £91.5.10d annually. His earnings remained at this level until he retired in 1833 (WO54/542 and WO54/587) but he no longer received an allowance to train an Apprentice. A Return of Persons belonging to the Civil Establishment of the Ordnance Board dated the 31st January 1831, recorded that William Brown was one of the 3 Artificers to be employed at Waltham Abbey Powder Mills and the Small Arms Manufactory at Enfield; he was the Master Carpenter and was to be paid 5/10d per day. His duties were to work with the Artificers and Labourers in the Gunpowder Manufactory and "consequently great attention, sobriety, and steadiness of conduct are required" (WO54/570).

Under an Order of the Board dated the 15th March 1833, William Brown, Master Carpenter, was to be discharged and granted a pension of £31.10.9d per annum "until an opportunity to employ him again should arise" (Supply 5/208). William was retired on the 4th July 1833, and was still in receipt of a pension in 1837 (Supply 5/237).

William Buck was a Master Carpenter at the Powder Mills. Supply 5/238 dated the 15th September 1841 recorded that William Buck had died, and that his pension was to be paid to his widow, Susannah.

William Bunce was born circa 1770, trained as a Carpenter, and was initially employed by a Contractor who was engaged to undertake work for the Ordnance Board as early as the 3rd July 1791 (WO54/550). William then left the contractor and was employed direct by the Board. The earliest record of William working at the Royal Gunpowder Mills at Waltham Abbey was in 1809, when he was paid £1.9.9d for work carried out within the Manufactory by the Engineers' Department between the 15th and 21st July. He was then a Carpenter (First Class) (Supply 5/228).

It was another 14 years before his name appeared in the Waltham Abbey records again. A Return listing the personnel employed in the Engineers' Department dated the 1st April 1823, recorded that William Bunce was one of 7 Carpenters appointed to the Engineers' Establishment on the 8th March 1822. He was then a 52-year-old married man with 6 children, living in Waltham Abbey. The Return also noted that he had 35 years' continuous service with the Board, but gave no indication as to where this was (WO54/542). The 1825 valuation shows that he was living in one of the cottages at the junction of High Bridge Street and Powder Mill Lane, being one of the tenements in Plot No. 60 on the Town Map in Appendix 1. Sometime after that, William moved to one of the cottages in the old Tanyard, Tenement No. 54 in the same Appendix.

He was still receiving the same money in 1831 when he was on the Establishment to work at the Gunpowder Mills and the Small Arms Manufactories – see notes on William Brown. He then worked under William Brown, the Foreman Carpenter, and was paid 4/1d per day for 313 days in the year which gave him an annual income of £63.18.1d (WO54/542).

In October 1833, it was recorded that he was 63 years of age (WO54/587) and a Return of Properties owned by the Board dated the 20th December 1834, stated that Widow Bunce occupied a cottage in West Street (High Bridge Street) and that she (or her husband) had been in occupation since the 6th April

1829 (Supply 5/237). Another Return of the same date showing how vacant properties were proposed to be let, indicated that William Bunce had died and that his cottage had been leased to his widow on the 6th April 1829. However, another entry of the same date stated that his cottage was to be let to J. Lording, Labourer (Supply 5/237). The property has been identified as one of those purchased from Mr. Cannop in 1818 – see notes on Jeremiah Betts.

R. Burr was working as a Store House man in November 1789, earning 2/-d per day (Winters, *op.cit.* p.32)

George Butcher, born circa 1769, started his employment within the Engineers' Department on the 1st October 1815 as a Labourer. In February 1816, he was working as a casual Labourer, earning 2/4d a day. George was a 46-year-old married man without children, living in Epping (WO54/516).

Samuel Butler was born circa 1770 and worked as a Millwright in the Engineers' Department. He was paid £1.9.9d for work carried out within the Manufactory between the 15th and 25th July 1809 (Supply 5/228). His name is not associated with the Waltham Abbey Mills again until April 1825. He was still a Millwright in the Engineers' Department and paid 5/2d per day for 313 days in a year, which gave him an annual income of £80.17.2d. Samuel was then a 55-year-old married man with 2 children, and had served the Board for nearly 19 years (WO54/550).

John Butte was working as a Corning House man in August 1808, earning 2/6d per day. He was also allowed to watch in turn, for which he received one shilling (Supply 5/227).

Colonel John By's name appears on many documents and Returns made to the Royal Ordnance Board from the Powder

Mills at Waltham Abbey. Having studied at the Royal Military Academy, Woolwich (R. Legett, *John By, Builder of the Rideau Canal*, Ottawa, 1982, p.6) he was commissioned in the Royal Artillery in 1799 before being transferred to the Royal Engineers in the same year, serving in Canada and the Peninsular War. (WO54/241). In 1812 By was appointed Officer Commanding Royal Engineers at the Royal Gunpowder Mills, Waltham Abbey and Faversham, the Government Magazines at Purfleet and the Government Armoury at Lewisham, holding this post until 1821 when he retired (WO54/251). In 1812, he was given the important task of planning and erection of the Government's Small Arms Factory at Enfield Lock (WO55/753). (Legett, *op.cit.* pp.23-24). He also organised the official fireworks' display to commemorate the Peace of Paris in 1814. He was recalled to the Army in 1823, and promoted to Lt.Colonel in 1824.

In 1826, By was posted to Canada to carry out what represented the pinnacle of his career – the building of the Rideau Canal from the Ottawa River to the fortress at Kingston on Lake Ontario. The canal was built for strategic reasons, bypassing a section of the St. Lawrence River on the military supply route from Montreal to Kingston, which was vulnerable to American attack. By's operational centre, originally named Bytown, became the city of Ottawa. The Rideau Canal was completed in 1832 and is still in use today - a masterpiece of civil engineering by any standards. He died in 1836 at Frant, where he is buried (*FGPR,* p.18).

Robert Byner, born circa 1794, trained as a Cordwainer before being employed as a casual Labourer by the Engineers' Department on the 6th March 1813. In February 1816, he was earning 2/8d per day as a 21-year old-bachelor living in Waltham Abbey (WO54/516).

Thomas Byner was born circa 1796, and was employed as a casual Labourer in the Engineers' Department on the 14th

November 1812. In February 1816 he was earning 2/8d per day, and was a 19 -year-old bachelor living in Waltham Abbey (WO54/516).

W. C. Byres was born circa 1815, and appointed as a Clerk in the Engineers' Department on the 24th May 1837. Following the death of Thomas Littler, he was promoted to Second Clerk within the Manufactory on the 19th August 1839 with a salary of £80.0.0d per annum, and provided with a house (WO54/623). His name does not appear in the 1841 Census for Waltham Abbey.

C

John Cadwell started work as a casual Labourer in the Engineers' Department on the 21st August 1813. In February 1816, he was working as a casual Bricklayer's Labourer earning 2/8d per day. At that time he was a 50-year-old widower with 2 children, one of whom was married (WO54/516).

Charles Callensoe was born circa 1740, and was seconded from the Waltham Abbey Royal Powder Mills on the 17th December 1787 for training at the Royal Powder Mills at Faversham (Supply 5/70). At Faversham he was described as a Labourer marking powder barrels, and he returned to Waltham Abbey on the 8th March 1788 (Supply 5/113). He was working as a Millman in November 1788, and in January 1789, he was described as a Stove man who was paid 1/6d per day (Supply 5/212). In April 1789, in common with the majority of the workforce, he was "undertaking necessary works within the manufactory" (Supply 5/213). By September 1789, he was "Warding at the Refining House Field Gate and Bank of Canal" (Supply 5/214).

B. Camp was in the Corning Houses grinding saltpetre and charcoal in August 1793, having replaced John Hayes, who had been discharged for stealing coal (Supply 5/216). He continued in the Corning Houses throughout 1793 and 1794 earning 1/6d per day (Supply 5/216). On the 11th March 1794, he was chequered (fined) for striking George Pain in the Corning House. On the 7th May of the same year he enlisted as a Private in the Volunteer Company (Winters, *op.cit.* p.42). At the end of that year he was described as "separating gunpowder" (Supply 5/217) and in June and July 1795, he was working as a Puntman (Supply 5/217). No further entries relating to Mr. Camp were found after that date.

Henry Camps was born circa 1740, and had seen military service in America. Prior to the capture of Quebec in 1759, he had been taken prisoner by the French and confined in a fort situated on the Canadian lakes (Supply 5/229). During the American War of Independence (1778–1783) he was the Conductor of Artillery Stores, and on the orders of William Congreve (later Sir William), Deputy Comptroller, he was appointed to the position of Office Keeper at the Powder Mills on the 1st June 1788 (Supply 5/212). He was then 48 years' old, was to be paid 2/-d daily and "employed attending the office" (Supply 5/214). On the 30th September 1790, he was reimbursed 8/8d for postage by James Wright, the Storekeeper (WASC 1382).

On the 12th July 1792, Henry was transferred to the Stores as a Storehouse Man. He received the same pay (Supply 5/216) and remained associated with the Stores until his death in 1813 (Supply 5/229). His daily pay gradually rose to 3/10d by 1812 (Supply 5/229); from 1805 onwards he was also a Rounder, for which he was paid 1/6d every third night (Supply 5/223). He signed the Petition on Pay and Conditions at the Mill in February 1800, being one of the few employees who could write (Supply 5/220). A Return of the Marital State of the Employees at the Powder Mills in May 1801, recorded that he was a widower with three children (Supply 5/221). There were three cats on the Establishment, and on the 30th June 1805, an entry in the accounts reads, "keeping three cats 13 weeks [at] 4d – 13s. Henry Camps Storehouse Man" (Winters, *op.cit.* p.28).

A Petition to the Board dated the 17th April 1807, from the Storekeeper, Hugh Mathews, and the Clerk of the Cheque, William Breeze, recommended that Henry Camps be promoted to the position of "Foreman of General Storehouse" with a nominal increase in pay (Supply 5/226). The Petition went on to say that in the course of his duties, Henry had ruptured himself, necessitating the use of a truss. A statement from Robert Hilton, the Surgeon at the Powder Mills, was appended to the Petition stating that Henry Camps had suffered a serious injury which required the immediate use of a truss. There is no mention of the Board concurring with the request, nor does Camp appear to have had an immediate increase in his pay.

Another letter written by the Storekeeper, H. J. Mathews, and the Clerk of the Cheque, J. Wright, informed the Board that on the morning of the 27th June 1813, Henry was unloading a barge which had arrived with hoses from the Tower (of London), when a sudden and violent gust of wind blew the door of the barge house against him "by which accident the abdomen and parts adjacent were so much injured as to cause his death 24 hours afterwards" (Supply 5/229). The letter went on to say that Camps had 3 children, one son who was a Sergeant in the Army in Spain, and two daughters, the youngest of whom, Caroline, was unmarried and entirely dependant on her late father. They requested that the Board pay Caroline an allowance of 9d per day, and the request was granted commencing on the 30th September (Winters, *op. cit.* p.75).

William Campton was a Labourer by trade set to work by Daniel Cornish in October 1787, renovating the Powder Mills following their purchase from Mr Walton by the Ordnance Board; he was paid 9/-d per week (Winters *op.cit.* p.28).

John Cannon (1) was working as a Saltpetre Refiner in August 1812 at 2/8d per day and, when not working extra, he was allowed to watch in turn (Supply 5/229). In February 1814, he had moved to the Corning Houses where he was paid 3/3d daily and was still allowed to watch, for which he received 1/6d per night (Supply 5/230).

John Cannon (2) was employed as a Labourer "drawing and setting stoves and in the willow plantation" during August 1812, for which he was paid 2/8d per day. He was also allowed to watch in turn (Supply 5/229). By February 1814, he was a

Saltpetre Refiner earning 2/8d per day and still allowed to watch (Supply 5/230).

Joseph Cannon was born circa 1770, and in August 1812 was working as a Labourer at 2/8d per day for "drawing and setting stoves and in the willow plantation." In addition, he was allowed to watch in turn (Supply 5/229). By February 1814 he was working as a Puntman, earning the same pay and allowance to watch (Supply 5/230).

Joseph left the Ordnance, possibly at the end of the Napoleonic wars, but was re-employed as a Labourer in the Engineers' Department on the 27th August 1929, at which time he was paid 2/2d per day for 313 days, making an annual total of £33.18.2d (WO54/570). He was then a 40-year-old married man with 6 children. A Return dated October 1830 (WO54/570) recorded that he was one of 15 Labourers to be employed at Waltham Abbey Powder Mills and the Enfield Small Arms Manufactory. They were "to undertake different services as labourers in the manufactories where steadiness and sobriety were particularly required." He continued to work as a Labourer earning the same wage until at least October 1833 (WO54/587) after which his name does not appear in the records.

Lewis Capet was employed as a casual Labourer in the Engineers' Department on the 27th February 1815, earning 2/8d per day. He was then a 20-year-old bachelor living in Cheshunt (WO54/516).

John Carr was born circa 1799, and, according to a letter dated the 3rd October 1811 (Supply 5/229) he was approved as an Apprentice to the Master Worker, William Newton. The letter stated that John was to lodge with his father, also John Carr, a Shoemaker, living in Waltham Abbey. A Record dated the 1st April 1823, noted that his Apprenticeship started on the 30th

September 1811 (WO54/542). It is interesting to note that his father supplied the Mills with shoes to be worn within the manufactory areas, and during the years 1789-1790, John Carr, Snr., furnished the factory with magazine shoes (Winters *op. cit.* p.33). On the 30th September 1805, he was paid £12.12.0d for 36 pairs of shoes at 7/-d per pair (Winters *op. cit.* p.64).

In August 1812, John Junior was paid 6/-d per week, with his Master receiving the same sum (Supply 5/229). His pay gradually increased over the ensuing years and towards the end of his training he was earning 9/-d per week (Supply 5/231). When the Establishment was reduced in September 1818, John was retained as an Apprentice. However, towards the end of his Apprenticeship he was concerned as to whether he would be offered work, so on the 6th January he presented a petition to the Board in which he begged that he remain at the Mills to support his family, i.e. his parents and siblings (Supply 5/202), and the Board agreed to retain him as an Artificer under the Master Worker. In May 1819, he was working as a Brimstone Refiner earning 2/4d per day, and was allowed to watch in turn, for which he received 1/-d a night (Supply 5/231). The same document recorded that he was a bachelor, living in Waltham Abbey.

By an Order of the Board dated the 4th October 1819, he was appointed as a Saltpetre Refiner and paid £41.14.4d annually (Supply 5/232). When the Establishment was reduced still further in 1822, John was reclassified as a general Labourer to undertake whatever type of work was required within the Manufactory (Supply 5/233). He was still a Labourer in 1824 earning £39.0.0d annually, which included an allowance to watch (WO54/546). The same document recorded that he was still single and had been trained as a Gunpowder Maker.
WO54/554 of April 1826 stated that John was married. By October of that year he had one child (also WO54/554) and a second child was born between October 1828 and April 1829

(WO54/566). He continued to work as a general Labourer on the same pay until the 26th September 1832, when he was dismissed by the Board's Order 1082 (WO54/581). The 1841 Census showed that a John Carr, aged 41, was the Publican of the Three Tuns in the Market Square. His age, coupled with the age of his son, John (14) matches the details on the Employees' Returns at the Gunpowder Mills.

Abraham Carter was born circa 1802 and worked as a Labourer in the Engineers' Department between June and October 1825 on a temporary basis, for which he was paid 2/2d per day (WO54/550).

Charles Carter was born circa 1803 (Supply 5/232) and started an Apprenticeship under the Master Worker on the 14th August 1815 (Supply 5/233). During his Apprenticeship his weekly wage rose from 6/-d in 1815 to 7/-d in 1822 (Supply 5/232). The end of the Napoleonic wars saw a reduction in the manufacture and regeneration of gunpowder and, as a consequence, the workforce had to be cut back. A list of employees dated the 28th August 1818 sent from Waltham to the Board, indicated the names of the people the Storekeeper proposed to retain between the 4th September and the 31st December 1818 to meet the new production requirement, and Charles' name was on that list (Supply 5/231). However, having completed his Apprenticeship with the Master Worker in 1822, he was promptly discharged by an Order of the Board dated the 22nd May 1822 (Supply 5/233).

He was employed as a Labourer on a temporary basis within the Engineers' Department between June and October 1825 and paid 2/2d per day (WO54/550) and the same document recorded that he was a bachelor. In April 1833, Charles, together with William Taylor, was apprehended by the Thames police for being in possession of Government stores from the Waltham Abbey Powder Mills, although the outcome of the arrest is unknown

(Supply 5/208). Nevertheless, he was taken on again at the Mills on the 7th April 1837 as a general Labourer and paid £39.0.0d annually, which included an allowance to watch (WO54/623). Some time after 1837 he worked as a general Labourer in the Mixing House, still earning the same annual pay of £39.0.0d (WO54/623) and that document noted that by then he was a married man with one child. At the 30th November 1840, he was employed as a Millman (Supply 5/238).

The 1841 Census recorded that he and his wife, Ann, together with their children, Charles (4), George (3) and three-month-old Thomas, were living in Broomstick Hall Road. All were born in Essex, and he was described as a Labourer at the Gunpowder Mills.

Daniel Carter, born circa 1805, was employed as a General Labourer between April 1837 and October 1839 earning £39.0.0d per annum, which included an allowance to watch in turn (WO54/623).

Thomas Carter (1) was born in the mid-1760's, but his given age is inconsistent in the records. Before being employed as a Labourer at the Mills on the 8th March 1810, he had trained as a Shoemaker (Supply 5/232). By September of that year he was working as a Millman and paid 2/8d daily, with an extra 6d when on night duty (Supply 5/228). In August 1812 he was described as a Corning House Man who earned 3/3d per day, and he was also allowed to watch in turn, for which he received 1/6d per night (Supply 5/229). Thomas continued to work in the Corning Houses on the same pay and allowances until 1818, when cuts were made in the Establishment. However, Thomas was retained as a Saltpetre Refiner by an Order of the Board dated the 4th September 1818, with his pay reduced to 2/4d per day (Supply 5/232) although he was still allowed to watch, for which he received 2/-d per night. This gave him an annual take-home pay of £41.14.4d.

A Labour Return for September 1820 (Supply 5/232) recorded that Thomas was a married man living in Waltham Abbey who had 9 children. The number of children recorded in December 1821 was 8 (Supply 5/232) and only 7 in April 1833 (WO54/587). The ensuing Returns consistently recorded the number of offspring as 7.

In the spring of 1822 the Ordnance Board reduced production and regeneration of gunpowder still further, and the Establishment at Waltham was cut again. Empsom Middleton and James Wright drew up a list of people who were to be retained (Supply 5/232 dated the 21st March 1822). Thomas was to continue his employment as a Saltpetre Refiner, although his basic wage was to be reduced by some £2.10.0d per annum; he then earned £39.0.0d per annum, which included his watch allowance (Supply WO54/542). He continued to work in the Refining House on the same terms until the 24th February 1827 (WO54/558) when he returned to the Corning Houses with a basic rate of pay of £42.18.0d per annum. He was still allowed to watch in turn, which gave him an estimated annual income of £48.2.0d.

The Corning House was his workplace until at least October 1839, but his basic pay was reduced to £35.17.9d per annum between October 1833 and April 1834 (WO54/593) although he was still allowed to watch. A Return of Employees dated the 1st October 1839 (WO54/623) recorded that his employment as a Corning House Man had been reconfirmed on the 5th September 1837, and that his annual wage increased to £42.18.0d. In 1839 his given age was 72, and although he was still allowed to watch in turn, it appeared that due to his age, he declined. The 1841 Census recorded that a Thomas Carter of a similar age was living with his wife Elizabeth, aged 60, in North Upshire near the Green Man, and that both were born in the County. He was described therein as an Agricultural Labourer.

Thomas Carter (2) was born circa 1797 and was employed as a Cooper in August 1812. He earned 1/9d per day and his age and rate of pay suggested that he was being trained as a Cooper (Supply 5/229). Thomas continued to work at the Mills as a Cooper with his daily wage increasing to 3/6d by June 1818 (Supply 5/231). However, with peace in Europe following the cessation of the Napoleonic wars, he was discharged in September 1818 ((Supply 5/231). Nevertheless, he was re-engaged to make cement casks for Harwich on the 20th December 1824 (Winters *op.cit.* p.94), and this was confirmed by a Labour Return dated the 1st October 1825 (WO54/550). This Return also verified that he had been trained as a Cooper, and that he was paid £54.12.0d annually. It also stated that at that date he was married with 2 children.

Thomas Carter (3) was born circa 1797, and started work as a casual Labourer in the Engineers' Department on the 9th September 1815 at 2/8d per day (WO54/516).

William Carter was born circa 1764 and trained as a Butcher before starting work as a Labourer at the Powder Mills on the 21st November 1791 (Supply 5/232). In August 1794 he was refining and milling Saltpetre, for which he was paid 1/6d per day (Supply 5/216). He was still a Saltpetre Refiner when he died in 1826 (WO54/554).

William enlisted as a Private in the Military Volunteer Company on the 7th May 1794 (Winters, *op.cit.* p.42). In February 1800 he 'signed' the document relating to pay and conditions with a cross (Supply 5/220). A Return showing the Marital Status of the Employees in 1801 noted that he was a married man with 6 children (Supply 5/221). The number of children he had increased to 9 by February 1820 (Supply 5/232).

Over the ensuing years, his daily rate of pay gradually increased; in 1806 it was 2/-d per day (Supply 5/224) as it was in 1807, but he was then allowed "to watch in turn if not working extra" (Supply 5/226). In February 1814 his pay had risen to 2/8d per day, and he was still allowed to watch (Supply 5/230).

William survived the cuts to the Waltham Abbey Establishment in both 1818 and 1822, retaining his position as a Saltpetre Refiner. However, his annual take home pay had fallen from £41.14.4d in 1818 (Supply 5/232) to £39.0.0d by 1823 (WO54/542). For further details on reductions to the Establishment, see notes on Thomas Carter (1). WO54/554 dated the 1st April 1826 recorded that William Carter, Saltpetre Refiner, had died.

Isaac Cass was born circa 1732 and was a Labourer when he was set to work by Daniel Cornish in October 1787, renovating the Powder Mills following their purchase by the Ordnance Board from Mr Walton, and according to Winters (*op.cit.* p.28) he was paid 9/-d per week. In January 1789, he was "to be tried as a Millman having lately been employed by Mr Walton." He worked in the Corning Houses at 2/-d per day (Supply 5/212), but with little production taking place within the manufactory in April 1789, Isaac's job was described as "cutting and planting willow trees, cutting of a canal at the new Corning House, removing earth to the store, unloading barge of coals & charring wood" (Supply 5/213). By September of that year he was working as a Millman again (Supply 5/214) and continued to do so until at least December 1794 (Supply 5/217). During this period his pay remained unchanged at 2/-d per day.

By the 24th June 1795, Isaac was working in the Dusting House but his pay had been reduced to 1/6d per day (Supply 5/217). A

Petition on Pay and Conditions at the Mills forwarded to the Board in February 1800 showed that he was literate, and was then working as a Warder (Supply 5/220). A Return showing the Marital Status of the Employees in May 1801, recorded that he was not married (Supply 5/221) and a Return of Artificers and Labourers for November 1801 indicated that he was still employed as a Warder, "attending at the field gate, the Refining House and the upper part of the works." (Supply 5/221).

John Cass was working as a Saltpetre Refiner in August 1812, earning 2/8d per day. In addition, "when not working extra", he was allowed to watch in turn (Supply 5/229). He was still in the same position on the 13th February 1814 (Supply 5/230).

Luke Cawthorn worked as a Labourer in the Engineers' Department in May 1806, earning 1/6d per day with "one day extra allowed per week agreeable to the Board's Order dated the 12th March 1801" (Supply 5/222).

James Cellop was working as a Millman in February 1814, earning 3/-d per day with an additional 6d per night when on duty (Supply 5/230).

William Champness was born circa 1792, and in August 1812 he was working as a Saltpetre Refiner earning 2/8d per day, as well as being allowed to "watch in turn when not working extra" (Supply 5/229). On the 12th September 1815, he joined the Engineers' Department as a casual Labourer, still earning the same money (WO54/516). The same Labour Return showed that in February 1816 he was a 23-year-old married man with one child. In the 1841 Census, William Champness, Carpenter, and a daughter of similar age as above, were living in High Bridge Street.

Joseph Chapel, a single man, was working as a Labourer in May 1801, earning 1/6d per day (Supply 5/221).

John Chaplin was appointed as a general Labourer within the Manufactory on the 11th February 1834; he was then a 47-year-old married man with 7 children. He had worked in the Royal Ordnance Laboratory as a Labourer since the 1st May 1806, and had served for 28 years. At Waltham Abbey he was paid £28.5.6d per annum and allowed to watch in turn, which gave him an annual remuneration of £33.9.6d (WO54/593). On the 26th October 1836, he was appointed as a Millman and his total annual pay, including allowances, was then £46.16.0d (WO54/623).

The 1841 census recorded that John and his wife, Sarah, described as a Char-woman, were living in Camp's Alley with 5 of their children, John, who was aged 15 and a Labourer working at the Gunpowder Mills, Mary, also 15, Eliza (14) Rachael (11) and Richard (9). With the exception of Richard, they were all born in Essex.

Thomas Chaplin replaced Charles Carter as a general Labourer in the Mixing House on the 30th November 1840 (Supply 5/238).

William Chaplin was employed as a general Labourer on the 2nd October 1839, replacing Charles Horam, who had been discharged. He was paid £39.0.0d per annum, which included an allowance to watch in turn. (WO56/623).

William Chapman was working as a general Labourer on the 2nd February 1800 when he signed a Petition relating to Pay and Conditions with a cross (Supply 5/220). Since his name did not appear in the Waltham Abbey records again until August 1812, it is possible that he left the Ordnance Board's employment, returning as a Labourer "drawing and setting stoves and in the willow plantation" (Supply 5/229). He was then paid 2/8d per day and allowed to watch. In February 1814, he was employed as a Cooper earning 2/4d per day but, like all other Coopers, he was not allowed to watch (Supply 5/230).

Joseph Chapple started work at the Gunpowder Mills as a Labourer in the spring of 1805, and in January of 1806, he was earning 2/-d per day (Supply 5/224). During June 1807 he was "drawing and setting stoves, loading and unloading barges etc." (Supply 5/226). By August 1808, he was a Corning House Man earning 2/6d per day, and all Corning House men were, "in addition to their pay...allowed to watch in turn, for which they receive one shilling" (Supply 5/227).

Joseph continued to be employed in the Corning Houses, but at 11.15 a.m. on the 27th November 1811 there was a huge explosion at No. 4 Press House - for full details see the notes on Thomas Belsham. Among those killed was Joseph, a widower, who left a 17-year-old daughter, Sarah. Although she was in service, she was generally considered to be dependant "to a great measure" on her late father. Sarah petitioned the Board, saying that she "humbly prays an allowance in consequence of the death of her late father, Joseph Chapple, who was killed by the explosion of the corning house on the 27th November" (Winters *op.cit.* p.72). In a letter dated the 29th November 1811, the Board agreed to pay "a donation of ten guineas" to Sarah, "the daughter of Joseph Chapple" (Supply 5/199). A second letter from the Board dated the 3rd December 1811, stated that his other children were provided for (Supply 5/229) and confirmed that Chapple had been employed in the Corning House "at 2/6d per day."

Edward Chase was employed as a Labourer in April 1791 "setting and drawing stoves and in the punts", for which he received 1/6d daily (Supply 5/215).

Anthony Childs was employed as a Puntman in September 1810; he was paid 2/-d per day, and allowed to watch in turn

(Supply 5/228). By August 1812, he was working in the Corning Houses (Supply 5/229) and continued to do so until at least February 1814 (Supply 5/230). During this period he was earning 3/3d per day, with an additional 1/6d per night when it was his turn to watch.

James Chillis worked as a Brimstone Refiner in August 1812 until at least February 1814, earning 3/-d per day and, in addition, he was allowed to watch in turn, for which he received 1/6d (Supply 5/229 and Supply 5/230).

John Chillis started work as a Brimstone Refiner in January 1806 at 2/-d per day (Supply 5/224). By June 1807, he was refining Saltpetre on the same pay but "when not working extra… allowed to watch in turn" (Supply 5/226). John was still a Saltpetre Refiner in August 1812, but was then paid 2/8d per day and still allowed to watch in turn (Supply 5/229). This remained the case in February 1814 (Supply 5/230).

John suffered an injury at work, and the following is yet another example of how the Ordnance Board looked after their employees. In a letter dated the 3rd November 1817, James Wright, the Storekeeper at Waltham Abbey, wrote to the Board stating that Mr Hilton, the Ordnance Surgeon at Waltham Abbey, "represented the life of John Chillis, a Labourer ….to be in danger for want of a proper truss to be used by him in a case of Hernia occasioned by his work in the manufactory, and which cannot be reduced." As a consequence, the Board gave directions to the Director General of the Ordnance Medical Department "to cause two trusses of the description you have stated to be immediately forwarded to Waltham Abbey for the use of this man." (Supply 5/201).

William Chillis was working as a Saltpetre Refiner in August 1808 earning 2/-d per day, and all Refiners "in addition to their pay... are allowed to watch in turn, for which they receive one shilling" (Supply 5/227). William was still working as a Saltpetre Refiner in September 1810 on the same pay and conditions as before (Supply 5/228).

Benjamin Clark worked as a casual Labourer in the Engineers' Department in September 1812, earning 2/8d per day for a six-day week (WO54/512).

Daniel Clark was born circa 1794 and started as a casual Labourer in the Engineers' Department on the 14th October 1814. In February 1816 he was paid 2/8d per day, at which time he was a 21-year-old bachelor living in Waltham Abbey (WO54/516).

John Clark (1) started work as a Millman in the spring of 1805, and in January 1806, he was earning 2/3d per day (Supply 5/224). He continued as a Millman until at least September 1810 at the same rate of pay, but was "allowed 6d per night when on duty" (Supply 5/228).

John Clark (2) born circa 1793, started work on the 11th November 1815 as a casual Labourer in the Engineers' Department. In February 1816, he was paid 2/8d per day; he was then a 22- year-old married man with one child, living in Waltham Abbey (WO54/516).

Peter Clark, a married man with 5 children, worked as a Labourer in May 1801, earning 1/6d per day (Supply 5/221). On the 16th June 1801, Peter, with others, was repairing the Corning House when it caught fire following an explosion and 7 men, including Peter, were badly burnt. The fire was caused "from a blow of a copper hammer on a pit wheel" (Winters, *op.cit.* p.59). Full details of their suffering are given in the notes on Timothy Bates. In a letter to the Board dated the 29th July 1801, the men who were burnt requested that they were reimbursed for the loss of clothing. Peter Clark's claim amounted to £2.12.6d in all – for a hat (4/-d) stockings (2/6d) a shirt (5/6d) a coat (6/6d) breeches (4/-d) a waistcoat (6/-d) and sheets (£1.4.0d) Supply 5/221). He, together with the others, also requested financial assistance – see notes on Timothy Bates.

A Return of Artificers and Labourers dated the 3rd November 1801, indicated that Peter had returned to work when the majority of the workforce was repairing the riverbanks. It was noted that it would be dangerous, however, to expose him and the other severely burnt men to this type of work, and instead, they should perform other trifling jobs as they occurred (Supply 5/221). This is the last reference made of Peter Clark.

William Clark was born circa 1780, and was employed as a Labourer on the 13th June 1805 (Supply 5/232) "drawing and setting stoves etc." at 2/-d per day (Supply 5/224). By June 1807, he had transferred to the Corning Houses where he was earning 2/2d daily and allowed to watch in turn, for which he received 1/-d per night (Supply 5/226). William continued to work as a Corning House Man until September 1818. His wages had peaked at 3/3d per day in August 1812, and his watch allowance set at 1/6d per night (Supply 5/228). In June 1818, he was a 38-year-old married man with one child, living in Waltham Abbey. His pay was then 2/11d per day, and his watch money had been reduced to 1/-d per night (Supply 5/231).

The end of the Napoleonic Wars saw a reduction in the manufacture and regeneration of gunpowder, and as a consequence, the workforce and their wages were reduced. A list of names of the people the Storekeeper proposed to retain on the Establishment between the 4th September and the 31st December 1818 to meet the new production and cost requirements, was sent to the Board on the 28th August (Supply 5/231). William's name was not on that list. However, a second list was submitted on the

3rd September which rescinded his proposed dismissal, and a Board Order dated the 4th September 1818, confirmed his re-appointment as a Corning House Man with his pay remaining unchanged, but he was no longer allowed to watch (Supply 5/231).

A List of Employees dated the 6th February 1822, recorded that on the 4th October 1819, William Clark was appointed as a Saltpetre Refiner with annual pay of £41.14.4d, which included an allowance to watch. This List showed that William and his wife lived in Cheshunt, and that they still had the one child (Supply 5/232).

The Establishment at Waltham was reduced still further in 1822 – see notes on Thomas Carter – and William was included on the list of those to be dismissed on the 1st June 1822 (Supply 5/232). Several petitions were submitted by the men asking for financial assistance, and many of those concerned were long-service employees in their middle age, who pointed out that they had little hope of finding employment after the hay and corn harvest had been gathered. The Storekeeper was sympathetic and forwarded their petition to the Board. William was one of those awarded two weeks' pay to ease their financial burden (Supply 5/203).

Benjamin Clarke (also Clark) was born circa 1764 and started work as a Labourer in the Corning Houses on the 8th October 1794. He was paid 1/6d per day (Supply 5/217) and this was also the case in July 1795 (Supply 5/217). He had enlisted as a Private in the Military Volunteer Company on the same day as he joined the Ordnance, and in September 1798,he was described as a Refiner (Supply 5/219). A signed Petition on Pay and Conditions raised in February 1800 showed that he was illiterate and was still working as a Refining House Labourer (Supply 5/220). The following year, a Report on the Marital Status of the Employees recorded that he was a single man (Supply 5/221). On the 8th October 1801, Robert Coleman, the Clerk of the Cheque, recorded in his Minute Book that 24 men were required to work at the Faversham Mills or be discharged, and Benjamin agreed to go (Winters, *op.cit.* p.60). However, his name did not appear in the Faversham records, nor was it again recorded at Waltham Abbey until 1808, so it is assumed that his services were terminated, but that he was subsequently re-engaged.

In August 1808, a Benjamin Clarke was employed as a Saltpetre Refiner earning 2/-d per day, and "when not working extra, allowed to watch in turn" (Supply 5/227). He was still a Refiner in September 1810 (Supply 5/228) but by August 1812 he was employed as a Warder, who was paid 2/8d per day and still allowed to watch (Supply 5/229). A Return for June 1818 recorded that he was still a Warder with the same pay and allowance, and that he was then a 54-year-old widower with 3 children, living in Waltham Abbey (Supply 5/231).

Peace in Europe saw a reduction in the manufacture and regeneration of gunpowder, and as a consequence, the Board required the Establishment at the Royal Powder Mills to be cut back and expenditure reduced. A list sent from Waltham Abbey to the Board on the 28th August 1818, recorded the names of the people the Storekeeper proposed to retain between the 3rd September and the 31st December 1818 to meet the new production and financial requirements. Although Benjamin's name was on that list (Supply 5/231), a few days later, a second letter to the Board stated, "We respectfully beg leave to add the names and stations of those people whom it will be necessary to discharge in consequence of this arrangement" and Benjamin Clarke, Warder, was included on that list (Supply 5/231).

William Claverly was working as a common Labourer in the Engineers' Department in July 1809, and was paid 17/-d for 7 days' work carried out in the Manufactory (Supply 5/228). By

September of the following year, he was on the Storekeeper's payroll as a Labourer "setting and drawing stoves and in the willow plantations etc." for which he received 2/-d per day, and was allowed to watch in turn (Supply 5/228). In August 1812, he was working in the Corning Houses (Supply 5/229) where he remained until at least February 1814 (Supply 5/230). During this period he was paid 3/3d per day and 1/6d per night when it was his turn to watch.

Charles Clayden/Claydon/Clayton was born circa 1784 and started a life-long association with the Mills on the 24th October 1805 as a Puntman (Supply 5/232). By the end of January 1806, he had transferred to the Corning Houses where he worked for the next 16 years. In 1806 he was paid 2/2d per day (Supply 5/224) and the following year was allowed to watch in turn, for which he received 1/-d per night (Supply 5/226). Over the ensuing years his daily rate of pay and watch allowance gradually increased, and in August 1812, they were 3/3d and 1/6d respectively (Supply 5/229) with his wage peaking at 3/10d by February 1814 (Supply 5/230). In June 1818, he was a 33-year-old married man with 5 children living in Waltham Abbey. His pay was then recorded as 2/11d per day, but his watch-money had been reduced to 1/-d per night (Supply 5/231).

When the Storekeeper formulated his proposal for reduced production and economies in August 1818 – see notes on William Clark – Charles was to be retained. However, a few days' later, a letter from Waltham Abbey to the Board stated, "We respectfully beg leave to add to the names and stations of those persons it will be necessary to discharge in consequence of this arrangement" i.e., the reduction of the Establishment numbers, and Charles Claydon, Corning House Man, was then to be discharged (Supply 5/231). Nevertheless, he was reprieved by an Order of the Board dated the 4th September 1818, and reappointed a Corning House Man, retaining his daily rate of pay of 2/11d, and was still allowed to watch in turn, for which he received 1/-d per night. He continued to work as a Corning House Man, and by September 1820 his watch-allowance had been increased to 1/6d per night (Supply 5/232). A Return of Employees at the 31st December 1821, recorded that his watch money was then 2/-d per night, which gave Claydon an estimated annual amount of £51.16.11d (Supply 5/232).

A statement dated the 4th April 1822 "of monies to which the public were entitled to receive credit", recorded that Charles was one of several employees "having occupied their present residences previous to the Hon. Board purchasing the same, sanction will be asked for their future residing in them." Under an Order dated the 4th May 1821, the property was leased to him for an annual rent of £5.4.0d (Supply 5/232) but where the property was is unknown.

From a List of Employees dated April 1821 (Supply 5/232) it would appear that one of his children had died, but apart from that, there was no change on his circumstances. In the spring of 1822, the Ordnance Board decided to reduce the production and regeneration of gunpowder still further and the Establishment at Waltham was cut again. On the 21st March, Empsom Middleton and James Wright drew up a list of people who were to be retained (Supply 5/232) and this list included Charles Claydon, not as a Corning House Man but as a "Labourer for general purposes to be sent to any part of the Manufactory wherever their services may be required" (Supply 5/233). Further reductions to his pay were made by Board Orders dated the 27th December 1822 and the 15th January 1823, cutting them by £2.12.0d per annum (WO54/542). A further Return of Employees for April 1823 gave his basic wage as £33.16.0d per annum (WO54/542) which, with an allowance to watch, equated to £39.0.0d annually. The Return for October 1824 (WO54/546) recorded that he was then a widower.

124

In the spring of 1827, Charles moved to Romeland to another tenement owned by the Board off High Bridge Street, and a List of Properties prepared by the Royal Engineers' Office on the 20th December 1834, recorded that on the 6th April 1827, Charles Clayton was granted the lease of a Tenement, for which he was charged £5.4.0d per annum (Supply 5/237 and WO44/133). The cottage is Plot No. 71 on the Town Map shown in Appendix 1, and according to the 1825 Rateable Valuation for Waltham Abbey, had then been occupied by a Thomas Clayton (D/DHf B29). Charles continued to work as a General Labourer, and retained his right to watch in turn until October 1827, when he was classified as a "Leading Hand". This allowed him to act as a Rounder, which increased his annual income to £47.17.4d (WO54/558). Sometime between 1834 and 1840, he moved into a cottage within the Storehouse Yard following the death of Benjamin Archer, and this was Plot No. 21 on the Town Map in Appendix 1. By October 1829 he had remarried (WO54566) and on the 15th July 1833, he returned to the Corning Houses, replacing James Pallett, who had died (WO54/587). The Return recorded that his annual wage was then £53.16.0d, which included an amount for Rounding every third night of 2/-d. More reductions to wages were made by April 1934, and his annual pay, including his Rounder's allowance, was then only £48.1.9d (WO54/593). However, it appears that the pay structure was reviewed yet again on the 5th September 1837. Charles retained his position in the Corning House and was then allowed to watch in turn, which increased his annual pay to £55.0.08d, as was the case in October 1839 (WO54/623).

The 1841 Census showed that he was still employed at the Gunpowder Mills and still living in a cottage within the Saltpetre Refinery located on the south side of High Bridge Street, with his second wife, Elizabeth. Living with them was a Sarah Pegrum, aged 90, perhaps his Mother-in-Law.

Joseph Claydon worked as a Labourer in September 1810 "setting and drawing stoves and in the willow plantations etc.", for which he was paid 2/-d per day and allowed to watch (Supply 5/228). By August 1812, he was working in the Corning Houses earning 3/3d per day and 1/6d per night when it was his turn to watch (Supply 5/229) as was the case in February 1814 (Supply 5/230).

Thomas Claydon was working as a Labourer in June 1807 "setting & drawing stoves and loading and unloading barges etc", for which he was paid 2/-d per day (Supply 5/226).

John Clowdersly was born in 1753 and engaged by General Conway as a Clerk in the Ordnance Department at Portsmouth on the 12th October 1772. He was made an "Extra Clerk" on the 24th February 1776, being appointed to the permanent Establishment on the 1st April 1776, and was transferred to a similar position at Woolwich on the 24th April 1777. He became the Clerk of the Cheque at Purfleet on the 12th August 1780, and was appointed to the same position at Waltham Abbey on the 1st April 1788 with a salary of £90.0.0d per annum (WO54/217). John moved yet again on the 1st January 1793 to the Faversham Gunpowder Mills as the Clerk of the Cheque (WO54/217) and more information on this man can be found in the *Faversham Gunpowder Personnel Register*.

John Coal started work in the Engineers' Department on the 12th June 1813. In February 1816, he was working as a casual Bricklayer's Labourer earning 2/8d per day. At that date he was a 30-year-old married man with one child, living in Enfield (WO54/516).

Steven Cock was a Labourer by trade who was set to work by Daniel Cornish in October 1787 at 9/-d per week, renovating the Powder Mills following their purchase by the Ordnance Board from Mr Walton (Winters, *op.cit.* p.28). A Return dated the 27th January 1789, recorded that Stephen Cock was to be tried as a Millman, having previously been employed by Mr. Walton (Supply 5/212). However, it appears that he was unsuccessful, since in March 1789 he was undertaking Labourer's work "setting and drawing stoves etc.", for which he was paid 1/6d per day (Supply 5/212).

On the 12th September 1789, J. Wright and J. Clowdersly wrote to Major Congreve saying, "We beg leave to report that last night at 6 0'clock the 2nd of No. Head Mills blew up. The charge had not been upon the bed more than five minutes and the Mill did not receive any injury; it was set to work this day at 10 O'clock. The Master Worker has removed James Bennett and Stephen Cock out of the Mills as he found d them incapable of doing their business; we therefore desire to know if you would have them discharged. We have given notice to Richard Stevens and Thos Wright that they are not to be employed after the 20th instant which we hope will meet your approbation." (WASC 1392).

Abraham Cockham worked as a Saltpetre Refiner on the 29th August 1812 (Supply 5/229) and continued to do so until at least February 1814 (Supply 5/230). During this period he was paid 2/8d per day, and in addition, "when not working extra," he was allowed to watch in turn.

John Codwell was working as a casual Labourer in the Engineers' Department in September 1812, and was paid 2/8d per day for a six-day week (WO54/512).

William Colbert was trained as a musician in the Dragoons, commencing employment with the Ordnance Board on the 31st May 1800 (WO54/587) possibly at Faversham, since Georgina, daughter of William and Mary Colbert was baptised there on the 6th May 1801. In 1825 he was described as a Foreman at the

Royal Gunpowder Manufactory at Faversham, but was stopped 2/-d for medical attendance from the 1st July to the 31st December 1825. Between the 31st January and the 4th February 1828, he suffered from ague (Malaria) and was given 2 oz. of bark (quinine) according to Supply 5/116.

John came to the Waltham Abbey Powder Mills on the 18th May 1832 as the Foreman of Labourers in the Engineers' Department, and in April 1833, his daily rate of pay was 4/9d for 313 days, giving him an annual amount of £74.6.9d (WO54/587). The same document recorded that he had 33 years' service and that he was then aged 67, a widower with 6 children. Under an Order of the Board dated the 15th March 1833, William Colbert, Labourer in the Engineers' Department, was to be discharged and granted a pension of £29.14.9d per annum until an opportunity to employ him again should arise (Supply 5/208).

James Cole, born circa 1784, trained as a Pin Maker before starting work as a Corning House Man on the 8th September 1804 (Supply 5/232). He earned 2/2d per day in January 1806 (Supply 5/224) and by June 1807 was allowed to watch in turn, for which he received 1/-d each time (Supply 5/226).

By August 1808, he was the "Foreman of the Reeling Houses" and paid 2/10d per day with 1/6d extra when it was his turn to watch (Supply 5/227) as was the case in 1810 and 1811. A List of Employees for August 1812, recorded that he was still the Reeling House Foreman and that his daily wage had been increased to 3/10d, while his watch allowance remained unchanged (Supply 5/229).

With the cessation of hostilities in Europe, the Establishment was reduced, and by June 1818, James had returned to the Corning Houses with his daily wage and watch allowance cut to 2/11d and 1/-d respectively (Supply 5/231 and WO54/542). A List of

Employees sent from Waltham to the Board on the 28th August indicated the people the Storekeeper proposed to retain to meet new production and cost requirements. James Cole was on that List (Supply 5/231) and an Order of the Board dated the 4th September 1818 confirmed his position as a Corning House Man (Supply 5/232). He was to be paid 2/11d per day with an extra 1/-d per night when on watch, and this document recorded that he was then a 33-year-old married man with 4 children, living in Waltham Abbey. The Corning House was to remain his workplace for the next 15 years, surviving another reduction in the workforce in 1822 (Supply 5/232) although his annual wage, including his allowance to watch, gradually decreased from £50.16.1d in 1821 (Supply 5/232) to £41.1.9d in April 1834 (WO54/593). There was a small increase, however, in April 1839, making it £42.2.0d per annum (WO54/623).

James' name did not appear in the 1841 Census for Waltham Abbey; on the 13th April 1843, some 40 barrels of gunpowder exploded in the Corning House, together with another 20 in the Press House, killing 7 men, including James (Winters, *op.cit.* p.106). A graphic description of the explosion and damage caused, etc., was given in the *Illustrated London News* dated Saturday, the 22nd April 1843 (WAAC). James left a widow and 4 children.

Thomas Cole, born circa 1739, started work in 1790 in the Engineers' Department as a Labourer earning 1/6d per day. In August and September 1790, he worked in the Manufactory with his wages submitted by William Spry, Colonel Commanding the Royal Engineers, for payment by the Storekeeper, James Wright, and signed for his pay with a firm hand (WASC 1382). In May 1801, he was paid 1/9d per day, and was then a married man with one child (Supply 5/221). On the 18th April 1801, there was a huge explosion in the new Corning House whilst it was undergoing repair and Thomas was one of the men who were very badly burnt. Full details of the explosion and the suffering endured by Thomas and the other men are given under the notes on Timothy Bates.

Cole plainly recovered from his terrible burns, since a Return of Officers and others Employed on the 8th May 1806, showed he was still working as a Labourer in the "Engineers' Department Established" earning 1/6d per day with "one day extra allowed per week agreeable to the Board's Order dated the 12th March 1801" (Supply 5/222). In January 1806, Thomas was working as a Warder earning 2/-d per day (Supply 5/224) as was the case in 1807 and 1808, and he was also allowed to watch in turn (Supply 5/227). By August 1812, his daily rate of pay had increased to 2/8d, and remained so until April 1816.

It is clear from the notes on other employees that following the defeat of Napoleon at Waterloo and peace in Europe, the Storekeeper recommended that many of the long-service and older employees should be retired on a pension. On the 2nd March 1816, the Storekeeper recommended to the Board that Mr. Thomas Cole, who was a 76-year-old Warder who had served 27 years, should receive a daily superannuation of 2/8d. In the notes attached to the letter was the comment that Mr. Cole and others should be superannuated ".... because of the hurts they have received in this dangerous Manufactory." It was also stated therein that Mr. Cole "has been getting more feeble every month for several years past, and is now incapable of exertion and quite worn out." (Supply 5/230) The Board awarded Thomas a pension of 2/-d per day for a six-day week, commencing on the 1st April 1816 (Supply 5/200). In spite of his ill health and infirmity, Thomas was still receiving his pension of 12/-d per week in 1826 (Winters, *op. cit.* p.96).

George Coleman was employed as a Labourer at the Cylinder Houses in West Sussex. A Return showing the Marital Status of

Employees, recorded that he was a married man with one child, and that he was paid 1/6d per day. The same document said that since the cylinders were out of repair, Coleman had been employed stacking timber in the yards and levelling the ground where the cylinders were to be re-sited, but "...it is possible that he will go to Faversham as has been done heretofore, or his business will be terminated." All of this information has been taken from Supply 5/221.

Robert Coleman was appointed as an Extra Clerk at Purfleet on the 22nd July 1780, before transferring to Waltham Abbey Powder Mills as a Clerk on the 1st April 1788 (Supply 5/216). On the 7th May 1794, he enlisted as a First-Lieutenant in the Military Volunteer Company (Winters, *op. cit.* p.51). A Report on Pay and Allowances in July 1795, noted that he had been appointed the Clerk of the Cheque and gave his salary as £90.0.0d per annum, with a further £20.0.0d per annum for house rent (Supply 5/217). The Clerk of the Cheque acted as the Storekeeper's Deputy and often signed documents in his absence; one typical example was when Coleman produced a List of Members of the Military Volunteer Company which was signed by him as the "Storekeeper on duty" (Supply 5/219 dated September, 1798).

Between 1793 and 1796 he kept a Minute Book listing many small incidents relating to life and conditions at the Mills, which Winters used extensively in his *Centenary Memorial* (pp 36-48). His last entry on the 17th June 1796 read, "Discontinued these minutes, for it is impossible to keep them with accuracy in consequence of my frequency of going after the Cylinder Works and Charcoal Wood." The Cylinder Works were at Fisher Street and Fernhurst in West Sussex, and he made frequent "scouting" trips in Essex for charcoal wood.

Most of the letters leaving Waltham Abbey were signed in conjunction with the Storekeeper, James Wright, but a note on one which was dated the 17th May 1799, recorded, "Clerk of the Cheque absent on duty in Sussex" (WO13/2202). A letter from the Board dated the 19th August 1801, recorded that Henry Dugleby had been appointed as Clerk of the Cheque in place of Coleman, who had been promoted, although to where is unknown (Supply 5/195).

James Collop was employed as a Labour in 1805 "drawing and setting stoves etc.", at 2/-d per day (Supply 5/224). In August 1808 he was employed as a Puntman, still on a daily wage of 2/-d and allowed to watch in turn (Supply 5/227). He was to change his trade again in September 1810, when he became a Millman earning 2/3d per day, with an additional 6d when he worked "extra" (Supply 5/228). The same applied in 1812, except that he was then paid 3/-d daily (Supply 5/229).

Joseph Colver, born circa 1768, was employed a casual Labourer in the Engineers' Department on the 12th November 1811, and in February 1812, he was paid 2/8d per day for a six-day week (WO54/512). The same document recorded that he was a 48-year-old married man with 8 unmarried children, who lived in Waltham Abbey. Along with the rest of the workforce in the Engineers' Department, his wages had been cut by February 1817, when he then received 2/4d daily and worked "occasionally as the service required" (WO54/520). Joseph was still on the same rate of pay and conditions in April 1821 (WO54/536) and was possibly made redundant late in 1821 or early 1822, as there were no further entries for this man.

John Colverd was born circa 1787 and had been trained as a Carpenter (WO54/562). A Labour Return for October 1833 recorded that he worked for a private contractor on the 6th September 1804, who was employed to undertake work for the Ordnance Board at the Powder Mills (WO54/587). He then left the contractor and was taken on the Establishment by the Board, joining the Engineers' Department as a Carpenter (1st Class), probably in 1809, since he was paid £1.9.9d for work carried out by that department in the Manufactory between the 15th and 21st July of that year (Supply 5/228).

His name did not appear in the Powder Mills' records again until April 1825 when WO54/550 noted that he was employed as a Carpenter at 4/1d per day for 313 days in the year, giving him an annual income of £63.18.1d. According to this Return, he was a 38-year-old married man with 10 children who had 15 years' service with the Ordnance Board. Other Returns such as WO54/581 indicate that he was taken on the Establishment on the 23rd June 1823.

A Return of Persons belonging to the Civil Establishment of the Ordnance dated the 31st January 1831, recorded that John was one of 7 Carpenters to be employed at the Waltham Abbey Powder Mills and the Small Arms Manufactory at Enfield. It confirmed he was paid 4/1d per day, and required to undertake general services as a Carpenter where "great care, attention and sobriety etc. are required" (WO54/575). He was still working as a Carpenter in the Engineers' Department in April 1839 on the same pay (WO54/623).

In the 1841 Census it was recorded that John, a Carpenter, and his wife, Mary, together with their children Charles (20), also a Carpenter, James (15), a Shoemaker, Ann (15) who worked at the Small Arms Factory as a Percussion Cap Maker, and Elizabeth (13) and Rebecca (7) both of whom were Pin Makers, lived in Waltham Abbey. John was not born in Essex, but the rest of his family were. Another son may have been William, who was living in High Bridge Street with his wife, Martha.

Thomas Colverd was born in 1810 and trained as a Carpenter. However, when he joined the Engineers' Department on the 21st

May 1829, it was as a Labourer and not as a tradesman (WO54/566). He was a 19-year-old bachelor and was paid 2/2d per day. A Return dated the 31st January 183, recorded that Thomas was one of 15 Labourers retained in the Engineers' Department (see notes on Joseph Cannon). Thomas continued to be employed as a Labourer on the same pay until at least April 1834 (WO54/593).

Based on the 1841 Census and previous information regarding age and marital status, he may well have been the Thomas Colverd, a 30-year-old bachelor and Carpenter by trade, who was living in what appears to be a lodging house in Mr Hicks' yard in Sewardstone Street. It is possible that he was the son of John Colverd.

Sir William Congreve, 1st Baronet, instigated the purchase of the Waltham Abbey Powder Mills by the Crown. He was born on the 4th July 1742 at Walton, Staffordshire, and became a cadet at the Royal Military Academy, Woolwich at the age of thirteen. Congreve was commissioned in the Royal Artillery in 1759. In the War of the Spanish Succession he was at the siege of Louisville in 1758 which opened the way to Quebec, and later he served in the West Indies.

On the 9th December 1771 he married Rebecca Elmstone at St. Luke's, Old Street, London, and they had two sons, William and Tomas Ralf, as well as two daughters, Anne Catherine Penelope and Charlotte.

Congreve fought in the early stages of the first American War, and was wounded in the autumn of 1776. In 1788 he organised the Royal Military Repository, a school of instruction in Artillery exercises and machines. He became the Deputy Comptroller of the Royal Laboratory at the Arsenal at Woolwich, where research and development was undertaken on behalf of the Board of

Ordnance. His son, William, was later to occupy the same position.

After 24 years' service in 1783, he had risen to the rank of major and was given further responsibility for the manufacture of gunpowder. The only Government-owned Powder Mills were at Faversham, Kent, which the then Prime Minister, William Pitt the Younger was proposed to sell. Congreve, through the Master General of Ordnance, the Duke of Richmond, persuaded Pitt to reverse his decision, and to purchase he Mills at Waltham Abbey. The run-down Mills at Waltham Abbey were purchased in 1787 from the Walton family for £10,000, and over the next twelve months or so, were refurbished with new production facilities being added. As well as the modernisation works, Congreve introduced new management systems and procedures. Written rules covered many aspects of life within the Manufactory with emphasis laid on health and safety, and amongst these were included the elimination of sparks from grit or steel which could cause an explosion. This was tackled by leather floor covering, the use of bronze or copper tools, sewn boots without studs, wooden wheel rails and specially designed covered barges.

Congreve maintained that consistency of the finished product was of the utmost importance, and particular attention was paid to the preparation of the ingredients used in the manufacture of gunpowder. Saltpetre was refined three times at Waltham Abbey, and in collaboration with Dr. Watson, the Bishop of Llandaff, a Professor of Chemistry and a fellow of Trinity College Cambridge, invented a new way of making charcoal in iron vessels - the cylinder method as opposed to pit burning. Much of the practical development of this new system of making charcoal was undertaken by James Wright Snr., the Storekeeper at the Waltham Abbey Mills under the supervision of Congreve.

Gunpowder was stored in barrels each containing 100lbs, and its life in a magazine or ships' holds was short, due to the absorption of dampness. To extend its life, Congreve improved the quality of the barrels by closer supervision of the coopers making them, and the use of better wood in their construction. The regeneration of the powder following the return of a ship from a tour of duty, or storage in a land magazine, became an important operation. Congreve brought this process 'in house', whereas previously the spoiled powder had been sold off cheaply, and much of this work was carried out at the Waltham Abbey Mills.

Congreve himself did not get rich from his initiative and inventions, becoming, however, a favourite of the Prince of Wales, who made him a Baronet in 1812. He was still in Office as a Lieutenant-General when he died in 1812 at the age of 71, and was buried in St. Luke's Church at Charlton.

Joseph Conyerd was working as a Saltpetre Refiner in August 1812 earning 2/8d per day, and in addition, when not working extra, he was allowed to watch in turn (Supply 5/229). This was also the case in February 1814 (Supply 5/230).

John Cook started work as a Labourer in the Corning Houses on the 5th November 1789, earning 1/6d per day (Supply 5/214 dated the 27th March 1790). In the winter of 1792 he was "in the barges" (Supply 5/215) while in the summer months he was "in the country charring wood" and paid the same daily rate (Supply 5/216). In February 1793, John, together with William Fuller and John Turnham, was taking materials to London by barge along the River Lee, and was afraid of being "seized by the Press Gangs." Accordingly, the Rex Officers at the Waltham Abbey Mills wrote to the Duke of Richmond stating that John, William Fuller and John Turnham were Gunpowder Makers and Bargemen, and were apprehensive of the Impress Court on the River Thames, and "they request that you will be pleased to grant them protection." (WASC 0475). John continued to work on the barges, first as a Bargeman and then as Master Bargeman, until he was superannuated on the 1st April 1816. As a Bargeman he was initially paid 1/6d per day (Supply 5/216) which rose to 3/3d by May 1804 (Supply 5/222). A signed Petition on Pay and Conditions raised in February 1800 (Supply 5/220) showed that he was illiterate, and a Return in May 1801 (Supply 5/221) recorded that he was a married man with 2 children.

During November 1801, although employed as a Bargeman, "when not on the barges he was employed with the other men cleaning and deepening the river, canals, ditches and any other work necessary to be performed" (Supply 5/221). A Return of Employees in May 1804 (Supply 5/222) noted, "while transporting gunpowder to Pickets Field, Bargemen are allowed double pay." A List of Foremen, etc. on the Establishment dated the 28th March 1805, recorded that both John Cook and John Turnham were in charge of 19 men employed in shipping gunpowder, landing and drawing stores, transporting gunpowder and in the willow plantation." Each was paid 14/-d a week (Supply 5/223).

In January 1806, Cook is listed as a Master Bargeman (Supply 5/224), a position he retained until he retired in 1816. His pay in 1806 was 4/-d per day but by 1812 it had risen to 5/2d (Supply 5/229) continuing at this rate until his retirement (Supply 5/230).

A List of Persons in Employment dated the 2nd March 1816 stated that Mr Cook was a Master Bargeman with 26 years' service, and the Storekeeper recommended to the Board that he should receive a daily superannuation of 5/2d. In the attached notes was a comment that Cook, together with others, should be superannuated because "...of the hurts they have received in this dangerous Manufactory." It also stated therein that Mr. Cook had, "previous to his entry into the Ordnance, served in the employment of the Merchants at these works from his childhood." In addition, it was said that he had been "very much bruised in the Ordnance service at various periods, which has brought on complaints which render him unfit to continue his duty" (Supply 5/230). The Board awarded John Cook a pension of 3/6d per day for a six-day week commencing on the 1st April 1816 (Supply 5/200) which he was still receiving in 1837 (Supply 5/237).

A statement dated the 4th April 1822, "of monies to which the public were entitled to receive credit" recorded that John was one of several employees "having occupied their present residences previous to the Hon. Board purchasing the same, sanction will be asked for their future residing in them." Under an Order dated the 4th May 1821 the property was leased to him for an annual rent of £8.9.0d (Supply 5/232). The house was one in a row of five known as Bank Cottages on the north side of High Bridge Street to the west of Powder Mill Lane, and has been identified as Plot No. 48 on the Town Map in Appendix 1. A Return of Properties dated the 20th December 1834, showed that John had vacated the cottage owned by the Board, and that it had been occupied by Edward Essex in 1834 (Supply 5/237).

The 1841 Census recorded that John Cook, an Ordnance Pensioner, together with his wife, Jane, were living in Paradise Row in Waltham Abbey. Their rounded-down ages were 75 and 70 years respectively and both were born in Essex.

Thomas Cook was Apprenticed into the Mixing House in August 1789, and paid 1/-d per day (Supply 5/213). It would appear that he did not complete his training, since his name did not appear in the records for the Manufactory after August 1793 (Supply 5/216). However, it is possible that he returned to the Mills as a casual Labourer in the Engineers' Department in 1812, because a Thomas Cook was shown as earning 2/8d per day for a six-day week in WO54/512.

John Cooms was a Bricklayer who carried out work for the Engineers' Department between the 15th and 21st July 1809, for which he was paid £1.9.9d (Supply 5/228).

John Cooper was born in 1790 and trained as a Carpenter, but it was as a casual Labourer that he was first engaged by the Engineers' Department on the 3rd May 1815 (WO54/623). In February 1816, he was paid 2/8d per day, and was a 26-year-old married man with one child, living in Waltham Abbey (WO54/516).

He continued to work "occasionally as required" within the Engineers' Department, but in common with the rest of the workforce, his wages were reduced following the cessation of hostilities in Europe. In February 1817 his pay was 2/4d per day, and he now had 2 offspring to support (WO54/520). By April 1823, John's pay had been reduced to 2/2d daily, giving him an annual income of £33.18.2d (WO54/542). However, by April 1825, his fortunes had changed because he was appointed as a Carpenter in the Engineers' Department. This promotion practically doubled his wage since he was then paid 4/1d per day for a six-day week, which amounted to £63.8.1d annually (WO54/550). A Return dated the 31st January 1831, of Persons belonging to the Civil Establishment of the Gunpowder Mills and the Small Arms Manufactories at Waltham Abbey, Faversham and Enfield recorded that John Cooper was one of 7 Carpenters to be employed at Waltham Abbey and Enfield, all of whom were to be paid 4/1d per day. John was required to undertake general services as a Carpenter in the Manufactory, "requiring great care, attention, sobriety, etc." (WO54/575).

A Labour Return for April 1839 (WO54/623) recorded that Cooper had been appointed as a Millwright in the Engineers' Establishment on the 16th October 1834 at 5/2d per day, with estimated annual earnings of £80.17.2d. In addition, it stated that he was then a 49-year-old married man with 5 children, still living in Waltham Abbey.

The 1841 Census recorded that John, described as a Millwright (Journeyman), was living in Paradise Row, together with his wife, Mary, their 3 daughters Jemima, Susan and Mary (aged 20, 15 and 12 respectively) and son John (aged 10); all the family were born in Essex, and apart from his own family, John had two Journeymen Millwrights as lodgers.

William Coote was born circa 1802. In February 1814, he was working as a Cooper earning 1/9d per day (Supply 5/230) as was the case in June 1818 (Supply 5/231). His age and low rate of pay for a Cooper indicated that he was still undergoing training, and when the Establishment was reduced in numbers in September 1818, William was discharged (Supply 5/231).

Henry Coreham was born circa 1766. He began working as a Labourer in the Corning Houses on the 1st June 1793 at 1/6d per day (Supply 5/216) and the Corning House was to be his workplace until 1818, first as a Labourer and then as one of the working Foremen. He enlisted as a Private in the Military Volunteer Company on the 7th May 1798 (Supply 5/219). A signed Petition on Pay and Conditions in the Mills of February 1800 showed that he was illiterate (Supply 5/220). On the 23rd October 1801 Robert Coleman, the Clerk of the Cheque, recorded in his Minute Book that 24 men were required to go to Faversham or be discharged, and Henry agreed to go (Winters *op. cit.* p.60). However, his name did not appear in the Faversham records, and most of the subsequent service records for Waltham

Abbey indicate that he was retained at Waltham Abbey Mills rather than being discharged.

In May 1804, Henry's daily wage as a Labourer in the Corning Houses had risen to 2/1d and, in addition, he was allowed 1/-d per night when it was his turn to watch, which was, on average, every fifth night (Supply 5/222). By January 1806, he was one of 3 working Foremen in the Corning Houses, with his pay increased to 2/6d per day (Supply 5/224) and he was soon to become a Rounder, for which he received 1/6d every third night (Supply 5/226). In August 1808 his daily rate of pay and his Rounder's allowance had risen to 3/-d and 2/-d respectively (Supply 5/227). This remained the case in 1810 (Supply 5/228) until he received a further rise in his daily rate to 4/-d by August 1812 (Supply 5/230).

Wages were cut following the cessation of the Napoleonic and Peninsular Wars and production of gunpowder was reduced. A List of Officers and Others Employed dated the 25th June 1818, recorded that Henry Coreham was then the Reeling House Foreman; he was paid 3/-d per day and was in receipt of an additional 1/6d for acting as a Rounder every fifth night. It was also noted that he was a 53-year-old married man without issue, living in Waltham Abbey (Supply 5/231 and WO54/542). Further reductions to the Establishment were made in September 1818, but by an Order of the Board dated the 4th September 1818, Henry retained his position and continued as the Reeling House Foreman until May 1822 (Supply 5/231). During this period his pay was 3/4d per day, although his Rounder's allowance, then on average every third night, was increased to 2/-d, which gave him total pay of £57.7.4d per annum (Supply 5/232).

Further economies were proposed in March 1822, and by an Order of the Board dated the 22nd May 1822, Henry was demoted to a Corning House Man (Supply 5/232). A Return dated the 1st

April 1823 recorded that his annual pay was only £48.2.0d, which included his watch monies (WO54/542). On the 25th May 1825, Henry was promoted to the Corning House Foreman, and his earnings were increased again to £57.7.4d annually (WO54/550). Sometime between April and October 1826 his wife died (WO54/550) and it would appear that he had remarried by October 1827 (WO54/558). Under a Board Order dated the 30th June 1830, Henry again served as a Rounder, which increased his annual pay to £64.6.0d (WO54/581) and he continued as the Corning House Foreman, although he ceased to be a Rounder in 1833 when he was some 66 years' old (WO54/587).

A Return of Properties owned by the Board dated the 20th December 1834, recorded that Henry had been leasing a cottage in Powder Mill Lane from his employers since the 24th September 1829, his annual rent being £5.4.0d (Supply 5/237). According to WO54/570, Henry's second wife died sometime in 1830.

It would appear that Henry then moved to another house, also in Powder Mill Lane, according to a Return made by the Royal Engineers on the 20th December 1834, which related to how vacant houses owned by the Board were proposed to be occupied (Supply 5/237). A cottage previously occupied by George Redpath (1) was to be let to Henry Coreham, Corning House Man. The property has been identified as one of three forming Plot No. 62 on the Town Map in Appendix 1, and a similar Return made in 1840 confirmed that the cottage was in Powder Mill Lane. It also confirmed that following Henry's death, it was occupied by J. Gibbs (WO44/133).

A List of people to be either promoted or superannuated dated the 12th September 1837, noted that "Henry Coreham, aged 71, with an infirmed hand is now the Foreman in the Corning Houses but recognises his infirmity, proposed he is superannuated." (Supply 5/237). This was the last record found for Henry Coreham.

John Cornhill joined the Ordnance Board in late 1804 or early 1805, and was employed in the Corning Houses in January 1806, earning 2/2d per day (Supply 5/224). The same applied in June of the following year except that he was then allowed to watch in turn, for which he received 1/-d per night (Supply 5/226). The Corning House continued to be his workplace until at least February 1813, and by then, his daily rate of pay had increased to 3/3d and his watch allowance to 1/6d (Supply 5/230).

William Cornhill was working in the Corning Houses in August 1808, earning 2/6d per day and allowed to watch in turn, for which he received 1/-d each time (Supply 5/227). The same applied in September 1810, except that his watch allowance had by then been increased to 1/6d per night (Supply 5/228).

Benjamin Cornish was born circa 1796 and trained as a Cooper (WO54/550). He was possibly still 'serving his time' as an Apprentice in September 1810, when he was paid 2/6d per day as a Cooper (Supply 5/228). He continued to be employed in this trade with his daily wage peaking in 1814 at 4/-d, but in common with all other Coopers, he was not allowed to watch (Supply 5/230). Benjamin survived the cuts made to the Establishment in September 1818, but his wages were reduced to 3/-d per day (Supply 5/231). A List of Employees dated May 1819, recorded that he was a 22-year-old bachelor living in Waltham Abbey, still employed as a Cooper, but now earning 3/6d per day (Supply 5/231). His name, however, did not appear in a similar Return for September 1820 (Supply 5/232) so it would appear that he might have left the Mills.

However, a Labour Return for October 1825, recorded that he had been re-employed for 9 months, that he was earning £54.12.0d per annum, and that at that date he was a married man with 2 children (WO54/550). According to Winters (*op.cit.* p.94) Benjamin was reinstated as a Cooper on the 20th December 1825, to make cement casks for Harwich. It is clear, however, that this was a temporary appointment, since Benjamin was once again employed as a general Labourer on the 10th February 1826, with basic pay of £33.16.0d per annum, although he was allowed to watch in turn, for which he received an extra 2/-d per week. This gave him an annual income of £39.0.0d with which to support his young family of 3 children (WO54/554). Benjamin continued to work as a Labourer until 1834 when, by April of that year, he "had been removed to the Salt Petre Refinery", replacing William Turnham, deceased. It would appear, however, that he received no financial gain from this move (WO54/593).

Life on a Labourer's pay must have been hard because in October 1838, Benjamin appealed to the Board for additional money. He stated that he had been brought up as a Cooper but had had 14 years' service as a Labourer, being compelled to take a Labourer's place (job). He added that he had a large family of 6 children, and that he was only paid 10/10d per week. In his Petition he requested that he replace Thomas Sadd, a Cooper, who had been promoted to Master Mixer (Supply 5/237). His appeal seems to have been partially successful because the Storekeeper wrote to the Board on the 23rd March 1840, saying that Benjamin Cornish's services were more valuable than that of a common Labourer, for which he was paid 2/4d daily. He was employed as a Cooper occasionally, and often worked in the Proof House mending machinery. The Storekeeper recommended, therefore, that his pay be increased to 3/-d per day (Supply 5/238), but the outcome is unknown.

Returns of Domestic Properties for December 1834 (Supply 5/237) and May 1840 (WO44/133) recorded that Benjamin was living in High Bridge Street in the same house previously occupied by Daniel Cornish, Carpenter, possibly his father, who died in 1825, the same year as Benjamin returned to the Mills. The 1841 Census confirmed the location of Benjamin's home in High Bridge Street, and showed that besides Benjamin, his wife, Sarah, a Stay Maker, and their children Mary, Emma, Sarah, Benjamin, Edward and Eliza also lived there.#

Daniel Cornish was born circa 1750 and had worked with the Walton family at their Waltham Abbey Powder Mills since the year 1780 (Supply 5/217). When the Ordnance considered purchasing the Mills from the Waltons, the Comptroller, Major Congreve, wrote to Daniel Cornish as follows:

"Mr. Daniel Cornish, I am directed by his Grace the Duke of Richmond to desire you immediately hire the best of the Millmen and labourers who lately worked at Mr Walton's Powder Mills. They will be paid nine shillings for every week for a month certain, and for every week they may be continued in these Powder Mills if they [the mills] should be purchased by the Government; and they (the above mentioned men) will be allowed every advantage that has been hitherto given to the Millmen and labourers who work in the Royal Powder Mills at Faversham. (Signed) W. Congreve, Major of Artillery, Waltham Abbey, 21st September, 1787."

In addition, Winters, (*op.cit.* p.27) quoted:

"Mr Cornish, you will be paid fifteen shillings a week from the date hereof for one month certain. (Signed) W. Congreve."

Daniel was taken on the Engineers' Establishment on the 1st November 1787 (Supply 5/217) and according to Winters (*op.cit.* p.29), would have worked on the extensive alterations and repairs, coupled with the new buildings erected on the site. In addition to his daily pay of 2/6d In February 1789, Daniel was entitled to train an Apprentice, for which he received 7/-d per week (Supply 5/188). In April of that year he was "fitting up racks to the Store & preparing stuff for the Charcoal Mill, etc." (Supply 5/213). Throughout the rest of 1789 and until 1793, Daniel was engaged in carpentry work in various parts of the Manufactory such as "fitting sieve lines etc.", as well as general repairs to buildings and equipment (Supply 5/214).

On the 7th May 1794, he joined the Military Volunteer Company as a Private (Supply 5/219). A Petition on Pay and Conditions at the Mills in February 1800, recorded that he was literate (Supply 5/220) and the Return on the Marital Status of the Employees in May 1801, indicated that he was married, with 4 children (Supply 5/221). The same document noted that he was still a Carpenter earning 3/-d per day. In a further Labour Return in May 1806, Daniel was shown as a Carpenter in the "Engineers' Department Established" who was paid 4/1d per day, with an additional allowance of 6/-d for an Apprentice (Supply 5/222).

In a letter to the Board dated the 16th July 1806, the Storekeeper stated that Mr Cornish, Master Carpenter, should retire on 10/6d per week, which would be borne upon the Charity List. In addition, he also considered that William White should be "appointed as Master Carpenter in the room of (in place of) Daniel Cornish" (Supply 5/197). However, in a further letter dated the 19th November to the Board (also Supply 5/197) it appeared that Cornish had said that he was unable to support his family on the superannuation granted to him and "requested the indulgence of being allowed to make...articles for the Powder Mills at the prices stated against each." It would appear that the Board agreed to this request, because the reply stated the writer desired that the Storekeeper pay Cornish "periodically for such work as he may perform, quoting the date of this Order as the Storekeeper's authority for such payments."

Daniel's pension was increased to 12/-d per week on the 1st April 1816 and to 14/-d weekly with effect from the 1st January 1818 (Supply 5/231). A statement dated the 4th April 1822, "of monies to which the public were entitled to receive credit" recorded that Daniel Cornish, Pensioner, had been living in a Board of Ordnance house, Tenement No. 18, leased to him on the 13th June 1808 for £6.10.0d per annum (Supply 5/232). Sometime after May 1821, Cornish moved to another tenement owned by the Board; the property in question has been identified as forming part of Plot No. 49 on the Town Map in Appendix 1. The house was originally leased to James and Eliza Allsup who ran a Post Office there, and was subsequently divided to form two dwellings. Daniel lived in the western half while the Allsup family continued to occupy the half nearest Powder Mill Lane. In 1822, Daniel's pension was still 14/-d per week or £36.8.0d per annum (Supply 5/232) and Winters records in his *Centenary Memorial* (p.96) that Cornish had died in 1825. A Return of Domestic Properties prepared by the Royal Engineers' Office in May 1840 (WO44/133) confirmed the location of Daniel's property, which was then occupied by Benjamin Cornish, Cooper, who was Daniel's son.

James Cornish, born circa 1776, started an Apprenticeship as a Carpenter on the 16th February 1789 when he was 13 years old, and was paid 1/-d per day (Supply 5/213). In August 1790 he worked in the Manufactory with his wages submitted by William Spry, Colonel Commanding the Royal Engineers, for payment by the Storekeeper, James Wright. James signed for his pay with a cross (WASC 1382). He joined the Military Volunteer Company on the 7th May 1794 as a Drummer Boy, and was sent to Woolwich in July 1795, "to be perfected in the drums" (Supply 5/219). James was still an Apprentice in December 1794, but was then paid 1/10d per day (Supply 5/217). This was also the case in July 1795 (also Supply 5/217) but his pay at that date had risen to

2/-d per day. He finished his 7-year Apprenticeship on the 1st March 1796, and was taken on the Engineers' Establishment.

Signing the Petition on Pay and Conditions at the Powder Mills on the 2nd February 1800, it appeared that he was then one of the few employees able to write (Supply 5/220). A Return on the Marital Status of the Employees dated May 1801, recorded that he was a married man with 2 children, and that he was still working as a Carpenter (Supply 5/220). Three years later, his pay as a Carpenter in the "Engineers Department Established" was 2/6d per day (Supply 5/222).

James Cornish (2) worked as a Labourer in the Engineers' Department, and was to be paid 9d for half a day's work in the manufactory (document submitted by W. Spry, Colonel commanding the Royal Engineers, to J. Wright, Esq., Storekeeper – 10/08/1790 – WASC 1382).

John Cornish started work as an Apprentice Carpenter on the 3rd March 1796, and was paid 1/-d per day (Supply 5/219). He was still an Apprentice in May 1801, but was then married with one child (Supply 5/221).

William Cottage was working as a Puntman in August 1812; he was paid 2/8d per day and allowed to watch in turn (Supply 5/229).

John Crabb worked as a Labourer in February 1814 "setting and drawing stoves, and in the Willow plantations", for which he was paid 2/8d per day. In addition he was allowed to watch in turn (Supply 5/230).

James Creamer was employed as a casual Labourer in the Engineers' Department on the 18th July 1815, earning 2/8d per day. In February 1816 he was a 37-year-old married man without issue, living in Waltham Abbey (WO54/516).

William Creamer worked as a Mixing House Man earning 1/6d per day in January 1806, and was a married man with 6 children. He was still employed in the Mixing House in June 1807, and "in addition to his pay he is allowed to watch in turn, for which he receives 1/-d" (Supply 5/226). By August 1808 William was paid 2/3d daily, but his watch allowance was unchanged (Supply 5/227).

Walter Creek was recorded as a Cooper repairing barrels and charge tubs at Faversham in August 1789; he had been in service for 9 months and was then 31 years of age (Supply 5/114). In November 1789, he was working as a Cooper at Waltham Abbey Powder Mills earning 2/6d per day (Winters, *op.cit.* p.33).

Thomas Cross had been cutting weeds in the streams within the Mills in the autumn of 1806, and died on or about the 26th of October that year. His wife, Elizabeth, petitioned the Board on the 23rd January 1807, saying that her husband "Having been principally employed for four years in this capacity (cutting weeds) he had caught such a violent cold as to be the cause of bringing on Consumption from which he died," and she, therefore, requested financial assistance. In a letter dated the 16th February 1807, the Board replied that she should be allowed the sum of "Two guineas as some relief in her present necessity" (Supply 5/198). Cross was possibly a Water Warden.

John Cuttle was appointed Overseer of the Works in the Engineers' Department on the 17th July 1789 (Winters, *op.cit.* p.119). James Wright, the Storekeeper, paid him £18.8.0d for work carried out in the Manufactory between the 1st July and 30th September 1790 (WASC 1382).

William Cuttle was employed as a Saltpetre Refiner in August 1812 earning 2/8d per day, and, in addition, when not working extra, he was allowed to watch in turn (Supply 5/229). In February 1814, he was earning 3/-d per day as a Millman, with an additional 6d per night when on duty (Supply 5/230).

D

Edward Dabnam was born circa 1763 and employed as a Blacksmith in the Engineers' Department on the 22nd March 1813. In February 1816, he was earning 4/7d per day; at that date he was a 52-year-old widower living in Waltham Abbey, with 1 married and 11 unmarried children (WO54/516). He was still in the same position in February 1817 (WO54/520).

Samuel Dabnam was an 18-year-old bachelor from Waltham Abbey who worked as a casual Labourer in the Engineers' Department in September 1816, earning 2/8d per day (WO54/516).

Thomas Dane was the Master of the powder vessel *Wheatsheaf* serving the Waltham Abbey Powder Mills in 1799 (Winters, *op.cit.* p.55). More information on his family can be found in the *Faversham Gunpowder Personnel Register.*

John Daniel was working as a casual Labourer in the Engineers' Department in September 1812 earning 2/8d per day (WO54/512).

Clark Davie was employed as a Labourer in the Refining House, and in July 1792 was being paid 1/6d per day, continuing to refine Saltpetre throughout that year (Supply 5/216). Robert Coleman, the Clerk of the Cheque, recorded in his Minute book that on the 29th July 1793, "C. Davie, together with others, was chequered one day's pay for having gone across the Hoppit contrary to repeated orders" (Winters, *op.cit.* p.39). Another entry in Coleman's Minute book recorded that Davie, together with Ben Wall Junior and William Dunn, Labourers, was discharged on the 4th November 1793, having been suspected of stealing iron from a farmer's gate (Winters, *op.cit.* p.40).

William Davis was born circa 1750, training as a Butcher before being employed in the Mixing House on the 11th February 1793 at 1/6d per day (Supply 5/216). He enlisted as a Private in the Military Volunteer Company on the 7th May 1794 (Supply 5/219) and a Return on the Marital Status of the Employees dated May 1801, recorded that he was a married man without issue (Supply 5/220). The same document noted that he was still a Labourer mixing composition at the same rate of pay. In May 1804, he was working as a Saltpetre Refiner with his pay increased to 2/-d per day. All Refiners received an additional allowance of 1/-d per night when it was their turn to watch – on average every 5th night (Supply 5/222).

The Saltpetre Refinery remained his place of work and by August 1812, he had been promoted as one of two Foremen in charge of Saltpetre refining, at that date being paid 5/2d per day. He was also a Rounder every third night (Supply 5/229) and this was also the case in February 1814 (Supply 5/230). In June 1818 William was still a Foreman in the Salpetre Refinery, but in common with the rest of the workforce, his wages had been reduced and he was then only paid 4/2d per day with his Rounder's allowance remaining at 1/6d per night (Supply 5/231). Davis retained his position when the Establishment was reduced still further in September 1818 but with a further reduction in his pay, which was set at 3/8d per day. Again, his Rounder's pay remained the same (Supply 5/231).

A statement dated the 4th April 1822, "of monies to which the public were entitled to receive credit" recorded that William was one of several employees "having occupied their present residences previous to the Hon. Board purchasing the same, sanction will be asked for their future residing in them." Under an Order dated the 4th May 1821, the property was leased to him for an annual rent of £5.4.0d (Supply 5/232). His cottage was in

Powder Mill Lane, being part of Plot No. 63 on the Town Map in Appendix 1.

In a letter dated the 15th September 1821, Davis, amongst others, applied for his superannuation (Supply 5/232). In their letter of reply dated the 16th November, the Board agreed that he should be paid an annual pension of £15.15.7d, commencing from that date (Supply 5/236) which amount was still being paid in 1823 (Winters, *op.cit.* p.95). On the 14th March 1827, Davis advised the Board that he intended to quit his cottage on the 25th March, recommending that Henry Brown, Labourer, should occupy the property, to which the Board agreed (Supply 5/205).

J. Davy was working as a Labourer in the Royal Engineers' Department in May 1840, living in a cottage owned by the Board located in the old Tanyard, on the south side of High Bridge Street (WO44/133). In 1841, the cottage was occupied by Jeremiah Betts (see notes on Betts). It is possible that J. Davy is the same man as Joseph Davy detailed in the following note.

Joseph Davy, a bachelor, was born in 1798 and worked as a Labourer on a temporary basis between June and October 1825, during which period he was paid 2/2d per day (WO54/550).

J. Dawson had worked in the Corning Houses for a year in January 1806, being paid 2/2d per day (Supply 5/224).

Henry Dewes was born circa 1744, and in April 1789 he worked in the Refining House earning 1/6d per day (Supply 5/213). A List of Employees for September 1789 recorded that he was 45 years of age, employed as a Labourer, refining Saltpetre under John Baker (Supply 5/214). This was also the case in January 1792 (Supply 5/215).

On the 29th April 1792, Henry was involved in an horrific accident in the Saltpetre Refinery. Messrs. Wright and Clowdersly reported the accident to the Board in their letter dated the 2nd May. It stated that Dewes was standing in the Refining House between two coppers with the intention of removing a pump from one of them with a block and tackle, but he apparently forgot to hook the tackle to the pump, and that "he took hold of the fall, and not making any resistance, fell backwards into the copper of boiling Salt Petre." Although other Labourers pulled him out, he only lived for another 24 hours, dying on the 30th April. He had resided with John Baker, the Foreman Refiner, and had no living relatives. Before he died he requested that his effects be left to Baker. Wright and Clowdersly, therefore, requested that the Board pay Henry's April earnings of £2.18.6d to Baker, and permission was granted to that effect (Supply 5/216).

Francis Dimmock was employed as a Labourer in the Corning Houses in 1805. In January 1806 he was earning 2/2d per day, in addition to which, he was allowed to watch in turn, for which he received 1/-d (Supply 5/224) and this was also the case in June 1807 (Supply 5/226). In July 1809 he was working as a common Labourer with the Engineers' Department, and was paid 17/-d for work carried out within the Manufactory between the 15th and 21st July 1809 (Supply 5/228). He had returned to the Mills as a Saltpetre Refiner by August 1812 at 2/8d per day, and was allowed to watch when not working extra (Supply 5/229). The same details also applied in February 1814 (Supply 5/230).

Jeremiah Dimsey was working in the Corning House in January 1806 earning 2/2d per day, and by that date, had been employed by the Ordnance for one year (Supply 5/224).

Gray Dixon was initially employed in the Corning House on the 1st April 1792, receiving pay of 1/6d per day (Supply 5/216). By

February 1793, he was refining and melting Saltpetre (Supply 5/216) continuing as a Refiner until at least July 1795 on the same daily pay (Supply 5/217). Dixon enlisted as a Private in the Military Volunteer Company on the 7th May 1794 (Supply 5/219). On the 23rd April 1793, Robert Coleman recorded in his Minute Book, "Gray Dixon having left his watch for half an hour, chequered (fined) one day (viz. one day's pay) and ordered off the watch for the present" (Winters, *op.cit.* p.38). On the 24th January 1795, Coleman noted in his Minute book that "Gray Dixon, watchman, reported he saw 2 men on the New Corning House Platform this morning at 4 o'clock [but] he could not get over, the water being low and the punt froze. He called to them and they, he supposed, went away, as he saw no more of them." (Winters, *op.cit.* p.45).

Frederick Drayson, the son of William and Ann Maria Drayson, was born at Waltham Abbey on the 14th July 1810, and wrote A *Treatise on Gunpowder* when he was only 20 years' old. He had extensive knowledge of the manufacture of gunpowder, was a first-class draughtsman, and clearly had formal training, possibly as a 'superior apprentice' at one of the government's establishments such as the Tower of London. However, Frederick's name does not appear in the records relating to the Powder Mills at Waltham Abbey. Sally Wilks, a descendant of his brother Alfred Wilks-Drayson, believes he died on the 7th May 1854 at Framfield, Sussex, and that he worked as a Surveyor preparing parish maps in the area.

William Drayson was the son of Charles and Mary Drayson. He was born at Faversham on the 5th September 1776, and married Ann Maria Hodges at Faversham on the 24th December 1803. William and Ann were blessed with 16 children of which, 13 survived (*Faversham Gunpowder Personnel Register*, pp.27-28).

A Board of Ordnance Order dated the 19th September 1804, appointed William as the Overseer of Works at the Faversham Gunpowder Mills. He was transferred to the Waltham Abbey Mills on the 19th September 1806, in the same position. In September 1812 it was recorded that William was on the Establishment, paid 7/-d per day and provided with a house in Powder Mill Lane, together with an allowance of £12.10.0d annually for coal and candles (WO54/512).

By February 1816 William, then a 39-year-old with 8 children, was paid 10/-d per day and was still provided with an apartment, together with the same allowance for fuel and light (WO54/512). His pay and allowances remained unchanged until April 1827 (WO54/558).

A statement "of monies to which the public were entitled to receive credit between the 1st January and the 31st December, 1821, showing the amounts received by the Storekeeper" recorded that William had been living rent-free in a Board of Ordnance house since the 29th September 1809 (Supply 5/232). This house was within the Engineers' yard off Powder Mill Lane, being Plot No. 73 on the 1825 Waltham Abbey Town Map in Appendix 1.

William was awarded a pay rise in April 1827 when he was upgraded to a Clerk of Works 2nd class, and then earned 13/6d per day, which, with allowances, gave him an annual salary of £246.7.6d (WO54/566). Details of the duties expected of him were recorded in a Return of "persons belonging to the Civil Establishment of the Ordnance at the Gunpowder and Small Arms Manufactories at Waltham Abbey, Faversham and Enfield showing in detail the several points of information called for by the Master General and Board's Order dated the 31st January 1831." Drayson, as the Clerk of Works at the Waltham and Enfield Manufactories, was to carry out the orders of the

Commanding Officer of the Royal Engineers, maintain accounts, official papers, stores and fixtures, as well as having to be acquainted with the machinery associated with the manufacture of gunpowder and small arms. This was in addition to the ordinary qualifications (duties) of a Clerk of Works. He was also required to do the same duties at Faversham, by correspondence and occasional visits. His pay remained at £246.7.6d per annum and he was provided with a house (WO54/575).

William was still at Waltham Abbey on the 1st January 1834 (WO54/593) but had left the Engineer's Department sometime after the 11th July 1834, when Henry Wright was appointed as the Acting Clerk of Works at Waltham (WO54/593). This was confirmed by a Return made by the Royal Engineers showing how the vacant houses and cottages belonging to the Ordnance Board were to be let. It recorded that Drayson had left on the 14th December 1834, and that his house was to be occupied by Henry Wright, Acting Clerk of Works (Supply 5/237).

Drayson went to the Royal Engineers at H.M.Dockyard, Chatham, and remained there, since Ann Maria died at Brompton in 1857, followed by William on the 8th February 1863, and both were buried in nearby Gillingham. The Royal Engineers' School of Military Engineering was, and still is, based at Brompton, so it is clear that William and his family had settled there. Further information on the Drayson family may be found in P. J. Huggins' *Waltham Abbey Gunpowder People* and *The Faversham Gunpowder Personnel Register: 1573-1840* by Raymond Godfrey and Arthur Percival.

John Dudley was born circa 1813, and started his employment as a general Labourer at the Mills on the 3rd June 1833, earning £33.16.0d annually. He was also allowed to watch in turn which increased his pay to £39.0.0d per annum (WO54/587). In the summer of 1837, he replaced James Horam as a Corning House man (Supply 5/237) and in October of that year, his pay was recorded as £42.2.0d per annum (WO54/623). His name did not appear in the 1841 Census for Waltham Abbey.

On the 13th April 1843, some 40 barrels of gunpowder exploded in the Corning House, together with another 20 in the Press House; 7 men were killed and much damage was done in the town. Among those killed was John Dudley. His widow, Mary, was granted "a donation of £2 in her confinement, in consequent of the explosion." There was one child in their family (Winters, *op.cit.* p.106). A graphic description of the explosion and damage caused, etc., was given in the Illustrated London News dated Saturday, the 22nd April 1843 (*WAAC*).

William Dudley worked in the Corning House in January 1806, and was paid 2/2d per day. At that date, he had been employed by the Ordnance Board for some 9 months (Supply 5/224). By September 1810, he was a Brimstone and Saltpetre Millman and his daily rate of pay had dropped to 2/-d, although he was now allowed to watch in turn (Supply 5/228). He was still employed as a Millman in August 1812 with his pay increased to 3/-d per day, and he earned an additional 1/6d per night when it was his turn to watch (Supply 5/229). William was still a Brimstone and Saltpetre Millman in February 1814, but his wages had been reduced to 2/8d per day with his watch allowance unchanged (Supply 5/230).

In 1816 the Board formed 3 tenements out of the dwellings in the Tanyard on the south side of High Bridge Street. William, Saltpetre Millman, was allocated one of Plot Nos. 54 or 55 on the Town Map in Appendix 1, and the rental was 2/-d per week (Winters, *op.cit.*p.83*)*.

Thomas Dugard worked as a general Labourer for 1/6d per day in February 1800. The Petition submitted on the 2nd February of that year relating to pay and conditions in the Mills showed that he was illiterate (Supply 5/220). A Return of Marital Status of the Employees in May 1801 recorded that he was a married man with 2 children (Supply 5/221). Robert Coleman, Clerk of the Cheque, recorded in his Minute book on the 20th October 1801, that Thomas Dugard was one of 24 men who were required to work at Faversham or be discharged. Thomas agreed to go (Winters, *op.cit.* p.60). However, his name does not appear in the Faversham records, nor do the subsequent Waltham Returns show that he had a break in his service record, so it must be assumed that he remained at Waltham Abbey.

In May 1804, he was working in the Corning Houses as a Labourer earning 2/1d per day, and receiving an additional allowance of 1/-d per night when it was his turn to watch – on average every 5th night (Supply 5/222). By January 1806 he had transferred to the Dusting House, still earning the same monies (Supply 5/224). The Dusting House was to remain his workplace until at least February 1813, when his wages and watch allowance had increased to 3/-d per day and 1/6d per night respectively (Supply 5/230).

William Dugard was born circa 1753. In April 1789, he was employed as a Labourer earning 1/6d per day "cutting and planting willow trees, cutting of new canal at the new Corning House, removing earth to the Store, unloading barge of coals and charring wood" (Supply 5/213). He was appointed to the Establishment on the 1st May 1789 (Supply 5/217) and continued to work as a Labourer. In August 1789 he was employed "drawing and setting stoves" (Supply 5/213) as he was the following month, together "with sundries in different parts of the Manufactory" (Supply 5/214).

By March 1790, he was employed as a Millman at 2/-d per day (Supply 5/214) and this was to be his trade for the next 16 or 17 years. The Petition on Pay and Conditions presented on the 2nd February 1800 showed that he was literate (Supply 5/200) and the Return giving the Marital Status of the Employees the following year, recorded that he was a married man with one child (Supply 5/221). The same document stated that in November of 1801, although still a Millman, he was employed "cleansing and deepening the river, canals and ditches and other necessary works." He was paid 2/3d per day in May 1804, with an additional 3d per night when "duty working was called for" (Supply 5/222). This was also the case in January 1806 (Supply 5/224).

By June 1807 William had been transferred to the Dusting House; his pay was reduced to 2/-d per day but he was allowed to watch in turn (Supply 5/226). He continued to work as a Dusting House Man, and in August 1812 his daily rate of pay had risen to 3/-d with his watch allowance at 1/6d per night (Supply 5/229). Dugard was made a Warder at the end of the Napoleonic wars with his wages reduced to 2/8d per day (Supply 5/230). In March 1816 at 65 years of age and with 28 years' service, the Storekeeper recommended that he should receive a daily superannuation of 2/8d per day. In the notes sent to the Board was the comment that Dugard and others should be superannuated "because of the hurts they have received in this dangerous Manufactory." It also stated therein, "William Dugard has become very feeble and incapable of any hard work, and any violent noise or exertion appears to affect his senses." However, in a letter dated the 6th March 1816, the Board awarded him a pension of only 2/-d per day for six days in the week, commencing the 1st April 1816 (Supply 5/200), and he was still in receipt of a pension of 12/-d per week in 1826 (Winters, *op.cit.* p.96).

Henry Dugleby started work with the Ordnance Board at Woolwich on the 1st January 1781, and was appointed a Clerk there on the 22nd February 1783 before being transferred in the same position to Waltham Abbey on the 1st April 1788 (Supply 5/216). Winters, (*op.cit.* p.121) states Henry was paid £60 per annum in 1791, although, according to Supply 5/217, in July 1791 his salary was £70 per annum with an allowance of £15 for house rent. He joined the Military Volunteer Company as First Lieutenant in May 1794 (Winters, *op. cit.* p.51).

Sometime between 1793 and May 1795, Robert Coleman had been made Clerk of the Cheque at Waltham Abbey, and Dugleby was promoted to First Clerk in Coleman's place (Supply 5/217). A Directive from the Board dated the 2nd February 1800 appointed Dugleby Clerk of the Cheque, replacing Robert Coleman, who had been promoted and moved elsewhere (Supply 5/195). A Return of Employees dated the 8th May 1804, showed that his salary was then £150 per annum, in addition to which, he received a lodging allowance of £26 per annum, with a further £12.10.0d for "coals and candles" (Supply 5/222). Coupled with this Return was a list of the "Engineers' Department Established" which indicated that Dugleby was also an Overseer (of the Works) for the Engineers, and for this, he was to be paid 1/6d per day by the Storekeeper.

William Breeze replaced Henry Dugleby as Clerk of the Cheque on The 6th February 1805, but there is no indication as to where Dugleby was posted (Supply 5/223).

James Dunn was born circa 1762 and was appointed as a Labourer on the 13th August 1805 (Supply 5/232). In January 1806, he was working as a Brimstone Refiner earning 2/-d per day (Supply 5/227). He continued to refine Brimstone until at least 1814 (Supply 5/230) and during this period his daily wage peaked at 3/-d per day; in addition, he was allowed to watch in turn, for which he received 1/6d each time he was on duty (Supply 5/229). In June 1818, he was employed in the Dusting

House earning 2/8d per day and allowed to watch in turn, for which he received 1/-d; at that time, he was a 55-year-old single man, living in Waltham Abbey (Supply 5/231 and WO54/524). When the Establishment was reduced in numbers in September 1818, James retained his employment as a Brimstone Refiner by an Order of the Board dated the 3rd September, and this was reconfirmed in an Order dated the 4th October 1819 (Supply 5/232). However, his pay was reduced to a daily sum of 2/-d in 1818 (Supply 5/231) increasing to 2/4d the following year (Supply 5/231).

A statement dated the 4th April 1822, "of monies to which the public were entitled to receive credit" recorded that James was one of several employees "…having occupied their present residences previous to the Hon. Board purchasing the same, sanction will be asked for their future residing in them." Under an Order dated the 4th May 1821, the property was leased to him for an annual rent of £5.4.0d (Supply 5/232). The tenement was on the western side of the road junction of High Bridge Street and Powder Mill Lane, being Plot No.60 on the Town Map in Appendix 1.

The Establishment at Waltham was reduced still further in 1822 – see notes on Thomas Carter – and James was included on the list of those to be dismissed on the 1st June 1822 (Supply 5/232). The men asking for financial assistance submitted several petitions; many were long service-employees in their middle age, and they pointed out that they had little hope of finding employment after the hay and corn harvest had been gathered. The Storekeeper was sympathetic and forwarded their petition to the Board, with the result that James was one of those awarded two weeks' pay to ease his financial burden (Supply 5/203).

William Dunn (1) was working as a Labourer in February 1793, earning 1/6d per day. In March 1793, he was replaced by William

162

Cottage and transferred to the Dusting House (Supply 5/216). A Return of Employees dated August 1793, confirmed his new workplace (also Supply 5/216).

An entry in Robert Coleman's Minute book recorded that Dunn, together with Ben Wall Junior, and Charles Davie, Labourers, was discharged on the 4th November 1793, having been suspected of stealing iron from a farmer's gate (Winters, *op.cit.* p.40). A footnote to Supply 5/216 confirmed that he had been discharged and replaced by Mr. R. Wright.

William Dunn (2) was born circa 1793, and was working as a Puntman earning 2/8d per day in August 1812, when he was also allowed to watch in turn (Supply 5/229). By February 1814, he was employed as an additional Bargeman and paid 3/10d per day (Supply 5/230). In June 1818, William was described as a Master Bargeman earning 4/2d per day, and at that date he was a 24-year-old married man, living in Waltham Abbey with one child (Supply 5/231). The end of the Napoleonic Wars saw a reduction in the manufacture and regeneration of gunpowder, and as a consequence, the workforce had to be cut back. A list of employees dated the 28th August 1818 sent from Waltham to the Board, showed the names of the people the Storekeeper proposed to retain between the 4th September and the 31st December 1818 to meet the new production requirements; Dunn's name was on that list, but he was then described as a Bargeman, with his pay reduced to 3/-d per day. (Supply 5/231). However, a second letter sent to the Board a couple of days later stated, "We respectfully beg leave to add the names and stations of those persons whom it will be necessary to discharge in consequence of this arrangement." and the list included William Dunn, Master Bargeman (Supply 5/231).

William may have continued to work on the barges; the 1841 Census for Waltham Abbey recorded that a Sarah Dunn, wife of a

Bargeman, was living in Paradise Row. Her rounded-down age of 40 is comparable with that of William's, and it is possible that she was his wife.

James Dye was born circa 1796 and was employed as a casual Labourer in the Engineers' Department on the 8th November 1815, earning 2/8d per day. He was a bachelor and lived in Waltham Abbey (WO54/516).

John Dye was working as a Puntman in August 1812, earning 2/8d per day and allowed to watch in turn, for which he received 1/6d per night (Supply 5/229). This was also the case in February 1814 (Supply 5/230).

William Dyer was born circa 1764 and had worked for Mr Walton in his Gunpowder Mills before their purchase by the Government in 1787. In 1788 he was working as a Labourer for the Ordnance Board who promised, since he had previously worked for Mr Walton, that he was "to be continued" (Supply 5/212). In March 1789, he was paid 1/6d per day for working in the Corning House (Supply 5/212). In common with the majority of the workforce, he was undertaking essential renewal and maintenance works within the Manufactory during April 1789 (Supply 5/213) returning to "Corning Gunpowder" by September of that year. At that time, he was 25 years' old (Supply 5/214).

William continued to work as a Corning House Man and was allowed to watch in turn. However, on the 13th and 14th May 1793, Robert Coleman, Clerk of the Cheque, recorded in his Minute book, "William Dyer had gone away from his watch without leave and was ordered off his watch" (Winters, *op. cit.* p.39). Coleman also reported on the 31st May 1794, "Discharged Wm. Dyer for improper conduct at the *Club* respecting the Volunteer Corps by endeavouring to turn out those men who belonged to it that engaged in this Company" (Winters, *op. cit.*

p.43). However, it would appear that he was reinstated, since on the 15th January 1795, Coleman noted in his Minute Book, "All stopt by Frost, Dyer and Mold sent with two loaded wagons to Purfleet." (Winters, *op.cit.* p.44).

E

John Eason (also spelt Eaton) was born circa 1790. He was appointed as a Labourer on the 17th June 1829 in place of Thomas Freeman, Snr., who had died. His basic pay was £33.16.0d per annum, but as he was allowed to watch in turn, his earnings totalled £39.0.0d per annum. He was a widower with 5 children, and prior to joining the Ordnance, had been a Mariner (WO54/566). John continued to work as a general Labourer and it appeared that he had remarried by April 1830 (WO54/570). A Labour Return for April 1834 recorded that his basic pay as a Labourer had been cut to £28.5.6d per annum, although he was still allowed to watch in turn, which increased his annual pay to £33.9.6d (WO54/593). On the 16th April 1836, two Mills exploded and John Eaton, Watchman, was called before Lt.Colonel Moody as a witness (Winters, *op.cit.* p.103).

William Eason was working as a Millman earning 2/3d per day in June 1807, and was allowed 3d per night when on duty (Supply 5/226). This was also the case in August 1808, except that he was then "allowed 6d per night when on duty" (Supply 5/227). He continued to be employed as a Millman until at least February 1814, when his daily rate of pay was 3/-d, with his allowance for night duty remaining at 6d (Supply 5/230).

James Easton who was born circa 1728, first worked for the Ordnance Board at the Faversham Mills as a Millman and Labourer being paid 1/6d per day. In September 1787, he was "suspended for bad behaviour at the request of the Clerk of the Cheque." He was then 58 and had been in the Board's service for 16 years. James was working as a Labourer in the Corning House and "shifting powder" in October 1787 (Supply 5/113). On or about the 18th October 1787 he, together with Bartholomew Bennett, John Goodfellow and Mr Cowell, was ordered "to go immediately to Mr Walton's Mills at Waltham Abbey" (Supply

5/113). He was to have his pay doubled to 18/-d a week while working away from home at Waltham Abbey Mills, and was entitled to travel inside the coach (Supply 5/113). The men from Faversham were still at Waltham Abbey on the 15th November 1787, when it appeared that the purchase of Mr Walton's Mills had not been finalised. At a meeting at Faversham on that date, it was Major Congreve's opinion that William Sutton, James Easton and John Goodfellow should still be on the Faversham List of Employees and receive double pay (Winters, *op. cit.* p.28). This may well explain why they were not on the List of Employees working at Waltham during October 1787, and, according to Winters (*op. cit.* p.28), they were not on the Establishment.

James Easton remained at Waltham Abbey, and In January 1789 he was working as a Charcoal and Sulphur Millman, earning 1/6d per day (Supply 5/212). In April 1789 he was described as "cutting and planting willow trees, cutting of canal at the new Corning House, removing earth to the Store, unloading barge of coals and charring wood" (Supply 5/213). In September 1789 James, then 63, was attending the Stoves Supply 5/214) as he was in December 1790, at which time he was still being paid 1/6d per day (Supply 5/215).

Nathaniel Easton was born circa 1762, and was appointed as a casual Bricklayer within the Engineers' Department on the 7th May 1808 (WO54/516). In September 1812, he was paid 4/3d per day for a six-day week (WO54/512). By February 1816 his daily wage had risen to 4/7d, and he was then a 53-year-old widower, living in Cheshunt (WO54/516).

Benjamin Eaton was working as a Labourer in August 1808 "setting and drawing stoves and in the Willow plantations, etc." He received 2/-d per day and was also allowed to watch in turn (Supply 5/227). By September 1810 he was a Millman, with his pay increased to 2/3d per day and allowed an extra 6d if he was on night duty (Supply 5/228).

Charles Edwards started his employment on the 20th September 1815 as a casual Labourer within the Engineers' Department, earning 2/8d per day (WO54/516). He was then a 31-year-old married man with 4 children, living in Waltham Abbey. Prior to joining the Ordnance Board, he had been a Grocer.

Christopher Edwards was employed as a Labourer in the Engineers' Department earning 1/6d per day. In August until the 20th September 1790, he worked in the Manufactory with his wages submitted by William Spry, Colonel Commanding the Royal Engineers, for payment by the Storekeeper, James Wright. Christopher signed for his pay with a cross, "his mark" (WASC 1382). On the 21st September 1790, he transferred to the Storekeeper's Department, and by December of that year he was working in the Stores (Supply 5/215). Between April and June 1791 he was "setting and drawing stoves and in the punts", graduating to a Millman by January 1792 earning 2/-d per day, with an extra 3d when on night duty (Supply 5/215). Christopher continued to work as a Millman until at least January 1806, when he was paid 2/3d per day with the same allowance when on night work (Supply 5/226). The Petition on Pay and Conditions presented to the Board on the 2nd February 1800, showed that he was still illiterate (Supply 5/220) and the Return on the Marital Status of the Employees in May 1801, recorded that he was a married man with 3 children (Supply 5/221).

Isaac Edwards was a Labourer set to work by Daniel Cornish in October 1787, repairing and renovating the Mills prior to their purchase from Mr Walton (Winters, *op.cit.* p.29).

Samuel Edwards was a common Labourer who worked in the Engineers' Department and was paid 4/6d for work carried out in the Manufactory between the 15th and 21st July 1809 (Supply 5/228).

John Egleton was born circa 1793; he was appointed as a casual Labourer in the Engineers' Department on the 19th August 1815, and earned 2/8d per day (WO564/516). He was then a 22-year-old bachelor living in Waltham Abbey.

Samuel Ellenthorpe worked as a labourer in the Corning House in August 1790, earning 1/6d per day (Supply 5/215). A Labour Return dated the 11th December 1790, recorded that Samuel, along with Clark Rook, was "sick but receive their pay." In a footnote to this document, it stated that both had returned to work by the 18th December (Supply 5/215). A Labour Return for April 1791 indicated that Samuel was "Dusting and glazing powder", but a footnote recorded that he was to be discharged on the 21st May 1791 (also Supply 5/215).

George Elliott was born circa 1779, and in January 1806 he was working as a Stoveman on the Gloom Stoves earning 2/-d per day, having at that date one year's service (Supply 5/224). In June 1807, he was described as "Rex Officers Labourer" still earning 2/-d per day (Supply 5/226). A year later he was employed as a Cylinder Man working at Fisher Street in West Sussex, and still earning 2/-d per day (Supply 5/227). George remained in West Sussex making charcoal by the cylinder method, and by August 1812 he was paid 2/8d per day (Supply 5/229). This remained the case in February 1814 (Supply 5/230). A List of Employees dated the 25th June 1818, confirmed that he was still a Cylinder Man, but that he was then paid 2/4d per day. He was a 38-year-old married man with one child, living at Fernhurst in West Sussex (Supply 5/231). When the Establishment was reduced in September 1818 due to the downturn in the production and regeneration of gunpowder, George Elliott's services were no longer required (Supply 5/231).

Henry Elliott was born circa 1757 and was employed on the 17th January 1796 as a casual Labourer earning 2/8d per day in the Engineers' Department; he was then a 37-year-old married man with 5 children, living in Waltham Abbey (WO54/516). Henry was still working as a casual Labourer in April 1823, at which time he had 27 years' service, 6 children, and was paid £33.18.2d per annum (WO54/542).

Joseph Elliott, born circa 1807, started his employment with the Board on the 27th August 1829 as a Labourer at 2/2d per day, which equated to an annual sum of £33.1.2d. He was then a 22-year-old bachelor (WO54/570). Under an Order of the Board dated the 31st of January 1831, he was one of 15 Labourers to be employed at the Waltham Abbey Powder Mills and the Enfield Small Arms Manufactories to undertake "different services as a Labourer in the Manufactories where steadiness and sobriety are particularly required." He was still paid 2/2d per day (WO54/575). In April 1833 he was still a Labourer, then married, but without children (WO54/587) as was also the case in April 1834 (WO54/593).

Benjamin Ellis was born circa 1764 and was appointed as a Labourer at the Mills on the 17th November 1791 (Supply 5/232). On the 1st April 1792, he was working as a Labourer in the Refining House, almost certainly the Saltpetre House, earning 1/6d per day (Supply 5/216), and he was to work as a Refiner for the next 30 years.

He enlisted as a Private in the Military Volunteer Company on the 7th May (Supply 5/219). The signed Petition on Pay and Conditions at the Mills submitted to the Board on the 2nd February 1800, showed that he was literate (Supply 5/220) while the Return on the Marital Status of the Employees in May 1801, recorded that he was a married man with 2 children (Supply 5/221).

Benjamin's pay gradually increased during the Napoleonic and Peninsular wars; in May 1804 he earned 2/-d per day, and like all Refiners, was allowed to "watch in turn when not working extra" (Supply 5/222). His daily wage peaked to 2/8d by August 1814, and he was allowed to watch when not working overtime or on night work (Supply 5/230). With peace in Europe, the manufacture and regeneration of gunpowder were reduced and, as a consequence, the Establishment and its wages were cut back. In August 1818, Benjamin's daily pay was reduced to 2/4d, although he was still allowed to watch and paid 1/-d per night when performing this task (Supply 5/231). At this time he was a 53-year-old with 2 children, living in Cheshunt (WO5//524).

A list of names of the people the Storekeeper proposed to retain on the Establishment between the 4th September and the 31st December 1818 to meet the new production and cost requirements, was sent to the Board on the 28th August (Supply 5/231). Benjamin's name was on the list, and an Order of the Board dated the 4th September 1818, confirmed his continued employment as a Saltpetre Refiner earning 2/4d per day. He was still allowed to watch, for which he then received 1/-d (Supply 5/231).

A List of Employees dated the 6th February 1822, recorded that his position as a Saltpetre Refiner was reconfirmed on the 4th October 1819 with annual pay of £41.14.4d, which included an allowance to watch (Supply 5/232). In the spring of 1822 the Ordnance Board decided to reduce the production and regeneration of gunpowder still further, and the Establishment at Waltham was cut again. Empsom Middleton and James Wright drew up a list dated the 21st March 1822 of people who were to be retained or dismissed (Supply 5/232). Benjamin was included in the list of those to be dismissed on the 1st June 1822 after some 31 years' service (Supply 5/232). The men asking for financial assistance submitted several petitions; many were long service-employees in their middle-age, and they pointed out that they had little hope of finding employment after the hay and corn harvest had been gathered. The Storekeeper was sympathetic and forwarded their petitions to the Board. Benjamin, amongst others, was awarded two weeks' pay to ease his financial burden (Supply 5/203).

J. Ellis was working as a Labourer in the Engineers' Department in May 1801, earning 1/6d per day. He was then a bachelor (Supply 5/221).

John Ellis worked as a Millman between 1805 and at least August 1808. During this period he was paid 2/3d per day, with an additional 3d per night when on duty (Supply 5/224 and Supply 5/227). In September 1810, he was working in the Mixing House, still earning the same daily rate of pay, but his night allowance had doubled to 6d (Supply 5/228). By August 1812, he was earning 3/-d per day and was then allowed to watch in turn, for which he received 1/6d each time (Supply 5/229). In February 1814 he was a Saltpetre Refiner who was paid 2/8d per day, but his allowance to watch remained unchanged (Supply 5/230).

Richard Ellis was working as a Millman in January 1805, earning 2/3d per day (Supply 5/224).

Stephen Ellis was working as a Puntman in August 1808 earning 2/-d per day, and allowed to watch in turn (Supply 5/227). By September 1810, he was employed as a Labourer "setting and drawing stoves and in the Willow plantations etc." (Supply 5/228). This was also the case in August 1812 (Supply 5/229) and February 1814 (Supply 5/230). During this time his wages peaked at 2/8d per day as well as being allowed to watch.

Thomas Ellis was refining Saltpetre in August 1812 (Supply 5/229) and continued to do so until at least August 1814 (Supply

5/230). He was paid 2/8d per day, and in addition, when not working extra, he was allowed to watch in turn.

William Ellis worked as an extra Bargeman on three barges transporting gunpowder to Picket's Field and the Magazines. For this he was paid £2.2.0d per week (Supply 5/222).

William Ellison was born circa 1807, and was appointed as a general Labourer at Faversham on the 11th January 1830. He transferred to Waltham Abbey on the 5th October 1832, where he was paid £39.0.0d per annum, which included an allowance to watch in turn. He was then a bachelor (WO54/587). He continued to work as a Labourer, but his wage was cut to £33.9.6d in April 1834 (WO54/593). However, it had been restored to its former level by 1839, when he was a married man without issue (WO54/623). A Return of Properties owned by the Board dated the 28th May 1840 (WO44/133) recorded that William Ellison, Stoveman, had been living in a cottage identified as Plot No. 61 on the Town Map in Appendix 1, and noted that he had, "given it up." The 1841 Census recorded that he was born in Scotland, and that he and his wife, Betsy, together with their children William, 2, and Barbara, 6 months, were living in High Bridge Street.

Thomas Emery was employed as a Labourer in the Engineers' Department and paid 1/6d per day. In August and September 1790, he worked in the Manufactory with his wages submitted by William Spry, Colonel Commanding the Royal Engineers, for payment by the Storekeeper, James Wright. Thomas signed for his pay with a cross - "his mark" (WASC 1382).

James Enticknap was working as a Cylinder Man in West Sussex in June 1807, earning 2/-d per day (Supply 5/226). He continued to make charcoal until at least February 1814, at which time, he was paid 2/8d per day (Supply 5/230).

William Enticknap was working as a Cylinder Man in West Sussex in January 1806. He was paid 2/-d per day, and at that date had served the Board for ten years (Supply 5/224). He continued in the same position until at least February 1814, and by then, his pay had risen to 2/8d per day (Supply 5/230).

Edward Essex was born circa 1776, and trained as a Baker before starting a lifetime's work at the Waltham Abbey Gunpowder Mills on the 14th August 1793 (Supply 5/217). In August 1794 he was "dusting and glazing powder", for which he received 1/6d per day (Supply 5/216) and the following year he was employed in the Corning House at the same rate of pay (Supply 5/217) This was also the case in July 1795 (also Supply 5/217).

He enlisted in the Military Volunteer Company as a Private on the 4th May 1795 (Winters, *op.cit.* p.42) and a Petition on Pay and Conditions of the Employees submitted to the Board in February 1800, showed that he was illiterate (Supply 5/220). A Return of the Marital Status of the Employees dated the 8th May 1801, recorded that Edward was a married man with 2 children, and that he was employed as a Millman (Supply 5/221). In November 1801, although still a Millman, Edward was engaged in "cleaning and deepening the river, canals and performing sundry necessary work" (Supply 5/221). He was still a Millman in May 1804, but his pay had increased to 2/3d per day, and in addition, he had an allowance of 3d per night when on duty "working at the mill" (Supply 5/222); this was also the case in January 1806 (Supply 5/224).

By June 1807 he had returned to the Corning House, with his pay reduced to 2/2 per day, but he was allowed to watch, for which he received 1/-d each time it was his turn (Supply 5/226). The Corning House remained his work place until at least the end of the Napoleonic and Peninsular wars, with his wages and watch allowance peaking to 3/3d and 1/6d respectively in 1812 (Supply 5/229). In June 1818 he was employed as a Saltpetre Refiner with his pay reduced to 2/4d per day, coupled with a watch allowance of 1/-d. He was then a 43-year-old married man with 4 children, living in Waltham Abbey (Supply 5/231 and WO54/527).

Edward retained his position in the Saltpetre Refinery when the Establishment was reduced in September 1818, and continued to be paid the same rate of pay, together with his watch allowance (Supply 5/231). In May 1819, he was a Brimstone Refiner with his pay and watch allowance unchanged (Supply 5/231). By September 1820, he had returned to the Corning House (Supply 5/232) and his total remuneration, including an allowance to watch, was now £50.16.11d per annum (Supply 5/233). He worked in the Corning House for the rest of his life, but, in common with the rest of the Board's employees, his wages were reduced over the years and he earned only £48.2.0d annually in October 1839 (WO54/623).

On the 15th February 1832, Edward leased a cottage for £5.4.0d per annum. It was owned by the Board and was on the north side of High Bridge Street, being one of five known as Bank Cottages, part of Plot No. 48 on the Town Map in Appendix 1. It had previously been occupied by John Cook, a retired Bargeman (Supply 5/237). The 1841 Census recorded that Edward, together with his wife, Ester, and 2 young children (James Essex (8) and Mary Bennett (1) - possibly their grandchildren - were still living in Bank Cottages.

On the 13th April 1843, some 40 barrels of gunpowder exploded in the Corning House, together with another 20 in the Press House; 7 men were killed and a great deal of damage was done in the town. Among those killed was Edward Essex. A graphic description of the explosion and damage caused, etc., was given in *The Illustrated London News* dated Saturday, the 22nd April 1843 (WAAC).

John Essex was born circa 1745, and was promised to be started at the Mills on the 9th February1789 as a Labourer in the "Corning House and on the glazing engine." By the 21st March he was working as a Labourer earning 1/6d per day (Supply 5/212), and in April of that year, he was described as "cutting and planting willow trees, cutting of new canal at the new Corning House, removing earth to the Store, unloading barge of coals and charring wood." The following September he was "Corning gunpowder." and, according to Supply 5/213, at that time he was 44 years' old. John was promoted to a Millman in the early part of 1790, earning 2/-d per day (Supply 5/214). This was his trade until late1793 when he transferred to the Dusting House, but had reverted to being a Millman by March 1794 (Supply 5/216).

Robert Coleman, Clerk of the Cheque, reported in his Minute Book that on the 7th March 1794, John Essex, Millman, had been chequered (fined) for coming to work drunk at 6 p.m. (Winters *op.cit.* p.41). John obviously liked his tipple, since he and his fellow Millman, Benjamin Guinn, were also drunk when they came to work on Christmas Day, 1794, and were chequered 2 days' pay (Winters, *op.cit.* p.44).

He continued to work as a Millman, and in July 1795, Millmen were paid an extra 3d per night when on duty (Supply 5/217). The Petition submitted to the Board on the 2nd February 1800 relating to pay and conditions at the Mills showed that he was illiterate (Supply 5/220) while a Return on the Marital Status of the Employees in May 1801, recorded that he was a married man with 2 children (Supply 5/221). In November 1801, although still employed as a Millman, John was engaged in "cleaning and deepening the river, canals and performing sundry necessary work" (Supply 5/221). He was still a Millman in May 1804, but was then paid 2/3d per day, and in addition, he had an allowance of 3d per night when on duty "working at the mill." (Supply 5/222).

In January 1806, he was working as a Warder earning only 2/-d per day (Supply 5/224) yet by August of the following year he had returned to the Dusting House, with his daily pay again 2/3d. In addition to his pay, he was allowed to watch in turn, for which he received "one shilling" (Supply 5/227). He was still a Dusting House Man in August 1812, with his pay and watch allowance increased to 3/-d and 1/6d respectively (Supply 5/229).

William Essex worked as a Cooper in August 1812 earning 1/9d per day, which indicated that he may well have been under training, and like all Coopers, he was not allowed to watch in turn (Supply 5/229). He was still a Cooper in February 1813, but was then paid 2/4d per day (Supply 5/230).

William Etherington was working as a Cylinderman in June 1807 earning 2/-d per day (Supply 5/226).

Nathaniel Ethridge was a Labourer set to work by Daniel Cornish in October 1787 at 9/-d per week, renovating the Mills following their purchase from Mr Walton (Winters, *op.cit.* p.29) although he does not appear to have been retained. Winters recorded on page 69 of his book, *Centenary Memorial of the Royal Gunpowder Factory* that he was one of the first labourers to be employed at the Mills and that in May 1792, he was away on militia duty.

F

Charles Fenton was born circa 1770, and started his employment on the 10th November 1815 as a Labourer in the Engineers' Department at 2/4d per day. He was a married man with 3 children living in Enfield (WO54/516).

James Ferguson served in the Royal Artillery from the 7th August 1778 until the 30th June 1789, starting work as a Labourer in the Corning House at the Mills on the 26th January 1790 at 1/6d per day (Supply 5/214). He remained in the Corning House throughout 1790 and was still there in June 1791 (Supply 5/215). By January 1792 he was a Millman who was paid 2/-d per day, and he continued as such until his death in the autumn of 1801. During this period his pay remained at 2/-d, with an extra 3d per night if on duty (Supply 5/217). He joined the Military Volunteer Company as a Corporal (Supply 5/219) and the Petition submitted to the Board in February 1800 on Pay and Conditions at the Mills, showed that he was literate (Supply 5/220). A Return on the Marital Status of the Employees dated May 1801 confirmed that he was a married man with 6 children (Supply 5/221).

A letter to the Board from his wife, Mary, dated the 4th October 1809, (Supply 5/228) referred to the death of her husband James, a Millman, who died of a cold in the Autumn of 1801 while employed in cleaning gravel from the river. She requested financial help, and the Board awarded her a charitable pension of 7/-d per week (Supply 5/199) which was still being paid in 1826 (Winters, *op.cit.* p.96). Another entry in *Winters Centenary Memorial of the Royal Gunpowder Mills* (p.61) showed that the Storekeeper was sympathetic towards Mary, since on the 13th December 1801, she was paid 4d per pair for washing sheets; these sheets would have been from the Watch Houses.

John Ferguson was working as a "Rex Officers Labourer" in June 1807 receiving pay of 2/-d per day (Supply 5/226). By June 1808, Ferguson was employed in the Dusting House, earning 2/3d per day, and was allowed to watch in turn, for which he received 1/-d (Supply 5/227). In September 1810, John was employed as a Labourer "setting and drawing stoves and in the willow plantations" with his pay reduced to 2/-d daily, although he still received the same watch allowance (Supply 5/228). From at least August 1812 until February 1814, he was working as a Saltpetre Refiner with his pay increased to 2/8d per day, and, in addition, when not working extra, he was allowed to watch (Supply 5/229 and Supply 5/230).

James Ferris was working as a Labourer in the Engineers' Department in May 1804, earning 1/6d per day with "one day extra allowed per week agreeable to the Board's Order dated the 12th March 1801" (Supply 5/222).

William Feversham was working as a Labourer in August 1808 "setting and drawing stoves, and in the Willow Plantations, etc." earning 2/-d per day. In addition, he was allowed to watch in turn, for which he was paid 1/-d (Supply 5/227).

John Fewell was born circa 1785 and was employed as a casual Labourer in the Engineers' Department on the 13th September 1815, earning 2/8d per day. In February 1816, he was a 30-year-old bachelor living in Waltham Abbey (WO54/516).

William Field was a Carpenter, 2nd Class, who was paid £1.3.4d for work carried out by the Engineers' Department in the Manufactory between the 15th and 21st July 1809 (Supply 5/228).

John Finlay, Lieutenant in the Royal Engineers, was appointed Inspector of Gunpowder at the Royal Gunpowder Mills at Faversham and Waltham Abbey on the 31st January 1789, and was paid a salary of £200.0.0d per annum (Winters, *op. cit.* p.115). He wrote to the Royal Mills at Waltham Abbey enquiring as to whether any of the staff would wish to learn the use of arms; they assembled, agreed, and on the 1st May 1784, 56 men enrolled in the Waltham Abbey Volunteer Company (Winters, *op.cit.* p.41). More information on Lt. Finlay is given in the *Faversham Gunpowder Personnel Records* (p.32).

Henry Fish was born circa 1765, and was engaged on the 1st July 1796 as a Cylinderman in West Sussex at 1/6d per day (Supply 5/219). A Return on the Marital Status of the Employees made on the 8th May 1801 showed that he was a married man with 4 children (Supply 5/221). The cylinders were under repair in November 1801, so Fish was employed in stacking timber in the yards and levelling and preparing the ground where the cylinders were to be re-sited (Supply 5/221).

Henry continued to be employed as a Cylinderman in West Sussex and his daily rate of pay gradually increased; in 1806 it was 2/-d (Supply 5/224) and in 1812 it rose to 2/8d (Supply 5/229). On the 2nd March 1816 it was recommended to the Board that he should receive a daily superannuation of 2/8d, and in the notes attached to the recommendation was the comment that Henry Fish and others should be superannuated "because of the hurts they have received in this dangerous manufactory." It was also stated therein that the health of Mr. Fish, who by then was extremely ill, "has been so much impaired by the nature of his employment as to make it improbable that he can ever be again advantageously employed in the service" (Supply 5/230). In their reply on the 6th March, the Board agreed to pay Henry Fish a pension of 2/-d per day for six days in the week, starting on the 1st April 1813 (Supply 5/200). He was still in receipt of his pension in November 1818 and this pension was paid to him at the Cylinder Works (Supply 5/231).

Richard Fish was born circa 1767, and was possibly Henry Fish's younger brother; like Henry, he was employed as a Cylinderman in West Sussex on the 1st July 1796 at 1/6d per day (Supply 5/219). A Return on the Marital Status of the Employees made on the 8th May 1801, showed that Richard was a married man with 4 children (Supply 5/221). The cylinders were under repair in November 1801, so Fish was employed in stacking timber in the yards and levelling and preparing the ground where the cylinders were to be re-sited (Supply 5/221).

His wages mirrored those of Henry's, but following the end of the Napoleonic Wars, a List of Employees in June 1818, recorded that he was then paid 2/8d per day (Supply 5/231). The same list documented that he then had 7 children, and that he was living and working at the Fisher Street Cylinder Works in West Sussex. Richard Fish was discharged when the Establishment was drastically reduced in numbers in September 1818 (Supply 5/231).

John Fleming was born circa 1801 and on the 12th May 1830, was appointed as a Labourer "in the room of (in place of) Henry Brown". He was paid £33.16.0d per annum and allowed to watch in turn, which gave him a total amount for the year of £39.0.0d. John was a bachelor and was brought up in the Bakery Trade (WO54/570). Absenteeism was not tolerated at the Mills and a Report dated the 8th August 1832 indicated that John and three others had been cautioned for being absent from their work for a whole day without leave, and warned that a repeat would result in their dismissal (Supply 5/207).

John continued to work as a Labourer and, in common with the rest of the workforce, had his annual earnings cut in April 1834 to £33.9.6d (WO54/593). On the 12th July 1839 he transferred to the Stores, and as the Storeman was paid £57.7.4d per annum. He was still a bachelor in October 1839 (WO54/623). On the 13th December 1839, John was appointed as the Master Mixer

(Winters, *op.cit.* p.105) a position he still held in 1855 (Winters, *op. cit.,* p.112). The 1841 Census recorded that John, together with his wife, Elizabeth, and their 4-month-old son, William, were living in Romeland.

John Fordham was working as a Puntman in January 1806 earning 2/-d per day, and at that date he had 3 months' service (Supply 5/224). In June 1807, he worked as a Labourer "setting and drawing stoves and loading and unloading barges, etc" (Supply 5/226). By August 1808, he had become a Millman earning 2/3d per day and was "allowed 6d per night when on duty" (Supply 5/227). A Return of Employees for September 1810 indicated that John was then working in the Glazing Mill on the same rate of pay, but he was then allowed to watch in turn for 1/6d per night (Supply 5/228). He continued as a Glazing Millman until at least February 1814, when he was paid 3/10d per day (Supply 5/230).

Thomas Foreman commenced work as a general Labourer at the Mills on the 5th November 1789, earning 1/6d per day. In March 1790 he was "grinding salt petre and charcoal" (Supply 5/214) as was the case in August 1790 (Supply 5/215). Thomas continued to work as a Saltpetre Millman throughout the 1790's on the same rate of pay (Supply 5/219). A Petition submitted to the Board on Pay and Conditions in February 1800 showed that he was literate (Supply 5/220) while a Return on the Marital Status of the Employees in May of the following year, recorded that he was a widower with one child (Supply 5/221).

In November 1801, although still a Saltpetre Millman, he was engaged in "cleaning and deepening the river, canals and ditches and other work necessary to be performed" (Supply 5/221). By May 1804, he was working as a Warder with pay of 2/-d per day, and an allowance of 1/-d per night when it was his turn to watch, which was, on average, every 5th night (Supply 5/222). He continued in this situation until the 28th January 1811, when the Storekeeper wrote to the Board requesting approval for the retirement of Thomas, due to age and infirmity. This request was granted, and he was to be paid 2/- per day by the Storekeeper (Supply 5/199).

John Foxen was born circa 1782, and in June 1818, he was working as the Storekeeper's Labourer, i.e., acting as James Wright's gardener, etc. He was paid 2/4d per day and allowed to watch in turn, for which he received 1/-d per night. He was then a 35-year-old married man with 4 children, living in Waltham Abbey (Supply 5/231). He survived the cutback to the Establishment in September 1818, and was still in the same position in May 1819, earning the same pay and watch allowance (Supply 5/231).

William Franklin was born circa 1800, and was employed as a Labourer on a temporary basis in the Engineers' Department in June 1825, but was due to be discharged at the end of October 1825. He was paid 2/2d per day (WO54/550).

James Free had been working in the Corning House for three months in January 1806 and was paid 2/2d per day (Supply 5/224). He was still employed in the Corning House in February 1814, but was then paid 3/3d per day and allowed to watch in turn, for which he received 1/6d per night (Supply 5/230). The 1841 Census recorded that James was an Agricultural Labourer, who, together with his wife, Elizabeth, was lodging with Ann Hudson, an Ordnance Board Pensioner living in High Bridge Street.

Thomas Freeman (1) was born circa 1779 and started work at the Royal Gunpowder Mills, Waltham Abbey on the 1st September 1798, where he was paid 1/6d per day for "setting and drawing stoves and clearing willow plantation" (Supply 5/219). He enlisted in the Military Volunteer Company as a Private (Supply 5/219).

The Petition on Pay and Conditions at the Mills submitted to the Board in February 1800 showed that he was illiterate (Supply 5/220) while a Return on the Marital Status of the Employees made in May of the following year recorded that he was a married man with one child (Supply 5/221). It would appear that he transferred to the Engineers' Department for a while, since a List of Employees dated the 8th May 1804 noted that he was working as a Labourer in the "Engineers' Dept. Established" earning 1/6d per day, with "one day extra allowed per week agreeable to the Board's Order dated 12th March, 1801" (Supply 5/222).

However, he had returned to the Storekeeper's Department by January 1806, where he was employed as a Saltpetre Millman at 2/-d per day (Supply 5/224) as he was in June 1807, when he was allowed to watch in turn, for which he received 1/-d per night (Supply 5/226). The following year he was described as a Charcoal Millman at 2/3d per day and was still in receipt of the same watch allowance (Supply 5/227). Thomas changed his work place again, since in September 1810 he was working in the Mixing House for the same pay, and was still allowed to watch in turn, but then for 1/6d per night (Supply 5/228). He continued to work in the Mixing House and in August 1812, his daily wage was recorded as 3/-d (Supply 5/229).

With peace in Europe, the manufacture and regeneration of gunpowder were reduced and, as a consequence, the Establishment and wages were cut back at the Royal Gunpowder Mills. In June 1818, his pay as a Mixing House Man had been reduced to 2/8d per day and his watch allowance to 1/-d per night (WO54/524); this Return recorded that he was 37, married, with 5 children and living in Cheshunt.

A list of names of the people the Storekeeper proposed to retain on the Establishment to meet the new production and cost requirements was sent to the Board on the 28th August (Supply

5/231). Thomas's name was on the list, with a proposal that his daily pay should be reduced to 2/-d and that he should not be allowed to watch (Supply 5/231). A few days later, a second letter to the Board said, "We respectfully beg leave to add the names and stations of those people whom it will be necessary to discharge in consequence of this arrangement." and Thomas Freeman's name was included (Supply 5/231). However, he was reprieved by an Order of the Board dated the 4th September 1818, which confirmed his continued employment as a Mixing House Man earning 2/4d per day and he was still allowed to watch, for which he then received 1/-d (Supply 5/231). Thomas was still employed as a Mixing House Man on the same rate of pay in May 1819, and the size of his family remained unchanged (Supply 5/231). However, from this Return it would appear that he was living in Waltham Abbey, although in September of the following year, his abode was again shown as Cheshunt (Supply 5/231).

A List of Employees dated the 6th February 1822 confirmed his position as a Mixing House Man and that his annual pay including watch allowance, was £39.0.0d (Supply 5/232). In the spring of 1822, the Ordnance Board decided to reduce the production and regeneration of gunpowder still further and the Establishment at Waltham was cut again. Empsom Middleton and James Wright drew up a list dated the 21st March 1822 of people who were to be retained or dismissed; Thomas was retained (Supply 5/232).

He continued to work in the Mixing House, and in October 1823 his annual wage, including his watch allowance, was £39.0.0d. He then had 6 children (WO54/546). On the 27th May 1827, Thomas requested that he be allowed the tenancy of a cottage owned by the Board at a rental of 2/-d per week, being the same rent as paid by the woman who "has quitted the premises" (Supply 5/205). This was a cottage in Powder Mill Lane previously occupied by John Simpson and then granted to his widow for 12 months, and has been identified as Plot No. 62 on the Town Map in Appendix

1. Thomas was still working in the Mixing House on the same pay, and in October 1827, he was 44 years' old with 29 years' service (WO54/558). He died some time between April and October 1829 (WO54/566).

Thomas Freeman (2) was working as a Labourer in January 1806 "drawing and setting stoves", for which he was paid 2/-d per day. At that time he had 12 months' service with the Ordnance Board (Supply 5/224). In June 1807 he was working as a Warder, still earning 2/-d per day and allowed to watch in turn (Supply 5/226). This was still the case in August 1812 (Supply 5/229).

John Fullar was born circa 1770 and started work as a casual Labourer in the Engineers' Department on the 18th May 1811. He lived in Waltham Abbey and was a bachelor, his previous employment having been as a Butcher (WO54/516). In September 1812, he was earning 2/8d per day (WO54/512) as he was in February 1816 (also WO54/516).

Phillip Fullar was working as a Labourer in the Engineers' Department in September 1812, earning 2/8d per day for a six-day week (WO54/512).

Richard Fullar was born circa 1793 and started work as a casual Labourer in the Engineers' Department on the 10th July 1815. In February 1816 he was earning 2/8d per day; he was then an 18-year-old bachelor living in Waltham Abbey (WO54/516).

William Fullar was employed on the 10th July 1815 as a casual Labourer in the Engineers' Department, earning 2/8d per day. In February 1816, he was a 31-year-old bachelor living in Waltham Abbey (WO54/516).

Thomas Fuller was working as a Saltpetre Refiner in September 1810 earning 2/-d per day, and he was allowed to watch in turn when not on duty (Supply 5/228). Thomas was still a Saltpetre Refiner in August 1812, but he was then paid 2/8d per day, and, when not working extra, allowed to watch (Supply 5/229). This was also the case in February 1814 (Supply 5/230).

William Fuller was a Labourer who was set to work by Daniel Cornish in October 1787 at 9/-d per week, renovating the Mills following their purchase by the Government from Mr. Walton (Winters, *op.cit.* p.28). He was still employed as an occasional Labourer in November 1788 (Winters, *op. cit.* p.32 and Supply 5/212) and was working on a temporary basis within the Storekeeper's Department as a Warder in January 1789 "but has no promise to be continued" (Supply 5/212).

However, a William Fuller was employed in the Engineers' Department at 1/6d per day for work carried out within the Manufactory in August 1790. His wages were submitted for payment by William Spry, Colonel commanding the Royal Engineers to the Storekeeper, James Wright, and William signed for his pay with a cross (WASC 1382). He returned to work as an occasional Labourer in the Storekeeper's Department on the 21st November 1790 (Supply 5/212).

In February 1793, a William Fuller was working as a Bargeman, and with John Cook and John Turnham, was taking materials to London by barge along the River Lee. Fuller was clearly afraid of being "seized by the Press Gangs" because the Rex Officers at Waltham Abbey wrote to the Duke of Richmond stating that Fuller, John Cook and John Turnham were Gunpowder makers and Bargemen, who were apprehensive of the Impress Court on the River Thames. They requested, "You will be pleased to grant them protection" (WASC 0475).

William Fullham worked as a Labourer between January 1792 and December 1794 "in the punts and likewise drawing and

setting stoves and landing and shipping gunpowder and stores."
During this period he was paid 1/6d per day (Supply 5/212 –
Supply 5/217). He enlisted as a Private in the Military Volunteer
Company on the 7th May 1794 (Supply 5/219). In July 1795, he
was recorded as a Millman earning 2/-d per day with an additional
3d when on night duty (Supply 5/217). The Clerk of the Cheque,
Robert Coleman, recorded that on the 4th September 1795,
Fullham and Mason made a charge against John Ashwood, the
Master Mixer. On the 18th of the month he noted "Order to
discharge [William] Fullham and [James] Mason, not having
made good their charge against Ashwood" (Winters, *op.cit.* p.46).
Fullham was to be discharged on the 18th September 1795.

James Furlouger was working as a Puntman in February 1814;
he was paid 2/8d per day, and allowed to watch in turn (Supply
5/230).

G

Charles Gale (1) was born circa 1783, and trained as a Carpenter. He was employed by a Contractor who had worked at Waltham Abbey on the 17th May 1796 (WO54/550) and had been in "Contractors Employ" on the 27th July 1796 (WO54/587). In 1809, Charles was working as a Carpenter (1st Class) for the Engineer's Department at Waltham Abbey, and was paid £1.9.9d for work carried out in the Manufactory between the 15th and 21st July of that year (Supply 5/228). There are no records linking Charles to Waltham Abbey between 1809 and the beginning of 1822, but he returned to Waltham Abbey as a Carpenter in the Engineer's Department on the 8th March 1822, and was taken on the Establishment along with other Carpenters on that date. He was then paid 4/1d per day for 313 days, which gave him an annual income of £63.18.1d. WO54/542 recorded that he was then a 39-year-old married man with 6 children living in Waltham Abbey. The same document recorded that he then had 27 years' service which started on the 27th July 1796, and this date continued to be used for his length of service until October 1839, when his service with the Board is given as 17 years, i.e., he was "Established" with the Board in 1822 (WO54/623).

From 1822 until 1839 his rate of pay remained at £63.18.1d per annum. A Return of Employees dated the 31st January 1831 recorded that Charles was one of 7 Carpenters to be employed at the Waltham Abbey Powder Mills and the Enfield Small Arms Factory, where he was required to undertake general services as a Carpenter in the Manufactory "requiring great care, attention and sobriety, etc" (WO54/570). In October 1832, Charles had 9 children (WO54/581) but it would appear that one had died by October 1839 (WO54/623). The 1841 Census recorded that Charles Gale, Carpenter, and his wife, Ann, were living on the south side of High Bridge Street, together with their sons Edward

(20) who was a Brush Maker, and William (15) and their daughter Tabitha (11).

Charles Gale (2) was born circa 1806 and may have been the son of Charles Gale (1). He started work as a Labourer in the Engineers' Department on the 11th October 1823. In April 1825, he was being paid 2/2d per day for 313 days in the year, which gave him an annual income of £33.18.2d. At that date he was a 19-year-old bachelor (WO54/550). He was still working as a Labourer in April 1827 and paid the same wage (WO54/558).

William Galleon was appointed as a Labourer in the Corning House on the 21st May 1795, and paid 1/6d per day (Supply 5/217). In September 1798, he was employed as a Puntman according to Supply 5/219. He enlisted as a Private in the Military Volunteer Company (Supply 5/219) and a Petition on Pay and Conditions at the Mills submitted to the Board on the 22nd February 1800 (Supply 5/220) showed that he was literate, and working as a general Labourer. A Return on the Marital Status of the Employees in May 1801, recorded that he was a married man with 2 children (Supply 5/221).

On the 23rd October 1801, Robert Coleman, the Clerk of the Cheque, recorded in his Minute Book that 24 men were required to go to Faversham or be discharged. Galleon was one of those who agreed to go (Winters, *op. cit.* p.60). However, his name did not appear in the Faversham records, nor was there a break in his service record, so it is clear that he was not discharged. In May 1804, he was employed as a Saltpetre Refiner at 2/-d per day with an additional 1/-d per night when it was his turn to watch, which was, on average, every 5th night (Supply 5/222). In January 1806, he was working as a Stoveman and still earning 2/-d per day (Supply 5/224). In August 1808, he was described as "an Assistant to Steam Stoveman" with his pay increased to 2/6d daily (Supply 5/227). He changed his occupation yet again, since in September

1810 he was employed as "Assistant to the Coppersmith" (Supply 5/228) as he was in August 1812, but he was then paid 3/3d per day (Supply 5/229).

Thomas Gapes was working as a Labourer in August 1808 "setting and drawing stoves and in the Willow plantations" for which he was paid 2/-d per day; in addition, he was allowed to watch in turn (Supply 5/227).

George Garnett was taken on as a Labourer in the summer of 1805, and in January 1806, he was employed in "drawing and setting stoves etc." for which he was paid 2/-d per day (Supply 5/224). He was still undertaking the same sort of work in August 1808 for the same pay, but he was then allowed to watch in turn (Supply 5/227). In September 1810, George was working as a Collar Maker, with his wage then set at 2/6d per day (Supply 5/228).

Henry Gatenbury worked as a Labourer in the Storekeeper's Department. A Return on the Marital Status of the Employees made in May 1801, recorded that he was a married man with 3 children (Supply 5/221). On the 16th June 1801, Henry Gatenbury, with others, was repairing the Corning House when it caught fire following an explosion. The fire was caused "from a blow of a copper hammer on a pit wheel" (Winters, *op.cit.*p.59). Henry was not injured, but requested that he be reimbursed for the loss of his hat, for which he claimed 12/-d (Supply 5/221). Robert Coleman, Clerk of the Cheque, recorded in his Minute Book on the 23rd October 1801, that 24 men were required to go to Faversham or be discharged. Gatenbury refused to go and was, therefore, discharged (Winters, *op. cit.* p.60).

John Gayler was born circa 1779 and engaged as a Labourer in the Engineers' Department on the 9th September 1815 at 2/8d per day; in February 1816, he was a 36-year-old married man without issue, living in Waltham Abbey (WO54/516).

John Gelleoum was working as a Cooper in August 1812 at 1/9d per day, and, like all Coopers, he was not allowed to watch (Supply 5/229). He was still in the Cooperage in February 1814, but at that date his pay had increased to 2/4d per day (Supply 5/230).

Robert George was born circa 1789 and engaged as a Labourer on the 30th November 1815. In February 1816, he was paid 2/8d per day and at that date was a 27-year-old widower without issue, living in Enfield (WO54/516).

George Gibbs was born circa 1795 and was employed on the 27th May 1815 as a casual Labourer in the Engineers' Department, earning 2/8d per day; he was a bachelor, living in Waltham Abbey (WO54/516).

James Gibbs was born circa 1793 and employed on the 15th May 1815 as a casual Labourer in the Engineers' Department, earning 2/8d per day. He was a bachelor living in Waltham Abbey, and his previous trade was that of a Butcher (WO54/516).

John Gibbs, Snr. was born circa 1782 and trained as a Millwright. He was first employed as a casual Millwright for the Board on the 29th March 1806 (WO54/516) and was paid £1.9.9d for work carried out by the Engineers' Department within the Manufactory between the 15th and 21st July 1809 (Supply 5/228). In 1812 he was earning 5/2d per day (WO54/512) which had risen to 5/8d by February 1816 (WO54/516). At that date he was a 32-year-old married man with 4 children.

John continued to be employed "occasionally as the Service requires" until circa April 1823 when he was placed on the Civil

Establishment. He was then paid 5/2d per day for 313 days, giving him an annual income of £80.17.2d (WO54/542) and he was still receiving the same rate of pay in April 1834 (WO54/59). A Return for April 1826 recorded that he then had 9 children (WO54/554).

A Return of Personnel belonging to the Civil Establishment of the Ordnance at the Gunpowder and Small Arms Manufactories at Waltham Abbey, Faversham and Enfield dated the 31st January 1831, recorded that John Gibbs was one of 3 Millwrights employed at Waltham Abbey. He was still paid 5/2d per day, and his duties were the general services of a Millwright within the Manufactory, which "required great attention, skill and sobriety etc." (WO54/570). John died in the autumn of 1834 (Supply 5/237).

John Gibbs, Jnr., the son of John Gibbs, Snr., was born circa 1822. In a Petition to the Board dated the 7th March 1838, his mother, Sarah, the widow of Millwright John Gibbs, stated that her son had been Apprenticed to the Master Sulphur Refiner on the 1st October 1834 following the death of his father. She continued that her son was then doing a man's job and requested a pay increase for him. It was agreed by the Board to increase his money from 6/-d to 9/-d per week (Supply 5/237). In October 1839, after 5 years' service, John was paid £23.8.0d per annum (WO54/623). On the 20th March 1840, the Storekeeper wrote to the Board pointing out that although John was only an Apprentice, he was doing the work of a man, and recommended that the 6d being paid to James O'Brien, Master Refiner, be withdrawn and that Gibbs should be paid 2/4d per day (Supply 5/238).

According to a list prepared by the Royal Engineers' Office in May 1840 of property owned by the Board at that date (WO44/133) "J. Gibbs, Sulphur Refinery" was living in a cottage previously occupied by Henry Coram (Coreham). This would have been part of Plot 62 shown on the Town Map in Appendix 1, being located in Powder Mill Lane. This was confirmed by the 1841 Census, which recorded that a John Gibbs, a 20-year-old Brimstone Refiner, was living in Powder Mill Lane. In the same property were Ann Gibbs, a dressmaker, aged 20, together with Caroline Gibbs, aged 15, who was described as a female servant, and Kate Gibbs, aged 7 years. It is possible, therefore, that Sarah Gibbs, the mother, died, leaving John the head of the family, and this may account for John having been given the increase in pay.

Joseph Gibbs, along with 8 other men and 4 horses, was killed on the 18th April 1801 in a tremendous explosion when the new Corning House blew up (Supply 5/220). Full details of the explosion can be found under the notes of John Bailey. A Petition dated the 24th April 1801 stated that Joseph's mother, Elizabeth, along with the widows and another parent, requested "relief in their distress" (Supply 5/194). Another Report dated the 29th April 1801, stated that Joseph's mother, Elizabeth Gibbs, who was 47 and Joseph's next of kin, was infirm and had been supported by her son (Supply 5/220). Elizabeth was awarded a weekly pension of 2/-d (Winters, *op. cit.* p.58).

Paul Gibbs was employed as a Millwright in November 1789 earning 3/-d per day (Winters *op. cit.* p.32).

Robert Giffin started work as a Labourer "drawing and setting stoves" in the autumn of 1805, for which he was paid 2/-d per day (Supply 5/224).

William Gilham was a Labourer who was set to work by Daniel Cornish in October 1787, renovating the Mills following their purchase by the Government from Mr. Walton (Winters, *op. cit.* p.29). He was paid 9/-d per week, but does not appear to have been retained.

J. Gillham was working on the barges and punts in April 1789 earning 1/6d per day (Supply 5/213). He continued to do so until the 27th March 1790, when, through sickness, he was replaced by Edward Heddy (Supply 5/214).

Thomas Gilliam was working as a Stoveman in June 1807 with a wage of 2/-d per day, and in addition to his pay, he was allowed to watch in turn, for which he received 1/-d per night (Supply 5/226).

John Ginn was born circa 1797, and was employed by the Engineers' Department as a casual Bricklayers' Labourer on the 14th November 1815 at 2/8d per day. He was an 18-year-old bachelor living in Waltham Abbey (WO54/516).

Thomas Ginn was born circa 1777, and started his employment as a casual Bricklayer in the Engineers' Department on the 23rd July 1806 (WO54/516). Between the 15th and 21st July 1809 he was paid £1.9.9d for work carried out in the Manufactory (Supply 5/228). In February 1816 he was paid 4/7d per day as a Bricklayer. At the time he was a 38-year-old married man with 3 children, living in Waltham Abbey, (WO54/516).

Richard Gladwin was employed as a Carpenter (2nd Class) in the Engineers' Department, and was paid £1.8.4d for work carried out in the Manufactory between the 15th and 21st July 1809 (Supply 5/228).

Daniel Goats started work at the Royal Gunpowder Mills at Waltham Abbey as a Puntman in the summer of 1805 (Supply 5/224) and remained in this position for the next 3 years, earning 2/-d per day and allowed to watch in turn (Supply 5/227). In September 1810, Daniel was then a Corning House Man who was paid 2/6d per day and was allowed to watch for 1/6d per night (Supply 5/228).

At 11.15 a.m. on the 27th November 1811 there was a huge explosion at No. 4 Press House; the ensuing fire engulfed the Corning House, together with the Reel House which also exploded. There was much damage to the town with many windows shattered, and reports in the press recorded that the explosion was heard as far away as Hackney, Blackwall and Marylebone (Winters, *op.cit.* p.72). A graphic account of the explosion was reported in the *Cambridge Chronicle* on the 29th November 1811 and reads as follows:

"A Dreadful Accident. A powder mill at Waltham Abbey was blown up on Wednesday last, 8 lives were lost, and 7 of those persons left families. The whole town of Waltham was in great danger, as it was thought the magazine would have blown up. A man was, in consequence, sent through the streets of Waltham to caution the inhabitants to leave their houses instantly. No further explosion had, however, taken place at the date of our last account. At Stepney a mirror of plate glass was broken by the shock; at Hackney several panes of glass were forced in, and at Blackwall the windows throughout a whole street were shattered. Near the New Road, Marylebone, several houses were much broken; and the labourers who were excavating in the park felt the earth shake where they were at work. Even ships of the river were shaken. Some of the morning papers mistook it for an earthquake. This seems singular that the shock should be felt so much more in London, while the damage done in the town was but trifling, except that the current of air at that time might have directed the concussion from the town." (Winters, *op.cit.* p.72).

Among those killed was Daniel. On page 153 of his book *Centenary Memorial of the Royal Gunpowder Factory*, Winters recorded that although Daniel was killed in the explosion in the Corning House on Lower Island and a coffin "supposed to contain his remains was buried with the bodies of the rest of the unfortunate men," his body was not actually discovered until sometime afterwards. John Smith was given a reward of £1 for finding the body, and John Rowland, a Carpenter employed by the Engineers' Department, was paid £2.8.1d for funeral expenses. Daniel was single and "as far as was known, had no encumbrance" (Supply 5/229). However, his widowed mother, Ann, who lived in Bishops Stortford, came to Waltham Abbey to ask for a small allowance or donation as the Board "judged to be proper" (Supply 5/229). She was granted twenty guineas on the 25th March 1812 (Winters, *op.cit.* p.73).

John Goats was born circa 1771 and started life-long employment with the Board at Waltham Abbey on the 19th December 1792. Initially he worked in the punts and was "drawing and setting stoves" for which he received 1/6d per day (Supply 5/216). From at least January 1794 to July 1795, he worked in the Corning House (Supply 5/217) and during this period he enlisted as a Private in the Military Volunteer Company (Supply 5/217).

In September 1798 he was working as a Bargeman (Supply 5/219) and the Petition on Pay and Conditions at the Mills submitted to the Board on the 2nd February 1800 showed that he was literate, and confirmed he was still a Bargeman (Supply 5/220). A Return on the Marital Status of the Employees made in May 1801 noted that he was a married man without issue (Supply 5/221) and he and his wife were to remain so. On the 23rd October 1801, Robert Coleman, the Clerk of the Cheque, recorded in his Minute Book that 24 men were required to go to Faversham or be discharged. John Goats was one of those who agreed to go (Winters, *op. cit.* p.60). However, his name did not appear in the Faversham records, nor was there a break in his service record so it is clear that he was not discharged but continued to work at Waltham Abbey.

A List of Employees for January 1806 recorded that John was working as a Saltpetre Refiner at 2/-d per day (Supply 5/224) and like all Refiners "when not working extra, they are allowed to watch in turn" (Supply 5/227). By August 1812 he was a Foreman in the Saltpetre Refinery at 4/7d per day (Supply 5/229) and was still in this position in February 1814 (Supply 5/230). However, by June 1818, he had reverted to being a Refiner, with his pay reduced to 2/4d per day but allowed to watch in turn, for which he received 1/-d per night (Supply 5/231). He escaped redundancy when the Establishment was reduced in 1818 and again in 1822, retaining his position as a Saltpetre Refiner until at least 1839 (WO54/623) when his annual pay was £39.0.0d, which included his watch money.

In December 1821 John was living in Waltham Abbey (Supply 5/232) and by October 1822, he was living in a cottage belonging to the Board (Supply 5/233). A Return for October 1823 confirmed that he was still living in the same tenement "so that his wife could look after the water." The same document noted that he lived in Cheshunt which suggests that it was one of a pair of cottages at Aqueduct Lock which were located in that Parish, and confirmed in a List of Domestic Properties prepared by the Royal Engineers' Office dated the 20th December 1834, which clearly indicated that John Goats (as well as John Brown) was living on Aqueduct Island. The rent for the cottage was £5.4.0d per annum (Supply 5/237).

A Return for October 1839 (WO54/623) recorded that John was then a widower, and the 1841 Census recorded that he was then lodging in Powder Mill Lane with Elizabeth Pallett, the widow of James Pallett.

William Goats started work at the Mills on the 13th August 1793, filling one of 7 vacancies then available (Winters, *op. cit*, p.40).

Edward Godwin (1) was born circa 1765 and was working as a Storehouse Man in August 1789, earning 2/-d per day (Supply

5/213) as he was the following month, with his job description given as "looking after the storehouse and delivering out the stores etc." (Supply 5/214). He was then 29 years of age. Edward continued to run the Stores until he was replaced by Henry Camps circa July 1792 (Supply 5/216).

Edward Godwin (2) was born circa 1765 and worked in the Corning House in August 1789, earning 1/6d per day (Supply 5/213) until March 1790 (Supply 5/214). A Return for December 1790, recorded that he had been replaced by John Godwin, Snr., who was later severely burnt when the Corning Mill blew up in 1801 (Supply 5/214).

John Godwin Snr. was born in the parish of Alver in Gosport, and as a youth served in the Royal Navy for several years (Supply 5/222). He joined the Ordnance Board on the 1st April 1789 (Supply 5/219) and worked in the Corning House at Waltham Abbey, where he was paid 1/6d per day (Supply 5/215). This was his workplace for several years, but by August 1793, he had replaced Clark Davie in the Refining House (Supply 5/215) where he still received the same rate of pay (Supply 5/216). Robert Coleman, the Clerk of the Cheque, recorded in his Minute Book that on the 29th July 1793 John was chequered (fined), along with others, one day's pay for "having gone across the Hoppit contrary to repeated orders" (Winters op. cit. p.39). He enlisted as a Private in the Military Volunteer Company on the 7th May 1794 (Supply 5/219), and continued to refine Saltpetre, but by December 1794, he was "setting and drawing stoves" for which he was paid 1/6d per day (Supply 5/216).

John, together with John Cook, worked the barge *Bengal* in 1795 (Winters, *op. cit.* p.55). In June 1795 in Supply 5/217 he was described as a Bargeman and paid 1/6d per day, exclusive of extras when working the barge at night, and this was also the case in September 1798 (Supply 5/219). A Petition on Pay and

Conditions (Supply 5/220) submitted to the Board on the 2nd February 1800, showed that he was literate and still working as a Bargeman, while a Return on the Marital Status of the Employees dated May 1801, recorded that he was a married man with 3 children (Supply 5/221).

When not working in the barges he was expected to undertake other work within the Manufactory. On the 16th June 1801, John, with others, was repairing the Corning House when it caught fire following an explosion. The fire was caused "from a blow of a copper hammer on a pit wheel" (Winters *op.cit.* p.59). The Storekeeper sent a letter to the Board dated the 23rd June 1801, listing the names of the men who had suffered terrible burns, and sought permission to support the casualties; John's name was included. The letter went on to state "we beg to represent the situation of the poor men who were burnt when the Corning House took fire on the 16th instant when under repair." It continued, "…These men are burnt in a dreadful manner. Their pain is very great…." and "Our surgeon has represented the necessity of the men most burnt having immediate assistance in wine, as a considerable suppuration is come on their constitutions. They cannot support it without wine, and we have directed wine to be immediately provided to them. We request your permission for our continuing to support these poor men with such wine or other proper support as their surgeon may think their respective situations require" (Supply 5/195). It would appear that the Board responded immediately, replying the same day, and the writer said he had "the Board's commands to transmit to you on the other side hereof a list of the men who have been burnt and otherwise hurt by the fire which lately destroyed the Corning House at Waltham Abbey; and I am to desire the Storekeeper will pay the men all their pay until they are recovered" (Supply 5/195).

Another letter to the Board dated the 29th July 1801 (Supply 5/221) said that the men who had been burnt at the Corning House requested that they were reimbursed for the loss of clothing. The list included John Godwin, whose claim amounted to £2.14.0d in all – for a hat (5/-d) handkerchiefs (2/6d) stockings (2/6d) shirt (5/-d) waistcoat (8/-d) breeches (8/-d) another shirt (6/-d) and sheets (17/-d). The letter went on to say that Mr Godwin, amongst others, had suffered so much that he wished for death to release him from his torture, and that it was a matter of surprise that he was recovering. The constant attention the men needed meant that their wives could not undertake seasonal work (haymaking) at which they could earn sufficient to pay the rent. It was requested that financial allowances were made; no record of the Board's response has come to light. A Return of Artificers and Labourers dated November 1801 recorded that John, with others, had been so severely burnt in the old Corning House that it would be dangerous to expose him with the other men repairing the river banks at that time, but instead, he should perform trifling jobs as they occurred (Supply 5/221).

Letters dated the 24th April and the 2nd May 1804, recorded that John Godwin, Bargeman, had died, and that it was believed that his death was caused by the injury he had received when the old Corning House was burnt on the 16th June 1801. He left a wife, Hannah, aged 32, and children, John (8) - see notes on John Godwin Junior - William (6), Hester (3) and Elizabeth (16 months). James Wright, the Storekeeper, requested the Board provide financial assistance for Hannah, and they agreed to pay her a pension of 16/-d per week, being her husband's wage (Supply 5/222). Her pension commenced on the 17th April 1804 (Supply 5/231) and in December 1821, it was confirmed as being £41.12.0d per annum (Supply 5/232). However, by 1837 her pension had been reduced to 10/-d weekly, possibly because her family had grown up (Supply 5/237). The 1841 Census recorded that Hannah, an Ordnance Pensioner, and her daughter Ester

(Hester) were living in Silver Street, Waltham Abbey, and that both were born in Essex.

John Godwin, Jnr, the son of John Godwin, Snr., was a youngster of 8 when, on the 4th October 1804, he was Apprenticed to the Master Worker, John Newton, at 1/2d per day (Supply 5/223). However, under a Board Order dated the 12th March 1801, the Apprentices were allowed one day extra each week, which gave John a weekly wage of 8/2d (Supply 5/222). In 1807 his wage was 1/4d per day, but a document dated the 30th September 1808 recording the wages paid to and signed for by the Apprentices, showed that his wage had been cut to 6/2d per week; this document also showed that John was literate, and the reduction appeared to be in accordance with a Directive from the Board dated the 5th August 1808 (Supply 5/227). On the 1st September 1810, his pay had increased to 6/8d per week, while his Master was receiving 8/-d for teaching John his trade (Supply 5/228). He completed his Apprenticeship, and in August 1812 was employed as a Cooper at 1/9d per day (Supply 5/512).

William Godwin was born circa 1797 and was also possibly a son of John Godwin, Snr. He was Apprenticed to the Master Bricklayer on the 19th August 1811, and paid 6/-d per week (WO54/512). His pay remained the same until June 1818 when it increased to 6/4d weekly (WO54/524). William was time-served by May 1819, and was then employed by the Engineers' Department as a Bricklayer "occasionally as the service requires." He was then paid 4/1d per day (WO54/528) as was the case in April 1821, and at that date, he was a 23-year-old bachelor living in Waltham Abbey (WO54/536).

John Golding (Golden) was born circa 1721, and set to work as a Labourer renovating the Mills by Daniel Cornish in October 1787 at 9/-d per week (Winters *op. cit.* p.28). In January 1789 he was to "be tried as a Millman, having lately been employed by

Mr. Walton" (Supply 5/212). However, in March 1789, with his name spelt as Golden, he was undertaking Labourer's work "setting and drawing stoves etc," for which he was paid 1/6d per day (Supply 5/512) and he continued to work as a Labourer undertaking various tasks. In April 1789 he was "cutting and planting willow trees, cutting of canal at the new Corning House, removing earth to the Store, unloading barge of coals and charring wood" (Supply 5/213). In August of that year he was again "setting and drawing stoves" while in September, he was "attending at the Proof House to keep the fires, prove powder etc." (Supply 5/213).

An undated memo signed by William Congreve (No.191) stated, "old Golding is to have one month's notice and then be discharged" (Supply 5/189). His name did not appear in the List of Employees dated the 27th March 1790.

John Gooch was working as a Labourer at 1/6d per day in May 1801; he was then a married man with one child (Supply 5/221). Robert Coleman, the Clerk of the Cheque, recorded in his Minute Book on the 23rd October 1801 that 24 men were required to work at Faversham or be discharged. Gooch refused to go and was discharged (Winters, *op. cit.* p.60).

John Goodfellow was born circa 1745 and was one of 3 men in October 1787 sent from Faversham to Waltham Abbey on the orders of the Duke of Richmond, to set up the Mills there which were about to be purchased by the Government. Major Congreve was of the opinion that the Mills at Waltham "were not settled" and that the men should continue to be on the list at Faversham; consequently, Goodfellow was entitled to receive double pay, i.e. 18/- per week. For more information on John Goodfellow's career at Faversham, see the *Faversham Gunpowder Personnel Register 1573 – 1840* (p.35).

John was appointed as the first Master Mixer to the Establishment at Waltham on Sunday, the 1st February 1789 (Supply 5/188). As the Master Mixer of Composition he was paid 3/-d per day, and in addition to his wage, he was entitled to train an Apprentice, for which he received 7/-d per week (Supply 5/212). He continued in this position until 1793, although in April 1789 he was "Superintending the men planting willow, cutting canal etc." (Supply 5/213).

An anonymous letter sent to "His Majesties Honble. Board of Ordnance" in January 1791, made serious allegations against 3 men employed at the Mills, viz. John Goodfellow, John Ashwood and John White. The letter said, "men whose work was very dangerous were frequently found in public houses neglecting his Majesties duty and whose names ought to be reported." The charge against Goodfellow was that on the 12th January 1791 he was "incapacitated and incapable of his business all day and slept in the works all night." The matter was referred to Major Congreve and he was to "cause enquiry to be made and report the result to the Board" (Supply 5/190). Major Congreve judged that the complaints were without foundation (Winters, *op. cit.* pp.34-35).

On the 7th April 1793, Robert Coleman, the Clerk of the Cheque, discovered gravel adhering to the bottom of the shoes belonging to a Labourer working in the new Corning House; this was a danger so Goodfellow was ordered to examine people's footwear at frequent intervals (Winters, *op. cit.* p.37). This incident was only one of several of its type recorded in Coleman's Minute Book. Goodfellow was replaced as the Master Mixer on the 18th June 1793, by John Ashwood (Supply 5/217).

W. Goodhew worked as a Labourer until March 1792, earning 1/6d per day grinding Saltpetre and Charcoal; he was replaced at that time by John Spellor (Supply 5/216).

Alexander Gordon was working at the Royal Gunpowder Mills at Faversham in August 1789 "Employed at Sundry Places" (Supply 5/114). A letter dated the 29th December 1789 was sent from Faversham to the Mills at Waltham Abbey, advising them that Alexander Gordon, together with John Montague, "Labourers at this place" were to be transferred to Waltham Abbey. They would leave the next day and had been paid until the end of the month. Gordon had "frock and slippers" while Montague had been furnished with neither (WASC 0475). At Waltham, Gordon was employed as a Millman earning 2/-d per day (Supply 5/214) as he was in January 1792 (Supply 5/215).

From at least July to September 1792, he was working as a Labourer in the Corning House with his daily pay reduced to 1/6d (Supply 5/216). However, he was again working as a Millman in February 1793, with his pay restored to its former level (Supply 5/216). This was also the case in January 1794 (Supply 5/216).

On the 15th January 1794, Robert Coleman, Clerk of the Cheque, recorded in his Minute Book that Gordon was chequered (fined) one day's pay for fighting in the Watch House (Winters, *op. cit.* p.40). Gordon was in trouble again shortly afterwards because Coleman recorded on the 12th February 1794 that he was chequered 3 days' pay for "not coming on duty till past midnight, and having been refused entry at that time, he tried to gain admittance by getting over the ditch. It was agreed that for his next offence he would be discharged" (Winters, *op. cit.* p.41). Gordon's name does not appear in the List of Employees for the following August (Supply 5/216).

H. Gough started work at the Mills early in 1805, and by the 30th January 1806, he was employed in the Dusting House at 2/1d per day (Supply 5/224). This was also the case in June 1807 (Supply 5/226). Dusting House Men were allowed to watch in turn, for which they received 1/-d.

Stephen Gough was working as a Millman in August 1808, earning 2/3d per day and "allowed 6d per night when on duty" (Supply 5/227). He was still a Millman in September 1810, working for the same money (Supply 5/228).

John Grapes (1) was working as a Puntman in January 1806 earning 2/-d per day, and at that date, had 12 months' service with the Board (Supply 5/224). By June 1807, John was working in the Corning House earning 2/2d per day, and in addition, he was allowed to watch in turn, for which he received 1/-d (Supply 5/226). The Corning House remained his workplace, and in September 1810, his pay and watch allowance had increased to 2/6d and 1/6d respectively (Supply 5/228).

At 11.15 a.m. on the 27th November 1811, there was a huge explosion at No. 4 Press House; the ensuing fire engulfed the Corning House, together with the Reel House, which also exploded. There was much damage to the town with many windows shattered, and reports in the press recorded that the explosion was heard as far away as Hackney, Blackwall and Marylebone (Winters, *op.cit.* p.72). More details of Winters' account can be found under the notes on Daniel Goats. Among those killed was John Grapes, who left a widow, Sarah, but no children (Supply 5/229). A document dated the 8th November 1818 listing "persons to whom pensions or charitable allowances granted by the Hon. Board as widows, orphans or relations of those who have lost their lives in this manufactory" included Sarah Grapes, who was in receipt of a pension of 17/6d per week, which had commenced on the 28th November 1811 (Supply 5/231). Sarah was still receiving a pension in 1826, which was then given as £45.10.0d per annum (Winters, *op. cit.* p.96).

John Grapes (2) was born circa 1765, and was engaged as a casual Labourer in the Engineers' Department on the 16th January 1813 at 2/8d per day. In February 1816, he was a 50-year-old married man living in Waltham Abbey, with 5 children – 4 married and 1 single (WO54/516).

Robert Granger was a single man of 18, who was employed on a temporary basis as a Labourer in June 1825, at 2/2d per day. He was due to be discharged at the end of October 1825 (WO54/550).

Samuel Graves was engaged as a Puntman in the early months of 1804 earning 2/-d per day (Supply 5/224) as was the case in June 1807 (Supply 5/226). By August 1808, he was working as a Millman earning 2/3d per day and "allowed 6d per night when on duty" (Supply 5/227). Graves continued to be employed in the same position until at least February 1814, with his daily wage peaking at 3/-d in 1812 (Supply 5/230).

George Gray was engaged as a Millman on the 13th February 1814, with pay of 3/-d per day and an additional 6d per night when on duty (Supply 5/230).

James Gray was working as a Puntman in September 1810 earning 2/- per day, and was allowed to watch in turn (Supply 5/228). In August 1812, still as a Puntman, he was paid 2/8d per day (Supply 5/229) and this was also the case in February 1814 (Supply 5/230).

Thomas Grayling (Graylin) was born circa 1762. He was set to work on the 22nd October 1787 by Daniel Cornish, who, on the directions of the Duke of Richmond, had been asked by Major Congreve, to "hire the best of the Millmen and Labourers who lately worked at Mr Walton's Powder Mills. They will be paid nine shillings per week for a month certain." The directive went on to say that should the Mills be purchased by the Government then the men would be given every opportunity to remain employed there (Winters, *op.cit.* p.29). Thomas was taken on as a

Labourer, and in January 1789, he was "to be tried as a Millman having lately been employed by Mr. Walton." By the 21st March, he was working as Millman in the Corning House earning 2/-d per day (Supply 5/212). The following April, in common with the majority of the employees at the Mills, he was "cutting and planting willow trees, cutting of canal at the new Corning House, removing earth to the Store, unloading barges of coals and charring wood" (Supply 5/213).

A letter from Waltham Abbey to the Board described an explosion which took place on the 4th February 1790, stating "At one o'clock one this morning one of the Queens Meads Mills blew up, which entirely unroofed the same. The charge had been worked an hour. Thos. Grayling, Millman on duty, set fire to his jacket but he received no bodily harm" (WASC 0475). Thomas continued to work as a Millman, and by March 1795, the Millmen were working on a nightshift for which they received an extra 3d (Supply 5/217). Robert Coleman, Clerk of the Cheque, recorded in his Minute Book that on the 9th March 1795, the Rounder had found Thomas Graylin asleep on duty and that he was chequered (fined) (Winters, *op. cit.* p.45). A Petition on Pay and Conditions at the Mills presented to the Board on the 2nd February 1800 showed that he was illiterate and still working as a Millman (Supply 5/220). A Return on the Marital Status of the Employees made in May 1801 recorded that he was a married man with 1child (Supply 5/221). His daily wage peaked at 3/-d, and the allowance for working at night increased to 6d during the Napoleonic wars (Supply 5/229). Another entry on page 45 in Winters' *Centenary Memorial of the Royal Gunpowder Mills*, noted that Thomas was the father of the once well-known local celebrities "Georgie and Billie Graylin."

A Return of Employees dated the 2nd March 1816, confirmed that Thomas was paid 3/-d per day, that he was then 53-years of age, and had served the Board for 28 years. A footnote to this Return commented that Grayling and others should be superannuated "because of the hurts they have received in this dangerous Manufactory." It also stated therein that Mr. Graylin "had been very quiet and inoffensive in the discharge of his duty, had scarce ever lost any time through sickness or from any other cause, but has become so feeble as to make it improper to employ him in a Gunpowder Manufactory any longer." The Storekeeper recommended that his superannuation should be 3/-d per day. The Board awarded him a pension of 15/-d a week commencing the 1st April 1816 (Supply 5/200). In spite of being described as being "very feeble" Thomas Graylin was still receiving his annual pension of £39.0.0d in 1839 (Supply 5/237), and he died on the 7th October 1840 (Supply 5/238).

Phillip Green started work as a Charcoal and Brimstone Millman in the spring of 1805. He was earning 2/-d per day (Supply 5/224) and was still in the same position in June 1807, although he was then allowed to watch in turn, for which he received 1/-d per night (Supply 5/226). By August 1808, he was employed in the Corning House earning 2/6d per day and still allowed to watch for 1/-d per night (Supply 5/227). Although still working in the Corning House in August 1812, Phillip's daily wage and watch money had increased to 3/3d and 1/6d respectively (Supply 5/229). By 1814 he was employed as a Glazing Millman, but then only earned 3/-d per day, with his watch allowance unchanged (Supply 5/230).

William Greenfield was working as a Cylinderman in August 1808 earning 2/-d per day (Supply 5/227). This was also the case in August 1812 (Supply 5/229). He held the same position in February 1814, but by then his daily rate of pay had increased to 2/8d (Supply 5/230).

J. Gregg was working as a Labourer in 1800 and signed the Petition on Pay and Conditions at the Mills presented to the Board on the 2nd February of that year (Supply 5/220).

William Grenville was employed as a Cylinderman earning 2/-d per day between June 1807 (Supply 5/226) and August 1808 (Supply 5/227).

Thomas Griffin was born circa 1791. In February 1814, he was working as a Millman earning 3/-d per day with an additional 6d per night when on duty (Supply 5/230). Returns of Employees for June 1818 showed that Thomas was then a Saltpetre Refiner earning 2/8d per day and he was also allowed to watch in turn, for which he received 1/-d per night. He was then a 27-year-old married man with 2 children (Supply 5/231 and WO54/524).

As a result of peace in Europe a reduction in the production of gunpowder was made, and, therefore, the Establishment was reduced in number in September 1818. In a letter of that date it was stated "We respectfully beg leave to add the names and stations of those persons whom it will be necessary to discharge in consequence of this arrangement," and Mr. Griffin's name was included on the list provided (Supply 5/231).

Thomas Grover was working as a Labourer in August 1812 "drawing and setting stoves and in the willow plantation" for which he was paid 2/8d per day. He was also allowed to watch in turn (Supply 5/229).

John Gubby was engaged as a Millman in 1805 earning 2/3d per day (Supply 5/224). This was also the case in June 1807, except that he was then paid an extra 3d per night when on duty (Supply 5/226).

Benjamin Guinn (1) was born circa 1766/1767, and set to work on the 22nd October 1787 by Daniel Cornish, who had been asked by Major Congreve, on the instructions of the Duke of Richmond, to "hire the best of the Millmen and labourers who lately worked at Mr Walton's Powder Mills. They will be paid nine shillings per week for a month certain." The directive went on to say that should the Mills be purchased by the Government then the men would be given every opportunity to remain employed there (Winters, *op.cit.* p.29). Benjamin was taken on as a Labourer, and in January 1789 he was working as a Millman, grinding Saltpetre (Supply 5/212). In common with the majority of the employees at the Mills, the following April he was "cutting and planting willow trees, cutting of canal at the new Corning House, removing earth to the Store, unloading barges of coals and charring wood" (Supply 5/213). By March 1790, he was a Labourer refining Saltpetre under John Baker (Supply 5/214) and he continued to do so until December 1794, when he was promoted to a Millman, with his pay increased to 2/-d daily (Supply 5/217). Millmen were also paid an extra 3d a night when on duty (Supply 5/217).

It would appear that he celebrated Christmas 1794 in style since he went to work drunk on Christmas Day, and was chequered (fined) two days' pay by Robert Coleman, Clerk of the Cheque (Winters, *op. cit.* p.44). Benjamin enlisted as a Private in the Military Volunteer Company on the 7th May 1798 (Supply 5/219) and a Petition on Pay and Conditions at the Mills submitted to the Board in February 1800, showed that he was illiterate (Supply 5/220). A further Return in May 1801 giving the Marital Status of the employees at the Royal Gunpowder Mills, recorded that he was a married man with 3 children (Supply 5/221). By 1818 he had 6 children (Supply 5/231) all of whom were alive in the 1830's (WO54/587).

Benjamin remained a Millman at Waltham Abbey for the rest of his working life. His wages peaked between 1812 and 1814 when he was paid 3/-d per day, with an extra 6d for night work (Supply 5/228). He retained his position when the Establishment at Waltham was reduced in numbers in 1818 (WO54/524) and again in 1822 (Supply 5/232), but his pay fell to 2/8d per day, and night work had ceased. However, in addition, he was allowed to watch in turn, for which he was paid 2/-d a night.

A Statement dated the 16th February 1822, "of monies to which the public were entitled to receive credit between the 1st January and the 31st December 1821 shewing the amounts received by the storekeeper" recorded that Benjamin was one of several employees "having occupied their present residences previous to the Hon. Board purchasing the same, sanction will be asked for their future residing in them." Under an Order dated the 4th May 1821, his tenement, garden and shed were leased to him for an annual rent of £7.16.0d (Supply 5/232). His home was one of 3 tenements formed from the dwelling houses in the Tanyard purchased by the Board in 1817 from Mr. Cannopp, which were then let to Richard Hudson at 3/-d per week, Thomas Mason (3/-d per week) and William Dudley at 2/-d per week (Winters, *op. cit.* p.83). The Tanyard was on the south side of High Bridge Street opposite Powder Mill Lane, being part of Property 1972 on the 1826 Waltham Abbey Town Map or Plot No. 1415 on the 1842 Tithe Map. The 1825 Rateable Value of Waltham Abbey showed that Benjamin was living next to widow Hudson (D/DHF B29) so it appears that he had taken over the property from Thomas Mason, which was, therefore, Plot 52 on the Town Map in Appendix 1. However, from a Return of Domestic Properties prepared by the Royal Engineers on the 20th December 1834, it would seem that he had moved to Powder Mill Lane, leasing a cottage owned by the Board on the 6th April 1829, for an annual rent of £5.4.0d (Supply 5/237). This tenement was part of Plot 62 on the Town Map in Appendix 1.

In December 1821, Guinn's pay, including allowances, amounted to £46.18.8d, which, by April 1823, had been reduced to £39.0.0d as a basic wage, made up to £44.4.0d with his watch allowance (WO54/542). In April 1832, he had annual earnings of £46.16.0d (WO54/581). A Return dated the 1st April 1834, recorded that, although Benjamin was still a Millman, his basic wage had been cut to £32.12.6d per annum, but with his allowances to watch in turn, his "take home pay" was £39.3.0d per annum (WO54/593). This was also the case in October 1834, when he had served the Ordnance Board for some 47 years (WO54/593). In September 1837, the Storekeeper wrote to the Board saying that Benjamin, now 70 years' old, was too infirm to be trusted in supervising his Mill. It was proposed that he was superannuated which the Board agreed to, and his pension commenced on the 22nd October 1837 (Supply 5/237). Benjamin died on the 20th September 1840, and the balance of his pension was paid to his daughter, Sarah Adams (Supply 5/238). Confirmation of his death is given in a Return of Domestic properties owned by the Board dated the 20th May 1840 (WO44/133). An entry against the property in the Tanyard recorded that it was then occupied by W. Adams, and had previously been in the occupation of "Ben. Guin deceased." This possibly meant that Benjamin had spent his final years with his daughter. The cottage in Powder Mill Lane was then occupied by W. Alsop, Miller.

Benjamin Guinn (2) was not referred to as Benjamin Guinn, Jnr. within the records, so he was in all probability not the son of Benjamin Guinn the Millman. He was first mentioned in 1809, when he was paid 5/6d as a common Labourer for work carried out by the Engineers' Department between the 15th and 21st July (Supply 5/228). By September 1810, he was working within the Manufactory as a Saltpetre Refiner earning 2/-d per day, and allowed to watch "when not working extra" (Supply 5/228). Benjamin (2) continued to work in the Refinery, with his wages peaking at 2/8d daily from 1812 onwards and his other conditions still applying (Supply 5/229 & 5/230). Benjamin's name was on the list of people to be retained at the Mills between September and December 1821, but with his pay reduced to 2/-d per day (Supply 5/231). However, it appears that he did not continue his employment with the Ordnance Board.

George Guinn was working as a Labourer in August 1808 "setting and drawing stoves, and in the willow plantations, etc." earning 2/-d per day and, in addition, he was allowed to watch in turn (Supply 2/227). He was employed as a Cooper in September 1810 at 2/6d daily, but like all other Coopers, he was not allowed to watch (Supply 5/228). Coopers had to make a certain number of barrels a day to receive top money, so it would appear that in 1810 he was still learning the trade. George continued as a Cooper, and by the 29th August 1812 was earning 4/6d per day (Supply 5/229) as he was in February 1814 (Supply 5/230).

James Guinn worked for a short time in 1804 as a Labourer in the Engineers' Department, and was paid 1/6d daily (Supply 5/222).

John Guinn worked as a Saltpetre Refiner between 1812 and 1814. He was paid 2/8d per day and allowed to watch in turn when not working overtime (Supply 5/229 and 5/230).

Thomas Guinn (1) was born circa 1794/1795, and was working as a Puntman in August 1812 (Supply 5/229). He was paid 2/8d daily and allowed to watch in turn. The same Thomas was possibly employed within the Engineers' Department as a Labourer "occasionally as service required" on the 14th August 1820, for which he received 2/4d per day (WO54/536).

Thomas Guinn (2) worked as a casual Millwright for the Engineers' Department in 1812, earning 4/7d per day (WO54/512).

Thomas Guinn (3) was born circa 1790/1791. He joined the Engineers' Department as a Labourer on the 1st April 1822, and was paid £33.18.2d annually (WO54/542). In April 1827 he was a married man living in Waltham Abbey with 5 children (WO54/558). A Return of Persons belonging to the Civil

Establishment dated the 31st January 1831, recorded that Thomas was one of 15 Labourers to be employed to undertake different services at the Waltham Abbey Powder Mills and the Enfield Small Arms Manufactory, "where steadiness and sobriety are particularly required" (WO54/570). Thomas was still working as a Labourer in April 1833, on the same rate of pay (WO54/587).

William Guinn worked in the Corning House between 1812 and 1814. He was paid 3/3d per day and was allowed to watch in turn, for which he received 1/6d a night (WO54/512 and Supply 5/230).

John Guinstock was the Clerk of the Cheque's Labourer earning 2/8d per day in August 1812, as well being allowed to watch in turn (Supply 5/229).

Howard Gunn was working as a Dusting House Man in August 1808. He was paid 2/3d per day and allowed to watch in turn, for which he received 1/-d (Supply 5/227). He was still employed in the Dusting House in September 1810, but his pay and watch allowance had increased to 2/3d and 1/6d respectively (Supply 5/228).

George Gunnett was working as a Puntman in June 1807 at 2/-d per day. The description of his work was "setting and drawing stoves, loading and unloading barges, etc." (Supply 5/226).

James Guthrie was born circa 1786 and was working as a casual Millwright in the Engineers' Department in February 1817. He was then a 35-year-old bachelor living in Waltham Abbey and was paid 5/2d per day (WO54/520).

H

James Haismar, born circa 1789, was employed as a casual Millwright in the Engineers' Department on the 19th September 1809. In September 1812 he was earning 5/2d per day (WO24/512) which had increased to 5/8d by February 1816; he was then a 26-year-old bachelor living in Waltham Abbey (WO54/516). James was still employed on the same terms in 1817 (WO54/520).

Charles Hall started work as a Labourer in the "Engineers' Department Established" in 1803, earning 1/6d per day with "one day extra allowed per week agreeable to the Board's Order dated the 12th March 1801" (Supply 5/222). By January 1806, he had transferred to the Storekeeper's Department within the Manufactory where he worked in the Dusting House at 2/1d per day, and received an additional 1/-d when it was his turn to watch (Supply 5/226). Charles was still in the same position in August 1808, but was then earning 2/3d per day with his watch money unchanged (Supply 5/227).

Thomas Hall was a Sawyer by trade who was set to work by Daniel Cornish in October 1787 at 9/-d per week, renovating the Powder Mills following their purchase from Mr. Walton by the Government. He was not retained once his work was completed (Winters, *op.cit.*p.28).

Searing Hall was listed as the Master of the Barge *Betsey* in 1802 (Winters, *op.cit.* p.50).

Henry Hallet was working as a Labourer in the Corning House in July 1792 earning 1/6d per day (Supply 5/216). By February 1793, he was refining and melting Saltpetre for the same rate of pay (Supply 5/216).

Benjamin Halls (also Hall) in August 1812 was working as a Millman earning 3/-d per day, in addition to which, he was allowed 6d per night when on duty (Supply 5/229). On the 13th February 1814 his name was recorded as Hall, when he was still employed as a Millman with the same pay and conditions (Supply 5/230).

Henry Halsted was employed as a Clerk at the Royal Powder Mills. In 1795 he was paid £60.0.0d per annum, together with £15.0.0d annually as a lodging allowance, or house rent (Supply 5/217). On the 2nd February 1800, the workforce raised a Petition on the pay and conditions at the Mills, which was presented to the Board. Henry witnessed the signatures on the document and signed in his position of Second Clerk (Supply 5/220). By May 1804 he had been promoted to First Clerk, with his salary increased to £80.0.0d per annum and his housing allowance to £20.16.0d; in addition, he received another £8.0.0d allowance for coals and candles (Supply 5/222).

Dr. Hammond was appointed Surgeon at the Mills in 1784 (Winters, *op.cit.* p.122).

John Hampton was a 20-year-old-bachelor when he started work as a Labourer at the Mills on the 10th August 1789. In September of that year he was described as "setting and drawing stoves and sundries in various parts of the Manufactory" earning 1/6d per day (Supply 5/213). By March 1790, he was refining Saltpetre under Thomas Baker (Supply 5/213) and continued to work in the Refining House until at least 1810, by which time his daily wage had risen to 2/-d. In addition, he was allowed to watch in turn (Supply 5/228). He enlisted in the Volunteer Company as a Private on the 7th May 1794 (Winters, *op.cit.* p.42).

William Hampton (1) A William Hampton was employed as a Labourer in the Engineers' Department at 1/6d per day in 1790.

Between August and September 1790 he worked within the Manufactory, with his wages submitted by William Spry, Colonel commanding the Royal Engineers, and paid for by the Storekeeper, James Wright. He signed for his pay with a cross (WASC 1382).

A Return made in October 1825 recorded that a William Hampton, born circa 1773 and a married man with 4 children, was in June 1825 employed on a temporary basis as a Labourer at 2/2d per day. He was to be discharged at the end of October 1825 (WO54/550).

William Hampton (2) was born circa 1788 and started work as a Saltpetre Refiner at the Mills sometime in 1810. By 1812 he was earning 2/8d per day, and, when not working extra, was allowed to watch in turn (Supply 5/229). The same pay and conditions applied in February 1814 (Supply 5/230).

However, on the 2nd March 1816 when he was 27 years' old with 6 years' service, it was recommended that he receive a daily superannuation of 2/8d. On the Return in question was the comment that Mr Hampton and others should be superannuated because "of the hurts they have received in this dangerous Manufactory." It was also stated therein "this man [Hampton] will probably not live many weeks to receive the Board's bounty" (Supply 5/230). In a letter dated the 6th March 1816, the Board finally awarded William superannuation of 2/-d per day for a six-day week, commencing on the 1st April 1816 (Supply 5/200).

Samuel Hands worked as a Labourer in the "Engineers' Department Established" in May 1804 earning 1/6d per day, with "one day extra allowed per week agreeable to the Board's Order dated the 12th March 1801" (Supply 5/222).

John Hanes was a casual Labourer in the Engineers' Department in September 1812 earning 2/8d per day for a six-day week (WO54/512).

Henry Harbert was also a casual Labourer in the Engineers' Department in September 1812, earning 2/8d per day for a six-day week (WO54/512).

John Hardwick was employed in the Dusting House in January 1806, earning 2/1d per day (Supply 5/224).

John Harper was described as a Labourer in June 1807, "setting and drawing stoves, loading and unloading barges", earning 2/-d per day (Supply 5/226).

Edward Harris was a Corning House Man in February 1814, for which he was paid 3/3d per day. He was also allowed to watch in turn, for which he received 1/6d per night (Supply 5/230).

George Harris, born circa 1779, started his employment as a casual Labourer in the Engineers' Department on the 25th June 1815 at 2/8d per day. He was then a married man with 4 children living in Cheshunt (WO54/516) but by February 1817 he had moved to Waltham Abbey (WO54/520). In May 1819 it was recorded that he and his wife had another child (WO54/528). George remained a Labourer with the Engineers' Department until at least April 1834, but in common with the rest of the workforce at the Mills, his wages were cut following the cessation of the Napoleonic Wars and by February 1817, his daily rate of pay was only 2/4d (WO54/520). By April 1823, it had been cut still further to 2/2d, giving him an annual income of £33.18.2d (WO54/542).

A Return of Persons Belonging to the Civil Establishment of the Ordnance at the Gunpowder and Small Arms Manufactories at Waltham Abbey, Faversham and Enfield, showing in detail the several points of information called for by the Master General and Board's Order dated the 31st January 1831, recorded that George Harris was one of 15 Labourers to be employed at Waltham Abbey Powder Mills and the Enfield Small Arms factory. It confirmed that he was to be paid 2/2d per day and employed to undertake different services as a Labourer in the Manufactories, where steadiness and sobriety were particuliary required (WO54/575). The last Return to record his name was dated the 1st April 1834 when he was still paid £33.18.2d annually (WO54/593).

James Harris was a 20-year-old bachelor living in Waltham Abbey who was engaged as a casual Labourer in the Engineers' Department on the 20th July 1815 at 2/8d per day (WO54/516).

Thomas Harrison was first employed in the Engineers' Department on the 29th March 1806 (WO54/516) and, as a common Labourer, he was paid 17/-d for work carried out within the Manufactory between the 15th and 21st July 1809 (Supply 5/228). In September 1812, he was employed as a Cooper and paid 2/6d per day, and, in common with all other Coopers, he was not allowed to watch (Supply 5/228). He was then employed as a casual Bricklayer's Labourer in the Engineers' Department at 2/8d per day for a six-day week (WO54/512). He was still working as a casual Labourer for the Engineers in February 1816, and at that time was a widower without children, living in Enfield (WO54/516).

John Harrod was a Mixing House Man in September 1810 at 2/3d per day, and was allowed to watch in turn for 1/6d per night (Supply 5/228).

William Hasler was a 26-year-old bachelor when he was engaged to work at the Mills as a Labourer on the 3rd December 1838. He was paid £39.0.0d per annum, which included an allowance to watch in turn (WO54/623). The 1841 Census recorded that a William Hasler of the same age was then married, living and working as an Agricultural Labourer at Horseshoe Hill with his young family.

Arthur Hatby worked as a casual Labourer earning 2/8d per day in the Engineers' Department in September 1812 (WO54/512).

John Hawkins was working as a Labourer in the "Engineers' Department Established" in May 1804, earning 1/6d per day with "one day extra allowed per week agreeable to the Board's Order dated the 12th March 1801" (Supply 5/222).

James Hay worked as a Saltpetre Refiner who earned 2/8d per day in August 1812, and, in addition, when not working extra, was allowed to watch in turn (Supply 5/229). The same pay and conditions applied in February 1813 (Supply 5/230).

Thomas Haycock was employed as a Labourer in the Engineers' Department, and was paid 17/-d for work carried out within the Manufactory between the 15th and 21st July 1809 (Supply 5/228).

John Haycock was born circa 1765 and was engaged as a Labourer within the Engineers' Department on the 29th March 1806 (WO54/516). He was still employed as a Labourer in that Department in February 1816 and paid 2/4d per day, at which time he was a 50-year-old bachelor living in Waltham Abbey (WO54/516). His pay and other details remained unchanged in February 1817 (WO54/520).

John Haydon replaced Richard Hudson as a Charcoal Millman, circa 1798, and was also a Private in the Volunteer Company (Supply 5/219).

Patrick Hayes was born circa 1784. He trained as a tanner before joining the Ordnance Board as a Labourer at Tooley Street on the 27th May 1827 (WO54/587). He then transferred to Faversham where he was employed as a Charcoal Burner (Supply 5/207) and on the 19th November 1832, he was appointed as a Cylinder House Man at the Waltham Abbey Mills at £39.0.0d per annum ((WO54/587). The same document recorded that he was then a married man with 4 children.

Patrick was still employed as a Cylinder House Man in April 1834 but with reduced pay of £33.9.6d per annum, which included and allowance to watch in turn. He and his wife, Catherine, then had 5 children ((WO54/593). A Return made by the Royal Engineers' Office in December 1834 showing how the Board's houses and cottages were let, recorded that a cottage previously occupied by Michael Summers, was to be allocated to Patrick Hayes, Cylinderman (Supply 5/237). This cottage has been identified as being on the south side of High Bridge Street, formed out of dwellings in the old Tanyard, and is Plot No. 55 on the Town Map in Appendix 1. By October 1839, Hayes' total annual earnings had been restored to £39.0.0d (WO54/623). The following year, a list of Domestic Properties recorded that he had moved to the opposite side of High Bridge Street into one of the cottages known as High Bank, forming part of Plot 48 on the Town Map shown in Appendix 1 (WO44/133).

The 1841 Census showed that both Patrick and Catherine were born in Ireland, and that they were still living on the north side of High Bridge Street with their children Thomas (15), Edmund (11) and William (7).

John Haynes was born circa 1753. On the 27th November 1788, he was described as an occasional Labourer (Supply 5/212) and this was confirmed in a note in William Winters' book (p.32) which said that he was promised to be continued. During August and September 1789, he was "setting and drawing stoves in various parts of the Manufactory" earning 1/6d per day (Supply 5/213). From September 1789 until at least August 1790, as well as working on the stoves he was working in the punts conveying powder from the Mills to the Corning House (Supply 5/214). In 1791 he worked in the Corning House (Supply 5/215) and by January 1792 he was a Millman, continuing to work as such until 1793 (Supply 5/216).

On the 11th April 1793, Robert Colman, Clerk of the Cheque, recorded in his Minute Book that several men had seen Haynes put coal in his pocket while in the Watch House; evidence was given by Benjamin Wall, Snr. and C. Edwards, who claimed to have seen him do this. Others who gave evidence were A. Gordon, J. Ferguson, W. Dugard and J. Cass. Haynes denied the offence and said he only took them [the pieces of coal] to admire them. However, he was discharged on the 11th November 1793, and replaced by Mr. B. Camp (Winters, *op cit.* p. 38).

Thomas Hayward was born circa 1773, and trained as a Carpenter before joining the Ordnance Board in 1794 or 1795 (WO54/587). His name did not appear in the Establishment Returns for Waltham Abbey until the 1st April 1833 (WO54/587) yet at that date he had some 38 years' service with the Board, so it is not clear where he worked before coming to the Mills at Waltham. It is possible that he worked at Faversham, since a Carpenter bearing the same name appears on page 43 of the *Faversham Gunpowder Personnel Register,* and the Register stated that the Board appointed him Master Carpenter on the 23rd July 1806. The same information was given in the Return for the Waltham Abbey Engineers' Department for October 1839 (WO54/623). In March 1826, his duties at Faversham were listed as moving millstones, repairing punts, carts, wagons, doors, windows, ladders and fences, etc., as well as sawing timber (Supply 5/113). Between the 1st July and the 31st December 1825 he was stopped 2/-d for medical attendance (Supply 5/116). He was still at Faversham in 1832, and occupied 65, West Street.

Waltham Abbey Return WO54/587 dated the 1st April 1833, recorded that he earned £91.5.10d per annum, that he had 38 years' service with the Board and that he was a married man, aged 60, with 6 children. On the 14th October 1834, Hayward was appointed as the Acting Foreman of Works (WO54/623).

A Return of Domestic Properties prepared by the Royal Engineers' Office at the Mills dated the 20th December 1834, recorded the tenements owned by the Board, and stated that Thomas Hayward was living in one of three houses on Plot No. 64, paying a rent of £1.0.0d per annum (Supply 5/237). In October 1839, he was recorded as the Foreman of Works earning 5/10d per day, which gave him an estimated annual income of £91.11.8d. It was also stated that he was then a widower (WO54/623). Another Return of Domestic Properties dated the 28th May 1840, indicated that Mr Hayward, Foreman of Works, was living in one of three houses which had previously been occupied by Thomas Tamkin, "pensioned" (WO44/133). Tamkin was the Master Bricklayer within the Engineers' Department who was retired on the 4th July 1833 (Supply 5/208). The 1825 Valuation for Waltham Abbey recorded that Tamkin was living in a property of some 12 perches with a rateable value of £9 (ERO D/DHf B29), and this, coupled with information in the 1840 Waltham Abbey Poor Rates (ERO D/P 75/11/16) clearly indicates that the house was in Powder Mill Lane, at the northern end of Plot number 64 on the Town Map in Appendix 1.

The 1841 Census recorded that Thomas lived in Powder Mill Lane with Eleanor Hayward, aged 25, and Emma Hayward, aged 4; he is shown as a Carpenter, aged 60, with only Emma being born in Essex.

Thomas Henry Hayward was born circa 1809, and was possibly the son of Thomas Hayward referred to in the previous entry. He trained as a Carpenter and joined the Engineers' Department at Waltham Abbey on the 6th July 1830. As a 22-year-old bachelor he was paid 4/1d per day (WO54/570).

A Return of Persons Belonging to the Civil Establishment of the Ordnance at the Gunpowder and Small Arms Manufactories at Waltham Abbey, Faversham and Enfield, showing in detail the several points of information called for by the Master General and Board's Order dated the 31st January 1831, recorded that Thomas Henry Hayward was one of 7 Carpenters to be employed at Waltham Abbey Powder Mills and the Enfield Small Arms factory. It confirmed that he was to be paid 4/1d per day and employed to undertake general services as a Carpenter in the Manufactories, which required great care, attention and sobriety, etc. (WO54/575). The last Return to record his name was dated the 1st April 1834; it confirmed that he was paid the same monies and was still single (WO54/593).

Charles Hearn worked as a casual Labourer in the Engineers' Department in September 1812, earning 2/8d per day for a six-day week (WO54/512).

Thomas Heath was a general Labourer working within the Manufactory. He signed the Petition on Pay and Conditions within the Mills presented to the Board in February 1800, indicating that he was literate (Supply 5/220). A Return of the Marital Status of the Employees made in May 1801, noted that Heath was a married man, without issue (Supply 5/221).

J. Heather was an extra Bargeman who was employed on three barges in May 1804, transporting gunpowder to Picket's Field and the Magazines, for which he was paid £2.2.0d per week (Supply 5/222).

Edward Heddy, born circa 1728, worked for Mr. Walton as a Bargeman before the Mills were purchased by the Government in 1797 (Supply 5/229). He began working for the Board on the 28th May 1788 at 1/6d per day (Supply 5/217). Heddy was possibly transferred to the Engineers' Department between August and September 1790, since he worked as a Labourer within the Manufactory with his wages submitted by William Spry, Colonel commanding the Royal Engineers, and paid for by the Storekeeper, James Wright. He signed for his pay with a cross (WASC 1382).

Edward had returned to work on the barges by December 1790, and continued to do so until at least March 1792 (Supply 5/215) but in July and September of that year he was "in the country charring wood" (Supply 5/216). He returned to the Mills and continued to work on the barges, but was replaced by John Turnham on the 30th September 1793 (Supply 5/217). The following day he was appointed as a Warder "attending at the field gate, Refining House [Sulphur Refining House] in High Bridge Street and upper part of the works" (Supply 5/217). A Return on the Marital Status of the Employees recorded that he was a married man without issue (Supply 5/221). He continued to be employed as a Warder, and in May 1804, his pay had increased to 2/-d per day. As a Warder, he received an additional allowance of 1/-d per night when it was his turn to watch – on average every 5th night (Supply 5/222). In 1810, then in his 84th year, Edward was still a Warder and was allowed to "round" every third night, for which he received 2/-d (Supply 5/228).

Edward Heddy died in a tragic accident on the 19th November 1811 (Winters, *op.cit.* p.70). A Report to the Board dated the 2nd December 1811, described how Edward had left his post at the Refining House to wash his hands in the river, became giddy and fell in the water. He was rescued, taken to the Wardhouse and lived for another 30 minutes. His wife, Mary, upwards of 67 years, asked for a small allowance "for the remaining years of her life" (Supply 5/229). On the 6th December the Board agreed to pay Mary 5/-d a week "upon the charity list", commencing from the date of her husband's death (Supply 5/199).

J. Hedley worked as a Labourer in May 1804 in the "Engineers' Dept. Established". He was paid 1/6d per day, with "one day extra allowed per week agreeable to the Boards Order dated 12th March, 1801" (Supply 5/222).

George Herbert was employed as a Millman in August 1812 at 3/-d per day, in addition to which, he was allowed 6d per night when on duty (Supply 5/229). This was also the case in February 1814 (Supply 5/230).

William Hickman worked as a Saltpetre Refiner earning 2/8d per day in February 1814, and, when not working extra was allowed to watch in turn (Supply 5/230).

George Hicks (1) was born circa 1753 and started work at Faversham on the 1st November 1787. He transferred to Waltham Abbey on the 15th September 1788 (Supply 5/512) and was employed there as a Sieve Puncher at 1/6d per day (Supply 5/212). In April 1789, in common with the rest of the workforce, he was "cutting and planting willow trees, cutting of canal at the new Corning House, removing earth to the store, unloading barge of coals & charring wood" (Supply 5/213). He had returned to his normal trade by September of 1789 "punching parchment bottoms and mounting sieves" (Supply 5/214).

A memorandum signed by William Congreve on the 26th December 1789 stated, "Hicks, the puncher and mounter of sieves, is to do that duty in the Proof House and have the care of that building" (Supply 5/189). He was still "punching sieves and at the proving house" in March 1790 (Supply 5/214) as he was in

July 1795 (Supply 5/217). He enlisted as a Private in the Volunteer Company on the 7th May 1794 (Supply 5/217)).

In December 1795, George stole a considerable quantity of Saltpetre which he took to London; he was subsequently tried at Chelmsford Assizes, and a cart was sent to Chelmsford after the trial to collect the stolen Saltpetre. In March 1796, he was sentenced to 7 years' transportation (Winters, *op.cit.* pp. 46/47).

George Hicks (2) was born circa 1769, and was first employed by the Board on the18th July 1815 as a casual Labourer at 2/8d per day. He was then living in Enfield (WO54/516) but by February 1817 his daily rate of pay had been cut to 2/4d, and he had moved to Waltham Abbey (WO54/520).

Nathaniel Hicks was working as a Saltpetre Refiner in September 1810 earning 2/-d per day, and, in addition, he was allowed to watch in turn (Supply 5/228). By August 1812, his rate of pay had been increased to 2/8d per day and he was still allowed to watch (Supply 5/229). His pay and conditions were unchanged in February 1814 (Supply 5/230).

R. Hide was an extra Bargeman employed in May 1804 on three barges transporting gunpowder to Picket's Field and the Magazines, for which he was paid £2.2.0d per week (Supply 5/222).

Richard Higgins was born at Preston-next-Faversham in 1791 and trained as a Cooper; he was employed in this capacity at Faversham in 1806, possibly serving an Apprenticeship there. His service record indicated that he left the Ordnance Board for a short while, possibly to work in a dockyard, but that he was re-employed at Faversham as a Cooper on the 30th November 1808 until the 25th June 1824, when his occupation changed to that of a Charcoal Burner (FGPR p.44). A Return for April 1825 confirmed his new trade and that he was paid 2/4d per day. He was then a married man with 1 child (Supply 5/116). Between the 1st July and the 31st December of that year he was stopped 1/-d for medical attention, and during October 1826, he suffered from "ague" (Supply 5/116).

Richard was transferred to Waltham Abbey on the 30th July 1832, where he was employed as the Foreman Charcoal Burner and paid 4/-d per day (Winters, *op. cit.* p.44). The production of charcoal by the Cylinder method did not start at Waltham Abbey until 1831/1832 (Winters, *op.cit.* p.102), and it is possible that Richard went to Waltham Abbey to set the cylinders up, since 3 other Charcoal Burners from Faversham were transferred to Waltham Abbey on the 19th November 1832, namely, Hayes, Wraight and Wilday (Winters, *op. cit.* p.102). In April 1833 he earned £72.16.0d annually, and he and his wife still had 1 child. In the Return for April 1834, he was described as the Foreman of the Cylinder Works ((WO54/593). He was still in the same position in October 1839, and in receipt of the same annual wage (WO51/623).

A Return of Properties submitted by the Royal Engineers' Office dated the 20th December 1834 recorded that Higgins had been leasing one of the Board's cottages since the 10th July 1833, at a rent of £5.4.0d per annum (Supply 5/237). The cottage was in Powder Mill Lane forming part of Plot No.62 on the Town Map in Appendix 1. He was still receiving the same annual wage in October 1839 (WO51/623) and another Return of Domestic Properties prepared in 1840 confirmed that Richard was living in a small cottage in Powder Mill Lane previously occupied by widow Freeman.

The 1841 Census confirmed that Richard and his wife, Amy, were living in Powder Mill Lane; neither was born in Essex and their only child was not listed.

John Hill was employed as a Millman in 1805 at 2/3d per day (Supply 5/224).

John Hilton, the youngest son of Joseph Hilton, was born at Waltham Abbey circa 1826. The 1841 Census recorded that he was living with his parents in Silver Street. In 1855, he was employed within the Manufactory as a Millman (Winters, *op.cit.* p.112), and the 1861 Census confirmed he was still in the same position (David Bishop's *Family History)*.

Joseph Hilton was born circa 1788 at Great Munden in Hertfordshire, and worked as a Millman in January 1805, earning 2/3d per day (Supply 5/224). This was also the case in June 1807 (Supply 5/226) when he was also allowed 3d per night when on duty. He was still a Millman in August 1808 on the same rate of pay, but was then allowed 6d per night when on duty (Supply 5/228).

He married Elizabeth Webb at Waltham Abbey on the 26th August 1810, and a son, William, was born and baptised at the Abbey Church in 1813, followed by Thomas in 1815 and Joseph, Jnr. In 1818. It is known that they also had 2 other sons as well as 2 daughters (David Bishop, *Family History*).

By February 1814 Joseph was no longer a Millman but employed as the Labourer to the Storekeeper, H. S. Matthews, at 2/8d per day (Supply 5/230). Mathews was replaced as Storekeeper on the 1st January 1818 by Empson Middleton, who apparently preferred his own Labourer, for he replaced Joseph Hilton with John Foxen. Joseph then returned to the Manufactory, and in June 1818 was working as a Saltpetre Refiner at 2/4d per day, as well as being allowed to watch in turn, for which he was paid 1/-d per night (Supply 5/231). At that time, he was a married man with 2 children, living in Waltham Abbey.

With the output of gunpowder reduced following the end of the wars in Europe, the workforce was cut back. The Storekeeper drew up lists of people to be made redundant, and initially Joseph was to be retained. However, in a letter to the Board dated September 1818 it was stated, "we respectfully beg leave to add the names and stations of those persons whom it will be necessary to discharge in consequence of this arrangement." and the list included Joseph Hilton (Supply 5/231).

The 1841 Census recorded that a Joseph and Elizabeth Hilton were living in Silver Street with their sons, William, John and Benjamin. Elizabeth died in 1843 and John in 1862. (David Bishop, *Family History*).

Robert Hilton was born circa 1766 and appointed Surgeon at the Mills on the 1st April 1791, holding the position until 1839 (Supply 5/217 and Winters, *op.cit.* p.122). Between 1791 and 1822 his annual salary was £63.17.6d, and in addition, every Foreman, Artisan and Labourer paid Hilton 6d per month for medicines, the amount in question deducted from their wages by the Storekeeper (Supply 5/229). This arrangement continued until 1814 when Hilton's terms were changed insomuch as he received a lump sum of £50 per annum from the Board in lieu of stoppages from the men for medicines (Supply 5/230).

A Return for 1818 confirmed the date of his appointment, his salary and his allowance for medicines. It also recorded his age as 52, stated that he was married with 7 children, and that, although he was 'Upon the Establishment', he did not live in a house owned by the Board (Supply 5/231). In February 1822, he was still paid £63.17.6d per annum, but the extra money for providing medicine to the workforce as necessary had been reduced to £48.8.0d (Supply 5/232). In June 1822, the Establishment at Waltham was reduced and, with the decrease in numbers, the Board ordered the Storekeeper to reduce Hilton's salary to £40 per annum, with the allowance for medicines to be discontinued (Supply 5/232). A second document in April 1823 confirmed that these instructions had been put into effect (WO54/542).

Edwin Wheble replaced Robert as Surgeon at the Mills in 1839. It is probable that Robert had died, since the 1841 Census recorded that Charlotte Hilton, Independent, aged 70, together with Frederick Hilton, Surgeon, aged 45 years and born in Essex, were living in Sewardstone Road, together with a young female servant.

Thomas Hilton, the second son of Joseph and Elizabeth Hilton, was born at Waltham Abbey in 1815. He possibly married Ann Bardell, the widow of William Bardell, who died in 1834 aged 23. At the time of William's death, Ann was pregnant and went into the workhouse. The 1841 Census recorded that Thomas was a 25-year-old man working as a Labourer at the Gunpowder Mills, and that he and his wife, Ann, also 25 years old (rounded down) were living in Blackboy Alley, together with William Bardell, then aged 7, and their daughter, Elizabeth, aged 1. Although Thomas was born in Essex, Ann was born out of the county.

William Hilton, the eldest son of Joseph and Elizabeth was baptized at the Abbey Church in 1813. He joined the Ordnance Board on the 22nd December 1830 when he replaced Thomas Martin, Snr. as a Saltpetre Refiner, with basic pay of £33.16.0d per annum (WO54/623). He was also allowed to watch in turn, which increased his annual pay to £39.0.0d (WO54/575)). It was recorded on the 8th August 1832, that William Hilton and 3 others had been cautioned for being absent from their work for a whole day without leave, and warned that a repeat would result in their dismissal (Supply 5/207). William continued to work as a Saltpetre Refiner, but his basic wage had been cut to £28.5.6d per annum by April 1834, although he still retained his allowance to watch, which increased his annual pay to £33.9.6d (WO54/593). His wage was restored to its former level by October 1839, and it was confirmed he was still a bachelor at that date (WO/54/623).

He was described as a Labourer who was living with his parents in Silver Street in the 1841 Census, although there is no reference to the Gunpowder Mills. Nevertheless, according to Winters, (*op.cit*.p.112) William was still working at the Mills in 1855 where he was the Granulating House Foreman.

Samuel Hobbs was employed as a Millwright in the Engineers' Department at 3/6d per day. In August 1790 he worked in the Manufactory, and his wages – amounting to £1.13.3d - were submitted by William Spry, Colonel commanding the Royal Engineers, and paid by the Storekeeper, James Wright. He signed for his pay "with a firm hand" (WASC 1382).

Henry Hodgson was a Labourer who started work in the Corning House on the 11th December 1792 at 1/6d per day (Supply 5/216). The Corning House was to be his work place until his death on the 18th April 1801. Robert Coleman, Clerk of the Cheque, recorded in his journal on the 15th May 1783, that Henry Hodgson had been chequered (fined) for "coming to work in liquor" and was ordered off his watch until the 1st June (Winters, *op. cit.* p.39). Henry enlisted in the Volunteer Company as a Private on the 7th May 1794 (Supply 5/217). By July 1795 he had been promoted as a Foreman in the Corning House and, "as a rounder every third night paid 1/6d" (Supply 5/217). A Petition relating to pay and conditions in the Mills submitted to the Board on the 2nd February 1801, recorded that Henry was still a Foreman in the Corning House and indicated that he was illiterate (Supply 5/220).

A Report dated the 19th April 1801 from the Storekeeper to the Board, informed them that the new Corning House blew up on the 18th April with a tremendous explosion. Nine men, including

Henry Hodgson, were in the building and were killed, together with four horses (Supply 5/220). A Petition sent to the Board dated the 24th April, signed by the widows, and, in two cases, the men's mothers, requested "relief in their distress" (Supply 5/194). A statement dated the 29th April quoting the ages of the children and the circumstances of the widows and children, noted that Henry left a widow, Francis, aged 57 (another source says 51) and two sons, "the oldest in deep decline, and the youngest, an Apprentice who is kept in clothing by the widow" (Supply 5/220). On the 5th May, the Board said that pay and allowances were to be continued to Mrs Hodgson "until her eldest son shall recover his health, or until his decease, after which, she is to receive half her husband's pay" (Supply 5/194). The Board queried the payments made to the widows; Hodgson's basic pay was 12/-d per week, plus 1/6d "on account of the severity of the times" and decreed that the widow's pension should be based upon her husband or son's basic pay, and should not include the extra allowance for the hardship of the time. On the 23rd May 1801, the Board agreed that the pension awarded to Mrs Hodgson should be 12/-d per week (Supply 5/194).

Daniel Holden was working as a Millman in June 1807 (Supply 5/226) and in August 1808, he was earning 2/3d per day as well as being "allowed 6d per night when on duty" (Supply 5/227). In September 1810 he was a Dusting House Man who was still paid 2/3d per day, and allowed to watch in turn for 1/6d per night (Supply 5/228). By August 1812, Daniel was working as a Puntman with increased earnings of 2/8d each day, as well as still being allowed to watch (Supply 5/229). He continued to work in the punts, and in February 1814, he was in receipt of the same pay and allowances (Supply 5/230).

Thomas Holden was born circa 1756. He started employment as Foreman of Labourers within the Engineers' Department on the 1st August 1806, and was paid 5/3d per day for a six-day week. If he worked on a Sunday, he was paid one and a half days' pay (WO54/512). Between the 15th and 21st July 1809, he supervised the Engineers' Department's Labourers in the Manufactory, for which he was paid £1.4.6d (Supply 5/228). He was still working as a Foreman in April 1816, although his pay had been reduced to 4/9d per day (WO54/516). By early April 1818, he was "established" and it was recorded that he was a married man living in Waltham Abbey with 4 unmarried children (WO54/524).

On the 21st April 1818, Thomas petitioned the Ordnance Board for a cottage, stating that he had entered the army in 1772 and was made a Sergeant in 1774, whereby he was at the Battle of Camden in South Carolina at the defeat of Generals Gates and Green, and that on the night prior to the engagement, he was stationed with a party of men at an outpost about a mile from the battle in order to guard a Corn Mill (the only one in that station to supply the troops) when the enemy advanced with a party with lighted matches to set the same on fire. Mr. Holden, having posted his men, attacked the party and routed them, forcing them to flee and throw away their matches, for which action Colonel Doyle (afterwards Sir John) warmly recommended him to Lord Moira, who for good conduct appointed him in 1804 to the situation he held at the date of the Petition. Mr. Holden further stated that he had never asked any favour whatsoever during the 17 years he had been employed, and that in the whole of that time no complaint had ever been made against him for neglect of any kind. He stated that he had a wife and 4 children – all females – and, therefore, could not but feel that the reduction made in his pay should be viewed with dismay. He further stated that cottages had been assigned to several of the Foremen in the different departments, and, therefore, he humbly requested that he should be granted the same, a cottage being much nearer the works than the dwelling he occupied at that time. Mr. Holden also mentioned that should he be granted a cottage, it would enable him in case of any accident, to attend his duty with more expedition (Supply 5/231).

The Ordnance Board referred his Petition back to Waltham Abbey for investigation and comments, which were submitted on the 7th May 1818. It was recorded, "having received the Hon. Board's Commands of the 1st instant to report on the Petition of Thomas Holden, Foreman of Labourers. Praying that on account of his services and the reduction made in his pay, Mr. Holden be allowed to inhabit a cottage, the property of the Board, it was found that a Mr. Mathews was in possession of the house which Holden desired to occupy, and that Mr Mathews signified that he had obtained the Board's permission to deposit therein portions of furniture and other articles, his property, until he had an opportunity of removing same, and that it was quite impossible for him to give up possession of this house until he was finally to remove." The house was, in any case, under orders to be divided into two tenements to be let to Labourers or others in the Department, but this division was then to be delayed until Mr Mathews could give up possession. In addition, it was stated that the property was much too large for a person in Holden's situation, even should the Board be desirous of granting a cottage to him for his residence. The Mr. Mathews mentioned in the Report may possibly have been H. S. Mathews, the Storekeeper, who had been replaced by Epsom Middleton early in 1818.

The Report continued to give a résumé of Holden's carer at the Powder Mills and gave reasons why the employees' pay was generally increased "across the board "in 1812. Holden was first employed as a Labourer on the 1st September 1804 and continued as such until the 31st July 1804 at 1/6d per day, and afterwards, as Foreman of Labourers at 2/6d per day from the 1st August 1804 to the 11th July 1806. His pay was increased in consequence of an application to Lord Moira from 2/6d per day to 4/9d per day. In April 1812, he received an additional 6d per day on account of

236

the high price of provisions in common with all other Foreman, and he only had a reduction of that 6d by the Board's order of the 19th April 1816, again, in common with all other Foreman. His pay in May 1818 was 4/9d per day for a six-day week, in addition to which, he was paid a considerable military pension, which was conceived to be ample for his services in the army. It was concluded, therefore, that there were many Foremen in the Powder Works who were much more entitled to a residence at the public expense than Holden (Supply 5/231).

Thomas Holden continued to work at the Mills as the Foreman of Labour, until at least April 1821 when he was 65 years of age, living in Waltham Abbey with, possibly, his 4 spinster daughters.

John Holmes was a Labourer at Faversham in November 1787 (Supply 5/219) and the *Faversham Gunpowder Personnel Records* (p.48) state that he was at Waltham Abbey in February 1798, although nothing can be found in the Waltham Abbey records to corroborate this.

Thomas Holmes (1) was born circa 1764, and started his employment with the Ordnance Board at Faversham on the 1st November 1787, before transferring to the Waltham Abbey Powder Mills as a Labourer in the Storekeeper's Department on the 1st February 1789, where he was paid 1/6d per day (Supply 5/212). In April 1789, in common with the rest of the workforce, he was "cutting and planting willow trees, cutting of canal at the new Corning House, removing earth to the store, unloading barge of coals & charring wood" (Supply 5/213). In August of the same year, Thomas was " setting and drawing stoves and sundries in various parts of the Manufactory," while in the following month he is described as "a collier" (Supply 5/214). William Congreve, the Comptroller, explained how a Collier was to be employed in an undated instruction around this time (Supply 5/189). In this he recorded, "two colliers are to be employed in the Powder Works until the season for charring," in other words, it would seem they were to be given work within the Manufactory during the winter months, rather than be discharged.

Holmes was undertaking similar tasks in 1790, but during the summer of that year, he was "in the country bagging alder wood", Alder wood being used to produce charcoal (Supply 5/215). In the winter months of 1790 he worked in the Corning House (Supply 5/215) and a similar cycle of working in the countryside in the spring through to the autumn and returning to work in the Manufactory in the winter, was repeated until 1795. During the winter months he had worked in various parts of the Powder Mills, including the Dusting House, the Storekeeper, thereby, complying with Congreve's instructions (Supply 5/215 – 5/217).

During this period he had married, and he joined the Volunteer Company as a Private on the 7th May 1794 (Supply 5/217). In June 1795, he was described as a Charcoal Burner at 1/6d per day (Supply 5/217) and on the 25th October of that year, Robert Coleman, Clerk of the Cheque, noted in his journal, "Holmes and [Richard] Jameson sent to Faversham". Subsequent entries in the records show that both Holmes and Jameson were appointed as Foremen of Cylinders (Supply 5/219). Faversham was producing charcoal by the cylinder method, so it is possible that they were sent there to learn the production methods which were to be implemented at Fisher Street and Fern Street in West Sussex.

Coleman wrote to Faversham on the 22nd March 1796, asking for their return (Winters, op.cit. p.47). The Cylinder Works at Fisher Street were certainly operational by the 5th April 1796, since a note in Winters, (op.cit. p.52) stated that the travelling expenses from Waltham Abbey to West Sussex were 9d per mile, and Holmes and Jameson were possibly transferred to Fisher Street around this date. A Return on the Marital Status of the

Employees made on the 8th May 1801 recorded that Thomas Holmes, Foreman of Cylinders in Sussex, was a married man with 4 children (Supply 5/221). The cylinders were under repair in November 1801, and Thomas supervised the men stacking timber in the yards and levelling and preparing the ground where the cylinders were to be re-sited (Supply 5/221). In May 1804, he was paid 3/1d per day and an extra 6d per month (Supply 5/222) rising to 3/6d per day by January 1806 (Supply 5/224). A Return for June 1807 noted that he had "apartments at Fishers Green and Fernhurst" (Supply 5/226). His pay had risen to 4/-d per day in August 1808 (Supply 5/227).

Subsequent Returns recorded the he was re-designated in August 1812 as the "Overseer of Cylinders" at Fernhurst, with his pay set at 5/8d per day, and remained so until 1818 (Supply 5/229). In 1818 he was 50 years of age and had 7 children (Supply 5/231). When the Establishment was reduced in numbers in August 1818 Thomas was retained, but his daily wage was cut to 4/8d (Supply 5/231).

Thomas Holmes (2) was working as a Hoop Maker in June 1818 at 3/6d per day, and allowed to watch in turn, for which he received 1/-d per night. He was born circa 1774, and was a married man with 3 children, who lived in Cheshunt (Supply 5/231). When the Establishment was trimmed down in September 1818, Thomas was one of the men discharged (Supply 5/231).

Charles Horam worked as a Labourer within the Manufactory, but was discharged at the end of September 1839 (WO54/623).

James Horam was born circa 1787, starting work with the Board as a Labourer on the 28th August 1806. In August 1812, he was a Bargeman earning 3/-d per day (Supply 5/229) as he was in February 1814, when his pay had increased to 3/10d per day (Supply 5/230). In common with the rest of the workforce whose wages were reduced following the defeat of Napoleon at Waterloo, so were James', and in April 1816, he was paid only 3/-d per day. In June 1818, it was recorded that James was a married man without children living in Enfield (Supply 5/231). He retained his position as a Bargeman at the same rate of pay when the Establishment was reduced in September 1818 (Supply 5/231). In May 1819, he was living in Cheshunt (Supply 5/231) but had moved to Waltham Abbey by September 1820, with his wife and first-born child (Supply 5/232). As a Bargeman, his pay was then £46.19.0d per annum.

In the spring of 1822, the Ordnance Board decided again to reduce the production and regeneration of gunpowder at the Establishment at Waltham Abbey. Accordingly, Empson Middleton and James Wright drew up lists of people to be dismissed on the 1st June 1822, and James Horam's name was included (Supply 5/232). However, a List of Employees dated the 10th October 1822 (Supply 5/233) showed that he had been retained and was required to carry out any type of work anywhere within the Manufactory. This was confirmed in another Return dated the 1st April 1823, which recorded that he was classified, "as a Labourer for general purposes to be sent to all parts of the Manufactory wherever their services may be requested."

His pay for the year was £39.0.0d, which included an allowance for watching in turn (WO54/542). This was then reduced by £2.12.0d per annum in accordance with the Board's Orders of the 27th December 1822 and the 15th January 1823 (WO54/542) but had been restored to its former level by October 1824 (WO54/546). The same document noted that by then he had 2 children and that he continued to work as a Labourer. In October 1825, he was setting and drawing stoves (Winters, *op. cit.* pp.93-95) with his pay and allowances unchanged (WO54/550).

James was promoted to being a Corning House Man on the 27th February 1827, which increased his basic pay to £42.18.0d per annum, and he was still allowed to watch in turn, which further increased the amount he earned to £48.2.0d (WO54/558). He continued to work in the Corning House on the same pay and conditions, but became a widower with 4 young children in 1827. He returned to the barges late in the summer of 1837, replacing James Boswell, who had been appointed as the Master Bargeman (Supply 5/237). He was still a Bargeman in October 1839 at £39.0.0d per annum (WO54/623). James's name does not appear in the 1841 Census for Waltham Abbey.

John Horam (1) was employed as a Cooper in September 1810, and, in common with all other Coopers, he was not allowed to watch (Supply 5/226). By August 1812 his pay had risen to 4/-d per day (Supply 5/229) and had increased again to 4/6d daily by February 1814 (Supply 5/230).

John Horam (2) was a Millwright's Assistant who was paid £1.1.3d for work carried out by the Engineers' Department between the 15th and 21st July 1809 (Supply 5/228).

John Horam (3) was born circa 1793, starting work as a casual Labourer with the Engineers' Department on the 26th November 1815. In February 1816, he was paid 2/8d per day, and he was then a 22-year-old bachelor living in Cheshunt (WO54/516).

R. Horam worked as a Brimstone Refiner in January 1806, with a rate of pay of 2/-d per day (Supply 5/224).

Samuel Horam worked as a Punt Man earning 2/-d per day, and at the 30th January 1806, he had 3 months' service (Supply 5/224). By August 1812 he was employed as a Corning House Man who earned 3/3d per day, in addition to which, he was allowed to watch in turn, for which he was paid 1/6d per night

(Supply 5/229). His pay and allowance remained unchanged in February 1814 (Supply 5/230).

James Horn was born circa 1756 and was first employed as a casual Labourer in the Engineers' Department on the 29th March 1806 (WO54/516). As a common (casual) Labourer, he was paid 17/-d for work carried out by the Department within the Manufactory between the 15th and 21st July 1809 (Supply 5/228). In September 1812, James was described as an occasional Labourer in the Engineers' Department, earning 2/8d for a six-day week (WO54/516). At that date he was a 59-year-old married man, with 2 married children and 1 unmarried child, who lived in Waltham Abbey. He was still employed in February 1817, but his pay had been reduced to 2/4d per day (WO54/520).

Henry Horne, born circa 1798, worked as a Cooper in February 1814 earning 1/9d per day, and, in common with all other Coopers, was not allowed to watch (Supply 5/230). His rate of pay indicated that he was not achieving the daily output expected of a fully trained artisan. He was still employed as a Cooper in June 1818 then earning 4/-d per day, and was a bachelor, aged 19, who lived in Waltham Abbey (Supply 5/231). With the output of gunpowder reduced following the end of the wars in Europe, the workforce was cut back. The Storekeeper drew up lists of people to be made redundant, and in a letter to the Board dated September 1818, he stated, "we respectfully beg leave to add names and stations of those persons whom it will be necessary to discharge in consequence of this arrangement." The list included Henry Horne (Supply 5/231).

James Horne started work in the Manufactory as a Saltpetre Refiner in September 1805, earning 2/-d per day (Supply 5/224). There appears to be no other mention of James Horne within the Mills' records until the Establishment was reduced in numbers, when a James Horne, Bargeman, was one of those discharged

(Supply 5/231) but it is unclear whether or not this was the same person.

Nathaniel Horne worked as a Millman in January 1806 and was paid 2/3d per day. At that date, he had 1 year's service, (Supply 5/224). In June 1807, he was refining Brimstone at the same 2/3d per day, in addition to which, as a Brimstone Refiner, he was allowed to watch in turn, for which he received 1/-d (Supply 5/226). The following year he was employed as a Millman on the same daily rate of pay, but he was then allowed 6d per night when on duty (Supply 5/227) and this was also the case in September 1810 (Supply 5/228). He was refining Saltpetre in August 1812, for which he was paid 2/8d per day, and in addition, when not working extra, he was allowed to watch in turn (Supply 5/229). These details also applied in February 1814 (Supply 5/230).

John Horrod (also Horod) worked as a Puntman at 2/-d per day in June 1807 (Supply 5/226). In August 1808 he was employed in the Mixing House, earning 2/3d per day. Mixing House men "in addition to their pay, they are allowed to watch in turn, for which they receive one shilling" (Supply 5/227). John was a witness to a fight in the Watch House on the 8th April 1809, when Barnard Presland killed Noah Sayer. Sayer left a widow, Ann, and Presland was discharged from the Mills, but it is not known what punishment he received for killing Sayer (Winters, *op. cit.* pp.67-68).

William Hounson was working as a Labourer in the Cylinder Houses in West Sussex in May 1801, earning 1/6d per day. At that date the cylinders had been out of repair, and Hounson was employed in stacking timber in the yards and levelling and preparing the ground where the cylinders were to be re-sited (Supply 5/221). In January 1806, he was carrying out the tasks of a Cylinder Man, for which he was paid 2/- per day (Supply

5/224). This Return also recorded that he then had 3 years' service, which suggests that he had left the Cylinder Works in 1801, returning in 1803. His pay in August 1812 was 2/8d per day (Supply 5/229), and he continued to make charcoal by the cylinder method until at least February 1814, when he was on the same rate of pay according to Supply 5/230.

Edward Howe started work as a Refiner in the Saltpetre House in 1805. In January 1806, he was paid 2/-d per day (Supply 5/224).

Richard Hudson was born circa 1760, training as a Baker before being employed by the Ordnance Board on the 1st April 1788 at 1/6d per day (Supply 5/232). He was promised to be continued as a general Labourer, since he had previously worked for Mr. Walton (Supply 5/212). In March 1789, he was working in the Mixing House (Supply 5/212) and continued to do so until at least January 1792 (Supply 5/215) except for a short period in April 1789, when the majority of the workforce was engaged in "cutting and planting willow trees, cutting of canal at the new Corning House, removing earth to the store, unloading barge of coals & charring wood" (Supply 5/213). By August 1793, he was "marking barrels" (Supply 5/216) as well as "attending the magazine" (Supply 5/217) which he continued to do until at least September 1798 (Supply 5/219) although for an unknown period, he was a Charcoal Millman who was replaced by Jon Haydon (Supply 5/219). During this period he joined the Volunteer Company as a Private, and a Petition on Pay and Conditions in the Mills submitted by the workforce to the Board on the 2nd February 1800, recorded that he was literate (Supply 5/220). A Return of the Marital Status of the Employees dated the 8th May 1801, recorded that he was a married man without issue (Supply 5/221).

When not working in the Magazine or marking barrels, he was expected to undertake other work within the Manufactory, and on the 16th June 1801, Richard, with others, was repairing the Corning House when it caught fire following an explosion. The fire was caused "from a blow of a copper hammer on a pit wheel" (Winters, *op.cit.* p.59). The Storekeeper sent a letter to the Board on the 23rd June, listing the names of the men who had suffered terrible burns, seeking permission to support the casualties, and Richard's name was included. The letter went on to state, "we beg to represent the situation of the poor men who were burnt when the Corning House took fire on the 16th instant when under repair" and continued, "...these men are burnt in a dreadful manner. Their pain is very great...." and "Our surgeon has represented the necessity of the men most burnt having immediate assistance in wine, as a considerable suppuration is come on their constitutions. They cannot support it without wine, and we have directed wine to be immediately provided to them, we request your permission for our continuing to support these poor men with such wine or other proper support as their surgeon may think their respective situations require." (Supply 5/195).

It would appear that the Board responded the same day, the writer saying that he had "the Board's commands to transmit to you on the other side hereof a list of the men who have been burnt and otherwise hurt by the fire which lately destroyed the Corning House at Waltham Abbey; and I am to desire the Storekeeper will pay the men all their pay until they are recovered" (Supply 5/195).

Another letter to the Board dated the 29th July 1801 (Supply 5/221) recorded that the men who had been burnt at the Corning House requested that they be reimbursed for the loss of clothing. The list included Richard Hudson, whose claim amounted to £2.4.6d in all – for a hat (4/-d) handkerchiefs (5/-d) stockings (3/6d) shirt (6/-d) coat 6/-d breeches (6/-d) and sheets (15/-d).

The same letter went on to say that Mr. Hudson, amongst others, suffered so much that he wished for death to release him from his torture, and that it was a matter of surprise that he was recovering. The constant attention the men needed meant that their wives could not undertake seasonal work (haymaking), at which they could earn sufficient to pay the rent. It was requested that financial allowances be made, but no record of the Board's response has come to light. A Return of Artificers and Labourers dated November 1801 recorded that Richard, with others, had been so severely burnt in the old Corning House that it would be dangerous to expose him with the other men repairing the river banks at that time, but instead, he should perform trifling jobs as they occurred (Supply 5/221).

Richard recovered from his burns, and in May 1804, was working as a Refiner earning 2/-d per day as well as being allowed to watch in turn every fifth night (Supply 5/222). In January 1806 he was marking barrels for the same pay (Supply 5/224). By August 1808 he was the Office Keeper, with his pay increased to 2/6d per day, and was a Rounder, for which he received an extra 2/-d for each night that he fulfilled this duty (Supply 5/227).

However, soon after this he was promoted to The Foreman of the Stoves, with his pay increased to 5/2d per day, and he still acted as a Rounder (Supply 5/229). He occupied this position until his death in 1822, although his daily rate of pay had by then been reduced to 4/2d (Supply 5/232).

In 1816 the Board formed 3 tenements out of the dwellings in the Tanyard on the south side of High Bridge Street. Richard Hudson, Foreman of the Stoves, was allocated one, the rental being 3/-d per week (Winters, *op.cit.*p.83)   This was confirmed by a statement "of monies to which the public were entitled to receive credit between the 1st January and the 31st December, 1821, shewing the amounts received by the storekeeper" which recorded that Richard had been living in a Board of Ordnance house, Tenement No. 23, from the 24th December 1816, and that his rent at the time was £7.16.0d per annum. The property has been identified as Plot No. 53 on the Town Map in Appendix 1, being opposite Powder Mill Lane (Supply 5/232).

Richard died in January 1822, and the Storekeeper forwarded a petition from his wife, Ann, for assistance. In the petition, Ann pointed out that the late General Congreve had sent Richard to Waltham Abbey as a Labourer on the 1st April 1788. By good conduct and activity in the service he was made Office Keeper. In the year of 1808, he was promoted to the situation of Foreman of Stoves, in which post he continued until his death. On the 16th June 1801, he was severely burnt in the fire at No. 3 Corning House, and, thereafter, never enjoyed a good state of health. Ann, then aged 60 and in a 'hapless' situation, requested that the Board grant her a small charitable pension, or allow her to live rent-free in the cottage which belonged to the Board. The Board requested clarification from the Mills on Richard's health; it was agreed that Hudson had been severely burnt in the explosion at the Corning House in 1801, although the Surgeon, Robert Hilton, did not think that this was a contributory factor to his death at the age of 64. To alleviate her financial hardship, however, Middleton and Wright requested the Board allow Mrs. Hudson to continue to live in her cottage with the rent reduced from 3/-d to 1/-d per week, to which the Board agreed (Supply 5/232).

A Return of Properties owned by the Board dated the 20th December 1834 recorded that Ann was still living in the same cottage and that she had been the tenant since the 1st March 1822, with her rent confirmed at 1/-d per week (Supply 5/237). The 1841 Census revealed that Ann Hudson, Ordnance Pensioner, aged 70, was living on the south side of High Bridge Street, with James and Elizabeth Free as lodgers.

William Hudson worked as a Labourer for 2/8d per day in August 1812, "drawing and setting stoves and in the willow plantation." He was also allowed to watch in turn (Supply 5/229). This was also the case in February 1814 (Supply 5/230).

John Hughes started work as a Brimstone Refiner in September 1805 (Supply 5/224) and continued to do so until at least August 1808 (Supply 5/227). During this period he was paid 2/-d per day and, when not working, was allowed to watch in turn.

John Huken was employed as a Labourer in the Engineers' Department at 1/6d per day. In August 1790, he worked within the Manufactory with his wages submitted by William Spry, Colonel commanding the Royal Engineers, and paid for by the Storekeeper, James Wright. He signed for his money with a "bold hand" (WASC 1382).

J. Hunch worked in the Dusting House at 2/1d per day. At the 30th January 1806, he had served the Ordnance Board for one year (Supply 5/224).

William Hunns was employed as a Millwright in the Engineers' Department at 3/6d per day. Between August and September 1790, he worked in the Manufactory with his wages submitted by William Spry, Colonel commanding the Royal Engineers, and paid for by the Storekeeper, James Wright. He signed for his pay with a firm hand (WASC 1382).

John Hunt was born circa 1784 and worked as a Saltpetre Refiner in May 1804 at 2/-d per day, with an additional 1/-d when it was his turn to watch, which was, on average, every 5th night (Supply 5/222). In January 1806, he was employed as an extra Bargeman at the same daily rate, and at that point, he had two years' service (Supply 5/224). In June 1807 he was described as a Bargeman on the same rate of pay, but this rose to 3/-d by

August 1808 (Supply 5/226). His pay details were also the same in September 1810 (Supply 5/228). John was classified as a Master Bargeman in 1812, with his pay at 5/2d per day (Supply 5/229) but by June 1818, his wage had been reduced to 4/2d (Supply 5/231). He was then a 32-year-old married man with 3 children, living in Cheshunt. The last record relating to John being employed by the Ordnance was in May 1819, when his circumstances remained unchanged (Supply 5/231).

The 1841 Census recorded that a John Hunt of a similar age, a Bargeman, was living in Romeland with his wife, Sarah, aged 50, son James - who was a 20-year-old Shoemaker - and 15-year-old daughter, Ellen. None of the family was born in Essex.

Richard Hunt was a Cylinderman earning 2/8d per day in August 1812 (Supply 5/229) and this was also the case in February 1814 (Supply 5/230).

Thomas Hunt was working as a Puntman in June 1807, earning 2/-d per day (Supply 5/226). By August 1808, he was employed as a Millman earning 2/3d per day, and was "allowed 6d per night when on duty" (Supply 5/228). He continued to work as a Millman, and by August 1812, his daily rate of pay had risen to 3/-d (Supply 5/229). This was also the case in February 1814, and during this period his night-work allowance remained unchanged (Supply 5/230).

William Hunt started his employment with the Ordnance Board early in the year of 1805, and in January 1806, he was working in the Corning House earning 2/2d per day (Supply 5/224). In addition, he was allowed to watch in turn, for which he received one shilling. In June 1807 he was still in the Corning House earning the same amount (Supply 5/226).

I

Mead Ingle started work as a casual Labourer in the Engineers' Department on the 22nd April 1815. In February 1816 he was earning 2/8d per day, and at that date, he was a 48-year-old married man who lived in Cheshunt, and had 1 married and 5 unmarried children. (WO54/516).

James Ingles joined the Ordnance Board as a general Labourer on the 20th October 1787. In September 1788, he was working in the Magazine earning 1/6d per day, and had joined the Volunteer Company as a Private (Supply 5/219). The signed Petition on Pay and Conditions at the Mills presented to the Board on the 2nd February 1800, indicated that he was illiterate (Supply 5/220) and a Return of the Marital Status of the Employees dated May 1801, showed that he was a married man with one child (Supply 5/221).

William Irons was working as a Labourer in the Dusting House in March 1790, earning 1/6d per day (Supply 5/214). By August of that year he was employed as a Millman who then earned 2/-d per day, as he did in April 1791 (Supply 5/215). The last record for William was in February 1793 when his position was that of a Barrel Marker, with his daily rate of pay increased to 1/6d (Supply 5/216).

Joseph Ives was working as a Labourer in the Corning House in May 1804, and was paid 2/1d per day with an additional 1/-d when it was his turn to watch, which was, on average, every 5th night (Supply 5/222). In January 1806, he was employed as an extra Bargeman at the same daily rate, and at that date he had 2 years' service (Supply 5/224). In June 1807, he was described as a Bargeman on the same rate of pay (Supply 5/226) but was promoted to a Master Bargeman earning 4/-d per day by August 1808 (Supply 5/227). He held the same position and pay in September 1810 (Supply 5/228).

William Izzard joined the Ordnance Board circa 1799. A Return on the Marital Status of the Employees dated the 8th May 1801, recorded that he was a married man with 1 child (Supply 5/221).

In November 1801, in common with the majority of the workforce, he was engaged in "cleaning and deepening the river, canals and ditches and other work necessary to be performed" (Supply 5/221). In May 1804, he was employed as a Refiner at 2/-d per day, in addition to which, he was allowed to watch in turn, on average every 5th night, for which he received one shilling (Supply 5/222).

In January 1806, he was working as a Charcoal Millman, still earning 2/-d per day (Supply 5/224) and held that position until at least February 1814, when his daily rate of pay had risen to 3/-d (Supply 5/230). He was still allowed to watch in turn during this period, with his watch money set at 1/6d per night.

J

R. James was a Carpenter by trade who was set to work at 9/-d per week by Daniel Cornish in October 1787, renovating the Powder Mills following their purchase from Mr. Walton by the Government. He was not retained once his work was completed (Winters, *op.cit.* p.28).

William James was a Sawyer who was paid £1.9.9d for work carried out by the Engineers' Department in the Manufactory between the 15th and 21st July 1809 (Supply 5/228).

Richard Jameson served in the Artillery from November 1779 to 1790 (Supply 5/217) and shortly after leaving the Army, he started work in the Mills as a Labourer in the Mixing House at 1/6d per day (Supply 5/215). He continued to "mix composition" until he became a Millman on the 31st January 1792 (Supply 5/215) and continued in that trade until October 1795. During that period he was paid 2/-d per day with an additional 3d for night work (Supply 5/217). He joined the Volunteer Company as a Sergeant on the 7th May 1794 (Supply 5/219).

On the 25th October of that year Robert Coleman, the Clerk of the Cheque, noted in his journal "Jameson and (Thomas) Holmes sent to Faversham" (Winters, *op. cit.* p.47). Subsequent entries in the records showed that both were appointed as Foremen of Cylinders (Supply 5/219). Faversham Mills were producing charcoal by the cylinder method so, presumably, they were sent there to learn the production methods, using the processes which were to be implemented at Fisher Street and Fernhurst in West Sussex. Coleman later wrote to Faversham on the 22nd March 1796 asking for their return (Winters, *op.cit.* p.48). Jameson and Holmes were probably transferred to Fisher Street around that date, since a note in Winters (p.52) recorded that the travelling expenses from Waltham Abbey to West Sussex were 9d per mile.

The Cylinder Works at Fisher Street were certainly erected by the 9th May 1796 (Winters, *op. cit.* p.53). Under a Board directive, Richard was appointed as the Senior Foreman in the Cylinder Houses on the 1st October 1796 (Winters, *op. cit.* p.92). In September 1798 Richard was described as "the foreman of cylinders" at Fernhurst and was paid 2/6d per day (Supply 5/219).

A Return on the Marital Status of the Employees made on the 8th May 1801, recorded that Richard Jameson, Foreman of Cylinders in Sussex, was a married man with one child (Supply 5/221). The cylinders were under repair in November 1801 with Richard supervising the men stacking timber in the yards, and levelling and preparing the ground where the cylinders were to be re-sited (Supply 5/221). In May 1804 he was paid 3/1d per day and an extra 6d per month (Supply 5/222) and in March 1805 his wage was recorded as £1.2.0d per week, with an additional allowance of 6d per month (Supply 5/223). A note to this Return stated that his appointment was at Fisher Street and Fernhurst. In January 1806, his daily pay was 4/-d (Supply 5/224) and a Return for June 1807, noted that he had "apartments at Fishers Green and Fernhurst" (Supply 5/226). His pay had risen to 4/6d per day in August 1808 (Supply 5/227). Subsequent Returns showed that he was re-designated as the "Senior Overseer of Cylinders" at Fernhurst, with his pay set at 6/3d per day in June 1818 (Supply 5/231) and he still was married with one child. When the Establishment was reduced in numbers in August 1818 Richard retained his position between the 3rd September and the 31st December of that year, but with his daily wage cut to 5/3d (Supply 5/231).

W. Jasamine was working on the 27th November 1788 as an occasional Labourer in the Engineers' Department, earning 1/6d per day Supply 5/212) and "under promise to be continued" (Winters, *op. cit.* p.32). In August and September 1790, he worked within the Manufactory with his wages submitted by William Spry, Colonel commanding the Royal Engineers, to be paid by the Storekeeper, James Wright (WASC 1382).

James Jasper was working as a casual Labourer in the Engineers' Department in September 1812 and was paid 2/8d per day for a six-day-week (WO54/512).

J. Jenkins worked as a Foreman in the Corning Houses in November 1789, being paid 1/6d per day (Winters, *op. cit.* p.33).

J. Jenner was a bachelor working as a Cylinderman in Sussex in May 1801 (Supply 5/221). The cylinders were under repair in November 1801, and Jenner was stacking timber in the yards and levelling and preparing the ground where the cylinders were to be re-sited (Supply 5/221).

Thomas Jennings started his employment as an occasional Labourer with the Engineers' Department on the 4th December 1815, being paid 2/8d per day. He was then a 22-year-old bachelor living in Waltham Abbey (WO54/516).

James Jessop was appointed as a Junior Clerk at Sheerness on the 26th May 1787, and transferred to Waltham Abbey as the Second Clerk on the 14th March 1805, where he was paid £80.0.0d per annum (Supply 5/223).

Thomas Jieps was born circa 1796 and started his employment as an occasional Labourer with the Engineers' Department on the 7th April 1815 at 2/8d per day. He was a bachelor living in Waltham Abbey (WO54/516).

George Johnson (1) was a common (casual) Labourer who was paid 8/6d for work carried by the Engineers' Department within the Manufactory between the 15th and 21st July 1809 (Supply

5/228). He was still employed on a casual basis in September 1812, earning 2/8d per day (WO54/512).

George Johnson (2) was a casual Labourer in the Engineers' Department in September 1812, and was paid 2/8d per day for a six-day week (WO54/512).

Henry Johnson, born circa 1752, trained as a Millwright and was working as such in the "Engineers' Department Established" in May 1804; he was then paid 3/6d per day and "allowed 6d a month in addition" (Supply 5/222). Henry was appointed as the Foreman Millwright on the 16th November 1804 (WO54/512). In November 1804, he was paid £1.15.0d for work carried out in the Manufactory, and was then described as a Master Millwright, a position which allowed him to train an Apprentice (Supply 5/228).

His wage in September 1812 was 6/4d per day for a six-day-week and one and a half days' pay for working on a Sunday. He was also entitled to 6/-d per week to train an Apprentice (WO54/512).

A Return for February 1816 confirmed that his pay and allowances were unchanged, and that he had one married and five unmarried children (WO54/516). With the end of hostilities in Europe, his wage had been cut to 5/10d per day by February 1817 but his allowance to train an Apprentice had increased to 7/-d weekly, and at that date, another of his children had married (WO54/520). Henry was retained when the Establishment was reduced in numbers in September 1818 (WO54/524) as he was in similar cutbacks in 1820 and 1822. During this period his wage remained static, but his allowance to train an Apprentice increased to 8/-d weekly (WO54/532). A Return dated October 1823 recorded that he was paid 5/10d per day for 313 days work in the year, which equated to an annual income of £91.5.10d. His family details remained unchanged at that time (WO54/542).

A Return of Persons belonging to the Civil Establishment of the Ordnance at the Gunpowder and Small Arms Manufactories at Waltham Abbey, Faversham and Enfield, showing in detail several points of information called for by the Master General and Board's Order dated the 31st January 1831, recorded that Henry Johnson was one of 3 Master Artificers to be employed at Waltham Abbey and Enfield; he was the Master Millwright and was paid 5/10d per day. His duties were to work with Artificers and Labourers in the Gunpowder Manufactory, which, consequently, required great attention, sobriety, and steadiness of conduct (WO54/575). Under a Board Order dated the 15th March 1833, Henry Johnson, Master Millwright, was to be discharged and granted a pension of £36.10.0d per annum, until an opportunity to employ him again should arise (Supply 5/208). He was 81 years of age when he retired.

James Johnson was a Labourer who was set to work by Daniel Cornish in October 1787 at 9/-d per week, possibly renovating the Mills following their purchase by the government from Mr. Walton (Winters, *op. cit.* p.29). He does not appear to have been retained.

John Johnson was born circa 1761 and started his career as a Labourer with the Ordnance Board at Woolwich on the 1st April 1780 (Supply 5/232). He transferred to Faversham on the 1st June 1793 where he worked as a Saltpetre Refiner, and by 1795, he was the Foreman Refiner there (Supply 5/72). On the 4th December 1798, he moved to the Mills at Waltham Abbey as the Master Saltpetre Refiner (Supply 5/232) where he replaced John Baker who had died, and his pay was set at 3/-d per day (Supply 5/220). He occupied this position until his own death on the 27th June 1823. A Petition on the Pay and Conditions at the Mills presented to the Board on the 2nd February 1800 showed that John was literate, and a Return made in the following year on the Marital Status of the Employees recorded that he was a married man without issue (Supply 5/221). In November 1801, the Comptroller, William Congreve, directed him to "take care of the Refining House and the Saltpetre Store House due to the considerable depot of salt petre etc," (Supply 5/221).

In December 1801, Johnson was allowed £4.4.0d per annum for coal and candles (Winters, *op. cit.* p.61). In May 1804 he was earning 4/3d per day with an extra allowance of 6d per month (Supply 5/222). By June 1807 John was in receipt of 5/-d per day, and it was noted that he was then entitled to take an Apprentice. The Mills were apparently working long hours and Johnson was spending considerable time there, for, on the 20th July 1807, he petitioned the Board for "a house on the premises to ensure the necessary degree of heat at which the liquor in the boilers must be kept" and went on to say that the Master Refiner at Faversham was provided with a house. The Board agreed with his request (Supply 5/198). Initially he was not provided with a property owned by the Board, since a Return dated the 23rd August 1808 recorded that he was in receipt of an allowance of £20.0.0d for house rent, coupled with a coal and candle allowance of £4.4.0d per annum (Supply 5/227). The same document noted that his pay was still 5/-d per day and that he was entitled to receive 7/-d per week to train an Apprentice.

A statement "of monies to which the public were entitled to receive credit between the 1st January and the 31st December 1821" recorded that under an Order of the Board dated the 7th March 1810, John was entitled to live rent-free in a house located within the Saltpetre Refinery (Supply 5/232). The Refinery and the house were located on the north side of High Bridge Street, shown as Plot No. 39 on the Town Map in Appendix 1. John continued as the Master Saltpetre Refiner with his wages peaking at 8/1d per day by August 1812, with his allowance to train an Apprentice unchanged. He was still provided with a rent-free house as well as his coal and candle allowance (Supply 5/229). In common with the rest of the workforce at the Mills, his wages were reduced following the defeat of Napoleon, and in June 1818 he was paid 7/1d per day, with his allowances remaining unchanged (Supply 5/231 & WO54/524). The same documents noted that he was a married man with 3 children.

John retained his employment when the Establishment was reduced in numbers in September 1818 (Supply 5/231) and again in March 1822, when the Establishment was set to produce only 100 to 200 barrels of gunpowder and regenerate another 2000 barrels annually. During this period, his pay and allowances were unchanged (Supply 5/232).

John was killed by lightning on the 27th June 1823 (Winters, *op. cit.* p.90). Henry Wright's memories of the Powder Mills at Waltham Abbey as related to Winters, said, "I knew perfectly well Mr Johnson, Master Refiner of salt petre, who was killed by lightning in the presence of my father and myself; the only two persons that were with him in his office. The electricity passed down his side and out of his shoe bursting it. He did not fall from his chair for a few seconds. My father immediately opened the vein in his arm; the blood was solid, not a drip came. At this terrible flash his wife was dreadfully alarmed; she was at home in a small room near the refinery now occupied by Mr Knowler. We were told she exclaimed 'My dear husband,' and I am under the impression she died very shortly afterwards" (Winters, *op. cit.* p.143). He was reading at his desk close to the window, looking towards the chrystalizing house; he was struck on the left side of his head; he was wearing his hat at the time; this was shattered.).

Richard Johnson was working as a Puntman in August 1812; he was paid 2/8d per day as well as being allowed to watch in turn (Supply 5/229). In February 1814 he was employed as an additional Bargeman at 3/10d per day (Supply 5/230).

Thomas Johnson was a Millwright in the "Engineers' Department Established" in May 1804. He was paid 3/6d per day and allowed 6d a week in addition (Supply 5/222).

Evan Jones was working as a Labourer earning 1/6d per day "setting and drawing stoves and in the boats as well as planting willow trees" in March 1790 (Supply 5/214). A letter from the Comptroller, William Congreve, to the Rex Officers at Waltham Abbey, requested that Evan Jones be sent to the Royal Laboratory, and that the bearer of the letter, Phillip Sherren, be "entered as a Labourer in his place" (WASC 0475).

Hugh Jones was born circa 1761 and served in the Artillery between May 1784 and January 1790 before joining the Ordnance Board as a Labourer at Waltham Abbey on the 4th May 1790 (Supply 5/232). He spent the rest of his working life at the Mills, retiring in 1838 after 48 years, service (Winters, *op. cit.* p.104).

In August 1790, he was listed as a Millman earning 2/-d per day but by the end of the year, he was described as a Labourer working in the Corning House (Supply 5/215) as he was in January 1791 (Supply 5/215). The following January he was "grinding salt petre, charcoal and brimstone" (Supply 5/215). Although Hugh was made the Office Keeper on the 11th July 1792, his pay remained at 2/-d but he was appointed as a Rounder at the same time, a duty he undertook every third night (Supply 5/215). He joined the Volunteer Company as a Corporal on the 7th May 1794, but had been promoted to Sergeant by 1798 (Supply 5/219). The Petition on Pay and Conditions at the Mills presented to the Board on the 2nd February 1800, showed that he was literate (Supply 5/220) while a Return on the Marital Status of the Employees dated May 1801, recorded that he was then a married man with 2 children (Supply 5/221).

Hugh continued to be employed as the Office Keeper "attending the office" until January 1808. During this period his wage had increased to 2/3d daily, with his Rounder's wage set at 1/6d per night when on duty (Supply 5/222). In January 1808, the Board approved a recommendation by the Storekeeper that he be made the Foreman of the Stoves drying the gunpowder (Supply 5/198). His pay then was 4/-d per day, he was still allowed to be a Rounder every third night at 2/-d, and he was still in the same position in 1810 (Supply 5/227). On the 28th February 1812, Hugh was employed as the Master Mixer of Composition with his pay increased to 6/4d per day (Supply 5/229). He continued to be the Master Mixer for the next 13 years, but In August 1818 his daily rate of pay, in common with the rest of the Establishment, had been cut and he then only received 5/10d per day. However, as the Master Mixer, he was entitled to receive 6/-d per week to train an Apprentice (Supply 5/231 & WO54/524). The same documents recorded that he only had one child and that he was entitled to a house owned by the Board.

A Return of Employees to be retained between the 3rd September and the 31st December 1818 to meet the reduced outputs of gunpowder at the Mills included Hugh, who retained his same rate of pay and allowances (Supply 5/231). On the 21st October 1818 the Board "grants Mr Thomas Austen, the conductor of the Cornmill, the privilege of living in the Pin Factory House, and Hugh Jones, the master mixer, to reside in the house now occupied by Thomas Austen, at one pound per year" (Winters, *op. cit.* p.85).

A very faint copy of a letter dated the 6th November 1818, indicated that Jones requested that he be allowed to live rent free in a cottage he had recently occupied. The Board were of the opinion that "as an indulgence to Hugh Jones" it should be let to him at a rent of £5 per annum (Supply 5/202). However, subsequent records indicated that he occupied a property rent-free. He continued to be employed as the Master Mixer with the same rate of pay, but in September 1820, his allowance to train an Apprentice was 7/-d per week (Supply 5/232). A statement "of monies to which the public were entitled to receive credit between the 1st January and the 31st December 1821" recorded that under an Order of the Board dated the 6th November 1818, Hugh had been living rent free in Tenement No. 11 (Supply 5/232). The Royal Engineers produced similar lists of properties owned by the Board in 1834 (Supply 5/237) and 1840 (WO44/133) and followed the numbering system used by Frederick Drayson, who produced a map of the Royal Gunpowder Manufactory in 1830. Drayson numbered each building starting at Lower Island and ending with the pair of cottages at Aqueduct Lock. By comparing details on contemporary maps such as the 1825 Parish Map, the 1826 Town Map and the 1842 Tithe Map, the majority of the tenements owned by the Board can be located. It is clear that Hugh was living in one of 3 houses built from materials salvaged from the old Horse Mills within the Manufactory, and ready for occupation on the 29th August 1815 (Winters, *op. cit.* p.82). From the 1st September 1815, two were occupied by Samuel Knowler, Master Refiner, and Thomas Tamkin, Master Bricklayer, with an annual rental of £1.0.0d, while Thomas Austen, Millwright and Engineer, took occupation of another tenement owned by the Board around this date. Another document dated May 1840 (WO44/133) recorded that Jones, Tamkin and Knowler had occupied these 3 cottages which were located in Powder Mill Lane, with their position confirmed by the 1841 Census. Jones' house, together with its large garden of 22 perches, is shown as being at the northern end of Plot No. 64 on the Town Map in Appendix 1.

A list dated March 1822 of persons to form an Establishment at Waltham Abbey to regenerate 2,000 barrels of gunpowder as well as to make 100 or 200 barrels of gunpowder annually, indicated that Hugh Jones, Master Mixer of Composition, was to be retained (Supply 5/232). John Johnson, the Master Saltpetre Refiner, was killed by lightning on the 27th June 1823, and Hugh Jones was appointed in his place on the 30th September, so Jones was then the Master Saltpetre Refiner as well as being the Master Mixer of Composition (WO54/546) In October 1823 his total pay for the year, including an allowance of £23.18.0d to train an Apprentice, amounted to £142.1.7d (WO54/546).

William Newton, the Master Worker, died in February 1825 and Hugh was appointed in his place on the 23rd of that month, relinquishing the two previous posts he had held (Winters, *op. cit.* p.92). He then earned a   basic salary of £130.0.0d per annum (WO54/550) and did not move to Newton's House on Horse Mill Island, but remained in Powder Mill Lane. Newton's house, always referred to as the Master Worker's House, was soon divided into two dwellings.

 Henry Wright, relating his memories to William Winters, recalled that on one occasion, Jones, who resided in Powder Mill Lane, was superintending proving the powder and the mortar placed near the barge house and bridge when a "great mistake was made by putting in a double charge of powder, sending the ball over the left lodge at the entrance crossing the lane and river, and some distance into the marsh" (Winters, *op. cit* p.148). With regular annual increments Jones was earning £220.0.0d per year by October 1834 (WO54/593). In the same year he was paid £1.19.6d for instructing Frederick Wright, an Apprentice to the Rex Officers (Winters, *op. cit.* p.103). Hugh Jones retired soon after this, since his name did not appear further in the records seen. The 1841 Census recorded a Hugh Jones of a similar age, together with Judith Hogg, Housekeeper, living in Sewardstone Street. Neither was born in the County.

John Jones started an Apprenticeship as a Millwright at the Mills on the 3rd March 1796, and was still serving his apprenticeship in May 1801. He was being paid 1/10d per day, and at that date was a bachelor (Supply 5/221). He also served as a Private in the Volunteer Company (Supply 5/219).

Samuel Jones was born in 1775, joining the Ordnance Board at Waltham Abbey Powder Mills as a 14-year-old Apprentice Millwright on the 16th July 1789 at 1/-d per day (Supply 5/213). After serving his seven-year Apprenticeship he was taken on the Establishment on the 1st March 1796. He signed the Petition on Pay and Conditions at the Mills presented to the Board on the 2nd February 1800 with a firm hand (Supply 5/220) and the Return on the Marital Status of the Employees the following year recorded that he was single (Supply 5/221). He was then paid 3/-d per day.

On the 16th June 1801 Samuel, with others, was repairing the Corning House when it caught fire following an explosion. The fire was caused "from a blow of a copper hammer on a pit wheel" (Winters, *op.cit.* p.59). The Storekeeper sent a letter dated the 23rd June to the Board, listing the names of the men who had suffered terrible burns, seeking permission to support the casualties. Samuel, employed as a Millwright in the Engineers' Department, was one of the men on the list. The letter went on to state, "we beg to represent the situation of the poor men who were burnt when the Corning House took fire on the 16th instant when under repair." It continued, "these men are burnt in a dreadful manner. Their pain is very great..." and "Our surgeon has represented the necessity of the men most burnt having immediate assistance in wine, as a considerable suppuration is come on their constitutions. They cannot support it without wine, and we have directed wine to be immediately provided to them, we request your permission for our continuing to support these poor men with such wine or other proper support as their surgeon may think their respective situations require" (Supply 5/195). In further correspondence with the Board on the 29th July 1801, Samuel requested that he be reimbursed 5/-d for a hat lost in the fire (Supply 5/221). Samuel was paid 17/6d for work carried out by the Engineers' Department within the Manufactory between the 15th and 21st July 1809 (Supply 5/228).

John Judd was working as a Puntman in February 1814, earning 2/8d per day and allowed to watch in turn (Supply 5/230).

K

James Keens was working as a Corning House Man in August 1812 (Supply 5/229) as he was in February 1814 (Supply 5/230). During this period he was paid 3/3d per day and allowed to watch in turn for 1/6d per night.

John Keens (1) had been working in the Dusting House for a year in January 1806 earning 2/1d per day (Supply 5/224). He was employed as a Millman in June 1807 with pay of 2/3d per day, and an additional 3d per night when on duty (Supply 5/226). He was still a Millman in August 1808, with the same pay and allowance (Supply 5/227).

John Keens (2) was working as a Puntman in August 1808, earning 2/-d per day and allowed to watch in turn (Supply 5/227). **Thomas Keens** was working as a Millman in August 1812 (Supply 5/229) as he was in February 1814 (Supply 5/230). During this period he was paid 3/-d per day with an additional 6d per night when on duty.

Jacob Kegbread was born circa 1769, and started his employment wit the Board as a Labourer on the 23rd September 1815 at 2/8d per day. In February 1816 he was a 48 year-old bachelor living in Waltham Abbey (WO54/516).

Samuel Kennarley, born circa 1765, started his employment in the Engineers' Department as a casual Labourer on the 16th October 1815, earning 2/8d per day. In February 1815 he was a 50-year-old married man with 6 unmarried children living in Waltham Abbey (WO54/516).

Joseph Kent was working as a Sieve Puncher and Proof House Man in September 1810 earning 2/-d per day, in addition to which, he was allowed to watch in turn (Supply 5/228). In

August 1812, he was being paid 2/8d per day as a Puntman and was still allowed to watch (Supply 5/229) while in February 1814, he was a Corning House Man earning 3/3d per day with an additional 1/6d per night when it was his turn to watch (Supply 5/230).

William Kent (1) was working as a casual Labourer in the Engineers' Department in September 1812, earning 2/8d per day for a six-day-week (WO54/512).

William Kent (2) was born circa 1806, and in October 1825 he had been employed as a Labourer on a temporary basis for 4 months at 2/2d per day, but was due to be discharged at the end of that month (WO54/550). He was a single man, possibly the son of William Kent (1).

George Kestfield started his employment as a Cylinderman in Sussex on the 1st October 1796, and also served as a Private in the Volunteer Company (Supply 5/219).

John Kimble was born circa 1768 and started work at the Powder Mills on the 10th May 1791 as a Labourer refining Saltpetre, earning 1/6d per day (Supply 5/216). The Refining House was to be his work place for the next 10 years, and a Return on the Marital Status of the Employees in May 1801 stated that he ws a married man with one child (Supply 5/221). Robert Coleman, the Clerk of the Cheque, recorded in his Minute Book on the 23rd October 1801 that 24 men were required to work at Faversham or be discharged, and Kimble was one of those who agreed to go (Winters, *op.cit.p.*60). On the 28th April 1809, Kimble wrote to the Storekeeper at Waltham Abbey applying for relocation from Faversham to Waltham Abbey, because it would be better for his health, and his transfer was confirmed (Supply 5/199). Shortly after he was replaced at

Faversham by Stephen King, a Saltpetre Refiner from the Mills at Waltham Abbey (Supply 5/199).

John Kimble was working as a Saltpetre Refiner in September 1810, and was paid 2/-d per day as well as being allowed to watch in turn (Supply 5/228). A List of Employees dated the 29th August 1812 confirmed that Mr. Kimble was still a Saltpetre Refiner who at that date earned 2/8d per day, and, in addition, when not working extra was allowed to watch in turn (Supply 5/229). The same pay and terms applied in February 1814 (Supply 5/230). A Return of Employees dated the 25th June 1818 recorded that Kimble was still refining Saltpetre but that his wage was only 2/4d per day, in addition to which, he was still allowed to watch in turn for 1/-d per night (Supply 5/231). At that date he was a 50-year-old married man, then with 3 children, living in Waltham Abbey. When the Establishment was reduced in numbers in September 1818, John Kimble was one of those who were discharged (Supply 5/231).

Stephen King was working as a Saltpetre Refiner in January 1806 earning 2/-d per day, and at that date, he had twelve months' service (Supply 5/224). He was still refining Saltpetre in August 1808 with the same rate of pay, and, "when not working extra allowed to watch in turn" (Supply 5/227). A letter dated the 28th April 1809 showed that he was relocated to Faversham to replace John Kimble in the Refining House there, Kimble returning to Waltham Abbey (Supply 5/199).

William King was listed as the Master of the barge *Hunter* working out of Waltham Abbey Mills in 1802 (Winters *op. cit.* p.45).

Henry Kingshott was born circa 1742 (Supply 5/230) and started work as a Labourer at the Mills on the 3rd July 1796 earning 1/6d per day. He served as a Private in the Volunteer

Company, and at some stage transferred to West Sussex as a Cylinderman (Supply 5/219). A Return on the Marital Status of the Employees dated the 8th May 1801 recorded that he was a married man without children (Supply 5/221). The cylinders were under repair in November 1801, and Kingshott was stacking timber in the yards and levelling and preparing the ground where the cylinders were to be re-sited (Supply 5/221). He continued to work as a Cylinderman earning 2/-d per day in January 1806 (Supply 5/224) rising to 2/8d by August 1812 (Supply 5/229).

On the 2nd March 1816 it was recommended to the Board that Henry Kingshott, then aged 73 and with 20 years' service, should receive a daily superannuation of 2/8d per day (Supply 5/230). The notes attached to the recommendation commented that Henry Kingshott, "both from his age and the effects of his employ, is no longer capable of exerting himself." A letter from the Board dated the 16th April 1816, however, awarded Mr. Kingshott a pension of only 2/-d for 6 days in the week, commencing on the 1st April 1816 (Supply 5/200). A supplement to the Return dated the 8th November 1818 listing the names of persons who had been superannuated included "Henry Kingshott, Cylinderman" who received a pension of 12/-d per week which commenced on the 1st April 1816 (Supply 5/231).

John Kipping was a Labourer set to work by Daniel Cornish in October 1787 at 9/-d per week. He was probably renovating the Mills following their purchase by the government from Mr. Walton (Winters, *op.cit.* p.28). It appears that he was not retained.

William Kirby started work at the Mills as a Labourer on the 21st April 1794. In August of that year he was working in the punts earning 1/6d per day (Supply 5/216) and in December he was working in the Corning House, as he was in July 1795 (Supply 5/217). By September 1795, he was a Labourer in the Refining

House (Supply 5/219) as he was when he signed the Petition on Pay and Conditions at the Mills presented to the Board on the 2nd February 1800. This document showed that he was illiterate (Supply 5/220). The Return showing the Marital Status of the Employees in May 1801 recorded that he was a married man with one child (Supply 5/221).

John Knight started his employment in the Engineers' Department as a casual Labourer on the 29th March 1806 (WO54/516). He was, as a common Labourer, paid 17/-d for work carried out by the Engineers' Department in the Manufactory between the 15th and 21st July 1809 (Supply 5/228). In February 1816 he was still employed as an occasional Labourer earning 2/8d per day, at which time, he was a 59-year-old married man with 3 children, one unmarried and two married, who lived in Waltham Abbey (WO54/516). He continued to work "occasionally as required" with the Engineers' Department until at least May 1819, when his daily pay was 2/4d (WO54/528).

Henry Knowler, the brother of Samuel Knowler Snr. (WASC 2180, p.111) started work at the Mills as a Labourer on the 5th April 1791 (Supply 5/215). Initially, he was working "in the punts and setting and drawing stoves" for which he was paid 1/6d per day. In May 1791 he was "dusting and glazing powder," and between January 1792 and September 1793, he worked in the Corning House until he was replaced by William Speller (Supply 5/216). On the 29th July 1793, Robert Coleman, the Clerk of the Cheque, recorded in his Minute Book that Henry Knowler (and others) was chequered (fined) one day's pay for "having gone across the Hoppit contrary to orders" (Winters, *op. cit.* p.39). January 1794 saw Henry working as a Labourer in the Refining House and he continued to do so until at least October 1801, during which time he was paid 1/6d per day (Supply 5/216 – 5/221). He enlisted as a Private in the Volunteer Company on the 7th May 1794 (Supply 5/219) and the Petition on Pay and

Conditions at the Mills presented to the Board in February 1800 showed that he was literate (Supply 5/220). The Return on the Marital Status of the Employees recorded that in May 1801 he was a married man with one child (Supply 5/221).

Robert Coleman recorded in his Minute Book on the 23rd October 1801 that 24 men were required to work at Faversham or be discharged. Henry, together with his brother, Samuel, agreed to go (Winters, *op.cit*.p.60). However, the Faversham records did not record their names; additionally, Samuel's records did not show a break in his service with the Ordnance, so it can it can only be assumed that Henry either didn't go to Faversham and was discharged, or that he left of his own accord, either from Waltham or Faversham. On the 16th February 1814, a Henry Knowler was recorded as a Labourer "setting and drawing stoves and in the willow plantations," earning 2/8d per day and allowed to watch in turn (Supply 5/230). It is possible that this was one and the same man.

John Knowler started work as a Labourer in the Corning House on the 15th March 1798. He was also a Private in the Volunteer Company (Supply 5/219).

Samuel Knowler, Snr. was born circa 1764 (Supply 5/212) and trained as a Baker (Supply 5/230) before being engaged as a Labourer at Faversham on the 1st February 1787 (Supply 5/212). He was transferred to Waltham Abbey on the 1st February 1789 (Supply 5/113) and in April 1789 he was, "cutting and planting willow trees, cutting of canal at the new Corning House, removing earth to the Store, unloading barge of coals and charring wood" for which he was paid 1/6d per day (Supply 5/213). In September of that year he was "dusting and glazing powder," and was then 25 years' old (Supply 5/214). Samuel appeared to frequently move around the different sections of the Manufactory; in March 1790 he was in the Corning House

(Supply 5/214) in the Dusting House by September 1790 and he returned to the Corning House at the end of 1790, where he remained until September 1793 (Supply 5/216). In September 1793 he was transferred to the Refining House, replacing Benjamin Wall, who had been sacked (Supply 5/217). On the 7th May 1794 he joined the Volunteer Company as a Private (Supply 5/219). In June 1795, he was working as a Labourer, "setting and drawing stoves etc." (Supply 5/217) while a month later, he was a Millman at 2/-d per day with an extra 3d when on night duty (Supply 5/219).

By September 1798 he had returned to the Refining House as a Labourer (Supply 5/219) and this was to be his work place until he retired in 1821. The Petition on Pay and Conditions at the Mills submitted to the Board in February 1800 showed that he was literate (Supply 5/220) while the Return on the Marital Status of the Employees dated May 1801 noted that he was a married man with 3 children (Supply 5/221). Robert Coleman, the Clerk of the Cheque, recorded in his Minute Book on the 23rd October 1801 that 24 men were required to work at Faversham or be discharged. Samuel Knowler, together with his brother Henry, was one who agreed to go (Winters, *op.cit*.p.60). However, his name was not recorded at Faversham and there was no break in his service record, so it has to be assumed that either his stay there was brief, or that he never left Waltham Abbey. In 1804 his pay was 2/-d per day, and he was allowed to watch in turn – on average every 5th night – for which he received 1/-d (Supply 5/222). The Parish Poor Rates for 1805 recorded that he was living in High Bridge Street adjacent to the Cock Inn, being Plot No. 2158 on the 1825 Parish Map (WASC 2180, p.111).

At the end of the Napoleonic War, Samuel, in common with the rest of the workforce, suffered a reduction in his pay, and in August 1818 it was 5/10 per day as the Assistant Master Refiner. It was also recorded that he and his wife (Sarah) then had 6 children (Supply 5/232 & WO54/524). They were all baptised at Waltham Abbey as follows: - Edward Samuel (9th July 1794) Catherine Mary (7th September 1796) Samuel John Jones (17th May 1799) Mary Jones (25th May 1801) Thomas William (9th March 1805) and Frances Elizabeth (5th December 1810). When the strength of the Establishment was reduced in September 1818, Samuel retained his position but with his daily rate reduced to 5/4d (Supply 5/232). A Schedule of Properties owned by the Board at the end of December 1821 (Supply 5/232) recorded that Samuel was still living in the house and its garden which were located second from the northern end of the terrace of houses and cottages in Powder Mill Lane, forming part of Plot No. 64 on the Town Map in Appendix 1.

Empson Middleton, the Storekeeper at Waltham Abbey, wrote to the Board of Ordnance on the 15th September 1821 requesting that Samuel Knowler, Assistant Master Refiner of Saltpetre, be granted a pension. The Storekeeper went on to say that during his 32 years' service at the Gunpowder Mills, Knowler had received "severe concussion on the chest by the falling of a quantity of Saltpetre bags upon him, which occasions, at times, severe indispositions if he takes cold." The Board agreed in their letter of the 16th November that he should receive a superannuated sum of £20.17.4d per annum, and allowed him to continue to live in his cottage, paying a small rent of £1.0.0d annually (Supply 5/232). Samuel continued to receive his pension and live in Powder Mill Lane, but after Sarah died in June 1833, Samuel went to live with his son, Samuel Jnr., in the Refinery House, possibly in September 1834 when he was appointed the Master Refiner. His cottage in Powder Mill Lane was then let to Robert Simes, Millwright (Supply 5/237). The 1841 Census showed that Samuel, Snr. was still living with his son in High Bridge Street. Samuel died in 1843 at the age of 73 years.

Samuel Knowler Junior, the second son of Samuel Knowler Snr., was baptised at Waltham Abbey on the 17th May 1799. He was Apprenticed to the Master Refiner of Saltpetre, John Johnson, on the 3rd June 1811 (WO54/550) being paid 6/-d per week, with his Master receiving the same money for teaching him the trade (Supply 5/230). Towards the end of his seven-year Apprenticeship Samuel was paid 7/-d per day (Supply 5/231). A letter from the Board dated the 12th June 1818 confirmed that he had completed his Apprenticeship and that he was entered as a Saltpetre Refiner earning 2/4d per day (Supply 5/202). The letter also stated that approval was given by the Board for the Master Refiner to take on John Simpson, Jnr. as an Apprentice in place of Samuel Knowler.

Apart from a short period, circa May 1819, when he was described as a Brimstone Refiner (Supply 5/231) Samuel was associated with the Saltpetre Refinery for the remainder of his working days. His pay rose from 2/-d per day in 1818 to 2/4d by September 1820, with an additional 1/6d when he was allowed to watch in turn at that time (Supply 5/232). He retained his employment when the Establishment was reduced in numbers in 1818, and again in 1822. In February 1822 his yearly basic pay was £36.10.4d, which, with his night duties, equated to £41.14.4d per annum (Supply 5/232) although this had been reduced to £39.0.0d by October 1823 (WO54/546).

He and his wife, Elizabeth, had one child (WO54/550) a daughter, Mary Anne, who was baptised at Waltham Abbey on the 25th September 1825. On the 14th October 1828, Samuel was paid 16/-d for travelling from Waltham Abbey to Woolwich "for the purpose of instruction as to the mode of proof, and practical use of a new gun Epreuvette." The amount covered 48 miles at 4d per mile (Winters, *op. cit.* p.99). A Return of Employees dated the 1st October 1829 confirmed that his pay was unchanged and that he now had a second child (WO54/566) John Thomas, who was baptised at Waltham Abbey on the 16th May 1830.

Samuel was promoted to the position of Master Refiner on the 5th September 1834 following the retirement of John Braddock. He was then entitled to a house, and his annual pay, including allowances, amounted to £118.13.7d (WO/54/623). Samuel had moved into the house within the confines of the Saltpetre Refinery in High Bridge Street by December 1834 (Supply 5/237) which is shown as Plot No, 39 on the Town Map in Appendix 1, and his father moved there also.

The 1841 Census confirmed that Samuel and his wife, Elizabeth, their children, Mary and John, his father, and a Donald Blackmore, aged 15, an Apprentice at the Gunpowder Mills, all lived in the house.

In an article 'How Explosives are Made' by William G. Fitzgerald, whilst referring to a visit to the Gunpowder Mills and the Saltpetre Refinery in particular (date of visit unknown) Fitzgerald related that Mr. Knowler was known as the father of the factory "from the fact of his forty-three years' service (*The Strand Magazine*, Vol.IX - January to June, 1895). More information on the Knowler family after 1841 can be found in WASC 2180, pp.111-116.

L

Henry Lagdon (Lagden) was born circa 1787 and employed by the Ordnance Board as a Labourer on the 7th October 1805, but where is unknown (Supply 5/232). However, in August 1812, he was working as a Brimstone Refiner at Waltham Abbey earning 3/-d per day, and, in addition, he was allowed to watch in turn, for which he received 1/6d per night (Supply 5/229). He continued to refine Saltpetre, but by June 1818, his pay and allowances had been reduced to 2/8d and 1/-d respectively. He was then a married man with 3 children, living in Waltham Abbey (Supply 5/231 and WO54/524). When the Establishment was reduced in numbers in September 1818, Henry retained his position as a Brimstone Refiner, and this was confirmed by Orders of the Board dated the 4th September 1818 and the 4th October 1819. In January 1822, he was paid 2/4d per day and allowed 2/-d per night when on watch, and he was then living in Enfield (Supply 5/232). In the spring of 1822, the Ordnance Board decided to lower production and regeneration of gunpowder, and the Establishment at Waltham Abbey was consequently to be reduced. Accordingly, Empson Middleton and James Wright drew up lists of people to be dismissed (Supply 5/232) one of whom was Henry Lagdon. The men were subsequently made redundant on the 1st June, and several Petitions were submitted by them asking for financial assistance. Many were long-service employees in middle age, and they pointed out that they had little hope of finding employment after the corn harvest had been gathered. The Storekeeper was sympathetic and forwarded the petitions to the Board for their consideration. Henry Lagdon, signing with a cross, was one of the Petitioners, and he was awarded two weeks' pay to ease his financial burden (Supply 5/232).

John Lagdon joined the Ordnance Board at Waltham Abbey in June 1805 as a Labourer, "drawing and setting stoves etc.," at 2/-

d per day (Supply 5/224). In June 1807, the description of his work was, "Labourer in various parts of the Manufactory and setting & drawing stoves, and in the willow plantations, etc." (Supply 5/226). John was undertaking similar work as a Labourer in August 1808, but was then paid 2/-d per day and still allowed to watch (Supply 5/227). In September 1810, he was working as a Brimstone Refiner and paid 2/3d per day, as well as 1/6d per night when on watch (Supply 5/228).

John Lake was working as a Labourer when he signed the Petition on Pay and Conditions at the Mills in February 1800 (Supply 5/220). The new Corning Mill blew up on the 18th April 1801 and 9 men in the building, including John Lake, were killed, together with 4 horses (Supply 5/220). A Report on the circumstances of the victims stated in Lake's case, "the nearest relation is a brother, but we do not think him entitled to claim." (Supply 5/202).

George Lamb was working as a Labourer earning 1/6d per day in February 1793 (Supply 5/216). Robert Coleman, Clerk of the Cheque, recorded in his Minute Book that on the 12th August 1793, "G Lamb went away without leave. Chequered (fined) and ordered him off watch. N.B. He never came again to work till 19th, when agreed to discharge him" (Winters, *op. cit.* p.40). Corning Mills were often named after their operative, and on the 11th February 1793, *Lambs Mill* blew up. It may possibly be that George Lamb had a relative who was a Millman for Mr. Walton (Winters, *op. cit.* p.35).

James Lamb was working as a Saltpetre Refiner in January 1806, and at that time had 1 year's service (Supply 5/224). The Saltpetre Refinery continued to be his workplace, and "when not working extra allowed to watch in turn." His pay in August 1808 was 2/-d per day (Supply 5/227) and rose to 2/8d by August 1812 (Supply 5/229) as it was in February 1814 (Supply 5/230). James would appear to have suffered some sort of injury and petitioned the Board for assistance, because a letter from the Board to the Storekeeper dated the 18th March 1818 stated, "having laid before the Board your letter dated yesterday reporting upon the Petition of James Lamb, late a Salt Petre Refiner, soliciting some relief in consideration of his service and injury he received in the Department under your superintendence, I am directed to desire the Storekeeper will pay James Lamb the sum of two guineas as a donation agreeably for your recommendation" (Supply 5/202).

Anthony Lambert was an Apprentice Cooper at Waltham Abbey in 1821, but discharged himself (Supply 5/204).

Henry Lambert was employed as a Cooper between September and October 1825; he was paid 4/6d per day (£54.12.0d per annum) for making cement casks for Harwich, presumably for gunpowder. He was then a 24-year-old single man (Supply 5/205 & WO54/550).

Robert Lammon was working as a casual Labourer in the Engineers' Department in September 1812, earning 2/8d per day for a six-day week (WO54/512).

William Larby worked as a Millman in August 1812 and continued to do so until at least February 1814. During this period he was paid 3/-d per day, in addition to which, he was allowed 6d per night when on duty (Supply 5/229 and Supply 5/230). In September 1814, he left the Storekeeper's employment and joined the Engineers' Department as a casual Labourer. By February 1816 he was earning 2/8d per day, and at that date, he was a 25-year-old married man with 1 child living in Waltham Abbey (WO54/516).

John Latch started his employment as a casual Labourer in the Engineers' Department on the 16th February 1816, and in

February 1817 he was being paid 2/4d per day. He was then a 40-year-old married man with 3 children, living in Waltham Abbey (WO54/520).

Robert Lowman was working as a Puntman in August 1812 at 2/8d per day, as well as being allowed to watch in turn (Supply 5/229). By February 1814, he was a Corning House Man earning 3/3d per day, and was still allowed to watch in turn, for which he received 1/6d per night (Supply 5/230).

Thomas Lawrence was an extra Bargeman on 3 barges transporting gunpowder to Picket's Field and Magazines. In May 1804, he was paid £2.11.6d per week (Supply 5/222).

James Lee was born circa 1780, and was first employed as an occasional Labourer in the Engineers' Department on the 9th September 1815, earning 2/8d per day. In February 1816, he was a 35-year-old bachelor living in Waltham Abbey (WO54/516).

Michael Lee was working as an occasional Labourer in the Engineers' Department during September 1812, earning 2/8d per day for a six-day week (WO54/512). He was in the same employment in February 1816 at the same rate of pay, and at the time, was a 42-year-old married man with 3 children who lived in Waltham Abbey (WO54/516).

Edward Leopold had 10 years' service with the Ordnance Board in January 1806, when he was recorded as working as a Cylinder Man at Fisher Street in West Sussex, although where his previous employment was is unknown (Supply 5/224). In January 1806 he was paid 2/-d per day, which rose to 2/8d by August 1812 (Supply 5/229). In common with the majority of the employees, his wage was reduced at the end of the Napoleonic wars and in June 1818, his daily rate was 2/4d. He was a married man of 46 with 2 children, and still lived at Fisher Street ((Supply 5/231). In

September 1818, the Storekeeper wrote to the Board stating "We respectfully beg leave to add the names and stations of those persons it will be necessary to discharge in consequence of this arrangement," i.e., a reduction in the Establishment due to a downturn in work, and the list included Edward Leopold (Supply 5/231).

Joseph Leserf filled one of the 7 vacancies available at the Mills in August 1783 and was employed as a Labourer in the Corning House, where he earned 1/6d per day (Winters, *op. cit.* p.40). He enlisted as a Private in the Volunteer Company on the 7th May 1794 (Supply 5/219) and was still working in the Corning house the following August (Supply 5/216). In December 1794, John was described as "separating gunpowder" (Supply 5/217) but by the following July he had returned to the Corning House (Supply 5/217).

Richard Lewis was born circa 1784 and started his employment as a casual Labourer in the Engineers' Department on the 18th January 1816, earning 2/4d per day. At that date he was a married man, had 6 unmarried children, and lived in Waltham Abbey (WO54/520). He continued to work within the Engineers' Department "occasionally as required" until at least April 1821, and during this period, his pay remained unchanged. He still lived in Waltham Abbey, but by then had 7children (WO54/536).

Samuel Lincoln was born circa 1746 and trained as a Butcher. He joined the Engineers' Department as a Labourer on the 29th March 1806 (WO54/516) and as a common Labourer, was paid 17/-d for work carried out within the Manufactory by the Engineers' Department between the 15th and 21st July 1809 (Supply 5/228). In September 1812, he was paid 2/8d per day for a six-day week (WO54/512). A Return dated February 1816 recorded that he was a 62-year-old widower living in Waltham Abbey, and that he had 4 married children and 1 unmarried child

(WO54/516). The last record relating to Samuel is dated February 1817, when his pay at that date had been reduced to 2/4d per day (WO54/520).

George Lindsay was born circa 1768 (Supply 5/214) and in March 1789, he was a Labourer grinding Saltpetre and Charcoal at 1/6d per day (Supply 5/212). The following month George was "cutting and planting willow trees, cutting of canal at the new Corning House, removing earth to the Store, unloading barge of coals & charring wood" (Supply 5/213). By August 1789 he was "marking powder barrels" (Supply 5/215) a task he continued to doing until December 1791 (Supply 5/215). Between January and March 1792 he was working "in the punts, and likewise drawing and setting stoves, loading and shipping gunpowder and stores etc" (Supply 5/215).

Thomas Littler was born on the 19th February 1759 at Waltham Abbey, being one of Edmund and Elizabeth Littler's 9 sons. Thomas married Sarah Preston on the 20th July 1786, and they had 8 daughters, one of whom died in infancy (WASC 2180, p.124). Thomas served with the Royal Navy at Dover before joining the Royal Ordnance on the 8th June 1805, and was posted to Waltham Abbey on the same day as an extra (assistant) Clerk with a salary of £70.0.0d per annum (Supply 5/226). On the 1st August 1807, he was transferred to the Ordnance at Dover as the First Clerk (Supply 5/232) before returning to Waltham Abbey on the 26th February 1812 to occupy the same position there, replacing James Wright. His salary was then £90.0.0d per annum, with a £20.16.0d lodging allowance and a further £12.10.0d for coal and candles (Supply 5/229). Thomas was granted rent-free accommodation by an Order of the Board dated the 13th March 1812 in a house owned by them, which was Tenement No. 4 on a List of Properties dated the 16th February 1822 (Supply 5/232). Whether Thomas and his family moved there straight away is debatable, since a Return of Properties prepared by the Royal

Engineers' Office on the 20th December 1834, indicated that Littler occupied this house (then listed as Tenement No. 70) on the 11th April 1815. It was described as "House and garden at Romeland – West Street, area 0 acres-2 roods-24 perches" (Supply 5/237), and has been identified as located on the north east corner of Romeland, being Plot No. 70 on the Town Map in Appendix 1. The house was purchased by the Board in June 1809, being part of the Corn Mills, and was designated as the First Clerk's dwelling. It was to be Littler's home for the remainder of his life.

Several months after their return to Waltham Abbey, his wife, Sarah, died, leaving Thomas to raise 7 daughters, viz., Sarah (born 1788) Elizabeth (born 1792) Sophia (born 1794) Thirza (born 1798) Charlotte (born 1801) Harriet, and Mary. Another child, also Elizabeth, had died in infancy (WASC 2180, p.125). He continued to be employed as the First Clerk with his pay increasing over the years, and in 1818 his annual salary, including allowances, was £137.10.0d (Supply 5/231). In 1822 it was £152.10.0d (Supply 5/232) and by 1828 he was receiving £177.0.0d (WO54/562). His salary remained at this level until his death in 1839. In June 1827, Littler wrote to the Board requesting payment of two guineas for auctioning timber at the Mills (Winters, *op. cit.* p.97). Three of his daughters married, one becoming a widow at an early age (WASC 2180, p.125) and the four spinsters had left Waltham Abbey by the time the 1841 Census was taken. Thomas died on the 17th July 1839, and was buried at Waltham Abbey. A couple of months previously he had given his age as 76 years, but in reality he was nearer 81 (WO54/623). There is much more to his life; he invented a new and more efficient rifle in 1808, and further reading in the *Waltham Abbey Gunpowder People* by P. J. Huggins is recommended.

Charles Livermore was taken on in June 1807 as "a Labourer in various parts of the Manufactory drawing & setting stoves, loading and unloading barges etc." for which he was paid 2/-d per day (Supply 5/224).

James Livermore (1) was working as a Millman earning 2/3d per day in January 1806, and had then been employed by the Ordnance Board for one year (Supply 5/224). He was paid the same money in June 1807, and was allowed 3d per night when on duty (Supply 5/226). Livermore continued to be employed as a Millman, but in September 1810, although on the same daily rate of pay, his allowance for night work had been increased to 6d per shift (Supply 5/228).

James Livermore (2) was employed as a Labourer in the autumn of 1805 "drawing and setting stoves etc." at 2/-d per day (Supply 5/224). In August 1808 he was employed as one of the "Respective Officer's Labourers," i.e., he worked as a Labourer for one of the senior staff. He still earned 2/-d per day, but was then allowed to watch in turn (Supply 5/227). By September 1810, James was a Millman earning 2/3d per day, and allowed 6d per night when on duty (Supply 5/228).

William Livsey was born in Lancashire in 1790, and trained as a Weaver before joining the Royal Regiment of Artillery, Rochdale, as a Gunner on the 18th June 1808, his eighteenth birthday. During his military career he saw service in the Peninsular War for 3 years and nine months, and a further 6 years and 3 months in Canada. He was promoted to the rank of Corporal on the 1st June 1813, that of Sergeant on the 1st June 1825 and, finally, as a Sergeant-Major on the 1st April 1830.

On the 11th September 1839, Livsey appeared before a Medical Board at Woolwich where he was diagnosed with chronic Rheumatism and judged unfit for military service, and, therefore, should be discharged. His military service had spanned 31 years and ended on the 8th October 1839 (Soldiers' Documents WO97/1243).

He took the position of Warder at Waltham Abbey in 1840 when John Smith (1) and as retired regular soldier, was also acting Sergeant Major to the Cadet Company (Supply 5/238). The 1841 Census recorded that he and his wife, Isobella, and their 5 children were then living in the Gatehouse – John Smith's old house – being Plot No. 91 on the Town Map in Appendix 1.

William Lock was first employed by the Board as an occasional Labourer in the Engineers' Department on the 13th May 1815, earning 2/4d per day. In February 1816, he was a 43-year-old married man with 4 children, who lived in Enfield (WO54/516).

John Lockyer, Snr., the son of John and Mary Lockyer, was baptised at Faversham on the 25th April 1769 (*FGPR*, p.57) and started work as a Labourer at the Gunpowder Mills, Faversham, on the 5th May 1792, training to be a Saltpetre Refiner (Supply 5/232). He and his wife, Elizabeth, had a son, John Richard, baptised at Faversham Church on the 6th August 1797 (*FGPR*, p.57). John transferred to Waltham Abbey as the Foreman Brimstone Refiner between April 1805 and January 1806, and at Waltham he was paid 4/-d per day (Supply 5/224). He petitioned the Board in January 1807, pointing out that he came to Waltham Abbey from Faversham, and, since he had taken over refining following Mr. Townsend's death, production costs using the methods employed at Faversham had fallen, so he asked the Board for financial recognition. The Board agreed to increase his pay to 5/-d per day (Supply 5/198). John petitioned the Board again on the 5th May 1808, requesting that he be allowed an Apprentice, the same as the Master Brimstone Refiner at Faversham. The Board agreed to his proposition on the 23rd May (Supply 5/198) with the conditions and rates of pay for both the

Master and their Apprentices clearly laid out in a directive dated the 5th August 1808 (Supply 5/198). A Return dated the 23rd August 1808 recorded that John Lockyer was still paid 5/-d per day, with an allowance of £20.0.0d per annum for house rent, coal and candles. He also received an allowance of 6/-d per week to train an Apprentice, who so happened to be his son, John, Jnr. (Supply 5/227).

Lockyer's pay had been increased to 6/4d per day by August 1812 (Supply 5/229) and remained the same in February 1814 (Supply 5/230). A letter from Lockyer to the Storekeeper dated the 6th September 1814, stated that his son and Apprentice, John Lockyer, Jnr., had "served his legal time of his Apprenticeship, and humbly solicited The Honourable Board to grant me another Apprentice." Messrs. Mathews, Breeze and Wright confirmed in a letter that the facts were as stated, and "requested the Board direct the Assistant to the Ordnance Solicitor to prepare the usual kind of Indentures for Apprenticing a Thomas Martin Junior, the son of Thomas Martin Senior, to be Mr. Lockyer's new Apprentice." Master Thomas Martin Jnr. was described as "a stout lad about thirteen years' old" (Supply 5/230) who started his Apprenticeship on the 8th April 1815 (Supply 5/232). By June 1818 following the end of the Napoleonic wars, John's daily pay had been reduced to 5/10d (Supply 5/231) and the same document recorded that he and his wife, Elizabeth, still had one child, as well as confirming that he lived in Waltham Abbey.

When the production and regeneration of gunpowder was reduced and the Establishment trimmed to suit a lesser output John was retained, with his position as the Master Brimstone Refiner confirmed on the 4th September 1818 (Supply 5/232). His pay was still 5/10d per day (£91.5.10d per annum) and remained so until his death in 1829. He was still allowed to train an Apprentice which added another £21.13.5d to his annual pay, but after Thomas Martin had "served his time" on the 22nd May 1822, this allowance ceased.

A statement dated the 16th February 1822 of "monies to which the public were entitled to receive credit between the 1st January 1821 and the 31st December 1821 showing the amounts received by the Storekeeper", recorded that John Lockyer was residing in a house purchased by the Board – Tenement No. 37 – at a rental of £5.4.0d per annum. This document further stated that John Lockyer had occupied the premises prior to their purchase by the Board, and that "sanction will be asked for their future residing in them" which was granted by the Board on the 4th May 1821 (Supply 5/232). The property, together with its small garden, has been identified as being one of a terrace in Powder Mill Lane, forming part of Plot No. 63 on the Town Map in Appendix 1.

John continued as the Master Brimstone Refiner and in March 1822, when the Establishment was reformed to regenerate some 2000 barrels of gunpowder and was producing only 200 barrels of new powder annually, his pay remained unchanged (Supply 5/232). John died at the age of 59 on the 10th January 1829, (Winters, *op. cit.* p.101) and was replaced as the Master Brimstone Refiner by James O'Brien (WO54/566).

John Richard Lockyer, the son and only child of John and Mary Lockyer, was baptised at Faversham on the 6th August 1797, and came to Waltham Abbey circa 1805 when his father was appointed as the Foreman Brimstone Refiner there (*FGPR,* p.57). At nearly 11 years of age on the 23rd May 1808, John Richard started a seven-year Apprenticeship as a Brimstone Refiner under the tuition of his father; John, the Master, was paid 6/-d per week to teach his son the trade, with John Richard receiving the same amount Supply 5/227). The corresponding allowances and rates of pay in August 1812 were 6/6d and 6/2d respectively (Supply 5/229) increasing to 8/-d and 6/8d respectively by February 1814

(Supply 5/230). A letter from the Storekeeper to the Board dated the 6th September 1814, stated that John Lockyer Junior had "served his legal time of his Apprenticeship" (Supply 5/230) and was subsequently paid 2/8d per day and allowed to watch in turn, for which he received 1/-d per night (WO54/524 and Supply 5/231). He was retained as a Brimstone Refiner in September 1818 when the Establishment was decreased in numbers, but with his daily wage reduced to 2/6d per day. The last entries found for John Richard are dated the 19th May 1819; he was still a Brimstone Refiner who was paid 2/4d per day and still allowed to watch, and was a single man, aged 22, living in Waltham Abbey (Supply 5/231).

When writing his book *Centenary Memorial of The Royal Gunpowder Factory at Waltham Abbey* in 1887, William Winters noted on page 101 that John Lockyer, Master Refiner of Saltpetre, John Richard's father, died on the 10th January 1829. Winters speculated on the name and wrote, "possibly Mr Lockyer (viz. John Richard), whose 'Sulphur hair restorer' is now so celebrated, is the descendant of John Lockyer, the old brimstone refiner of Waltham Abbey."

Jacob Lofts was born circa 1778, and in February 1814, was working as a Labourer "drawing and setting stoves and in the willow plantations" for which he was paid 2/8d per day. In addition, he was allowed to watch in turn, for which he received 1/-d per night (Supply 5/230). In June 1818, he was employed as a Hoop Bender, paid 3/6d per day and was still in receipt of his watch allowance (Supply 5/231). The same document recorded that he was a married man with 6 children living in Cheshunt. In September 1818, the Storekeeper wrote to the Board stating "We respectfully beg leave to add the names and stations of those persons it will be necessary to discharge in consequence of this arrangement" i.e., a reduction in the Establishment due to a downturn in work. The list included Jacob Lofts (Supply 5/231).

John Lording was born circa 1799, and joined the Engineers' Department as an Apprentice Millwright on the 13th July 1810 (WO54/587). Whether he completed his Apprenticeship or not is unknown, since a Return of Employees dated the 1st April 1833 recorded that at that date he earned 2/2d per day for 313 days in the year, which gave him an annual income of £33.18.2d, a Labourer's wage (WO54/587). At that date he was a married man with 4 children living in Waltham Abbey. A Return of Properties owned by the Board prepared by the Royal Engineers' Office on the 20th December 1834, recorded that William Bunce had died and that it was proposed to let his cottage to John Lording, Labourer (Supply 5/237). John was still working as a Labourer in the Engineers' Department in October 1839 earning the same money, but left soon afterwards for London where he commanded a higher wage (WO54/623). His cottage was then let to J. Davy, which locates it as being one of the tenements in the old Tanyard on the south side of High Bridge Street (WO44/133), No. 54 on the Town Map in Appendix 1.

George Lovell was employed as the general Superintendent at the Royal Small Arms Manufactory at Enfield, but lived in a house owned by the Board in High Bridge Street Waltham Abbey, which was set in an acre of land. The house had previously been occupied by William Breeze, whose position within the Gunpowder Manufactory had been abolished in 1821 (Supply 5/231 and WO44/133).

James Luck was born circa 1817, and in December 1838 was a bachelor who was employed as a general Labourer within the Manufactory earning £39.0.0d per annum, which included an allowance to watch in turn. (WO54/623). The 1841 Census recorded that James and his young wife, Eliza, were living in Sewardstone Street and that both were born in Essex. On the 13th April 1843, some 40 barrels of gunpowder exploded in the Corning House, together with another 20 in the Press House.

Seven men were killed and much damage done in the town. Among those killed was James. In a note dated June 2nd, "Elizabeth Luck was to receive a donation of £2.0.0d in her confinement, consequent of the explosion" (Winters, *op. cit.* p.106). A graphic description of the explosion and damage caused, etc., was given in the *London Illustrated News* dated Saturday, 22nd April 1843 (*WAAC*). Besides his widow, James left a baby son.

John Luck was working as a Saltpetre Refiner in August 1812 (Supply 5/229) and this was also the case in February 1814 (Supply 5/230). During this period he earned 2/8d per day, and when not working extra, was allowed to watch in turn.

John Lumath was employed as a Labourer within the Engineers' Department, earning 1/6d per day. He worked within the Manufactory between August and September 1790, and his wages were submitted to, and paid by, the Storekeeper, James Wright, by William Spry, Colonel commanding the Royal Engineers. John signed for his pay with a cross (WASC 1382).

M

James Madell started his employment as an occasional Labourer in the Engineers' Department on the 20th November 1815, and was paid 2/8d per day. He was then a 20-year-old bachelor living in Waltham Abbey (WO54/516).

John Madgwick started his employment in the summer of 1805, and in January 1806 he was working in the Dusting House earning 2/1d per day (Supply 5/221). In June 1807, he was refining Saltpetre with pay of 2/-d per day, and, when not working extra allowed to watch in turn Supply 5/226). By August 1808, he worked as a Cylinderman making charcoal at Fisher Street in West Sussex, and was in receipt of the same pay (Supply 5/227). James was still working in Sussex in September 1810 (Supply 5/228) but had returned to Waltham Abbey by August 1812, when he was working in the Saltpetre Refinery at 2/8d per day (Supply 5/229). However, by February 1814, it was recorded that he was a Cylinderman, although he earned the same 2/8d per day (Supply 5/230).

Jerimiah Mahony was born circa 1797. He started his employment as a Labourer in the Engineers' Department on the 18th May 1826 and was paid 2/2d per day, which gave him an annual income of £ 33.18.2d. He was then a 33-year-old married man with one child (WO54/554). Jerimiah was still in employment on the 1st April 1828, with the same remuneration (WO54/562).

Levi March was a Labourer set to work by Daniel Cornish in October 1787 at 9/-d per week, possibly renovating the Mills following their purchase by the Government from Mr. Walton (Winters, *op. cit.* p.28).

W. Marchant was the Surgeon at the Mills between 1787 and 1791 (Winters, *op. cit.* p.122).

John Marr was a common Labourer who was paid 17/-d for work carried out by the Engineers' Department in the Manufactory between the 15th and 21st July 1809 (Supply 5/228). By August 1812, Mr. Marr was working in the Storekeeper's Department as a Brimstone and Saltpetre Millman who earned 2/8d per day, and in addition, he was allowed to watch in turn, for which he received 1/6d per night (Supply 5/229). In February 1814, John was employed in the Dusting House where he was earning 3/-d per day, and was allowed to watch for the same money (Supply 5/230).

William Marshall was an extra Bargeman on 3 barges transporting gunpowder to Picket's Field and Magazines. In May 1804, he was paid £2.11.6d per week (Supply 5/222).

Henry Martin was working in the New Corning House on Horse Mill Island during the afternoon of the 18th April 1801, when it blew up with a tremendous explosion. Nine men were in the building at the time and all, including Henry, were killed, along with four horses (Supply 5/220). Henry, who was single, lived with and had supported his 54-year-old mother since his father had left them several years earlier (Winters, *op.cit.* p.58 and Supply 5/220). A Petition dated the 28th April 1801 stated that Henry's mother, Mary, along with others, requested "relief in their distress" (Supply 5/194). A Report on the ages of children and circumstance of the widows and children said, "Mary Martin, the deceased's mother, is aged 54. Her husband had left her several years ago and she was supported by her son, Henry, who lived with her" (Supply 5/220). Mary was eventually awarded a pension of 2/-d with effect from the 19th April 1801 (Winters, *op. cit.* p. 58). There were no previous records relating to Henry so he must have been a relatively new employee. For more details on the explosion, see the notes on John Bailey.

Michael Martin, born circa 1745, started his employment as the Office Keeper in the Engineers' Department at the Waltham Abbey Powder Mills on the 29th March 1806 (WO54/512). In September 1812, he was paid 2/8d per day (WO54/512) and was in receipt of the same money in February 1816 (WO54/516). The same document revealed that he was a 60-year-old widower living in Waltham Abbey, with 4 married children. By 1817, following the cessation of the Napoleonic wars, his pay had been reduced to 2/4d daily (WO54/520. His name does not appear in the Engineers' records after the 19th May 1819 (WO54/528).

Thomas Martin, Senior was born circa 1770; he worked as a Labourer within the Engineers' Department, where he was paid 1/6d per day. Between August and September 1790 he worked within the Manufactory, with his wages submitted to and paid by the Storekeeper, James Wright, by William Spry, Colonel commanding the Royal Engineers (WASC 1382). On the 21st September 1790, he joined the Storekeeper's Department (Supply 5/232) where he worked in the Corning House still earning 1/6d per day (Supply 5/215). In August 1793, he was in the country felling wood (Supply 5/216) but had returned to the Corning House by August of the following year (Supply 5/216). In December 1794, he was employed in the Dusting House (Supply 5/217) before becoming a Refiner (Saltpetre Refiner) in June 1795 (Supply 5/217). During this period he was paid 1/6d per day.

Thomas continued to work in the Refinery and joined the Volunteer Company as a Private in September 1798 (Supply 5/219). A Petition on Pay and Conditions in the Mills submitted to the Board in February 1800 showed that he was illiterate (Supply 5/220). A Return on the Marital Status of the Employees in May 1801 revealed that he was a married man with 2 children (Supply 5/221). By 1818, his family had grown to 8 (Supply 5/231) one of whom died between 1822 and 1823 (WO54/524). On the 23rd October 1801, Robert Coleman, Clerk of the Cheque, recorded in his Minute Book that 24 men were required to go to the Gunpowder Mills at Faversham or be discharged. Thomas was one of those chosen and agreed to go (Winters, *op. cit.* p.60). However, there is no evidence to show that he either went to Faversham or was discharged, since his records do not reveal a break in his service.

A Return dated the 8th May 1804, recorded that he was working as a Labourer, possibly in the Saltpetre Refinery, earning 2/-d per day. In addition, he was allowed to watch, on average every 5th night, for which he received 1/-d (Supply 5/227). From then on Thomas was described as a Saltpetre Refiner and his daily wage peaked between 1812 and 1814 at 2/8d and he was still allowed to "watch in turn" (Supply 5/229 and 5/230). A letter dated the 23rd May 1818 to Mr. Middleton, the Storekeeper, from Mr Lovell, Superintendent of the Small Arms Manufactory at Enfield, read, "Mr. Lovell presents his compliments to Mr. Middleton and begs to acquaint him that the bearer, Thomas Martin, is the person who is to receive extra pay for bags during the period he was employed providing the articles for the Corn Mill at Waltham Abbey" (Supply 5/202).

Thomas survived the redundancies the Board made in 1818 and again in 1822 (Supply 5/232 and Supply 5/231) and apart from a short period when he refined Brimstone (Supply 5/231) retained his position as a Saltpetre Refiner. During this period his pay was gradually reduced from 2/8d to 2/4d daily, although he was still allowed to watch in turn (Supply 5/232).

At the age of 60 he became a Stoveman, replacing Isaac Webb, who died on the 24th December 1830. He was then paid £44.4.0d annually, which included his watch money (WO54/575). There was a further cut in wages in 1834 when, as a Labourer "attending the stoves", his annual pay was reduced to £37.16.6d (WO54/593). The last record found relating to Thomas is dated the 1st October 1834, when, at the age of 64, he was still working as a Stoveman (WO54/593).

Thomas Martin Jnr., the son of Thomas Martin, was born circa 1802/1803. On the 8th April 1815, upon the recommendation of the Storekeeper and the Clerk of the Cheque, he started an Apprenticeship under the Master Refiner of Brimstone, John Lockyer, (Supply 5/232). In the recommendation, Thomas was described as "a stout lad about thirteen years' old" (Supply 5/230). A Return dated the 25th June 1818, recorded that he was a 15-year-old living in Waltham Abbey, and as an Apprentice, was earning 6/-d per week (Supply 5/231) which gradually rose to £17.13.0d annually by the 31st December 1821 (Supply 5/232). Thomas finished his Apprenticeship under the Master Refiner of Brimstone in 1822, and was discharged by the Board's Order of the 22nd May 1822.

William Martin, born circa 1796, started work as an occasional Labourer in the Engineers' Department on the 30th June 1815, being paid 2/8d per day. He was a bachelor living in Waltham Abbey (WO54/516).

James Mash was a Labourer set to work by Daniel Cornish in October 1787 at 9/-d per week, possibly renovating the Mills following their purchase by the Government from Mr. Walton (Winters, *op. cit.* p.29). However, he does not appear to have been retained.

Daniel Mason worked as a Puntman between August 1812 and February 1814, and during this period was paid 2/8d per day (Supply 5/229 &5/230).

John Mason was described as "an occasional Labourer at the Royal Laboratory in the last war" (American War of Independence) and came to the Waltham Abbey Mills on the 13th April 1789 (Supply 5/213). He was then working in the Refining House under John Baker (Winters, *op. cit.* p.33). He was still refining Saltpetre in March 1790 (Supply 5/214) but in August and September of that year, he was working in the Corning House (Supply 5/215). In the spring and summer of 1791, he was "setting and drawing stoves and in the punts" (Supply 5/215). The following year, he worked in the Dusting House (Supply 5/216) before becoming a Millman in August 1793, with his pay increased from 1/6d to 2/-d per day (Supply 5/216). On the 21st February he was chequered (fined) by Robert Coleman, Clerk of the Cheque, for being insolent to him and not going to the Corning House when ordered (Winters, *op. cit.* p.45). Mason was still working as a Millman in July 1795 and still paid 2/-d per day, but he then received 3d per night when on duty (Supply 5/217). The Storekeeper received an anonymous letter of complaint against John Ashwood, the Master Mixer, in August 1795, details of which are not known, but "two men discharged, John Mason and (William) Fulham, the charge being non-proven" (Winters, *op.cit.* p.52). Mason left the Mills on the 18th September 1795.

Thomas Mason (1) worked as a Labourer in the Corning House in May 1804 for 2/1d per day and was allowed to watch in turn, which was, on average, every 5th night, for which he received 1/-d (Supply 5/222). He continued to be employed in the Corning House, with his pay increased to 2/6d per day by August 1808 (Supply 5/227) and his watch allowance to 1/6d a night by September 1810 (Supply 5/228). By August 1812, Thomas had been promoted to the position of Reeling House Forman and was then paid 3/10 per day and still allowed to watch in turn, earning 1/6d per night for that duty (Supply 5/229). Thomas was performing the same tasks in February 1814, for the same remuneration (Supply 5/230).

In 1816 the Board formed 3 tenements out of the dwellings in the Tanyard on the south side of High Bridge Street. Thomas, Foreman of the Reeling House, was allocated one of Plot Nos. 54 or 55 on the Town Map in Appendix 1, and the rental was 3/-d per week (Winters, *op.cit*.p.83*)*.

Thomas Mason (2) was engaged as an occasional Labourer by the Engineers' Department on the 30th July 1814, and paid 2/8d per day. In February 1816, he was a 20-year-old bachelor living in Waltham Abbey (WO54/516).

William Mason was refining Saltpetre in September 1789, and was then aged 36 (Supply 5/214).

James Mathanns started his employment as an occasional Labourer in the Engineers' Department on the 17th July 1815, and was paid 2/8d per day. In February 1816 he was a 43-year-old widower with no children, living in Waltham Abbey (WO54/516).

H. S. Mathews started his employment with the Ordnance Board on the 1st July 1785, and was appointed as the Storekeeper at Waltham Abbey on the 7th March 1805. On the 18th June 1807, he was paid £300.0.0d per annum, provided with a house, received an allowance of £25.0.0d for coal and candles, and was getting a £65.0.0d gratuity (Supply 5/226). By February 1814 his salary had risen to £350.0.0d per annum, and his annual gratuity was £110.0.0d. He was still provided with a house and heat and light allowances (Supply 5/230). However, Empson Middleton replaced him as Storekeeper on the 29th January 1818 (Supply 5/231).

It would appear that Mr. Mathews either retired or left the Ordnance Department, since in May 1818, Thomas Holden, the Foreman of Labourers, desired to occupy the house Matthews had been occupying. Mathews signified that he had obtained the Board's permission to deposit therein portions of furniture and other articles until he had an opportunity of removing the same, and that it was quite impossible for him to give up possession of this house until he was enabled finally to remove. The Board did not accede to Holden's wishes, since they intended to divide the house into two dwellings anyway (Supply 5/231). Where this house was located is unknown.

W. Mayaer started work as a Labourer in the Corning House on the 19th February 1798, and was also a Private in the Volunteer Company (Supply 5/219).

Benjamin Mayall was employed as one of the "Respective Officer's Labourers," in August 1808, i.e., he worked as a Labourer for one of the senior staff. He was earning 2/-d per day, and was also allowed to watch in turn (Supply 5/227).

James Maynard was working as a Saltpetre Refiner in September 1810 (Supply 5/228) as he was in February 1814 (Supply 5/230). During this time, his pay rose from 2/-d per day to 2/8d, and he was allowed to watch in turn when not working extra.

John Maynard was born circa 1800. He was employed as a general Labourer on the 26th October 1839, at £39.0.0d per annum, which included an allowance to watch in turn. He was a married man with 3 children (WO54/623) and the 1841 Census recorded that John and his wife, Eleanor, were living in Sewardstone Street with 2 of their children, John (15) and Elizabeth (9).

J. Maynerd started work at the Mills on the 23rd June 1797 as a Labourer, "setting and drawing stoves and clearing the willow plantation". He was also a Private in the Volunteer Company (Supply 5/219).

Donald McLean, an ex-soldier, started work at Faversham on the 1st November 1787, transferring to Waltham Abbey as a Warder on the 1st February 1789. In March of that year he was "grinding salt petre and charcoal, etc." and was paid 1/6d per day (Supply 5/212). He was described as "cutting and planting willow trees, cutting of canal at the new Corning House, removing earth to the Store, unloading barge of coals and charring wood" in April 1789 (Supply 5/213). An entry in Winters on the 22nd June 1789, recorded that McLean would be discharged for "ill-treating a young servant maid to the Clerk of the Cheque in one of the watch houses" and this was confirmed in a letter of the 23rd June 1797 from the Storekeeper and the Clerk of the Cheque, clearly stating that McLean would not be replaced (WASC 0475).

William Mears started his employment as an occasional Labourer in the Engineers' Department on the 16th July 1815, earning 2/8d per day. In February 1816, he was a 55-year-old married man with 3 children, living in Enfield (WO54/516).

James Meridith was working as a Labourer in the "Engineers' Dept. Established" in May 1804, earning 1/6d per day with "one day extra allowed per week agreeable to the Board's Order dated 12th March, 1801." (Supply 5/222).

John Meridith had been a Millman for 2 years in January 1806. At that time he was earning 2/3d per day (Supply 5/224) as he was in June 1807, when he was also allowed an extra 3d per night when on duty (Supply 5/226). By September 1810, he had transferred to the Dusting House (Supply 5/229) where he was still working in August 1812. As a Dusting House Man he was initially paid 2/3d per day (Supply 5/228) rising to 3/-d daily by August 1812 (Supply 5/229). During this period he was also allowed to watch in turn for 1/6d per night (Supply 5/228).

William Meridith was working in the Dusting House in February 1814 earning 3/-d per day and allowed to watch in turn, for which he received 1/6d per night (Supply 5/230).

John Merrit was appointed Foreman of the Stoves and Magazines on the 7th May 1825, replacing John Braddock (Winters, *op. cit.* p.92). However, it would appear that Winters is incorrect, or that Merrit never took up the appointment, since John Brown was appointed as the Foreman of Stoves and Magazines on the 28th May 1825 (WO54/ 554).

John Messer was born circa 1763. He trained as a Coppersmith before joining the Ordnance Board at Waltham Abbey on the 22nd July 1805 (Supply 5/232). In March 1805, he was working as the Stoves' Foreman with pay of £1.2.0d per week (Supply 5/223). In January 1806, he was paid 4/-d per day (Supply 5/224) as he was in June 1807 (Supply 5/226). In August 1808, he was described as "Coppersmith and Steam Stoveman" and paid 4/5d per day (Supply 5/227). On the 1st January 1810, he was appointed as the Coppersmith at the Mills (Supply 5/232) the inference being that prior to this date he was a Coppersmith on a part-time basis. As a Coppersmith his pay was then 5/-d per day (Supply 5/228) and was increased to 6/4d by August 1812 (Supply 5/229) remaining the same in February 1814 (Supply 5/230).

In common with the majority of the employees his wage was reduced at the end of the Napoleonic wars, and in June 1818, his daily rate was 5/4d (Supply 5/231). The same Return recorded that Messer was a married man with 3 children, living in Waltham Abbey. With reduced demand for new and regenerated gunpowder, the Board decreed that the Establishment was to be reduced in numbers and in August 1818, the Storekeeper drew up lists of people who were to be retained between the 3rd September and the 31st December 1818. John Messer was on this list and was to be paid 5/4d per day (Supply 5/231). However, a few days later, the Storekeeper proposed further redundancies and wrote to the Board stating, "We respectfully beg leave to add the names and stations of those persons it will be necessary to discharge in consequence of this arrangement" and John's name was on this second list (Supply 5/231). However, he was not discharged, since subsequent entries in the records show no break in the length of his service with the Board.

He was still being paid 5/4d per day in May 1819 (Supply 5/232) and the same record noted that at that date he had 4 children, with a fifth being born by September 1820 (Supply 5/232). John retained his position as the Coppersmith in March 1822 when the Establishment was reformed to regenerate some 2000 barrels of gunpowder and produce only 200 barrels of new powder annually (Supply 5/232). His position was re-affirmed on the 1st October 1824 (Supply 5/232) and his pay remained unchanged at 5/4d per day, or £83.9.4d annually. This Return recorded that he only had 3 children. John Messer died between April and October 1826 ((WO54/554).

Empson Middleton, born circa 1766, was appointed as the Superintendent of Ordnance Tradesmen at Birmingham on the 31st December 1813, and the Storekeeper at Gravesend on the 1st January 1817 (Supply 5/232). He was employed as the Storekeeper at Waltham Abbey on the 20th January 1818, and at the time was a 52-year-old married man, with 3 children. His salary was £350.0.0d per annum, and he was given an annual allowance of £25 for coals and candles as well as a house upon the Establishment (Supply 5/231). Middleton was also entitled to an Attendant Labourer, but this privilege was withdrawn in 1822 when he was paid an additional £13.16.0d for 6 months in lieu (Supply 5/232).

A statement "of monies to which the public were entitled to receive between the 1st January and the 31st December 1820" indicated that Middleton had been living rent free in a Board of Ordnance house under an order dated the 4th February 1818, and that in addition, he was renting some 6 acres of grass land from the Board at a cost of £11.17.0d per annum (Supply 5/232). His house and gardens are shown as Plot No. 57 on the Town Map in Appendix 1, on the south side of High Bridge Street opposite Powder Mill Lane. Mr. Middleton's basic salary was still £350.0.0d per annum in October 1824, and in addition, he received a gratuity of £52.2.6d, an annual coal and candle allowance of £25.0.0d and a further £27.7.6d in lieu of an Attendant Labourer, which gave him a total income of £454.10.0d (WO54/546). Empson Middleton died in June 1826 (Winters, *op.cit.* p.93).

Benjamin Miles was born circa 1785, and in June 1807 was working as a Millman earning 2/3d per day as well as being allowed 3d per night when on duty (Supply 5/226). He was still working for the same rate of pay in August 1808, but was then allowed 6d per night when on duty (Supply 5/227). This was also the case in September 1810 (Supply 5/228), but his pay had risen to 3/-d per day by August 1812 (Supply 5/229) and remained so in February 1814 (Supply 5/230). By June 1818, he was employed as a Saltpetre Refiner earning 2/4d per day, and in addition, he was then allowed to watch in turn at 1/-d per night. He was a married man living in Waltham Abbey with 1 child (Supply 5/231).

John Miles was working as a Labourer in the New Corning House on Horse Mill Island during the afternoon of the 18th April 1801, when it blew up with a tremendous explosion. Nine men were in the building at the time and all, including John, were killed, along with 4 horses (Supply 5/220). In a Report dated the 29th April 1801 in respect of the ages of children and circumstances of widows and children, it was stated that John Miles' father was Benjamin Miles, aged 60, who was infirm. Benjamin had 5 children and his son John, who was killed, had allowed his father a weekly sum (Supply 5/220). A List of Persons to whom Pensions or Charitable Allowances had been granted by the Board as widows, orphans or relations of those who had lost their lives in the Manufactory, included Benjamin Miles, who received a pension of 2/-d per week commencing the 19th April 1801 (Supply 5/231). Benjamin was still in receipt of a pension of £5.4.0d in 1826 (Winters, *op. cit.* p.96).

J. Miles was working as a Corning House Man in January 1806 earning 2/2d per day, and at that time had been employed with the Ordnance for 3 months (Supply 5/224).

George Miller, born circa 1765, trained as a Harness and Collar Maker (Saddler) before he was engaged as an occasional Labourer by the Engineers' Department on the 16th July 1816 at 2/4d per day. He was then a 51-year-old married man without issue living in Waltham Abbey (WO54/520). George was still employed as a casual Labourer earning the same money in April 1818 (WO54/524) as he was in May 1819 (WO54/528). However, by December 1821, he was described as "Repairer of Hose and Band" and was receiving 4/6d per day which, for 313 working days a year, gave him an annual income of £70.8.6d (WO54/536). He was still receiving this sum when he retired in 1833 (WO54/587).

A statement "of monies to which the public are entitled to have credit between the 1st January and the 31st December 1821" recorded that George Miller, by an Order of the Board dated the 4th May 1821, was renting a cottage owned by the Board together with its garden of 2 perches, for £5.4.0d per annum (Supply 5/232). The cottage with its small garden was located at the junction of West Street (High Bridge Street) and Powder Mill Lane, part of Plot No.61 on the Town Map in Appendix 1. George's wife died between October 1827 and April 1828 (WO54/562). A Return of Persons belonging to the Civil Establishment of the Gunpowder and Small Arms Manufactories at Waltham Abbey, Faversham and Enfield showing in detail the several points of information called for by the Master General and the Board's Order dated the 31st January 1831, recorded that George Miller was the repairer of millbands, hose, reels and fire engines, etc. at the Waltham Abbey and Enfield Manufactories, for which he was paid 4/6d per day (WO54/575). George retired on the 21st August 1833 and was given a pension, which he was still in receipt of in 1837 (Supply 5/237).

James Millington was employed as a Saltpetre Refiner in February 1814 earning 2/8d per day, and, when not working extra, was allowed to watch in turn (Supply 5/230).

George Mitchell was born circa 1749 and served in the Artillery from the 1st January 1771 to the 17th December 1784. From May 1785 until the 1st November 1787, he worked as a Labourer in the Corning House and the Glazing Engine at the Faversham Mills, starting work at Waltham Abbey on the 1st January 1789. (Supply 5/212). In March 1789, he was working as a Warder at the field gate and on the bank of the canal, and paid 1/6d per day (Supply 5/214). In November 1801, he was, "attending the field gate, refining house and upper part of the works" (Supply 5/229) and this was his station until at least August 1812 (Supply 5/229). During this period his pay started at 1/6d per day rising to 2/-d, in addition to which, he was allowed to watch in turn, for which he was paid 1/-d per night. From September 1810 onwards he was a Rounder receiving 2/- every third night (Supply 5/228).

George joined the Volunteer Company, an Artillery unit, on the 7th May 1794, and soon became a Corporal (Supply 5/219). The Petition of Pay and Conditions at the Mills submitted to the Board in February 1800 indicated that he was illiterate (Supply 5/220) while a Return on the Marital Status of the Employees submitted in May 1801, recorded that he was a married man with 1 child (Supply 5/221). He appears to have either left the Board or retired after August 1812.

Joseph Mitchell started his employment with the Ordnance on the 15th December 1788, being one of the first Bargemen at the Mills (Winters, *op. cit.* p.69). In January 1789, he was described as a sole Master Bargeman, earning 1/6d per day (Supply 5/212) as he was in September 1789 (Supply 5/214). In 1789 he was the Master of the *Resolution* (Winters, *op. cit.* p.55).

A statement "of monies to which the public are entitled to have credit between the 1st January and the 31st December 1821" recorded that by an Order of the Board dated the 23rd April 1819, Joseph Mitchell rented a house and garden owned by the Board for £27.0.0d per annum (Supply 5/232). The 1840 Tithe Map for Waltham Abbey recorded that Joseph Mitchell occupied Plot No.1414 on the south side of High Bridge Street to the west of Powder Mill Lane; it was a relatively large plot backing onto the old River Lee to the east of the Mills' Cooperage and is Plot No. 50 on the Town Map in Appendix 1. A Minute from the Mills' Letter Book dated the 22nd April 1819, noted that Mr. Mitchell was not to navigate the old River Lee above the Cooperage Yard - in other words Mitchell did not "park" his barge at the bottom of his garden (Winters, *op. cit.* p.86). A Return of Domestic Property owned by the Board prepared by the Royal Engineers' Office on the 20th December 1834, recorded that J. Mitchell, Bargemaster, had occupied a property in West Street (High Bridge Street) since the 23rd April 1819 when it was purchased by the Board (Supply 5/237); this was confirmed in a similar Return for 1840 (WO44/133).

The 1841 Census recorded that Joseph Mitchell (aged 70), Independent, and his wife, Harriett, aged 60, were living on the south side of High Bridge Street, together with John Mitchell, Coal Merchant aged 30, and his family.

Thomas Mitchell was a Labourer set to work by Daniel Cornish in October 1787 at 9/-d per week, possibly renovating the Mills following their purchase by the Government from Mr. Walton (Winters, *op.cit.* p.28). Thomas was retained as a Bargeman in 1788, and promised continuity of work since he had previously worked for Mr. Walton (Supply 5/212). In 1788 "the coal barge of Mr Tho. Mitchell carries 10 tons" (Winters, *op.cit.* p.55). Thomas died suddenly in December 1788.

Edward Mold possibly worked in Mr. Walton's Gunpowder Mills before their purchase by the Government, because he had a promise to be employed when the Mills were set to work. He was subsequently engaged as a Millman in March 1789, with pay of 2/-d per day (Supply 5/212). However, he was soon in trouble because in September 1789 the Storekeeper, James Wright, and the Clerk of the Cheque, John Cloudesly, wrote to the Duke of Richmond, "we beg to report that Edwd. Mold, a Millman employed at this place, has several times found to have drunk rather more than he should have done, for which we have admonished him and told him that he would certainly be discharged if he continued to be so indiscreet. Notwithstanding the repeated caution given to him, he came to take his turn of duty to work two mills (from 6 to 12 o'clock at night) so much in liquor that we were obliged to send him home [and] we have suspended him until we receive your commands whether he is to be discharged from the Service" (WASC 0475). No further records have been found for Edward Mold.

Henry Mold was working as a Labourer in the Engineers' Department in May 1801 at 1/6d per day, and was then a married man with 4 children (Supply 5/221). He was still employed in 1804 as a Labourer in the "Engineers' Dept. Established" and still being paid 1/6d per day with "one day extra allowed per week agreeable to the Board's Order dated the 12th March, 1801" (Supply 5/222). However, soon after this, he transferred to the Storekeeper's Department where, in January 1806, he was employed in the Dusting House, earning 2/1d per day. By then he had 2 years' service (Supply 5/224).

Thomas Mold started an Apprenticeship under the Master Millwright at 6/-d per week on the 5th January 1814 when he as 14 or 15 years old (WO54/542 & WO54/516). In September 1820, he was still Apprenticed to the Master Millwright and was then paid 7/-d per week (WO54/532). Although trained as a Millwright, he was appointed to the Establishment as a Carpenter on the 8th March 1822 (WO54/542). In April 1823, he was still employed as a Carpenter in the Engineers' Department, but then earned 4/1d per day, which, for 313 days, gave him an annual income of £63.18.1d (WO54/542).

He was a married man with 1 child in April 1826, but, sadly, by the following October, both mother and child had died (WO54/554). A Return of Persons belonging to the Civil Establishment of the Gunpowder and Small Arms Manufactories at Waltham Abbey, Faversham and Enfield, showing in detail the several points of information called for by the Master General and the Board's Order dated the 31st January 1831, recorded that Thomas Mold was one of the 7 Carpenters to be employed at Waltham Abbey Powder Mills and Enfield Small Arms Factory, for which he would be paid 4/1d per day. He was required to undertake general service as a Carpenter in the Manufactories, which required great care, attention and sobriety, etc. (WO54/575).

Thomas had married for a second time by April 1833 (WO54/575) and was still employed as a Carpenter earning £61.18.1d per annum. However, in April 1833, although described as having trained as a Millwright, he was employed as a Labourer, with his annual income then set at £33.18.2d. He had a child to support (WO54/587) with a second by April 1834 (WO54/593) and a third by October 1839 (WO54/623). The 1841 Census recorded that Thomas and his wife, Hester, were living in Baker's Entry with their son, William, aged 9. Thomas was described as a Carpenter.

William Mold, born circa 1762, was working as a Labourer in the Corning House earning 1/6d per day in August 1789 (Supply 5/213) as he was in March 1790, when he was described as "grinding salt petre, charcoal etc. (Supply 5/214). William worked in the Corning House until at least March 1792 (Supply 5/215) but by the following July he was a Millman earning 2/-d per day (Supply 5/216).

He continued to work as a Millman, but was soon in trouble with Robert Coleman, the Clerk of the Cheque, for on the 6th May 1793, he was caught wearing nailed shoes on duty and chequered (fined) one days' pay (Winters, *op. cit.* p.38). In September of that year, Coleman chequered him again for refusing to get up at 12 o'clock to attend to his Mill duty (Winters, *op. cit.* p.40). On the 4th May 1794, he enlisted as a Private in the Volunteer Company (Supply 5/219).

There was a severe frost in January 1795 which prevented barge transport, and work stopped in the Mills. Robert Coleman noted in his Minute Book, "Dyer and Mold sent with two loaded wagons to Purfleet" (Winters, *op. cit.* p.44) and it is possible that Coleman sent Mold to Purfleet because of his ill discipline in the Mills. Thomas was soon in trouble yet again, since on the 30th June 1795, Coleman recorded, "Mold was discharged for sleeping on duty, and abuse etc. to E. Jones, Rounder." Mold re-entered the Factory July 7th" (Winters, *op.cit.*p.46). A Petition on Pay and Conditions in the Mills submitted to the Board in February 1800 showed that Mould was illiterate (Supply 5/220). A Return on the Marital Status of the Employees in May 1801 revealed that he was a married man with 1 child, and was still employed as a Millman (Supply 5/221). This appears to be the last record relating to William Mold.

William Mold was working as a Labourer in August 1812, earning 2/8d per day "setting and drawing stoves and in the willow plantation." He was also allowed to watch in turn (Supply 5/229). By February 1814, he was described as a Puntman, still earning 2/8d per day and allowed to watch (Supply 5/230).

Joseph Mole was a Sawyer by trade, set to work by Daniel Cornish in October 1787 at 9/-d per week, possibly renovating the Mills following their purchase by the Government from Mr Walton. He was not retained once his work was complete (Winters, *op. cit.* p.28).

George Montague had been working as a Millman in January 1806, earning 2/3d per day (Supply 5/224). By June 1807 he was employed in the Corning House at 2/2d per day, and was allowed to watch in turn, for which he received 1/-d (Supply 5/226). George was still a Corning House Man in August 1808, but his pay had increased to 2/6d per day, with his watch allowance unaltered (Supply 5/227). He had changed his workplace again by September 1810, and was then employed as a Saltpetre Refiner with his daily rate of pay reduced to 2/-d, but still allowed to watch (Supply 5/228). He was still refining in August 1812, but was then paid 2/8d per day, and in addition, when not working extra, he was allowed to watch in turn (Supply 5/229). The same pay and conditions applied in February 1814 (Supply 5/230).

John Montague was working as a Labourer at Faversham in 1789. A letter dated the 29th December 1789 from the Royal Powder Mills at Faversham to the Mills at Waltham Abbey, advised them that John Montague and Alexander Gordon, "labourers of this place" were to be transferred to Waltham Abbey the next day, and that they had both been paid until the end of the month. Gordon had "frock and slippers" while Montague had been furnished with neither (WASC 0475). At Waltham Abbey, Montague was employed as a Labourer grinding Saltpetre for 1/6d per day (Supply 5/215 and 5/216). Robert Coleman, Clerk of the Cheque, recorded that on the 13th and 14th May 1793, John Montague had "gone away from his watch without leave and was ordered off his watch" (Winters, *op. cit.* p.39).

Thomas Montague was born circa 1765, and as a Labourer in March 1789, was paid 1/6d per day for dusting and glazing gunpowder (Supply 5/212). The following month Thomas was " was cutting and planting willow trees, cutting of canal at the new Corning House, removing earth to the Store, unloading barge of coals & charring wood" (Supply 5/213) returning to dusting and glazing gunpowder in September 1789 (Supply 5/214). Between March 1790 and June 1791 he was "grinding salt petre and charcoal" (Supply 5/215), while in January 1792, he was "mixing composition" (Supply 5/215). By July 1792 Thomas was employed in the Corning House, where he remained until March 1793 (Supply 5/216).

Lt.Col. Thomas Moody was, on the 7th November 1828 as Major Thomas Moody, appointed to command the Engineers' Department at Waltham Abbey and Faversham "in the room of" [in place of] Captain Boteler, who was promoted to the rank of Lt.Colonel, Royal Engineers (Winters, *op. cit.* p.100). Moody was promoted to the rank of Lt.Colonel, Royal Engineers, on the 28th October 1831, and appointed "to have general superintendence of the Establishment at Waltham Abbey" because the office of Storekeeper had been abolished (Winters, *op. cit.* p.102). He was given a house owned by the Board which had previously been occupied by Empson Middleton, being Plot No. 57 on the Town Map in Appendix 1.

William Morgan was employed as a Millwright in the Engineers' Department at 3/6d per day. In August 1790, he was working within the manufactory, and his wages, amounting to £1.1.0d, were submitted to and paid by the Storekeeper, James Wright, by William Spry, Colonel Commanding the Royal Engineers. Morgan signed for his pay "with a firm hand" (WASC 1382).

William Morley was employed as a Marker of Barrels in February 1812, earning 3/3d per day. He was also allowed to watch in turn, for which he received 1/6d per night (Supply 5/230).

Daniel Morrier was born circa 1755 and started his employment as an occasional Labourer in the Engineers' Department on the 8th September 1812, earning 2/8d per day. In February 1816, he was a 60-year-old widower with 4 children, who lived in Waltham Abbey (WO54/516).

James Morris was employed as an occasional Labourer with the Engineers' Department on the 1st July 1812 at 2/8d per day (WO54/512). He was still in this position in February 1816, and was then an 18-year-old bachelor living in Waltham Abbey (WO54/516).

John Morris was working as a Labourer in February 1814 "setting and drawing stoves and working in the willow plantation." He was paid 2/8d per day and allowed to watch in turn (Supply 5/230).

William Morris was working as a Saltpetre Refiner in February 1814 at 2/8d per day, and when not working extra, was allowed to watch in turn (Supply 5/230).

William Murrel was employed as a Puntman. In September 1810, he was paid 2/-d per day and allowed to watch in turn (Supply 5/228).

Michael Murrey started his employment as a Corning House Man early in 1805 (Supply 5/224) and was still in the same position in February 1814 (Supply 5/230). Initially, he was paid 2/2d per day which rose to 3/3d by 1814, and he was also allowed to watch in turn, for which he was paid 1/6d per night.

Richard Murton was born circa 1770 and joined the Engineers' Department as a casual Millwright on the 2nd January 1818 at 5/2d per day. He was then a 46-year-old married man with 3 children living in Waltham Abbey (WO54/520).

Henry Myres, born circa 1784, was working as a Labourer "drawing and setting stoves" earning 2/8d per day in 1813 (Winters, *op. cit.* p.77) In February 1814, he was employed as a Warder, and although still paid the same daily rate, in addition he was a Rounder every third night, for which he received 2/6d (Supply 5/230). He was still employed as a Warder in June 1818, but with his pay reduced to 2/4d per day, and at that date, he was a 34-year-old married man without issue, living in Waltham Abbey (Supply 5/231).

With reduced demand for new and regenerated gunpowder, the Board decreed that the Establishment was to be reduced in numbers and in August 1818, the Storekeeper drew up lists of people to be retained between the 3rd September and the 31st December 1818. Henry Myres was on this list and was to be paid 2/4d per day as the Warder at the Lower Island (Supply 5/231). A

Return dated the 3rd September 1821 (Supply 5/231) showed that he continued to be employed as a Warder at Lower Island where he lived in the Watch House marked as Plot No. 16 on the Town Map shown in Appendix 1, and that he was still paid 2/4d per day. Another Return of Employees made in January 1822, noted that he had served the Board for 11 years, was 37 years old and that he and his wife were childless (Supply 5/232). The next Return was dated the 6th February 1822, and listed the names of the people employed at Waltham Abbey as at the 31st December 1821. Henry's name had been replaced by that of Joseph Myers (Supply 5/232). Joseph's name does not appear in the Records after February 1814, and this, coupled with other details, can only mean a clerical error and that the entry referred to Henry Myers. The information given in this Return recorded that the Board had first employed Henry on the 20th June 1811, that his position as a Warder had been re-confirmed on the 4th September 1818 and that his annual pay, including his watch allowance, was £44.14.4d.

In the spring of 1822, the Ordnance Board decided to reduce the production and regeneration of gunpowder at the Establishment at Waltham Abbey again. Accordingly, Empson Middleton and James Wright drew up lists of people to be dismissed and Henry Myres, Warder, was on that list (Supply 5/232). The men were subsequently made redundant on the 1st June, and several Petitions were submitted by them asking for financial assistance. Many were long service employees in middle age, and they pointed out that they had little hope of finding employment after the corn harvest had been gathered. The Storekeeper was sympathetic and forwarded the Petitions to the Board for their consideration. Henry was one of the Petitioners and he was awarded two weeks' pay to ease his financial burden (Supply 5/232).

Joseph Myres was working as a Millman in August 1808 earning 2/3d per day, and "allowed 2/6d per night when on duty" (Supply 5/227). He continued to be employed as a Millman until at least February 1814, when his pay was 3/-d per day with an extra 6d if he worked at night (Supply 5/230). This is the last record found relating to Joseph Myres.

N

John Newland was born circa 1782 (WO54/254) and started his employment as a Puntman at the Mills on the 12th September 1805 (WO54/546). In January 1806, he was working in the Corning House earning 2/2d per day (Supply 5/224). The Corning House was to be his work place until at least September 1810, when his rate of pay was 2/6d per day, and, in addition, he received 1/6d per night for watching in turn (Supply 5/228). By August 1812, he had been promoted to one of 3 Reeling House Foremen earning 3/10d per day, and he was still allowed to watch for the same money (Supply 5/229). With the same pay and watch allowance, John was still in the Reeling House in February 1814 (Supply 5/230) but by June 1818, he had reverted to being a Corning House Man with his daily pay and watch allowance reduced to 2/11d and 1/-d respectively (Supply 5/231 and WO54/524). At that date he was a 36-year-old married man with 5 children living in Waltham Abbey.

John was retained when the Establishment was reduced in numbers in 1818, and his position in the Corning House was confirmed by a Board Order dated the 4th September 1818 (Supply 5/232). He continued as a Corning House Man until 1822, and during this period, his annual remuneration was £50.6.11d. At that time he had 7 children (Supply 5/232). In the spring of 1822, the Ordnance Board decided to lower production and the regeneration of gunpowder, and the Establishment at Waltham Abbey was to be reduced accordingly. On the 1st June 1822 Empson Middleton and James Wright drew up lists of people to be retained or dismissed (Supply 5/232) and John was retained as a Labourer to carry out any type of work required within the Manufactory (Supply 5/233). In April 1823 his annual pay, including an allowance to watch in turn, was £39.0.0d (WO54/542) but by October 1823, he had returned to the Corning House, with his total pay rising to £48.2.0d per annum. It was also recorded that he then had 8 children (WO54/546). A Return for 1831 (WO54/575) showed that he then had 9 children, but, according to WO54/593 dated April 1834, he only had 8, so it is presumed that one died or that there had earlier been a clerical error. The 1841 Census recorded that John (55) and his wife Mary (50) lived in Sewardstone Street with 2 of their children, Charles (20) a Butcher, and Thomas (15) a Cordwainer, and all were born in Essex.

On the 13th April 1843, some 40 barrels of gunpowder exploded in the Corning House, together with another 20 in the Press House; 7 men were killed, including John Newland, and much damage was caused in the town (Winters, *op.cit.* p.106). A graphic description of the explosion and the damage caused, etc., was given in the *London Illustrated News* dated Saturday, the 22nd April 1843 (*WAAC*). John left a widow and 8 children, most of whom were adults.

Samuel Newland was the Clerk of the Cheque's Labourer in February 1814 and earned 2/8d per day (Supply 5/230).

James Newton was employed on the 24th November 1788 as one of the first Bargemen (Winters, *op.cit.* p.69) and confirmed as an assistant Bargeman in January 1789 (Supply 5/212).

William Newton was born circa 1744, and appointed Master Worker at Waltham Abbey in 1787. There was some doubt as to when his service had commenced, and in this respect the Administration Clerks at Waltham questioned him at length in 1812. He told them that he had been requested to attend the Comptroller at Charlton at the end of 1787 and had arrived there from Lincolnshire on the 25th December, seeing the Comptroller the next day, when he was retained for his Majesty's service. He was informed that he would not receive any pay until he returned from Lincolnshire where he had to settle his affairs. He also said that the Comptroller gave him a month's leave for this purpose, and maintained that his service, therefore, commenced on the 26th December 1787 (Supply 5/229). His statement was accepted, and confirmed by subsequent documents such as WO54/528 and Supply 5/232. To occupy the Master Worker's position, William, presumably, must have had previous experience in the manufacture of gunpowder. However, it was not until 1823 that a Return of Employees noted that he had been trained as a Gunpowder Maker, although the document did not say where (WO54/542). Nevertheless, 2 of William's 3 children had been baptised at Waltham Abbey prior to his appointment to the Ordnance (WASC 2180, p.108) so it would seem possible that he had worked for John Walton before the Government purchased Walton's Mills.

Before William returned from Lincolnshire, he was told to go to Faversham for a while. Instructions were given to Faversham that William, "was to see your method of manufactory of gunpowder, keeping accounts, and every branch of duty, as far as he may require as Master Worker until the powder makers to be transferred from Faversham are ordered up" (*FGPR*, p.61). 7 powder workers were "ordered up" to Waltham on the 27th January 1788, but refused to stay due to the low wages being paid and difficulty in obtaining lodgings (see notes on Thomas Bates). It would appear that William did not go to Waltham until April 1788, since a report dated the 5th April 1788 stated, "Mr. Newton's family to occupy part of the master worker's house when convenient" (Winters, *op.cit.* p.30). The Master Worker's house was then within the Manufactory, being building No. 21 on the 1781 map of the Mills (WASC 2180, p.25). Following the death of James Ridpath in 1804, the Board purchased the old Turnpike House from the executors of Mr. Ellis Were (WO44/681A). The Turnpike House was previously known as *The Chequers,* or *The Turnpike Inn* which ceased to be licensed premises in 1796 (*Licensed Victuallers' Returns*) and Newton moved in soon after. *Turnpike House* was at Edmondsey at the northern end of the Manufactory, near a large pond known as "Newton's Pool" (WASC 2180, p. 24).

On the 29th January 1789, Newton was paid £90.0.0d per annum and, in addition, he was allowed to train an Apprentice, for which he received 7/-d per week (Supply 5/188). He was also allowed £5.5.0d per annum for coal and candles (Supply 5/217). William also signed several of the early Personnel and Labour Returns submitted to the Board in 1789 (Supply 5/212) and over the years his salary and allowances gradually increased; in January 1805, it was £100.0.0d per annum, and on the 8th May of that year he was awarded a pay increase of £10.0.0d per year, coupled with a gratuity of £8.0.0d. He was still entitled to a house, with a coal and candle allowance set at £12.0.0d (Supply 5/222) and entitled to train an Apprentice. In 1807 John Godwin Jnr. was his Apprentice (Supply 5/227) and in 1811, John Carr was receiving tuition under Newton (Supply 5/229). By August 1812, his salary had risen to £130.0.0d per annum, coupled with a gratuity of £55.0.0d (Supply 5/229).

In 1815 the Board purchased the Cornmill in Romeland, and it was suggested that this should become the residence for the Master Worker. However, it was decided that it should remain a Cornmill and instead of moving into the town, William moved in 1815 into a refurbished stable on Horse Mill Island or Marsh Side (Supply 5/232) which is building No.96 on the Town Map in Appendix 1. A Return of Personnel at Waltham Abbey dated the 25th June 1818 (Supply 5/231) recorded that William was then a 73-year-old widower with 3 children. At that time his salary remained at £130.0.0d per annum with a service gratuity of £150.0.0d, and he was still entitled to train an Apprentice, which added a further £22.8.0d per annum to his pay. His salary and allowances remained unchanged until he died in office in February 1825, aged 81 years, after 38 years of continuous service at the Royal Gunpowder Mills, Waltham Abbey. For a while after his death, his son, Charles, was allowed to stay in his father's house with his invalid sister until in 1828 it was converted into two dwellings. His 3rd child may possibly have been James Newton, a Bargeman at the Mills in 1788. For further reading on William Newton and his family, see *Waltham Abbey Gunpowder People* by P J Huggins.

S. Nichol was working as a general Labourer in February 1800 when he signed a Petition on Pay and Conditions at the Mills which was presented to the Board (Supply 5/220).

Zachariah Nicholls was a Labourer at 9/-d per week, set to work by Daniel Cornish in October 1787, possibly repairing the Mills following their purchase by the Government from Mr. Walton. However, he does not appear to have been retained (Winters, *op.cit.* p. 29).

Thomas Nicholls (Nicholl) was working as a Saltpetre Refiner in August 1812 at 2/8d per day, and, when not working extra, was allowed to watch in turn (Supply 5/229). This was also the case in February 1814 (Supply 5/230).

John Nigh, born circa 1766, was engaged as a Labourer to work in the Corning House on the 13th August 1793 at 1/6d per day, filling one of the 7 vacancies then available at the Mills (Winters, *op.cit*, p.40 and Supply 5/216). He enlisted in the Volunteer Company on the 7th May 1794 (Supply 5/219) and in June 1795, he was working as a Charcoal Millman with the same daily rate of pay (Supply 5/217). The Petition on Pay and Conditions at the Mills submitted to the Board in February 1800 showed that he was illiterate (Supply 5/220) while the Return on the Marital Status of the Employees for 1801 recorded that, although he was married he was without issue (Supply 5/221). In October 1801, 24 men were required to go to the Gunpowder Mills at

Faversham or be discharged. John was one of those chosen and he agreed to go (Winters, *op.cit*, p.60). However, there is no evidence to show that he either went there or was discharged, since his records do not reveal a break in his service. In 1804, John was working as a Saltpetre Refiner at 2/-d per day and allowed to watch in turn, on average every 5th night, for which he received 1/-d (Supply 5/222).

By June 1807, John was employed as a Bargeman with his rate of pay unchanged (Supply 5/226) but this had risen to 3/-d daily by August 1808 (Supply 5/227). By August 1812, he was described as a Master Bargeman in receipt of 5/2d per day (Supply 5/229) and he retained this position for the rest of his working days, surviving the cuts to the Establishment in 1818 and 1821. A Return of Employees in 1821 confirmed he was a married man without issue and that he was living in Enfield. His annual pay at that date was £65.4.2d (Supply 5/232). A Return of Properties owned by the Board dated the 20th December 1834 revealed that John was living in a cottage on Lower Island with an annual rent of £5.4.0d (Supply 5/237). A proviso to the lease was, "his wife to look after the water" (WO54/546) i.e., to ensure that water was not wasted through the locks by the bargemen. The cottage is marked as Plot No. 16 on the Town Map shown in Appendix 1. A similar List of Properties for December 1840 confirmed this, but also recorded that John had died and that the tenement was then occupied by William Nottage (WO44/133). John Nigh, Master Bargeman, died on the 20th August 1837, and at some time between December 1834 and the 20th August 1837, had moved to High Bridge Street to one of the properties forming Plot No. 60 on the Town Map in Appendix 1, where his widow still resided in May 1840.

Thomas Nigh was engaged as an occasional Labourer in the Engineers' Department on the 5th December 1814, and in February 1816, he was paid 2/4d per day. He was then a 45-year-old married man without issue, living in Waltham Abbey (WO54/516).

Isaac Norris was engaged as an occasional Labourer in the Engineers' Department on the 20th June 1815. In February 1816, his pay was 2/8d per day; he was then a 40-year-old bachelor living in Cheshunt (WO54/516).

John Norton was a Labourer set to work by Daniel Cornish in October 1787 at 9/-d per week, possibly repairing the Mills following their purchase by the Government from Mr. Walton. However, he does not appear to have been retained (Winters, *op.cit.* p.28).

William Nottage (1) was working as a Corning House Man earning 2/2d per day in January 1806, at which time he had served the Board for a year (Supply 5/224). He continued to work in the Corning House, and by February 1814, his rate of pay was 3/3d per day. In addition, he was allowed to watch in turn, for which he received 1/6d per night (Supply 5/230).

William Nottage (2) lived in a cottage and engine house on Lower Island, and was employed in a private capacity by Lt.Col. Moody. The cottage was owned by the Board, and had been occupied by John Nigh, Master Bargeman, who died on the 20th August 1837 (WO44/133) and is marked as Plot No. 16 on the Town Map shown in Appendix 1. The 1841 Census recorded that William Nottage, Gardener, aged 50, his wife, Mary, and their children, Sarah and William, lived on the south side of High Bridge Street.

O

James O'Brien was the eldest son of James and Jane O'Brien of Faversham, where he was baptised on the 30th January 1801. His father was born in Ireland and worked as a Saltpetre Refiner at the Royal Gunpowder Manufactory at Ballincollig. Like his father, James Edward trained as a Saltpetre Refiner at Faversham before being made redundant in 1821. He married his wife, Martha, in 1823 at Hadlow in Kent, before rejoining the Ordnance at Faversham on the 19th February 1825, by which time, they had 3 children (WO54/623).

He was transferred to Waltham Abbey as the Master Brimstone Refiner by an Order of the Board dated the 23rd January 1829, following the death of John Lockyer (*FGPR*, p.62). He was paid a basic remuneration of £54.12.0d per annum and was allowed to watch in turn, which gave him another 2/-d per week, increasing his annual pay to £59.16.0d. A Return of Properties dated the 20th December 1834 prepared by the Royal Engineers' Office listing the houses and cottages owned by the Board, recorded that James had been living in a cottage in Powder Mill Lane from the 11th February 1829, and that his annual rent was £5.4.0d (Supply 5/237) i.e., in the same tenement as occupied by John Lockyer, being Plot No. 63 on the Town Map in Appendix 1. James continued to be employed as the Master Brimstone Refiner on the same pay and allowances, and moved to the Master Refiner's house, Plot No. 44 on the Town Map in Appendix 1, following the death of Samuel Britton.

The 1841 Census confirmed that he lived on the north side of High Bridge Street with his wife, Martha, and their 7 children. James died in 1866 at Sulphur Cottage, Eleanor Road, Cheshunt, and Martha died some years later. Both were buried in the old cemetery in Waltham Abbey (Article by a descendant, Simon Malone, in *The Strand Magazine,* 1999).

Robert Oldwell (Odwell) was working as a Stoveman in January 1806, earning 2/-d per day (Supply 5/224). This was also the case in June 1807, when, in addition to his pay, he was allowed 1/-d per night when it was his turn to watch (Supply 5/226).

Simeon Oldwell (Odwell) was employed as a "Respective Officer's Labourer" in September 1810 at 2/-d per day, and in addition, was allowed to watch in turn (Supply 5/228). In August 1812, he was described as the Clerk of the Survey's Labourer with pay of 2/8d per day and, in addition, he was still allowed to watch (Supply 5/229). In February 1814, he was employed as a Puntman on the same pay and allowances (Supply 5/230).

William Osbourne was employed as a Labourer in the Engineers' Department earning 1/6d per day, and worked in the Manufactory for 2 days in August 1790. His wages were submitted to and paid for by the Storekeeper, James Wright, by William Spry, Colonel commanding the Royal Engineers. William signed for his money with a cross (WASC 1382).

John Oswell was employed in September 1812 as a casual Labourer in the Engineers' Department at 2/8d per day (WO54/512).

Edward Ovenden, Carpenter 1st Class, was paid £1.9.0d for work carried out by the Engineers' Department within the Manufactory between the 15th and 21st July 1809 (Supply 5/228).

John Ovenden (1) was a Millwright in the Engineers' Department who was paid £1.5.6d for work carried out in the Manufactory between the 15th and 21st July 1809 (Supply 5/228).

John Ovenden (2) was appointed as a Cooper in September 1810 and paid 2/6d per day (Supply 5/228). He was still working as a

Cooper in August 1812, but was then paid 4/-d daily (Supply 5/229). This was also the case in February 1814 (Supply 5/230).

John Oxley was working as a Millman in June 1807 (Supply 5/226) and was still employed in that trade in February 1814 (Supply 5/230). During that period his rate of pay increased from 2/3d per day to 3/11d and, initially, if he worked at nights, he received an additional 3d, which had doubled to 6d by August 1808 (Supply 5/227).

William Oxley was working as a Millman in January 1806 earning 2/3d per day, and at that date, he had 2 years' service with the Board (Supply 5/224). He was still employed as a Millman in February 1814, but was then earning 3/-d per day, with an additional 6d when on night duty (Supply 5/230).

P

Daniel Page was a Sawyer set to work by Daniel Cornish in October 1787 at 9/-d per week, possibly repairing the Mills following their purchase by the Government from Mr. Walton. However, he does not appear to have been retained (Winters, *op.cit.* p.28).

John Page was employed by the Engineers' Department repairing the Corning House when it was engulfed by fire on the 16th June 1801. His name was forwarded to the Board as one of the men badly burnt, and it would appear that the Board responded immediately, with the writer saying he had "the Board's commands to transmit to you on the other side hereof a list of the men who have been burnt and otherwise hurt by the fire which lately destroyed the Corning House at Waltham Abbey; and I am to desire the Storekeeper will pay the men all their pay until they are recovered" (Supply 5/195). More information on the fire is given in the notes on Peter Page.

A John Page was working as a Labourer within the Storekeeper's Department in August 1812, "drawing and setting stoves and in the Willow Plantation" at 2/8d per day. He was also allowed to watch in turn, as was the case in February 1814 (Supply 5/229 and Supply 5/230 respectively).

Peter Page was employed as a Carpenter in the Engineers' Department. On the 16th June 1801, with others, Peter was repairing the Corning House when it caught fire following an explosion. The fire was caused "from a blow of a copper hammer on a pit wheel" (Winters, *op.cit.* p.59). The Storekeeper sent a letter to the Board dated the 23rd June listing the names of the men who had suffered terrible burns, seeking permission to support the casualties, and Peter's name was included. The letter went on to state "we beg to represent the situation of the poor men who were burnt when the Corning House took fire on the 16th instant when under repair." It continued, "...these men are burnt in a dreadful manner. Their pain is very great...." and "Our surgeon has represented the necessity of the men most burnt having immediate assistance in wine, as a considerable suppuration is come on their constitutions. They cannot support it without wine, and we have directed wine to be immediately provided to them; we request your permission for our continuing to support these poor men with such wine or other proper support as their surgeon may think their respective situations require" (Supply 5/195).

It would appear that the Board responded immediately. Replying the same day, the writer said he had "the Board's commands to transmit to you on the other side hereof a list of the men who have been burnt and otherwise hurt by the fire which lately destroyed the Corning House at Waltham Abbey, and I am to desire the Storekeeper will pay the men all their pay until they are recovered" (Supply 5/195). Another letter to the Board dated the 29th July 1801, stated that the men who had been burnt at the Corning House requested that they were reimbursed for the loss of clothing. The list included Peter Page, whose claim amounted to £2.17.6d in all – for a hat (10/-d) handkerchiefs (3/6d) waistcoat (6/-d) shirt (6/-d) coat 6/-d, coat (12/-d) breeches (14/-d) and pillowcases (6/-d). The same letter went on to say that Mr. Page, amongst others, suffered so much that he wished for death to release him from his torture, and that it was a matter of surprise that he was recovering (Supply 5/221). The constant attention the men needed meant that their wives could not undertake seasonal work (haymaking) at which they could earn sufficient to pay the rent. It was requested that financial allowances were made, but no record of the Board's response in that respect has come to light.

George Pain was born circa 1771 and began employment with the Ordnance Board at Waltham Abbey on the 8th September 1793 (Supply 5/232) where he spent the next 33 years of his working life (WO54/556). In January 1794, he was working in the Corning House (Supply 5/216) and in May of that year he enlisted as a Private in the Volunteer Company (Supply 5/219). George had changed his workplace by August 1794, becoming a Mixing House Man earning 1/6d per day (Supply 5/216). In September 1798, he was described as "drawing and setting stoves and clearing willow plantation" (5/219).

A Petition on Pay and Conditions within the Mills submitted to the Board in 1800 showed that George was illiterate (Supply 5/220). A Return of the Marital Status of the Employees in May 1801, recorded that George was a married man without issue (Supply 5/221). In common with the majority of the workforce In November 1801, George was employed in "cleaning and deepening the river and canals, as well as performing other necessary sundry works" and during this period his pay remained at 1/6d per day (Supply 5/221). By May 1804, he was employed as a Refiner, paid 2/-d per day and, in addition, was allowed to watch in turn, which was, on average, every 5th night, for which he received 1/-d (Supply 5/222).

In January 1806, Pain was "drawing and setting stoves" earning 2/-d per day (Supply 5/224) and continued to be employed as a Stoveman practically for the rest of his life. In June 1807, he is listed as "working in any part of the Manufactory setting & drawing stoves and loading and unloading barges etc." (Supply 5/226). As a Stoveman (sometimes described as a Steam Stoveman) his pay rose from 2/-d per day in August 1808 (Supply 5/227) and peaked at 3/3d daily in February 1814 (Supply 5/230). This amount fell to 2/4d by June 1818 when he was also allowed to watch in turn, again for 1/-d each night. It was also noted that he was then a 44-year-old married man who lived in Waltham Abbey, and that he was still without issue (Supply 5/231). The same Return recorded that he resided in accommodation owned by the Board, linking him with Benjamin Poulter, who, it is known, lived on Aqueduct Island. This might be a clerical error for several reasons. Firstly, the Island was in Cheshunt and not Waltham Abbey, secondly, the adjoining cottage to Poulter's had been occupied by John Brown since 1810 and was his home until the 1830's, and, finally, George Pain's name does not appear in any Lists of Properties owned by the Board.

When the Establishment was cut back in 1818 because of the reduced demand for gunpowder, George retained his position as a Stoveman by an Order of the Board dated the 4th September 1818. His pay and allowances remained unchanged, and he had an annual income of £41.14.4d (Supply 5/231 and 5/232). In the spring of 1822, the Ordnance Board decided to cut production and regeneration of gunpowder still further, so the Establishment at Waltham Abbey was reduced yet again. Accordingly, Empson Middleton and James Wright drew up lists of people to be dismissed on the 1st June 1822, and George Pain's name was included on those lists (Supply 5/232). However, a List of Employees dated the 10th October 1822 showed that he had been retained, and was required to carry out any type of work anywhere within the Manufactory (Supply 5/233). This was confirmed in another Return dated the 1st April 1823, which showed that he was classified as "a Labourer for general purposes to be sent to all parts of the Manufactory wherever their services may be requested." His pay for the year was £39.0.0d, which included an allowance for watching in turn (WO54/542). This amount was reduced by £2.12.0d per annum in accordance with the Board's Orders of the 27th December 1822 and the 15th January 1823 (WO54/542) but had been restored to its former level of £39.0.0d per annum by October 1824 (WO54/546). The same documents noted that Pain was still a married without children. In October 1825, he had been restored as a Stoveman (Winters, *op.cit.* pp.93-95) with his pay and allowances unchanged (WO54/550). George died sometime between October 1825 and April 1826 (WO54/550 and WO54/554).

James Pallet was born circa 1786 and commenced his employment as a Labourer with the Ordnance Board at the Waltham Abbey Mills on the 20th February 1805 (Supply 5/232). In June 1807, he was working in the Corning House earning 2/2d per day and, in addition, he was allowed to watch in turn, for which he received 1/-d per night (Supply 5/226). James continued to work in the Corning House and in September 1810, he was paid 2/10d per day and 1/6d when it was his turn to watch (Supply 5/228).

By August 1812, he was employed as the Office Keeper (sometimes described as the Office Keeper and Messenger) at 3/3d per day, and he was still allowed to watch in turn (Supply 5/229). This was also the case in February 1814 (Supply 5/230). Although still the Office Keeper in June 1818, his daily rate of pay had been reduced to 2/11d. He was then a married man with one child (Supply 5/231). When the Establishment at Waltham was reduced in numbers in September 1818, although James was retained, it was not as the Office Keeper but as a Bargeman, and he was paid 3/-d per day to support his family which then comprised 2 children (Supply 5/232). He had in fact changed jobs with Joseph Brown, who was then the Office Keeper. However, a Return of Employees for September 1820 disclosed that James was at that time working in the Corning House earning 2/11d per day, and, together with his allowance to watch, his annual pay amounted to £50.16.11d (Supply 5/232).

A Statement dated the 16th February 1822 of "monies to which the public were entitled to receive credit between the 1st January 1821 and the 31st December 1821 showing the amounts received by the Storekeeper", recorded that James Pallet was residing in a house purchased by the Board – Tenement No. 39 – at a rental of £5.4.0d per annum. The document further stated that James Pallet had occupied the property prior to its purchase by the Board, and that "sanction will be asked for their future residing in them" which was granted by the Board on the 4th May 1821 (Supply 5/232). The property and its small garden has been identified as being one of a terrace in Powder Mill Lane forming part of Plot No. 63 on the Town Map in Appendix 1.

In the spring of 1822, the Ordnance Board decided to reduce the production and regeneration of gunpowder at the Establishment at Waltham Abbey still further. Accordingly, Empson Middleton and James Wright drew up lists of people to be retained, and Pallet was included, not as a Corning House Man but as a Labourer "drawing and setting stoves" (Supply 5/232). In April 1823 his annual pay, including his watch allowance, was £39.0.0d (WO54/542) and he then had 3 children to support. He replaced George Ridpath as a Corning House Man on the 25th May 1825 with his annual pay and allowance increased to £48.2.0d (WO54/550) and at that date it was recorded that he had 4 children. His pay remained at the same level until his death in 1833 (WO54/587).

A Return of Properties owned by the Board dated the 20th December 1834 (Supply 5/237) showed that Widow Pallet was living in Powder Mill Lane, having become the tenant by an Order of the Board dated the 16th July 1833. A similar Return made in May 1840, confirmed that Elizabeth Pallet was living in the same house following the death of her husband (WO44/133). The 1841 Census recorded that Elizabeth Pallet, Laundress, (aged 50); James Pallet (13) and Ann Pallet (11) were living in Powder Mill Lane, along with John Goats (65) as a lodger. John Goats had worked at the Mills as a Saltpetre Refiner and his wife had died by 1839.

Thomas Pallet, born circa 1766, was set to work by Daniel Cornish in October 1787as a Labourer at 9/-d per week, possibly renovating the Mills following their purchase from Mr. Walton by the Government (Winters, *op. cit.* p. 29). Pallet started work as a Labourer in the Refining House on the 10th August 1789, and was paid 1/6d per day (Supply 5/213); apart from a short spell in 1790, the Refining House was to be his workplace until 1818. A Return for March 1790 recorded that he was refining Saltpetre under the Master Refiner, John Baker, (Supply 5/214) and a footnote to a Labour Return for August 1790 stated, "Thomas had been bagging alder wood in the country but had now returned to the Refining House" (Supply 5/215). In May 1784 he enlisted as a Private in the Volunteer Company (Supply 5/219).

A Petition on Pay and Conditions at the Mills submitted to the Board in February 1800, showed that Thomas was illiterate (Supply 5/220) while a Return on the Marital Status of the Employees dated May 1801 recorded that he was a married man with 6 children (Supply 5/231). Both documents recorded that he was still a Saltpetre Refiner. Robert Coleman, Clerk of the Cheque, noted in his Minute Book on the 23rd October 1801, that 24 men were required to work at Faversham or be discharged. Thomas Pallet was one of these men, but the Storekeeper, James Wright, intervened, and requested that as Pallet was very ill and had young children, he should be allowed to stay at Waltham (Winters, *op.cit.* p.60).

A Return of Articifers and Labourers for November 1801 showed that, while Thomas was still employed as a Refining Labourer, he and others "having been employed in cleaning the river etc. but have taken cold and are now very unwell, when recovered [they] may be employed as before" (Supply 5/221). Thomas had returned to the Refining House by January 1806 with his pay increased to 2/-d per day, and, in line with all Refiners, received an additional allowance of 1/-d per night when it was his turn to watch – on average every 5th night (Supply 5/222).

On the 22nd April 1806, the Board purchased 13 houses in West Street (High Bridge Street) and Powder Mill Lane, and one of the sitting tenants was a Thomas Pallet (WO44/681a). As mentioned previously, Thomas was a sick man, and this is the last entry found in the records relating to him. It is possible that Thomas died, for by an Order dated the 13th June 1808, a William Pallet was admitted as a tenant to a cottage in Power Mill Lane (Supply 5/232), and this could have been Thomas's son, who would have been 15 or 16 years of age at the time. The same information was repeated in a similar Return made the following year, and the cottage in question with its small garden has been identified as part of a terrace located in Powder Mill Lane, forming part of Plot No. 62 on the Town Map in Appendix 1.

William Pallet (1) started employment at the Mills as a Saltpetre Refiner on the 16th July 1790 earning 1/6d per day, and the Refining House was to be his workplace until at least November 1801, at the same rate of pay (Supply 5/221). He enlisted as a Private in the Volunteer Company on the 4th May 1794 (Supply 5/219) and the Petition on Pay and Conditions at the Mills submitted to the Board in February 1800 showed that he was illiterate (Supply 5/220). A Return of the Marital Status of the Employees made in May 1801, noted that he was then a single man (Supply 5/221). A Return of Articifers and Labourers for November 1801 recorded that while Thomas was still employed as a Refining Labourer, like Thomas Pallet and others, "having been employed in cleaning the river etc. but have taken cold and are now very unwell, when recovered [they] may be employed as before" (Supply 5/221). This is the last reference found relating to William at the Mills in the early 1800's.

William Pallet (2) was born circa 1793, and may well have been the son of Thomas Pallet. William first appeared in a Return of Employees in August 1812, when he was working as a Labourer "drawing and setting stoves and in the willow plantation" and was paid 2/8d per day. In addition, he was allowed to watch in turn (Supply 5/229) as he was in 1813 (Winters, *op.cit.*p.77).

In February 1814, William Pallet was employed as an extra Bargeman earning 3/10d per day (Supply 5/230). He was still a Bargeman in June 1818, but with his pay reduced to 3/-d daily (Supply 5/231). This Return stated that he was then a married man of 24 with one child, and that he lived in Waltham Abbey. A list of names of the people the Storekeeper proposed to retain on the Establishment to meet the new production and cost requirements between the 4th September and 31st December 1818, was sent to the Board on the 28th August, and William's name was included on the list (Supply 5/231). A few days later, a second letter to the Board stated, "We respectfully beg leave to add the names and stations of those people whom it will be necessary to discharge in consequence of this arrangement" and William Pallet's name was included (Supply 5/231).

Although William (2) appears to have been dismissed, nevertheless, a William Pallet was recorded in a Statement dated the 16th February 1822 "of monies to which the public were entitled to receive credit between the 1st January and the 31st December 1821 shewing the amounts received by the storekeeper." This document recorded that a William Pallet had been leasing a cottage owned by the Board, Tenement No. 20, at a rent of £5.4.0d per annum and was confirmed by an Order dated the 13th June 1808 (Supply 5/232). The same information was repeated in a similar Return made the following year. Allowing for a slight delay in preparing the legal papers, this can only be the tenement where Thomas Pallet lived. The cottage and small garden have been identified as being in Powder Mill Lane, forming part of Plot No.62 on the Town Map in Appendix 1. A William Pallet was still living in the same cottage in 1825 (1825 Valuation of Waltham Abbey – D/DHf B29) on the Waltham Abbey Town Map of 1825.

J. Palmer was an extra Bargeman employed on 3 barges transporting gunpowder to Picket's Field and Magazines in May 1804, for which he was paid £2.2.0d per week (Supply 5/222).

Samuel Palmer was working as a Millman in June 1807 with pay of 2/3d per day, in addition to which, he was allowed 3d per night extra when on duty (Supply 5/226). By August 1808, Palmer was employed as a Puntman earning 2/-d per day, and, in addition, he was allowed to watch in turn (Supply 5/227). This was also the case in September 1810 (Supply 5/228).

James Parish was working as a casual Labourer in the Engineers' Department in September 1818, with pay of 2/8d per day for a six-day week (WO54/512).

John Parish was working as a casual Labourer in the Engineers' Department in September 1812, with pay of 2/8d per day for a six-day week (WO54/512). In February 1814, he replaced James Oldwell as the Clerk of the Survey's Labourer, and was still paid 2/8d per day as well as being allowed to watch in turn (Supply 5/230).

Joseph Parish was employed as a Labourer in February 1814, "drawing and setting stoves and in the willow plantation." He was paid 2/8d per day and, in addition, allowed to watch in turn (Supply 5/230).

Benjamin Parker was employed as a Labourer in the Engineers' Department earning 1/6d per day. In August 1790, he worked within the Manufactory with his wages submitted to and paid for by the Storekeeper, James Wright, by William Spry, Colonel commanding the Royal Engineers. He signed for his pay with a cross (WASC 1382). He joined the Storekeeper's Department in January 1805, and was employed in the Corning House where he was paid 2/2d per day in January 1806 (Supply 5/224). He was still working in the Corning House in September 1810, but was then paid 2/6d per day and allowed to watch in turn, for which he received 1/6d per night (Supply 5/228).

At 11.15 a.m. on the 27th November 1811, there was a huge explosion at No. 4 Press House; the ensuing fire engulfed the Corning House together with the Reel House, which also exploded. There was much damage to the town with many windows shattered, and reports in the press recorded that the explosion was heard as far away as Hackney, Blackwall and Marylebone (Winters, *op.cit.* p.72). A graphic account of the explosion was reported in the *Cambridge Chronicle* on the 29th November 1811, and reads as follows:

"A Dreadful Accident. A powder mill at Waltham Abbey was blown up on Wednesday last, 8 lives were lost, and 7 of those persons left families. The whole town of Waltham was in great danger, as it was thought the magazine would have blown up. A man was, in consequence, sent through the streets of Waltham to caution the inhabitants to leave their houses instantly. No further explosion had, however, taken place at the date of our last account. At Stepney a mirror of plate glass was broken by the shock; at Hackney several panes of glass were forced in; and at Blackwall the windows throughout a whole street were shattered. Near the New-road, Marylebone, several houses were much broken; and the labourers who were excavating in the park felt the earth shake where they were at work. Even ships of the river were shaken. Some of the morning papers mistook it for an earthquake. This seems singular that the shock should be felt so much more in London, while the damage done in the town was but trifling, except that the current of air at that time might have directed the concussion from the town." (Winters, *op.cit.* p.72).

Supply 5/229 recorded that among those killed was Benjamin Parker, who left a widow, sons John (12) Benjamin (5) and Jacob (Job) aged 2, and daughters Leonora (Laura) aged 7 and Sarah (6). Another daughter, Ann, was born after his death (Supply 5/232). The Board granted his widow, Ann, a charitable pension of 17/6d per week. A letter to the Board dated the 13th May 1818 disclosed that Ann Parker, the widow of Benjamin Parker, had received an offer to marry again, and she had requested that the pension of 17/6d per week which had been granted to her for the support of herself and her family, might now be divided among her 6 children in such proportions and for such terms as the Board might think proper (Supply 5/202). The Board agreed to this proposal and directed, therefore, that the pension of 17/6d granted to Mrs. Parker should be divided with effect from the 17th May 1818, as follows:

"John Parker, 17 years old, his pension to cease on his 18th birthday, the 11th March 1819 -

	2s.0d per week
Job (Jacob) Parker, 8 years old,	3s.0d per week.
Benjamin Parker, 12 years old,	3s.0d per week
Sarah Parker, 13 years old,	3s.0d per week.
Laura Parker, 15 years old,	3s.0d per week.
Ann Parker, 6 years old,	3s.6d per week"

It was stated that the allowances to the boys should be paid until they attained the age of 18 years, and the girls until they married. Ann, the widow, did remarry (Supply 5/232). Sarah married in 1825 (Winters, *op.cit.* p.96) but Ann, the daughter, was still in receipt of a pension of £9.2.0d per annum in 1837 (Supply 5/237).

James Parker was employed by the Engineers' Department as a Labourer on the 12th August 1815 at 2/8d per day; he was then an 18-year-old bachelor living in Waltham Abbey (WO54/516).

John Parker was working as a Cooper in August 1812, earning 1/9d per day (Supply 5/229). Although he was still employed in the same trade in February 1814, at that time he was paid 2/4d per day (Supply 5/230).

Thomas Parker was born circa 1775 and was employed as an occasional Labourer by the Engineers' Department on the 25th May 1811, earning 2/4d per day for a six-day week (WO54/516). In September 1812, his pay had increased to 2/8d per day (WO54/512) and was the same in February 1816, when he was described as a 40-year-old married man living in Waltham Abbey with his family of 5 children (WO54/516). By 1818, his daily wage as an occasional Labourer had been reduced to 2/4d (WO54/524), and a Labour Return for September 1820 recorded that he was then a widower (WO54/532). Wages were reduced still further, and in April 1823, his daily rate of pay had been cut to 2/2d, which amounted to an annual income of £33.18.2d (WO54/542). The same document recorded that he had remarried, and a Return for April 1830 noted that he then had 6 children (WO54/570). A Return of Persons belonging to the Civil Establishment of the Ordnance at the Gunpowder and Small Arms Manufactories at Waltham, Faversham and Enfield, showing in detail the several points of information required by the Master General and Board's Order dated the 31st January 1831, recorded that Thomas Parker was one of 15 Labourers to be employed at Waltham Abbey Powder Mills and the Enfield Small Arms Factory. He was to be paid 2/2d per day and employed to undertake different services as a Labourer in the Manufactories, where steadiness and sobriety were required (WO54/575). Thomas was still working as a Labourer for the same money in April 1834 (WO54/593).

William Parmenter was employed as a Millman in 1805; in January 1806 he was paid 2/3d per day, with 3d extra if he worked at night (Supply 5/224) and this was also the case in June 1807 (Supply 5/226).

William Passfield was born circa 1777. He worked as a common Labourer with the Engineers' Department, and was paid 17/-d for work carried out in the Manufactory by that Department between the 15th and 21st July 1809 (Supply 5/228). He joined the Storekeeper's Department on the 29th January 1811 (WO54/536) and in August 1812, he was working as a Labourer "drawing and setting stoves and in the willow plantation" at 2/8d per day, in addition to which, he was allowed to watch in turn (Supply 5/229). He was still employed in the same work in February 1814, earning the same money (Supply 5/230). When the Establishment was cut back in September 1818, William was retained as a Saltpetre Refiner by an Order of the Board dated the 4th September 1818, which was confirmed by a second Order of the 4th October 1819. His annual pay was £41.14.4d, which included his watch allowance (Supply 5/232). The same Record noted that he was then a widower, aged 41, with 6 children, and that he lived in Waltham Abbey.

In the spring of 1822, the Ordnance Board decided to reduce the production and regeneration of gunpowder at Waltham Abbey, and the Establishment was to be trimmed to an even lower level. Accordingly, Empson Middleton and James Wright drew up lists of people to be dismissed (Supply 5/232). The men were subsequently made redundant on the 1st June, and, asking for financial assistance, submitted several Petitions. Many were long service employees in middle age, and they pointed out that they had little hope of finding employment after the corn harvest had been gathered. The Storekeeper was sympathetic and forwarded their Petitions to the Board for consideration. William Passfield, signing with a cross, was one of the Petitioners, and he was awarded 2 weeks' pay to ease his financial burden (Supply 5/232).

William Paton (Peyton) (1) was a Carpenter 1st class who was paid £1.9.9d for work carried out in the Manufactory by the Engineers' Department between the 15th and 21st July 1809 (Supply 5/228). He was working as a Carpenter within the Manufactory on the 27th November 1811, when there was a tremendous explosion at No. 4 Press House, and the ensuing fire engulfed the Corning House and Reel House, which also exploded (for full details see the notes on Benjamin Parker). William was working at an adjacent Mill at the time, and noticed that a piece of burning rope had landed on the platform in front of the powder magazine near a door, which had wrenched from its hinges. He ran to the spot, extinguishing the rope and secured the door, therefore, preventing a huge explosion. Mr Mathews, the Storekeeper, recommended that he be rewarded for his prompt action (Supply 5/229) and he was given £20 (Winters, *op.cit*, p.71). It is clear that William was to be dismissed in 1818 but had made representation to be retained, because a letter from the Office of Ordnance dated The 27th February 1818, stated therein "Having laid before the Board your letter of the 30th ult. reporting upon the Petition from William Paton, Carpenter in the service of this Department at Waltham Abbey, I am directed to desire you will retain Mr. Paton, in consequence of the courage and conduct he evinced at the late explosion of the Mills in 1811" (Supply 5/202).

William Paton (2) commenced his employment at the Mills as a general Labourer in the Corning House on the 12th April 1798, and was paid 1/6d per day. He also enlisted as a Private in the Volunteer Company (Supply 5/219). The signed Petition on Pay and Conditions at the Mills presented to the Board in February 1800 showed that he was illiterate and still employed as a Labourer (Supply 5/220) while a Return on the Marital Status of the Employees dated May 1801, recorded that he was a married man with 1 child (Supply 5/221).

William Peach was working as a Labourer in the "Engineers' Department Established" (i.e., he was a regular employee and not a casual or occasional worker) earning 1/6d per day, with "one day extra allowed per week agreeable to the Board's Order dated the 12th March 1801" (Supply 5/222).

Thomas Pearce was engaged as an occasional Labourer in the Engineers' Department on the 4th November 1815 and paid 2/8d per day; he was then a 20-year-old bachelor living in Waltham Abbey (WO54/516).

John Pegrum was working as a Millman in September 1810. He was paid 2/3d per day, as well as being allowed 6d per night when on duty (Supply 5/228).

Joseph Pegrum was working as a Millman in August 1812 at 3/-d per day, in addition to being allowed 6d per night when on duty (Supply 5/229).

Thomas Pegrum was working in the Engineers' Department as a casual Labourer in September 1812, earning 2/8d per day for a six-day-week (WO54/512).

William Pegrum started work as an occasional Labourer in the Engineers' Department on the 16th May 1815 and was paid 2/8d per day; he was then a 24-year-old bachelor living in Waltham Abbey (WO54/516).

Edward Pellold is believed to have been a Millman because of his rate of pay. From the 13th April 1789 for an unknown period, the Millmen and general Labourers were engaged in cutting a new canal at the new Corning House, as well as cutting willow trees and loading barges, etc. (Supply 5/213).

Thomas Penfold was working as a Labourer in February 1814 "drawing and setting stoves and in the Willow Plantation". He was paid 2/8d per day, as well as being allowed to watch in turn (Supply 5/230).

Jesse Penfold was a Cylinderman in August 1812 earning 2/8d per day (Supply 5/229) as he was in February 1814 (Supply 5/230).

William Periment was employed as a Millman in August 1812 earning 3/-d per day, and in addition, he was allowed 6d per night when on duty (Supply 5/229).

George Perkins started his employment as a casual Bricklayer's Labourer in the Engineers' Department on the 27th May 1814, and was paid 2/8d per day. In February 1816, he was an 18-year-old bachelor living in Waltham Abbey (WO54/516).

Henry Perkins was a Labourer set to work by Daniel Cornish in October 1787 at 9/-d per week, possibly repairing the Mills following their purchase by the Government from Mr. Walton. However, he does not appear to have been retained (Winters, *op.cit.* p.29).

W. Perkins was a Bricklayer set to work by Daniel Cornish in October 1787 at 9/-d per week, possibly repairing the Mills following their purchase by the Government from Mr. Walton, but he does not appear to have been kept on (Winters, *op.cit.* p.29).

Robert Perkis, Snr. was born circa 1759. On the 1st June 1789, he started employment at the Powder Mills at Waltham Abbey, and this was to be his workplace for the next 46 years. Initially, he worked as a Labourer "setting and drawing stoves etc." for which he was paid 1/6d per day (Supply 5/213) and was undertaking the same work in September 1789 (Supply 5/214). By March 1790, he was "dusting and glazing powder" for the same pay (Supply 5/214) before transferring to the Corning House by February 1793 at the same daily figure (Supply 5/217). In September 1798, he was employed in the Proof House (Supply 5/219) where he remained until his retirement in 1834. In May 1794, he enlisted as a Private in the Volunteer Company (Supply 5/219). The signed Petition on Pay and Conditions at the Mills submitted to the Board in February 1800, showed that he was illiterate (Supply 5/220) while a Return of the Marital Status of the Employees recorded that he was a married man with 4 children (Supply 5/221). In November 1801, and in common with the majority of the workforce, Robert was employed in "cleaning and deepening the river and canals, as well as performing other necessary sundry works" (Supply 5/221). By 1806, his daily rate of pay had increased to 2/-d (Supply 5/224) and in September 1810, he was described as a Sieve Puncher and Proof House man but was still paid the same money. In addition, he was then allowed to "watch in turn" (Supply 5/228) and by August 1812, his remuneration had been increased to 2/8d per day (Supply 5/229).

A list of Employees dated The 25th June 1818 stated that Robert Perkis was employed as a Proof House Man, that he was a married man of 57 with 5 children, who lived in Waltham Abbey and earned 2/4d per day. He was also allowed to watch in turn, for which he received 1/-d per night (Supply 5/231). Robert was retained when the Establishment was reduced in numbers in 1818 and again in 1822, with his pay and allowances remaining the same until his retirement. These totalled £39.0.0d per annum, although this sum was reduced by £2.12.0d for a short period in 1823 (WO54/542).

A statement dated the 16th February 1822 "of monies to which the public were entitled to receive credit between the 1st January and the 31st December 1821 shewing the amounts received by the storekeeper" recorded that Robert Perkis was one of several employees "having occupied their present residences previous to the Hon. Board purchasing the same, sanction will be asked for their future residing in them." Under an Order dated the 4th May 1821, the tenement was leased to him for an annual rent of £5.4.0d (Supply 5/232). The cottage and its small garden have been identified as being on the north side of High Bridge Street to the west of its junction with Powder Mill Lane, forming part of Plot No. 60 on the Town Map in Appendix 1. The last entry for Robert in the Lists of Employees was dated the 1st October 1834, and recorded that he was then 71, with just over 46 years' service (WO54/593). A List of Properties owned by the Board submitted by the Royal Engineers' Office on the 20th December 1834, recorded that Robert had been superannuated, and that his cottage was "either to be let or removed" (Supply 5/237). A similar Return for 1840 indicated that the property was unoccupied and included a footnote saying, "refused to be occupied" (WO44/133).

Robert Perkis, Jnr. was Apprenticed to the Assistant Master Worker, John Ashwood, in August 1808. Robert was paid 6/-d per week, while his Master received 7/-d weekly (Supply 5/227). Towards the end of the seven-year Apprenticeship, Robert's pay had increased to 6/8d per week while Ashwood was receiving 8/-d (Supply 5/230). Together with another Apprentice, William Alsup, Robert was one of the casualties of the reduction in the workforce in 1818. They petitioned the Board stating that they were Articled Apprentices who paid £3.0.0d when first Articled, and that they had served 7 years, continuing 2 years after the term of Apprenticeship had expired, after which they were discharged upon the reduction. Having gone into the Works at an early age, they were then unable to earn a livelihood in any other employment. They further said that they had made themselves proficient in their several Departments and hoped that "their Lordships would take into their benign consideration their disagreeable case", and replace them again into their former situation in the Works, "in which case your humble Petitioners will as in duty bound to you for ever pray" (Supply 5/231).

The Board required more information from the Storekeeper at Waltham Abbey, who appeared to have been unsympathetic to the plea, giving preference to family men who were employed. In a letter to the Board dated the 7th April 1818 (Supply 5/231) the Storekeeper replied "In obedience to the Honourable Board's commands contained in your letter of the 1st instant desiring us to report upon the enclosed Petition of Robert Perkis and William Allsup, praying that they may be restored to their situations in the Royal Powder mills, having served their Apprenticeship in the Department from which they were discharged on account of the reduction. We beg leave respectfully to represent that Robert Perkis and William Allsup were taken as Apprentices, the one as Apprentice to the Assistant Master Worker, the other as Apprentice to the Master of Composition, [and] after serving their Apprenticeship they were employed as Labourers in the Manufactory." Further, "in forming an arrangement to comply with the Honourable board's commands of the 22nd December last that a reduction should take place at the Royal gunpowder Manufactory at Waltham Abbey, the beforementioned Robert Perkis and William Allsup were selected, amongst others, as junior labourers to be discharged, for if a preference had to be given to them to be retained, other Labourers with families who had been longer in the service than themselves who are single young men (would feel the same). We are therefore humbly of [the] opinion that they do not have cause for complaint." Nevertheless, in a letter dated the 10th April 1818 (Supply 5/202) it appears that the Board ordered that the two were to be "re-entered when any augmentation be required."

James Perry, possibly a cousin of Joseph Perry, was working as a Saltpetre Refiner in August 1812 earning 2/8d per day (Supply 5/229) as he was in June 1813 (Winters, *op.cit.* p.77). This was also the case in February 1814 (Supply 5/230).

Joseph Perry was the youngest son of William and Sarah Perry (nee Day) who were married by banns at Waltham Abbey on the 20th April 1777. Joseph was baptised at Waltham Abbey on the 13th May 1791. Joseph married Sarah Ann, circa 1812. They made their home in Sewardstone Street, where they raised their family of 5 children, William born in 1814, James in 1816, Henry in 1819, Mary Ann in 1832 and Joseph, Jnr. in 1827. Joseph died in 1860 and Sarah in 1878 in one of the town's almshouses (*Armes' Family History*) and she was the Mrs. Perry mentioned on page145 in Winters' *Centenary Memorial* book.

In February 1814, Joseph was working as a Labourer "drawing and setting stoves and in the Willow Plantation" at 2/8d per day and was allowed to watch in turn (Supply 5/230). By June 1818, he was employed as the Clerk of the Cheque's Labourer earning 2/4d per day (Supply 5/231). He was still in the same position the following year on the same pay, but was then allowed to watch in turn, for which he received 1/-d per night (Supply 5/231) which amount had risen to 1/6d per night by April 1824 (Supply 5/232). Joseph left the Mills shortly afterwards, but was re-engaged on the 22nd July 1825 as a general Labourer working within the Manufactory, replacing George Ridpath. He was paid £39.0.0d per annum, which included an allowance to watch in turn (WO54/550). On the 21st October 1827, he was paid 16/-d for travelling from Waltham to Purfleet and back to deliver a message, i.e., 48 miles at 4d per mile (Winters, *op.cit.* p.98).

Joseph continued to be employed as a general Labourer until the 3rd June 1833, when he was appointed as a Cylinderman at 2/2d per day, and was still allowed to watch (WO54/587). Upon the retirement of Benjamin Guinn, Joseph was appointed as a Millman on the 22nd October 1837, and his total annual pay rose to £46.16.6d (WO54/623). The 1841 Census recorded that Joseph and his wife, Sarah, were living in Sewardstone Street with their son, James, and he was still working as a Millman in 1855 (Winters, *op.cit.* p.112).

William Perry, the son of Joseph and Sarah Ann Perry, was baptised at Waltham Abbey on the 22nd May 1814. He was employed as a general Labourer within the Manufactory on the 26th October 1836, and earned a total of £39.0.0d per annum, which included an allowance to watch in turn (WO54/623). On the 16th May 1839, he married a widow, Mary Ann Winters of Walkern, near Stevenage. Mary's son was William Winters, the famous Waltham Abbey Historian and writer, whose works are referred to throughout these notes. The 1841 Census recorded that William, a Labourer at the Powder Mills, and his wife, Mary (aged 25) together with their daughter - also named Mary - (aged 1) and William Winters (aged 5) were living in a property in a lane leading to Sewardstone Street, William Perry's descendants continued to work at the Mills.

Richard Philpot was working as a casual Labourer in the Engineers' Department in September 1812, earning 2/8d per day for a six-day-week (WO54/512).

Joseph Pickett joined the Engineers' Department on the 11th June 1815. In February 1816, he was earning 2/8d per day as a 25-year-old married man with no children, and lived in Waltham Abbey (WO54/516).

Thomas Pickett was working as a Saltpetre Refiner in August 1812, being paid 2/8d per day, and in addition, when not working extra, he was allowed to watch in turn (Supply 5/229). This was also the case in February 1813, when the same pay and allowance applied (Supply 5/230).

Robert Picktall was employed as the 3rd Clerk at Waltham Abbey on the 23rd September 1812, with annual pay of £70.0.0d. He was not on the Establishment (Supply 5/230).

William Pierce (Pearce) was born circa 1777, and in January 1806, he was working as a Labourer "drawing and setting stoves etc." for which he was paid 2/-d per day. By that date he had some 6 months' service (Supply 5/224). By August 1808, he was one of the Foremen in the Reeling House earning 2/10d per day and, in addition, was allowed to watch in turn, for which he received 1/6d (Supply 5/227). In August 1812, Mr. Pierce was a Glazing Mill Foreman earning 3/10d per day, in addition to which, he was also a Rounder every 3rd night, which added another 2/-d to his pay (Supply 5/229). By February 1814, William had changed his workplace again, and was a Corning House Foreman, paid 4/-d per day and he still acted as a Rounder as before (Supply 5/230).

He remained employed in June 1818, but then as a Dusting House Foreman earning 3/4d per day. Although continuing as a Rounder, at that date he received only 1/6d every 5th night (Supply 5/231 and WO54/524). The same Returns noted that he was then a 41-year-old married man with 4 children, and that he resided in Waltham Abbey. When the Establishment was cut back in September 1818, William was retained as the Dusting House Foreman on the same pay, but was no longer a Rounder. However, he was allowed to watch in turn, for which he received 1/-d (Supply 5/231). William suffered another setback to his finances in September 1820 when he was employed as a Saltpetre Refiner, with his daily pay at 2/4d. Nevertheless, his watch allowance increased to 1/6d per night, but by then he had 5 children to support (Supply 5/231). He remained a Saltpetre

Refiner in April 1821 (Supply5/232) but appears to have left the Mills before the 21st March 1822 (Winters, *op.cit.* p.89).

John Piercy was listed in 1802 as the Master of the barge "The Peggy" (Winters, *op.cit.* p.55). *The Peggy* was a 28-ton vessel employed, but not owned, by the Ordnance at Faversham from the 10th December 1794, plying between Faversham and the Tower of London (Supply 5/72). *The Peggy,* also described as a Faversham Powder Hoy, went into service at Waltham Abbey in 1802. More details of John Piercy can be found in *FGPR* on page 65.

George Pittendrigh (1) was born circa 1749, and served in the Artillery from the 8th May 1776 to the 21st April 1783. He joined the labour force at Waltham Abbey on the 1st March 1788, but was seconded to the Mills at Faversham as a Labourer until January 1789 (Supply 5/70) returning as a Labourer to Waltham Abbey on the 1st February 1789 (Supply 5/217). In April 1789, he was "cutting and planting willow trees, cutting of canal at the new Corning House, removing earth to the store, unloading barge of coals and charring wood" (Supply 5/213). The following September he was employed as a Millman, as he was in March 1790 (Supply 5/214). A letter dated the 22nd May 1790 to the Board from the Storekeeper and the Clerk of the Cheque, described how between the hours of 10 and 11 o'clock the two Hoppit Mills blew up. The Millman, George Pittendrigh, had just laid a fresh composition on the beds and was just drawing water, and the runners had "scarce made two revolutions when the Lower Mill went off which communicated to the other." The letter went on to say that the Mills were "very old and decay" and that the fire had "great hold" on them, and much damage was done (WASC 0475).

George continued to work as a Millman until the 1st July 1793 when he was made the Labour Foreman "Superintending In different parts of the Manufactory, drawing and setting stoves and weighing powder etc." (Supply 5/217). He joined the Volunteer Company on the 7th May 1794, and held the rank of Sergeant by 1798 (Supply 5/219). The signed Petition on Pay and Conditions at the Mills submitted to the Board in February 1800 revealed that he was literate and that he was still the Labour Foreman (Supply 5/220). The Return of the Marital Status of the Employees recorded that he was married with 6 children (Supply 5/221) although subsequent Returns recorded only 5 children (WO54/524). In November 1801, he was supervising the Millmen and Labourers "cleansing and deepening the river, canal and ditches, and performing other necessary work" (Supply 5/221). In March 1805, his job description was "Foreman of Manufacturing" (Supply 5/224). This terminology continued to be used but was, in reality, the same as 'Labour Foreman'. By March 1808, he had been appointed as the Master Mixer of Composition, since it is recorded that William Allsup had started an Apprenticeship under George Pittendrigh, the Master Mixer, on the 26th of that month (Supply 5/232). His promotion was confirmed in a Return of Employees for August 1808, which noted that he was then Master Mixer of Composition, paid 5/-d per day, that he was entitled to a house, and was allowed 6/-d per week to train an Apprentice (Supply 5/227). By an Order of the Board dated the 28th February 1812, George Pittendrigh, Assistant Master Worker, was granted a rent-free house, being Tenement No.10 in a List of properties owned by the Board as at the 1st January 1821 (Supply 5/232). His cottage was in Powder Mill Lane and has been identified as part of Plot No. 62 on the Town Map in Appendix 1.

By August 1812, George was earning 6/4d per day in his capacity as the Assistant Master Worker under William Newton, the Master Worker. Besides an increase in pay, he was still entitled to a house and to train an Apprentice (Supply 5/229) which was also the case in February 1814 (Supply 5/230). In June 1818, his daily rate of pay had been cut to 5/10d but he was still allowed to train an Apprentice, which added £15.12.0d to his annual income (Supply 5/231). George retained his position when the Establishment was cut in September 1818, but it was proposed that he be discharged in March 1822 when further cuts were proposed (Winters, *op.cit.* p.89). However, the Storekeeper, Empson Middleton, wrote to the Board on the 15th September 1821, requesting that George Pittendrigh, Assistant Master Worker, be granted a pension. He had served the Board for 32 years, and was then in a very bad state of health with Consumption. In their letter of the 16th November The Board agreed that he should receive a superannuated sum of £31.19.0d per annum (Supply 5/203). George was allowed to live in his cottage (1825 Valuation for Waltham Abbey - D/DHF B29) and was still in receipt of his pension in 1826 (Winters, *op.cit.* p.95).

George Pittendrigh (2) was born circa 1797 and was probably the son of George Pittendrigh (1). He was appointed as a Cooper at Waltham Abbey on the 1st January 1812 (Supply 5/232) and in August of that year was earning 1/9d per day (Supply 5/229). George continued to be employed in his trade with his daily rate of pay increasing as he became more proficient. In February 1814, he earned 2/4d daily (Supply 5/230) which had risen to 4/-d per day by June 1818 (Supply 5/230). He was retained when the Establishment was cut in September 1818, but his pay dropped to 3/-d per day (Supply 5/231) although it had increased to 3/6d by May 1819 (Supply 5/231). He was married by February 1822, but was without issue. He lived in Cheshunt, and at that date his annual pay was £54.13.6d (Supply 5/232).

In the spring of 1822, the Ordnance Board decided that the Establishment at Waltham Abbey was to be cut back again since the production and regeneration of gunpowder at Waltham Abbey had fallen. Accordingly, Empson Middleton and James Wright drew up lists of people to be dismissed (Supply 5/232) and

George's name was included. The men were subsequently made redundant on the 1st June and, asking for financial assistance, submitted several Petitions. Many were long-service employees in middle age, and they pointed out that they had little hope of finding employment after the corn harvest had been gathered. The Storekeeper was sympathetic and forwarded the petitions to the Board for their consideration. George Pittendrigh, one of the Petitioners, signing with a cross, was awarded two weeks' pay to ease his financial burden (Supply 5/232).

James Pittendrigh was employed as a Cooper in February 1814, earning 1/9d per day (Supply 5/230).

John Pittendrigh was working as a Labourer in the Corning House in January 1806 (Supply 5/224). In June 1807, although still a Labourer, he was working in various parts of the Manufactory (Supply 5/226). By August 1808, he had transferred back to the Corning House, where he was paid 2/6d per day and allowed to watch in turn, for which he received 1/-d (Supply 5/227). John was a Glazing Mill Foremen by September 1810, but received the same money and allowance to watch (Supply 5/228).

Robert Pittendrigh was working as a Labourer in the Corning House in May 1804, and was paid 1/6d per day. In addition, he was allowed to watch in turn, for which he received 1/-d per night (Supply 5/222).

Charles Pitty was engaged as an occasional Labourer in the Engineers' Department on the 18th November 1815, and was paid 2/8d per day; at the time, he was a 20-year-old bachelor living in Waltham Abbey (WO54/516).

Benjamin Poulter, born circa 1775, was appointed as a Labourer at the Waltham Abbey Mills on the 19th July 1805 (Supply

5/232). In January 1806, he was "drawing and setting stoves" for which he was paid 2/-d per day (Supply 5/224) and in June 1807, the description of his work was "Labourer in various parts of the Manufactory and setting and drawing stoves, loading and unloading barges etc." (Supply 5/226). Benjamin continued "drawing and setting stoves" with his wages peaking at 2/8d per day by August 1812, and he was also allowed to watch in turn (Supply 5/229). In December 1810, Benjamin, together with John Brown, was provided with rent-free accommodation owned by the Board, but a condition to the property being rent free was that his family "had to look after the waters" i.e., that the Bargemen did not leave the lock gates open and waste water which was needed to power the Mills. Subsequent Returns recorded that his tenement was one of a pair on Aqueduct Island which lay in the Parish of Cheshunt – see notes on John Brown.

In June 1818, Benjamin was recorded as a Labourer "setting and drawing stoves" and was then paid 2/4d per day and 1/-d per night when it was his turn to watch. In addition, he was still entitled to a rent-free house (Supply 5/231). The same Return noted that he was a 42-year-old married man with 2 children. Benjamin retained his position when the Establishment was cut in September 1818 (Supply 5/231) and a Return for February 1822 (Supply 5/232) recorded that his annual pay was £39.0.0d, which included his watch allowance. It also confirmed that he was appointed as a Labourer setting and drawing stoves by an Order of the Board dated the 4th September 1818. The same Return noted that he then had 3 children and that he lived in Cheshunt.

The Ordnance Board decided in the spring of 1822 that the Establishment at Waltham Abbey was to be cut back again, since the production and regeneration of gunpowder at Waltham Abbey had fallen. Accordingly, Empson Middleton and James Wright drew up lists of people to be dismissed, which included Benjamin (Supply 5/232). The men were subsequently made redundant on the 1st June and submitted several Petitions asking for financial assistance. Many were long-service employees in middle age, and they pointed out that they had little hope of finding employment after the corn harvest had been gathered. The Storekeeper was sympathetic, and forwarded the Petitions to the Board for their consideration. Benjamin Poulter, who was one of the Petitioners, was awarded 2 weeks' pay to ease his financial burden (Supply 5/232).

Thomas Pratt was working as a Millman in January 1806 earning 2/3d per day, and at that date, he had 2 years' service with the Ordnance (Supply 5/224). On the 18th June 1807, Thomas was working as a Puntman (Supply 5/226) as he was in September 1810, when he was paid 2/- per day and allowed to watch in turn (Supply 5/228). In February 1816, he was paid 2/8d per day, and at that time, was a 46-year-old married man with 4 children, living in Waltham Abbey (WO54/516).

William Pratt was a common Labourer who was paid 17/-d for work carried out by the Engineers' Department in the Manufactory between the 15th and 21st July 1809 (Supply 5/228).

Barnard Presland was working as a Puntman in August 1808 earning 2/-d per day and, in addition, he was allowed to watch in turn (Supply 5/227). On the 8th April 1809 when Presland was working as a Saltpetre Millman, a fatal fight broke out in the Watch House between him and Noah Sayer, when the former struck the latter and killed him. Among those who witnessed the fight were John Horrod and James Rowley (who later became a sausage-maker in High Bridge Street). Sayer left a widow, Ann. Presland was discharged from the Mills, but it is not known what punishment he received for killing Sayer (Winters, *op.cit.* pp. 67/68).

James Preston was a Bed Stone Cutter by trade who was set to work by Daniel Cornish in October 1787 at 9/-d per week, refurbishing the Mills following their purchase by the Government from Mr. Walton. He was not retained once his work was completed (Winters, *op. cit.* p.28).

William Price was working as a general Labourer when he signed a Petition on the Pay and Conditions at the Mills submitted to the Board in February 1800 (Supply 5/220). A Return of the Marital Status of the Employees made in May 1801, recorded that he was a bachelor who earned 1/6d per day (Supply 5/221). Robert Coleman, the Clerk of the Cheque, noted in his Minute Book on the 23rd October 1801, that 24 men were to go to Faversham or be discharged and William Price's name was included in the 24. However, his name does not appear in the Faversham Rolls, so it can only be assumed that he was discharged.

John Prior was a Bricklayer's Labourer who was paid 17/-d for work carried out by the Engineers' Department within the Manufactory between the 15th and 21st July 1809 (Supply 5/228).

Thomas Pritchard was working as a Saltpetre Refiner in August 1812 earning 2/8d per day, and, in addition, when not working extra, was allowed to watch in turn (Supply 5/229). This was also the case in February 1814 (Supply 5/230).

Peter Puddick was employed as a Cylinderman in Sussex on the 1st June 1798 (Supply 5/219). A Return on the Marital Status of the Employees made in May 1801 noted that he was a married man without issue, and the same Return records his rate of pay as 1/6d per day (Supply 5/221). A Return of Artificers and Labourers for November 1801 said, "since cylinders have been out for repair Puddick has been employed in stacking timber in the yards, levelling and preparing the ground where the cylinders were to be re-sited" (Supply 5/221). He continued to work as a Cylinderman, and his pay had increased to 2/- per day by January 1806 (Supply 5/224). The same Return noted that he then had 10 years' service, but did not record where he worked prior to 1798. His name does not appear in the Labour Returns after August 1808 (Supply 5/227).

Robert Pugh was working at the Mills in January 1806 as a Labourer "drawing and setting stoves etc." at 2/-d per day. At that time, he had served the Board for some 6 months (Supply 5/224).

William Purkess (Purkiss) born circa 1793, joined the Engineers' Department as a casual Labourer on the 22nd July 1811 (WO54/516). In September 1812, he was paid 2/8d per day for a six-day week (WO54/512) as he was in February 1816, when he was a 22-year-old bachelor living in Waltham Abbey (WO54/516). In February 1817, it was recorded that he was a married man with 1 child, still living in Waltham Abbey. However, he was then paid only 2/4d per day (WO54/520).

R

George Radpath (Ridpath) was probably the son of James Ridpath according to Dr. D. L. Ridpath, a descendant of the Ridpath family. George was working as a casual Labourer in the Engineers' Department in September 1812, with pay of 2/8d per day for a six-day week (WO54/512). In February 1814, a George Ridpath was working as a Puntman earning 2/8d per day, and in addition, he was allowed to watch in turn (Supply 5/230).

Richard Ragees worked as a Corning House Man in February 1814 earning 3/3d per day, and he was allowed to watch in turn, for which he received 1/6d per night (Supply 5/230).

John Ran was working as a casual Labourer in the Engineers' Department in September 1812, with pay of 2/8d per day for a six-day week (WO54/512).

Edward Randall was born circa 1792. He commenced employment as a casual Labourer in the Engineers' Department on the 1st September 1815, and was paid 2/8d per day. In February 1816, he was a 23-year-old bachelor living in Waltham Abbey (WO54/516).

John Randall was a Labourer set to work by Daniel Cornish in October 1787 at 9/-d per week, possibly repairing the Mills following their purchase by the Government from Mr. Walton (Winters, *op.cit.* p.29). In November 1788, he was working as a Millman (Supply 5/212). A Return of Employees for January 1789, recorded that Randall was "sick and does not appear that he will be able to attend duty" and he was still sick in March 1789, "but still receives his pay" (also Supply 5/212).

Thomas Randall was employed by the Ordnance as a Corning House Man on the 6th November 1788 (Supply 5/219) and this was confirmed by Winters (*op.cit.* p.31). Thomas enlisted as a Private in the Military Volunteer Company (Supply 5/219), and the Petition on Pay and Conditions at the Mills submitted to the Board in February 1800, showed that he was literate (Supply 5/220).

There was a huge explosion at the new Corning House on the 16th June 1801, full details of which can be found under the notes of Peter Page. Thomas was one of those "burnt and otherwise hurt by the fire" and the Board agreed to pay his wages until he recovered. A letter to the Board requested that the men burnt at the Corning House be reimbursed for the loss of clothing, and the list included Thomas Randall. His claim amounted to £1.4.6d, and according to Supply 5/221, comprised of a hat (16/-d) stockings (4/-d) and handkerchiefs (4/6d). He continued to be employed at the Powder Mills, although not as a Millman, because in May 1804, he was recorded as a Refiner earning 2/-d per day, and allowed 1/-d per night when it was his turn to watch – on average every 5th night (Supply 5/222).

William Randall was a Bricklayer in the Engineers' Department, who was paid 17/-d for work carried out in the Manufactory between the 15th and 21st July 1809 inclusive (Supply 5/228). By the 29th August 1812, he was working in the Storekeeper's Department as a Millman earning 3/-d per day, in addition to which, he was allowed 6d per night when on duty (Supply 5/229). This was also the case in February 1813 (Supply 5/230).

William Randle was working as a Brimstone and Saltpetre Millman in September 1810, and, in addition, he was allowed to watch in turn (Supply 5/228).

Edward Rapley was working as a Saltpetre Refiner in June 1807 earning 2/-d per day, and "when not working allowed to watch in turn" (Supply 5/226). Edward was still refining Saltpetre in

February 1814, but was then paid 2/8d per day and still allowed to watch when not working extra (Supply 5/230).

John Rapley joined the Ordnance Board as a Saltpetre Refiner in June 1805. In January 1806, he was being paid 2/-d per day and "when not working allowed to watch in turn (Supply 5/224). This was also the case in June 1807 (Supply 5/226).

D. Ratty was working as a Labourer in May 1801, earning 1/6d per day. At the time, he was a married man with 1 child (Supply 5/221).

John Raynor was a Sawyer set to work by Daniel Cornish in October 1787 and paid 9/-d per week, possibly repairing the Mills following their purchase by the Government from Mr. Walton (Winters, *op.cit.* p.28). However, he does not appear to have been retained.

John Reason was born circa 1793, and in February 1814 was working as a Labourer, "drawing and setting stoves and in the Willow Plantation" at 2/8d per day. In addition, he was allowed to watch in turn (Supply 5/230). By June 1818, John was the Labourer to the Clerk of the Survey and paid 2/4d per day, and at the time, was a single man of 25 who lived in Waltham Abbey (Supply 5/231). He retained his position in September 1818 when the Establishment was reduced in numbers, was still the Clerk of the Survey's Labourer, and had married by May 1819. A statement dated the 4th April 1821 "of monies to which the public were entitled to receive credit between the 1st January and the 31st December 1820 shewing the amounts received by the storekeeper", recorded that John Reason had been leasing a cottage and its small garden, Tenement No. 37, owned by the Board, for which he was charged a rent of £5.4.0d per annum (Supply 5/232). The cottage was in Powder Mill Lane, being part of Plot No. 61 on the 1825 Town Map in Appendix 1.. Sadly,

John was a widower by September 1820 (Supply 5/232) and George Miller, the "Repairer of Hose and Band", then occupied his cottage. John was still in the same post in April 1821, receiving 2/4d per day and allowed to watch, for which he received 1/6d per night (Supply 5/232).

Richard Reason was working in the Corning Houses in January 1792 at 1/6d per day (Supply 5/215).

John Redman was working as a Millman in March 1789 earning 2/-d per day (Supply 5/212). In April of that year, in common with the majority of the workforce, he was "cutting and planting willow trees, cutting of canal at the new Corning House, removing earth to the store, unloading barge of coals and charring wood" (Supply 5/213). In March 1790 he was still a Millman at 2/-d per day (Supply 5/214) but by August 1790, he was in the Corning Houses with his pay reduced to 1/6d per day (Supply 5/215).

In a letter dated the 18th April 1792 from James Wright, the Storekeeper, to the Board, it was stated, "we humbly beg to report that on unloading a wagon of charcoal Jn. Redman a Labourer at this place was so much in liquor (when he came to work at 6 o'clock in the morning) that on going up the ladder with a sack of charcoal he fell down but received little injury. Jn. Mason, another Labourer said 'Redman you have had a drop of Mr. Ways Spring Water too much this morning' meaning Gin, on which Redman kicked Mason several times, which treatment he had prudence enough not to return." When all the coal was unloaded, Mason said to Mr. Goodfellow (the Master Mixer) "it's a pity you let Redman go up the ladder." Goodfellow answered, "If I was to say anything to him I should get myself abused and you had better hold your tongue." The Storekeeper asked the Board if Redman should be dismissed for coming to work in liquor and for fighting in the Works (WASC 0475). No reply could be found from the Board, but since no other record appears for Redman, it is assumed that he was dismissed.

George Reen was working in the Corning House in January 1806; at that time he had 6 months' service with the Ordnance, was paid 2/2d per day and was allowed to watch in turn, for which he received 1/-d per night (Supply 5/226). He continued to work in the Corning House until at least February 1814, when his pay and watch allowance had increased to 3/3d per day and 1/6d per night respectively (Supply 5/230).

Thomas Reeves was a casual Millwright who had first been employed by the Engineers' Department on the 10th July 1813. In February 1816, he was a 30-year-old married man who was paid 5/8d per day. He had 3 children and lived in Waltham Abbey (WO54/516).

Edward Reyley was an Apprentice in the Mixing House in July 1792, who earned 1/-d per day (Supply 5/216). He was still serving his Apprenticeship in July 1795, at which time his pay had increased to 1/4d per day (Supply 5/217).

Robert Rich was a casual Labourer who had first been employed in the Engineers' Department on the 7th November 1815. In February 1816, he was paid 2/4d per day, and was a 60-year-old bachelor living in Waltham Abbey (WO54/516).

Thomas Rickett was working as a Saltpetre Refiner in February 1814. He earned 2/8d per day and, in addition, when not working extra, he was allowed to watch in turn (Supply 5/230).

Richard Ricketts started work as a general Labourer in the Corning House on the 11th March 1797, and was paid 1/6d per day. He was a Private in the Volunteer Company and was still working in the Corning House in September 1798 (Supply 5/219).

On the 18th April 1801, there was a huge explosion at the Mills. Reporting the event to the Board of Ordnance in London the next day, the Storekeeper, James Wright, who witnessed the event, said that the new Corning House on Horse Mill Island had blown up with a tremendous explosion the day before at "1/4 past 3 o'clock." 9 men were in the building and all were killed, including Richard Ricketts, and 4 horses also perished (Supply 5/220). "The mangled bodies of the poor men were buried without a memorial stone in a high heap in the yard, near the path leading to Mr King's House and in front of the Wollard tombs" (Winters, *Centenary Memorial,* p.59). According to Winters, Mr King was a market gardener at the Abbey gardens. Richard Rickett's wife, Sarah, together with the other widows and two mothers of the deceased, sent a petition to the Board via the Storekeeper on the 24th April, requesting "...relief in their distress..." (Supply 5/194). In a Report dated the 29th April regarding the ages of the children and the circumstances of the widows and children, the Storekeeper stated, "Sarah, Richard's widow, was aged 32 and was left with three children, a boy aged 10, a girl aged 1, and another girl aged 5, who had been severely burnt when her clothes caught fire." The five-year-old girl's arm was injured so badly that she would not be able to use it for the rest of her life (Supply 5/220).

On the 5th May 1801, the Board agreed that Sarah was to receive the whole of her husband's back pay and that she should continue to receive his pay and allowances, which included an additional 1/6d per week on account "of the severity of the times" (Supply 5/194). However, the Board decided that the other widows' pensions should be based on their husbands' basic pay and should not include the extra "due to the severity of the times" (Supply 5/194). On the 4th September 1805, the Board agreed to pay

Sarah an additional 3/6d per week to each of her two girls until they were 18 or married. A document dated the 8th November 1818 listed the names of the people who were in receipt of pensions or charitable allowances at the time. Among the recipients was Ann Ricketts, whose father had worked in the Corning House and was killed on the 18th April 1801. She had received a pension of 3/6d per week commencing the 1st September 1805. Ann reached her 18th birthday on the 20th December 1818, when her pension duly ceased (Supply 5/231).

George Ridpath (1) was probably the youngest son of James Ridpath who was born in Scotland in 1725, and the youngest brother of James Ridpath Junior, according Dr. D. L. Ridpath, a relative and descendant. George was born circa 1770, and trained as a "Taylor" (WO54/524) before he joined the Ordnance Board as a Millman on the 1st November 1804 (Supply 5/232) and in January 1806, he was earning 2/3d per day with an additional 3d if he worked at night (Supply 5/224). He continued to work as a Millman, but by August 1812, he was a Saltpetre Refiner earning 2/8d per day, and "when not working extra was allowed to watch in turn" (Supply 5/229).

On the 30th June 1813, George was appointed as a Storehouse Man with his pay increased to 3/10d per day (Supply 5/230). He was still in the same position in January 1818, but, in common with the rest of the workforce, his pay had been reduced following the defeat of Napoleon. At the time he was paid 3/6d per day and was allowed to watch in turn, for which he received 1/-d per night (WO54/524). The same document recorded that he was then a married man with 3 children and that he lived in Waltham Abbey.

George was retained when the Establishment was reduced in numbers in 1818, and his position as a Storehouse man was confirmed by a Board Order dated the 4th September 1818

(Supply 5/232). He was still allowed to watch, and in April 1821 he was made a Rounder, for which he was paid 2/- per night – on average every 3rd night (Supply 5/232). He continued as a Storehouse Man until 1822, and during this period his annual remuneration, including his Rounder's allowance, was £52.3.4d per annum (Supply 5/232). The Return in question stated that he and his wife then had 4 children and were living in Enfield.

In the spring of 1822 the Ordnance Board decided to lower production and regeneration of gunpowder, and the Establishment at Waltham Abbey was to be reduced. Hence, Empson Middleton and James Wright drew up lists of people to be retained or dismissed on the 1st June 1822 and George Ridpath was on the list of people to be dismissed (Supply 5/232). However, under an Order of the Board dated the 22nd May 1822, George Ridpath, Storehouse Man, instead was to be retained as a Labourer, and this was confirmed in a Return of Employees for April 1823 where he was described as "a Labourer for general purposes to be sent to all parts of the Manufactory where their services may be required" (Supply WO54/542). His pay for the year, including an allowance to watch in turn, was then £39.0.0d per annum. Under Orders of the Board dated the 27th December 1822 and the 15th January 1823, his basic wage was then reduced by £2.12.0d per annum (WO54/542). However, WO54/546 dated October 1824, recorded that his pay had been restored to its previous level, and the same document said that George had only 3 children.

A Return of Properties prepared by the Royal Engineers' Office in December 1834 listing the tenements owned by the Board, recorded that George Ridpath had been living in a cottage in Powder Mill Lane from the 15th January 1825, paying the Board an annual rent of £5.4.0d (5/237). This tenement had previously been occupied by George Pittendrigh, and forms part of Plot No. 62 on the Town Map in Appendix 1. By the 1st October 1825,

George Ridpath had been restored as a Storehouse Man in place of Abraham Bell, who had been promoted to the position of Master Mixer. George was then paid £57.7.4d per annum, which included an allowance of 2/-d per night when it was his turn to watch, on average, once a week (WO54/550). Correspondence in January 1828, revealed that George had suffered an injury in the Cooper's Yard (Supply 5/237) and that the Director General of the Ordnance Medical Department had agreed that George should be provided with a truss to prevent him incurring further injury (Supply 5/202).

He continued to be employed as the Storehouse Man on the same pay until April 1834, when his basic wage was reduced to £43.10.0d per annum, which, with his allowance to watch, gave him an annual income of £48.14.0d (WO54/593). George died in the summer of 1837, and a Petition from his wife, Susannah, confirmed that on the 10th October 1827, her late husband, George, had had an accident in the cooperage in the performance of his duty, and had suffered a hernia. She continued that her husband had served the Board for 33 years and she had been left a widow with children. She, therefore, requested a charitable donation of £12.0.0d (Supply 5/237). Susannah left her cottage in 1837; a Return made by the Royal Engineers' Office showed that her cottage thereafter was to be let to Henry Coreham, Corning House Man (Supply 5/237).

James Ridpath (1) born in Scotland in 1725, replaced John Godwin in the Corning House circa 1793, and on the 11th November 1793, was "drawing & setting stoves and in the punts" earning 1/6d per day (Supply 5/216). Winters, writing in his *Centenary Memorial of the Royal Gunpowder Factory,* recorded on page 51 that Mr. Ridpath lived at "Newton's Pool" in Edmondsey in the old Turnpike House, a pub previously known as *The Chequers* or *The Turnpike Inn*, which ceased to be a licensed premise in 1796 (*Licensed Victuallers' Returns).* As well as working at the Mills, he cultivated a certain class of winter Kale, since called 'Ridpath Greens' (Winters, *op.cit*.p.51). He continued to undertake the same work throughout 1794 (Supply 5/217) and enlisted as a Private in the Volunteer Company on the 4th May 1794 (Supply 5/219). In June 1795, he was employed as a Puntman, still earning 1/6d per day (Supply 5/217). The Petition on Pay and Conditions at the Mills submitted to the Board in February 1800 (Supply 5/220) showed that he was literate, while the Return on the Marital Status of the Employees made in May 1801, recorded that he was a married man with 5 children (Supply 5/221).

There was a huge explosion at the new Corning House on the 16th June 1801, full details of which are recorded under the notes on Peter Page. Several men were badly burnt while others lost clothing. In a letter to the Board dated the 29th July 1801, it was stated that the men had requested that they be reimbursed for the loss of clothing, and James Redpath's (Ridpath) claim amounted to 5/-d for a hat (Supply 5/221).

In common with the majority of the workforce In November 1801, James was employed in "cleaning and deepening the river and canals, as well as performing other necessary sundry works" (Supply 5/221). He was working as a Labourer in the Saltpetre Refinery and in other parts of the Manufactory as required in May 1801, paid 2/-d per day and received an additional allowance of 1/-d per night when it was his turn "to watch" – on average every 5th night (Supply 5/222).

James was buried on the 24th November 1804, his widow, Mary, on the 31st May 1807, aged 70 *(*WASC 2180*, p.110) and the house they lived in was sold to the Board in 1805 by the executors of Mr. Ellis Were (WO44/681a).

James Ridpath (2) was most likely the eldest son of James Ridpath and was possibly born in West Ham. He married Susannah Jones at Waltham Abbey on Christmas Day 1788 (*Dr. D. L. Ridpath*).

Thomas Ridpath was baptised at Waltham Abbey on the 7th September 1791. In his teens, he scratched his name in the plaster of his Uncle George's house at 41, Sun Street. The signature in question appears in the *History of a Tudor House* (p.16) published by the Epping Forest District Museum in 1982 (Dr. D. L. Ridpath, a descendant, 2008). Thomas married Elizabeth Jones at Waltham Abbey Church on the 13th November 1814.

In September 1810, he was working as a "Respective Officer's Labourer" at 2/-d per day, and allowed to watch in turn (Supply 5/228). In August 1812, he was employed as the Storekeeper's Labourer earning 2/8d per day, and was still allowed to watch in turn (Supply 5/229). At that particular time, the Storekeeper (the Respective Officer) was Mr. H. S. Mathews. By February 1814, Thomas was refining Saltpetre, still at 2/8d per day, and when not working extra, he was allowed to watch in turn (Supply 5/230). Thomas remained in the Saltpetre Refinery in June 1818, but his daily rate of pay had been cut to 2/4d, although he was still allowed to watch, for which he received 1/-d per night. He was then aged 27, lived in Waltham Abbey, and he and his wife, Elizabeth, had 2 children (Supply 5/231). In September 1818, the Establishment was reduced in numbers, and Thomas Ridpath, Saltpetre Refiner, was discharged (Supply 5/231).

W. Rigsby was a general Labourer when he signed the Petition on Pay and Conditions presented to the Board on the 2nd February 1800, and the document showed that he was literate (Supply 5/200).

John Roberts was working as a Puntman in November 1806, earning 2/-d per day, and at that date he had 3 months' service with the Ordnance Board (Supply 5/224). In June 1807, he was employed as a Dusting House Man, paid 2/1d per day and, in addition, he was allowed to watch in turn, for which he received 1/-d per night (Supply 5/226).

John Robertson (also Robinson) was working in the Mixing House in January 1806 at 2/-d per day, and at that date he had 1 year's service (Supply 5/224). He was still employed in the Mixing House in June 1807, and, "in addition to his pay he is allowed to watch in turn for which he receives 1/-d" (Supply 5/226). By August 1808, his name was recorded as Robinson; he was still working in the Dusting House and earned 2/3d per day, in addition to which, he was still allowed to watch for the same 1/-d (Supply 5/227).

James Robinson, a Labourer at the Mills, together with his wife, Mary, lived in High Bridge Street North, with Thomas Baldock (1841 Census).

John Robinson was employed as a Millwright in the Engineers' Department, and paid 3/6d per day. On the 10th August 1790, he received £1.6.3d for seven and a half days' work in the Manufactory (WASC 1382).

Thomas Robinson was working as a Labourer in the "Engineers' Dept. Established" in May 1804, earning 1/6d per day with "one day extra allowed per week agreeable to the Board's Order dated the 12th March, 1801" (Supply 5/222). By June 1807, he was employed by the Storekeeper's Department as a Millman and paid 2/3d per day, with an extra 3d when on night duties (Supply 5/226). The following August, he was working as a Puntman with his pay reduced to 2/-d per day, but he was then allowed to watch in turn, for which he received 1/-d (Supply 5/227). By August

1812, he was a Saltpetre Refiner who earned 2/8d per day, and in addition, when not working extra, was allowed to watch (Supply 5/229). Thomas was a Millman in February 1814 with his pay increased to 3/-d daily, and an extra 6d when on night duty (Supply 5/230).

James Rogers joined the Engineers' Department as a casual Labourer on the 3rd July 1815. In February 1816, he was paid 2/8d per day; at the time, he was a 20-year-old bachelor living in Waltham Abbey (WO54/516).

Richard Rogers was working as a Labourer "drawing and setting stoves and in the willow plantation" in August 1812, and was paid 2/8d per day as well as being allowed to watch in turn (Supply 5/229). By February 1814, he was a Corning House Man earning 3/3d per day and was still allowed to watch, for which he received 1/6d per night (Supply 5/230).

William Rogers joined the Engineers' Department as a casual Labourer on the 16th October 1812. In February 1816, he was paid 2/4d per day; at that time he was a 23-year-old bachelor living in Waltham Abbey (WO54/516). He was employed as a casual Labourer "Occasionally as required" in the Department on the same rate of pay in April 1818 (WO54/524) and in May 1819 (WO54/528).

Samuel Rolf started as an occasional Labourer on the 9th April 1814 in the Engineers' Department, having been trained as a Collar Maker. In February 1816, he was being paid 2/8d per day, and at the time was a 28-year-old bachelor living in Waltham Abbey (WO54/516).

Edward Roof was working as a Millman in August 1812 (Supply 5/229) as he was in February 1814 (Supply 5/230).

During this period he was paid 3/-d per day, with an additional 6d per night when on duty.

John Rook was employed as a Bricklayer's Labourer in the Engineers' Department, and was paid 16/-d for work carried out in the Manufactory between the 15th and 21st July 1809 (Supply 5/228).

William Rook was working in the Corning House in January 1806, earning 2/2d per day, and at the time, had been employed by the Ordnance for 3 months (Supply 5/224). The Corning House remained his workplace until at least September 1810, when his daily rate of pay was 2/6d and, in addition, he was allowed to watch in turn, for which he received 1/6d per night (Supply 5/228).

Clark Rook(e) was working as a Labourer in the Corning House at the Faversham Royal Powder Mills in October 1787, and on the 4th January 1788, he expressed a wish to be transferred to the Waltham Abbey Powder Mills (Supply 5/113). He remained at Faversham for a while, working as a Labourer in the Corning House and Glazing Engine being "entered" for Waltham Abbey on the 8th March 1788 (Supply 5/113). Winters noted that Rook (spelt Rooke) was working as a Millman at Waltham Abbey on the 27th November 1788. He also recorded that Rooke had previously worked for Mr. Walton, from whom the Government had purchased the Waltham Abbey Mills (Winters, *op.cit.* p.31). This may explain why Clark wished for a transfer to Waltham Abbey.

In March 1789, Clark Rook was working in the Corning House, earning 1/6d per day (Supply 5/212). In April of that year, in common with the majority of the workforce, he was "cutting and planting willow trees, cutting of canal at the new Corning House, removing earth to the store, unloading barge of coals and charring wood" (Supply 5/213). In December 1790 Clark Rook and Sam Ellenthorpe were recorded as "sick but receiving their pay" (Supply 5/215). Rook continued to be described as "Corning gunpowder" or "at the Corning Houses" until at least June 1791 (Supply 5/215). By January 1792, he was described as a Millman at 2/-d per day, and this was to be his occupation and rate of pay until his untimely death on the 27th January 1795 (Supply 5/216).

A letter to the Board dated the 28th January 1789, referred to the death of Clark Rook and stated, "we are sorry to inform your Honours that yesterday afternoon as the Millwright (Edward Jones) and several Labourers were endeavouring to disengage the water gates at the mill head from ice, a great quantity of water which came down was let off to prevent the several buildings from being overflowed; in these endeavours Clark Rooke one of our millmen fell into one of the Gully streams (which was very rapid) and carried under the ice of the Tail Stream at the Refining House, when he was taken up and every endeavour used by the surgeons to restore him, but without effect" (Supply 5/217). The Board agreed to pay his widow a pension of 7/-d per week (Winters, *op.cit.* p.58).

James Rowland was born circa 1764, and trained as a Carpenter. He was employed by a contractor working at the Mills on the 4th February 1805, and his service record shows that he joined the Board shortly after this. In April 1825, James was working as a Carpenter in the Engineers' Department at 4/1d per for 313 days per year and this amounted to an annual income of £63.18.1d. At that date he had nearly 20 years' service, was 61 years old, was a widower with 5 children and lived in Waltham Abbey (WO54/550).

A statement dated the 16th February 1822 "of monies to which the public were entitled to receive credit between the 1st January and the 31st December 1821 shewing the amounts received by the storekeeper" recorded that James Rowland was one of several employees "having occupied their present residences previous to the Hon. Board purchasing the same, sanction will be asked for their future residing in them." Under an Order dated the 4th May 1821, the tenement was leased to James for an annual rent of £5.4.0d (Supply 5/232). The cottage, without a garden, was purchased by the Board by auction in 1808 from the executors of a Mr. Barwick. Part of Lot No. 2 in the sale was described by the Board's agent as follows: "It is on the corner of Powder Mill Lane and it is desirable to buy this to pull the corner down to make a better turning circle for the charcoal wagons, which, from the lightness of that article, are loaded so high as often they touch the eaves of the houses in Powder Mill Lane." (WO44/681a). The cottage forms part of Plot No. 61 of the Town Map in Appendix 1.

A Return of Persons belonging to the Civil Establishment of the Ordnance at the Gunpowder and Small Arms Manufactories at Waltham, Faversham and Enfield, showing in detail the several points of information required by the Master General and Board's Order dated the 31st January 1831, recorded that James Rowland was one of 7 Carpenters to be employed at Waltham Abbey Powder Mills and the Enfield Small Arms Factory. He was to be paid 4/1d per day and used to undertake general services as a Carpenter in the Manufactories, requiring great care, attention and sobriety etc. (WO54/575). The same document also recorded that James only had 4 children. This was repeated in subsequent Returns, so possibly one of the children died.

James was still working in October 1832, with his annual income unchanged at £63.18.1d. At that time, he was 68 years' old and had served the Board for 27 years (WO54/587). Under an Order of the Board dated the 15th March 1833, James Rowland, Carpenter, was to be discharged and granted a pension of £20 per annum, until an opportunity to employ him again should arise

(Supply 5/208). He was still living in his cottage in December 1834 (Supply 5/237) and in receipt of his pension in 1837 (Supply 5/237). The 1841 Census recorded that James Rowland was an Ordnance Pensioner, aged 75, and was living in Silver Street, with Emily Littler, a 12 year-old girl, as his servant. James was not born in Essex.

Thomas Rowles (also Roles and Rools) started employment with the Ordnance Board on the 11th July 1790, working "in punts & sett & draw stoves" for which he was paid 1/6d per day (Supply 5/215). In December 1790 he was described as "At the Corning House" and still earning the same pay (Supply 5/215). In January 1792, Rowles was "At the stoves", where he continued to work for the next 12 years or so (Supply 5/216). In 1795, he was allowed an extra 6d if he had to work at night (Supply 5/216). He joined the Volunteer Company on the 7th May 1794 and was made a Corporal, having served 30 years in the Dragoons (Supply 5/219). The Petition on Pay and Conditions at the Mills submitted to the Board in February 1800 showed that he was literate, while a Return of the Marital Status of the Employees in May 1801, recorded that he was a married man with 1 child (Supply 5/221).

Although still employed as a Stoveman in November 1801, Thomas, in common with the majority of the workforce, was "cleaning and deepening the river and canals, as well as performing other necessary sundry works" (Supply 5/221). He was still employed as a Stoveman in May 1804, but his pay had increased to 2/-d per day, and, in addition, he was allowed to watch in turn, on average every 5th night, for which he received 1/-d (Supply 5/222).

In January 1806,Thomas, with his name now spelt Roles, was working as a Warder, although he was still paid 2/-d per day and allowed to watch. At that date, he had 15 years' service, which agrees with the start date given in the first paragraph (Supply 5/224). He was still employed on the same terms in August 1810 (Supply 5/227). In September 1810, Thomas, now Thomas Rools, was still working as a Warder earning 2/-d per day, and, in addition, he was a Rounder every 3rd night, for which he received an extra 2/-d (Supply 5/228). He was still a Warder and Rounder in February 1814, but his daily pay had increased to 2/8d, with his Rounder's allowance unchanged (Supply 5/230).

James Rowley started his employment as a Mixing House Man in the spring of 1805, and in January 1806, he was paid 2/- per day (Supply 5/224). The Mixing House remained his workplace until at least February 1814, and during this time, his daily pay gradually increased to 3/-d per day. In addition, he was allowed to watch in turn, for which he received 1/6d per night (Supply 5/230).

Thomas Rowley was working as a Millman in August 1808, earning 2/3d per day and "allowed 6d per night when on duty" (Supply 5/228). He was still a Millman in August 1812, but was then paid 3/-d per day, with an extra 6d if he worked at night (Supply 5/229). This was also the case in February 1814 (Supply 5/230).

William Rowley was working in the Corning House in January 1806 at 2/2d per day, and at that date he had 6 months' service (Supply 5/224).

Thomas Rudge started work as an occasional Labourer in the Engineers' Department on the 17th June 1813. In February 1816, he was earning 2/4d per day, and at that date, he was a 44-year-old married man with 7 children, living in Waltham Abbey (WO54/516). He continued to work "Occasionally as required" although it would appear that he was taken on the Establishment as a Labourer in 1820. He still received the same rate of pay until

April 1823, when it was reduced to 2/2d per day for 313 days (WO54/542). This gave him an annual income of £33.18.2d, which he continued to receive until he retired with a pension on the 21st November 1834, which he was still receiving in 1837 (Supply 5/237). It is possible that he is the same Thomas Rudge who, in the 1841 Census, was aged 65 and lived in a lane leading from Fountain Place to Sewardstone Street.

William Rudge started his employment as an occasional Labourer in the Engineers' Department on the 5th August 1815. In February 1816, he was paid 2/4d per day, and he was then an 18-year-old bachelor, living in Waltham Abbey (WO54/516).

James Rumble was born circa 1766, and started work on the 27th November 1813 as a casual Bricklayer's Labourer in the Engineers' Department. In February 1806, he was paid 2/8d per day, and he was a 48-year-old married man with 1 child, living in Waltham Abbey (WO54/516).

Thomas Rumbold was a Labourer set to work by Daniel Cornish October 1787 at 9/-d per week, possibly renovating the Mills following their purchase by the Government from Mr. Walton (Winters, *op.cit. p. 28)*. In January 1789, having previously being employed by Mr. Walton, he was tried as a Millman, and was employed in that capacity in March 1789, receiving pay of 2/-d per day (Supply 5/212). In common with the majority of the workforce in April 1789, Thomas was "cutting and planting willow trees, cutting of canal at the new Corning House, removing earth to the store, unloading barge of coals & charring wood" (Supply 5/213).

On the 9th September 1789, the Storekeeper reported to the Board, "at 11 o'clock the two new Iron Mills blew up. Thomas Rumbold, the Millman on duty, had just liquored the charge and happened to be outside; he received no hurt. The master worker says that this mill has frequently blown up" (Winters, *op.cit.* p.33). In spite of the explosion, Thomas continued to work as a Millman, and in September 1789, his age was recorded as 67, and it was confirmed that he was still paid 2/- per day (Supply 5/214). Around June 1791, Thomas became a Warder, and he continued in this position until February 1793, when it was recorded "he was absent sick but he still receives his pay" (Supply 5/216). His name does not appear in the records after February 1793.

William Russell was an Overseer in the "Engineers' Department Established" and in May 1804, was paid 5/-d per day by the Storekeeper (Supply 5/222).

S

Thomas Sadd, born circa 1795 and trained as a Cooper, started his employment at Waltham Abbey on the 13th July 1809 (Supply 5/232) and continued to work in his trade until the 5th September 1834, when he was appointed as the Master Mixer of Composition (WO54/623). In September 1810, he was paid 2/6d per day (Supply 5/228) peaking to £62.12.0d per annum in October 1829 (WO54/566) and falling to £54.4.0d in April 1834 (WO54/593).

Thomas had married by February 1822 (Supply 5/232) with the first of two children being born by October 1822 (Supply 5/232) although one of the children died between October 1833 and April 1834 (WO54/593). He was admitted on the 10th July 1825 to a cottage and 6 perches of land owned by the Board on the south side of High Bridge Street, for which he paid an annual rental of £5.4.0d (Supply 5/237). The property had previously been occupied by John Braddock (see notes on Braddock for further details) who had been appointed as the Master Saltpetre Refiner. Following his promotion as the Master Mixer in September 1834, it was proposed that Thomas move to a tenement in Powder Mill Lane previously occupied by Samuel Knowler, Snr. (Supply 5/237). More details of this tenement can be found under the notes on Samuel Knowler Snr. On the 16th April 1836, "two Mills exploded when shut up and not at work. Thomas Sadd, Master Mixer, was called before Lt.Col. Moody as a witness." (Winters, *op. cit.* p. 103).

Further promotion followed on the 22nd October 1838, when Thomas was appointed as Master Worker following the retirement of Hugh Jones, and he was then paid £120.0.0d per annum (WO54/623). By April 1839, he was a widower (WO54/623). A Return of Properties owned by the Board dated the 28th May 1840 and prepared by the Royal Engineers, although showing that Thomas was still living in Powder Mill Lane, recorded that he was then residing in the adjacent tenement which was previously occupied by Jones (WO44/133). On the 1st July 1840, James Wright, the deputy Storekeeper, examined Sadd concerning the house once occupied by Mr. Newton, who had been the Master Mixer at Waltham Abbey for many years. The house, on Horse Mill Island, had originally been a stable, but since Mr. Newton's house at "Newton's Pond" was falling down, the stable was fitted out as a dwelling house. When Newton died in February 1825, his house was converted into two dwellings. Hugh Jones, the late Master Worker, chose to live in a house more convenient for his duty, preferring the quarters he occupied as the Master Mixer. This arrangement was approved and so matters remained for 15 years. Once Thomas Sadd became the Master Worker, the two cottages were to be converted back into one house for his use, forming Plot No. 96 on the Town Map in Appendix 1. The 1841 Census recorded that Thomas was aged 45, and living with his 15-year-old daughter, Mary, in the "marsh" next to David Wilkie; this immediately places him on Horse Mill Island, living in the house built for William Newton. Some time after the Census was taken Thomas re-married (*WAAC*).

On the 13th April 1843, some 40 barrels of gunpowder exploded in the Corning House, together with another 20 in the Press House. Seven men were killed and much damage was done to the town. Among those killed was Thomas Sadd, the Master Worker, aged 47 (Winters, *op.cit.* p.106). A graphic description of the explosion and the damage caused, etc., was given in *The London Illustrated News* dated Saturday, the 22nd April 1843 (WAAC).

B. Samson started his employment at the Mills on the 11th October 1796. In September 1798 he was working in the Corning Houses, and had also enlisted as a Private in the Volunteer Company (Supply 5/219).

Thomas Sarson was employed as a casual Labourer in the Engineers' Department on the 4th January 1817 at 2/4d per day. He was then a 31-year-old married man with two children living in Waltham Abbey. He had previously been trained as a Brass Founder (WO54/520).

James Savage was a Labourer set to work by Daniel Cornish in October 1787. He was paid 9/-d per week, possibly repairing the Mills following their purchase from Mr. Walton by the Government (Winters, *op.cit.* p. 29). However, he does not appear to have been retained.

Thomas Saxe worked as a casual Labourer in September 1812, earning 2/8d per day for a six-day week (WO54/512).

Noah Sayer was a Saltpetre Millman, as was Barnard Presland. Sayer got into a fight with Presland in the Watch House on the 8th April 1809, and was killed. John Horrod witnessed the fight, and Barnard Presland was dismissed a few days later, but what punishment he received is not known (Winters, *op.cit.* pp.67-68). Sayer left a widow, Ann.

William Sayer was born circa 1773, and was first employed on the 29th March 1806 as a casual Millwright by the Engineers' Department (WO54/516). He was paid £1.10.7d for work carried out by that Department in the Manufactory between the 15th and 21st July 1809 (Supply 5/228). William was still employed as a casual Millwright in September 1812 (WO54/512) as he was February 1816, with pay of 5/8d per day (WO54/516). At that date he was a 42-year-old married man with 2 unmarried children, living in Waltham Abbey. His wage had been reduced to 5/2d daily by February 1817, and his name does not appear in the records for the Engineers' Department after this.

However, a statement dated the 16th February 1822 "of monies to which the public were entitled to receive credit between the 1st January and the 31st December 1821, shewing the amounts received by the storekeeper" recorded that William Sayer was one of several, "having occupied their present residences previous to the Hon. Board purchasing the same, sanction will be asked for their future residing in them." Under an Order dated the 4th May 1821, the tenement was leased to him for an annual rent of £5.4.0d (Supply 5/232). Supply 5/237 recorded that the cottage, without a garden, was in West Street (High Bridge Street) forming Plot No.60 on the Town Map in Appendix 1.

A similar document dated the 20th December 1834, recorded that William Sayer still occupied the same house in West Street (Supply 5/237). Another Return of Properties dated the 28th May 1840 regarding properties owned by the Board, confirmed that William Sayer, Baker, had occupied a tenement in High Bridge Street since its purchase by the Board (WO44/133).

The 1841 Census recorded that William Sayer, Baker, and his wife, Joyce, both aged 70, were living in the same location. Bearing in mind that the given ages in the 1841 Census were rounded down, the William Sayer in the Census was the same age as William Sayer, the Millwright, and there appears to be little doubt that they are one and the same person.

B. Sayers was working as a Labourer in the Engineers' Department in May 1801 at 1/6d per day. He was a married man with 3 children (Supply 5/221).

Henry Sayle was working as a Labourer in the Corning Houses in August 1798. In addition, he was also a Private in the Volunteer Company (Supply 5/219).

John Scovell commenced his employment as a Saltpetre Refiner in 1805; in January 1806, he was earning 2/-d per day and, when not working extra, allowed to watch in turn (Supply 5/224). He continued to refine Saltpetre with the same pay and conditions, but by September 1810, he was employed as a Cylinderman (Supply 5/228). He continued to be a Cylinderman until at least February 1814, and at that time was paid 2/8d per day (Supply 5/230).

Petre Scovell was a Cylinderman earning 2/8d per day in February 1814 (Supply 5/230).

William Scrivener was working in the Dusting House earning 2/1d per day in January 1806, and at that date had 3 months' service (Supply 5/224).

Roger Seabrook, born in 1764, was a Cooper by trade. On the 27th February 1789, he travelled by coach to the Tower of London bearing a letter from James Clowdesly at Waltham Abbey to William Waverly, requesting three bundles of Frick Hoops for whole barrels (WASC 0475). In March of that year he was repairing barrels and paid 2/6d per day (Supply 5/212). Barrel repairing was his occupation until at least January 1792 (Supply 5/215).

John Seagar was a Labourer set to work by Daniel Cornish in October 1787 at 9/-d per week, possibly repairing the Mills following their purchase from Mr. Walton by the Government (Winters, *op.cit*.p.29). However, he does not appear to have been retained.

Samuel Sears was born circa 1785 and was working in August 1812 as a Labourer in the Storekeeper's Department, "drawing and setting stoves and in the willow plantations" for which he was paid 2/8d per day (Supply 5/229). In February 1814 he was classified as a Stoveman, still earning 2/8d per day (Supply 5/230).

On the 5th July 1816, he joined the Engineers' Department as a casual Labourer earning 2/4d per day; He was then a 35-year-old married man with 2 children living in Waltham Abbey (WO54/520). Samuel continued to be employed as a Labourer on the same rate of pay, but in April 1823, this had been reduced to 2/2d per day for 313 days in the year. This gave him an annual income of £33.18.2d (WO54/542). A Return of Persons belonging to the Civil Establishment of the Ordnance at the Gunpowder and Small Arms Manufactories at Waltham Abbey, Faversham and Enfield, showing in detail several points of information called for by the Master General and Board's Order dated the 31st January 1831, recorded that Samuel Sears was one of 15 Labourers to be employed at Waltham Abbey and Enfield. He was to be was to be paid 2/2d per day and employed to undertake different services as a Labourer in the Manufactories, where steadiness and sobriety were particularly required (WO54/575). He was still employed on the same terms in April 1834 (WO54/593).

George Sebe started work as a Corning House Man in 1805 (Supply 5/224) and continued to do so until at least February 1814 (Supply 5/230). His daily wage rose from 2/2d to 3/3d during this period, in addition to which, he was allowed to watch in turn with his watch allowance increasing from 1/-d per night in 1807 to 1/6d by 1814.

James Selby was a common Labourer who was paid 17/-d for work carried out by the Engineers' Department in the Manufactory between the 15th and 21st July 1809 (Supply 5/228).

Richard Serle was working in the Corning Houses in August 1790 earning 1/6d per day, and by December of that year he was grinding Saltpetre (Supply 5/215).

William Sewell started work as a Corning House Man in 1805 (Supply 5/224) and continued to be employed in that capacity until at least February 1814 (Supply 5/230). During that period, his daily wage rose from 2/2d to 3/3d, and in addition, he was allowed to watch in turn. The allowance for watching increased from 1/-d per night in 1807 to 1/6d by 1814.

John Sharp started his employment on the 7th April 1815 as an occasional Labourer in the Engineers' Department, and was paid 2/8d per day. In February 1816, he was a 50-year-old married man with 4 children living in Enfield (WO54/516).

Thomas Sharp started his employment as an occasional Labourer on the 14th November 1815 in the Engineers' Department at 2/8d per day. In February 1816, he was a 52-year-old married man with 4 children living in Enfield (WO54/516).

Joseph Sheaf was working in May 1804 as a Labourer in the "Engineers' Dept. Established", earning 1/6d per day "with one day extra allowed per week agreeable to the Board's Order dated the 12th March, 1801." (Supply 5/222).

Joseph Sheffield was working as a Saltpetre Refiner in August 1812, as he was in February 1814. During that time he was paid 2/8d per day, and in addition, when not working extra, he was allowed to watch in turn (Supply 5/229 & 5/230).

William Shelbourne was the Master of the barge *The Mary Ann* in 1805 (Winters, *op.cit.* p.56).

William Shepherd started his employment as an occasional Labourer in the Engineers' Department on the 4th November 1815, and was paid 2/8d per day. In February 1816, he was a 30-year-old bachelor living in Waltham Abbey (WO54/516).

Phillip Sherrin was the bearer of a letter from the Comptroller, William Congreve, to the Rex Officers at Waltham Abbey, requesting that Evan Jones be sent to the Royal Laboratory and that they take Sherrin as a Labourer in Jones' place (WASC 0475). In August 1790, Sherrin was dusting and glazing powder (Supply 5/215), and this was also the case in February 1793 (Supply 5/216).

John Shields was a Carpenter by trade working within the Manufactory on the 16th June 1801 where, along with others, he was repairing the Corning House when it caught fire following an explosion. The accident was caused "from a blow of a copper hammer on a pit wheel" (Winters, *op.cit.* p.59). The Storekeeper sent a letter to the Board on the 23rd June 1801, listing the names of the men who had suffered terrible burns, seeking permission to support the casualties. John's name was included, and the letter went on to state, "we beg to represent the situation of the poor men who were burnt when the Corning House took fire on the 16th instant when under repair." It continued, "…These men are burnt in a dreadful manner. Their pain is very great..." and "Our surgeon has represented the necessity of the men most burnt having immediate assistance in wine, as a considerable suppuration is come on their constitutions. They cannot support it without wine, and we have directed wine to be immediately provided to them. We request your permission for our continuing to support these poor men with such wine or other proper support as their surgeon may think their respective situations require" (Supply 5/195). It would appear that the Board responded immediately; replying the same day, the writer stated he had "the Board's commands to transmit to you on the other side hereof a list of the men who have been burnt and otherwise hurt by the fire which lately destroyed the Corning House at Waltham Abbey; and I am to desire the Storekeeper will pay the men all their pay until they are recovered" (Supply 5/195).

Another letter to the Board dated the 29th July 1801 (Supply 5/221) recorded that the men who had been burnt at the Corning House requested that they be reimbursed for the loss of clothing. The list included John Shields, whose claim amounted to £1.9.6d in all – for a hat (4/-d) shirt 4/-d) neck cloth (1/6d) jacket (6/-d) and sheets (14/-d). The letter went on to say that Mr Shields, amongst others, had suffered so much that he wished for death to release him from his torture, and that it was a matter of surprise that he was recovering. The constant attention the men needed meant that their wives could not undertake seasonal work (haymaking) at which they could earn sufficient to pay the rent. It was requested that financial allowances be made, but no record of the Board's response has come to light. From a letter to the Board dated the 29th February 1806 containing a petition from his widow, Elizabeth, aged 63, it is evident that John Shields had died some two months earlier, having been severely burnt in the Corning House fire of 1801. The surgeon was of the opinion that "his days were shortened therefrom." It also stated that Mrs Shields was "a hard working woman of an exceeding honest character and has a great many children, none of which are in circumstances to render her any assistance, and now through age and infirmities [she is] not able to work and, therefore, is greatly necessitated." She asked for "some small weekly allowance to keep her from poverty and want" (Supply 5/224). The outcome of her Petition is unknown.

John Shore was appointed as an Extra Clerk at Waltham Abbey on the 20th July 1807, and paid £70.0.0d per annum (Supply 5/227). On the 20th August 1807, he was appointed as the Third Clerk, at the same annual salary; he received no allowances, nor was he on the Establishment (Supply 5/228). On the 27th July 1812, he was promoted to the position of "second clerk" with his salary increased to £80.0.0d per annum, and in addition, he received £12.0.0d per annum for lodgings and a further £8.0.0d annually for coal and candles (Supply 5/229).

W. Sibthorpe started an Apprenticeship as a Cooper on the 21st July 1796 (Supply 5/219).

Martin Sillcock was born circa 1757 (Supply 5/214) and had worked as an occasional Labourer at the Royal Laboratory "during the last war", which was, presumably, the American War of Independence (Supply 5/217). He started his employment at Waltham Abbey on the 13th April 1789 as a Labourer in the Saltpetre Refining House under John Baker, and was paid 1/6d per day (Supply 5/213). Martin continued to work as a Saltpetre Refiner, but did not sign the Petition on Pay and Conditions at the Mills in February 1801 (Supply 5/220). The Return on the Marital Status of the Employees dated the 18th May 1801, recorded that he was a single man (Supply 5/221). Robert Coleman, Clerk of the Cheque, noted in his Minute Book on the 23rd October 1801, that 24 men were required to work at Faversham or be discharged. Sillcock was one who agreed to go (Winters, *op.cit.*p.60) but the Faversham records do not list his name, so it can only be assumed that his services were not terminated, because he was still employed as a Refiner at Waltham Abbey in May 1804 at 2/-d per day. In addition, he was allowed to watch in turn – on average every 5th night – for which he received 1/-d (Supply 5/222).

Robert Simes, born circa 1781, was first employed as a casual Millwright in the Engineers' Department on the 18th September 1816, having originally trained as a Smith. In February 1817, he was a 38-year-old bachelor living in Waltham Abbey, who was paid 5/2d per day (WO54/520). Robert had married by February

1818 (WO54/524) and by the following May, he and his wife, Sarah, had their first child (WO54/528) with 8 more to follow (WO54/623). He continued to work within the Engineers' Department "occasionally as the Service required" although it would appear that he was employed on a full-time basis in April 1823, since he was then paid 5/2d per day for 313 days, giving him an annual income of £80.17.2d (WO54/542).

A Return of Persons belonging to the Civil Establishment of the Ordnance at the Gunpowder and Small Arms Manufactories at Waltham Abbey, Faversham and Enfield, showing in detail several points of information called for by the Master General and Board's Order dated the 31st January 1831, recorded that Robert Simes was one of three Millwrights to be employed at Waltham Abbey and Enfield. He was to be paid 5/2d per day, and his duties were "in general service as a Millwright within the Manufactories where steadiness and sobriety were particularly required." (WO54/575). He was still employed on the same terms in April 1834 (WO54/593).

Following the promotion of Thomas Sadd to the position of Master Worker in 1838, Robert moved into Sadd's house in Powder Mill Lane (WO44/133). The house was owned by the Board and, together with its garden of some seven perches, was let to Robert for £12.10.0d per annum; details of the construction of the house can be found under the notes on Samuel Knowler who was the occupant prior to Thomas Sadd. His annual pay was still £80.17.2d in April 1839 (WO54/623). The 1841 Census recorded that neither Robert nor his wife, Sarah, were born in Essex, and that the couple were living in Powder Mill Lane with 8 of their children - Robert and Sarah (both 20) Elizabeth (15) James (11) Amelia (11) Christine (8) Help (6) and Josiah (3).

Frederick Simpson, born circa 1808/1809, was "appointed as a Salt Petre Refiner in the room of Samuel Turnham on the 12th

May 1830" (WO54/570) i.e., he had replaced Turnham who had been a Saltpetre Refiner. The same document revealed that he was a 22-year-old bachelor, was paid £39.0.0d per annum - which included an allowance to watch in turn - and that he had been trained as a "Smith". This information was confirmed by WO54/581, which recorded that he had been trained as a Gunsmith (possibly at the Royal Small Arms Factory in Enfield) and may indicate that he was the son of John Simpson (2) who was living in Enfield by 1818. In August 1832, Simpson, together with three others, was cautioned for being absent from his work for a whole day without leave, and warned that a repeat would result in his dismissal (Supply 5/207).

Frederick continued to work as a Saltpetre Refiner. By October 1833, he had married (WO54/587) and a Return for April 1834, recorded that he had one child, and that his annual pay had been reduced to £33.9.6d (WO54/593). A Return of Employees dated the 10th October 1839 (WO54/632) confirmed his position as a Saltpetre Refiner, and stated that from the 5th September 1835, his total pay had been restored to £39.0.0d per annum; it also recorded that he then had 2 children. A Return of Domestic Properties for 1840 recorded that Frederick Simpson, a Labourer, was occupying "cottage number 71 on the general plan previously occupied by C Clayden" (WO44/133) and the property has been identified as being in Romeland. Although he is not recorded in the 1841 Census for Waltham Abbey, an Elizabeth Simpson, aged 30, together with her 4 young children, was living in Romeland, and she was likely to have been Frederick's wife. Frederick's name was not included in this Census, but he was working at the Mills in 1855 as a Granulating House Man according to Winters (*op.cit.* p.112).

John Simpson (1), born circa 1753, trained as a "Taylor" (Supply 5/231) before starting work as a Labourer with the Royal Ordnance at Waltham Abbey on the 10th February 1790 (Supply

5/217). Initially he was employed "in the punts and sett & draw stoves etc." for which he received 1/6d per day. John improved his position, and by April 1791 was employed as a Millman, with his daily pay increased to 2/3d. Millmen were paid an extra 3d when working at night (Supply 5/217) a practice that operated in 1804 (Supply 5/226). On the 6th May 1793 Robert Coleman, the Clerk of the Cheque, caught him wearing nailed shoes while on duty, and he was chequered (fined) one day's pay for this serious breach of Manufactory Regulations (Winters, *op.cit.* p.41). The Petition on Pay and Conditions at the Mills presented to the Board in February 1800, showed that John was literate (Supply 5/220) and a Return the following year on the Marital Status of the Employees, recorded that he was a married man with 7 children (Supply 5/221). By 1819, he had 10 (Supply 5/232). In November 1801, although still employed as a Millman, in common with the majority of the employees at the Mills, he was engaged in "cleaning the river and canals and performing necessary work" (Supply 5/221). A Return dated the 30th January 1806, confirmed that he was still a Millman at 2/3d daily (Supply 5/224) as he was on the 18th June 1807 (Supply 5/226).

A letter directed to the Board dated the 4th January 1808, recommended that John be appointed as the Foreman of the Millmen (Supply 5/198). His pay increased to 3/-d per day, and equally as important, he was allowed a house (Supply 5/227). The Board purchased some 19 dwellings in 1808 in High Bridge Street and Powder Mill Lane, including 7 from William Hanscombe and his under tenants, who were not named, as they were in other purchases made at the same time (WO44/81a). A Statement "of monies which the public were entitled to receive" dated 1821, recorded that John Simpson had been living rent-free in a house owned by the Ordnance Board since the 29th June 1808 (Supply 5/232). An extract from Properties owned by the Board compiled from the Rateable Value for Waltham Abbey for 1825, located the property as at the southern end of Powder Mill

Lane near its junction with High Bridge Street, being part of Plot No. 62 on the Town Map in Appendix 1 on the 1825 Parish Map of the town (WASC 2180, p.147).

John continued to work as the Foreman Millman until he was superannuated in 1821. During that period his daily pay peaked at 4/-d in 1812 (Supply 5/229) and in addition, he was a Rounder every third night, for which he received 2/-d. However, In common with all Ordnance employees, his pay was reduced with the cessation of the Napoleonic wars; by 1819 he was receiving 3/4d per day, and his money as a Rounder was 1/6d (Supply 5/231). On the 15th September 1821, the Storekeeper, Empson Middleton, wrote to the Board requesting that John Simpson, Foreman Millman, be granted a pension. He went on to say that Simpson had served the Board for 31 years, but was now in a very ill state of health with debility (Supply 5/232). In their reply dated the 16th November, the Board concurred (Supply 5/232) and shortly afterwards he received a superannuated sum of £14.6.11d per annum (Supply 5/232).

William Newton, the Master Worker who lived on Horse Mill Island (Marsh Side or Wall) died in 1825 (WASC 2180, p.108) and soon after, his house was divided into two (WASC 2180, p.110). From a list of domestic properties owned by the Board in 1840, it seems clear that it was intended that John and his wife, believed to be Sarah, should move from Powder Mill Lane into Newton's former house soon after its conversion (WO44/133). From other documents such as WO54/554, it is evident that John died in the autumn of 1826. Another record dated the 19th February 1827, stated that John had died, and that the Board had agreed his widow could stay in the cottage where they had lived for another 12 months, on the condition that she paid 2/-d a week rent (Supply 5/205). This, coupled with details relating to Thomas Freeman (1) clearly indicates that neither John nor his widow moved to Horse Mill Island.

John Simpson (2) was born circa 1781/1782, and started work as an Apprentice under the Master Mixer of Composition on the 1st December 1792 (Supply 5/217) at 1/-d per day (Supply 5/216). By December 1794, his pay had increased to 1/6d daily (Supply 5/217). A list of employees who joined the Volunteer Company of the 7th May 1794, does not include his name, (Winters, *op.cit.* p.42) nor was he in a Roll of Volunteers of September 1798 (Supply 5/219). In a List of Employees dated the 30th January 1806, he is described as "John Simpson (2)" and employed as a Millman, earning 2/3d per day (Supply 5/224). It is apparent that John left the Mills before completing his Apprenticeship, and is explained by a Return for February 1822, which recorded that he had been trained as a Cutler (Supply 5/232).

John returned to work at the Mills on the 8th May 1805 (WO54/558) and in January 1806, he was employed as a Millman earning 2/3d per day (Supply 5/224). By June 1807, he was working as a Saltpetre Refiner earning 2/-d per day and, when not working extra, allowed to watch in turn (Supply 5/226). He continued to work in the Saltpetre Refinery, with his daily wage peaking at 2/8d in the years between 1812 (Supply 5/229) and 1814 (Supply 5/230). A Return of Employees dated the 25th June 1818, recorded that he was a married man with 5 children living in Enfield, but although still a Refiner, his wage had dropped to 2/4d daily. However, he was still allowed to watch, for which he received 1/-d when it was his turn (Supply 5/231).

When the Waltham Abbey Establishment was drastically cut in 1818 by an Order of the Board dated the 4th September, it was proposed that John's services be retained as a Brimstone Refiner (Supply 5/232). However, he remained at the Saltpetre Refinery by an Order of the Board dated the 4th October 1819, and in 1822 was being paid £41.14.4d per annum, which included an allowance for watching in turn. He still lived in Enfield with his wife and 5 children (Supply 5/232). He continued as a Saltpetre

Refiner, but suffered another cut in his pay in January 1823, when the production and regeneration of gunpowder was reduced further, and he then earned £39.0.0d per annum (WO54/524).

John Simpson (1) died in 1826, and from then on John Simpson (2) was referred to in various documents and Returns as John (1) to distinguish him from his own son, who was then known as John, Jnr. On the 6th April 1829, John moved from Enfield to Waltham Abbey, occupying one of 5 cottages owned by the Board known as Bank Cottages, on the north side of West Street (High Bridge Street) forming part of Plot No. 48 on the Town Map in Appendix 1, for which he paid 2/-d per week rent (Supply 5/237). He continued in his trade until the autumn of 1830 when he became a Millman, with his pay being increased to £41.4.0d annually (WO54/570). He was still a Millman the following spring (WO/575) but by October 1831, he was refining Saltpetre again, with a reduction in pay to £39.0.0d per annum (WO54/581). He had been demoted still further by October 1832, when it was recorded that he was a General Labourer within the Manufactory (WO54/581). It appeared that he finally left the Ordnance shortly after October 1834, when he was earning a basic wage of £28.5.6d per annum and still allowed to watch in turn, which increased his annual pay to £33.9.6d (WO54/593). A Return of Domestic Properties owned by the Board in May 1840, recorded that John was "dismissed for drunkenness," and that Patrick Hayes then occupied his cottage (WO44/133). The 1841 Census recorded that a John Simpson, an Agricultural Worker of the right age, was living with the Durridge family in Sewardstone Street, although his wife is not mentioned.

John Simpson, Jnr., the son of John Simpson (2) was born circa 1804/1805. He started work as an Apprentice on the 12th June 1818 under Samuel Knowler, Snr., Master Refiner of Saltpetre. He was paid 6/-d per week and lived in Waltham Abbey (Supply 5/231) and it was common custom for an Apprentice to live with his Master. In 1820 his weekly pay had risen to 6/4d, and he then lived in Enfield, which is logical since his father had moved there prior to 1818. By the time he had completed his Apprenticeship in 1825, he was earning £16.7.8d per annum (Supply 5/232 & WO54/524).

On the 25th May 1825 he replaced James Pallet as a Labourer "setting and drawing stoves," and was then paid £39.0.0d annually, which included an allowance to watch in turn (WO54/550). Following the death of John Simpson (1) in 1826, he was then referred to as "John Simpson Junior" in various documents and records. A Return of Employees dated the 1st October 1829 recorded that he was still a Stoveman, but that he was now married with one child (WO54/566). Sadly, it appears that both his wife and child had died, since by the following spring he is described as being single (WO54/570). In October 1833, it was recorded that he had married again and that he was still paid £39.0.0d annually (WO54/587). By April 1834, he and his wife had one child but, although still a Stoveman, his annual pay had been reduced to £33.9.6d (WO54/593). John returned to live in Waltham Abbey, possibly when he remarried, since a Return of Domestic Properties dated the 28th May 1840, showed that John Simpson, Jnr., Labourer, was living in one of 5 cottages in High Bridge Street known as Bank Cottages, two doors away from where his father lived prior to his dismissal.

The 1841 Census recorded that John and his wife, Mary, although still living in High Bridge Street, had moved to a small yard forming part of Plot No. 60 on the Town Map in Appendix 1. John continued to work at the Mills and by 1855 was the Foreman of Stoves with a family of 4 children. (Winters, *op. cit.* p.112).

William Skinner was working as a Millman in January 1806 (Supply 5/224) as he was in February 1814 (Supply 5/230). His pay in 1806 was 2/3d per day and had risen to 3/-d daily by 1814; in addition, he was allowed an extra 6d when on night duties.

James Slaker/Staker started employment with the Ordnance Board in 1805. By January 1806, he was working as a Saltpetre Refiner at 2/-d per day (Supply 5/224). His name does not appear in the records again until February 1814, when he was working as a Saltpetre Refiner earning 2/8d per day (Supply 5/230).

Alexander Smith worked as a Labourer within the Manufactory in August 1808 "setting and drawing stoves and in the willow plantations etc." earning 2/-d per day; in addition, he was allowed to watch in turn (Supply 5/227). By 1812 he was working in the Dusting House, where he was paid 2/3d per day and allowed to watch in turn, for which he received 1/6d per night (Supply 5/229). The last record relating to Alexander was dated the 13th February 1814, and listed him as a Corning House Man receiving 3/3d per day, as well as still being allowed to watch in turn (Supply 5/230).

Henry Smith was employed as the acting Surgeon in January 1841, and paid £60.0.0d per annum (Supply 5/238).

James Smith was working as an occasional Labourer within the Engineers' Department in September 1812 earning 2/8d per day for a six-day week (WO54/512). A Return for 1816 disclosed that he was a 52-year-old married man living in Waltham Abbey, and that he had 3 unmarried children (WO54/516). He was still employed as a Labourer in 1817, but his pay at that date had been reduced to 2/4d per day (WO54/520). His employment with the Board ceased after this entry.

John Smith, born circa 1762/1763, was working as a Labourer at Faversham attending the New Horse Mill in October 1787, and was to be transferred to the Royal Powder Mills at Waltham

Abbey on the 4th January 1788 (Supply 5/113). A second Faversham document dated the 8th March 1788, noted that he had gone to Waltham Abbey as a Labourer "glazing gunpowder" (Supply 5/113, p.357). His arrival at Waltham Abbey was confirmed by a List of Employees dated the 21st March 1789, which noted that he was working there as a Labourer "dusting and glazing gun powder" for which he received 1/6d per day (Supply 5/212). In April of that year in common with the majority of the workforce, he was "cutting and planting willow trees, cutting of a canal at the new Corning House, removing earth to the Store, unloading barges of coal and charring wood" (Supply 5/213). In August and September 1789, he was grinding saltpetre, charcoal and brimstone, and the same Return recorded that he was 26 years' old (Supply 5/214).

A letter dated the 10th October 1789 from the Storekeeper, James Wright, to the Comptroller of the Royal Laboratory, recorded that John Smith, a Labourer, came to Waltham Abbey from Faversham, and had been on the sick list since the 28th August 1789. It further related, "his disorder has been chiefly ague, I have frequently observed him to walk about at improper times for a person having that disorder upon him. Yesterday there was a Horse race at Enfield meadows and tho' the waters were so much out that no person could walk without being half a leg deep in water yet Smith was there and stayed several hours in the wet and Dirt which was dangerous for anyone in full health. The Labourers speak much of his behaviour and I am afraid it will be a bad precedent for others to play loose when they may not happen to be unwell. I have mentioned this matter to receive your directions in what manner this man is to be treated." The Comptroller's 'directions' are unknown, but it would seem that he was dismissed, since his name did not appear in the records for another three years.

John Smith (1) in the 1792-1802 records, was born circa 1771, and commenced his employment at the Royal Powder Mills at Waltham Abbey on the 14th April 1792 (Supply 5/219). In July of that year he was working in the Saltpetre House, for which he was paid 1/6d per day (Supply 5/216). In December 1794, he was employed in the Corning House and still paid 1/6d per day (Supply 5/217) but by June 1795, he had returned to the Dusting House (Supply 5/217). This document recorded that he had joined the Volunteer Company, so he was not one of the first volunteers to step forward on the 4th May 1784 (Winters, *op.cit* p.42). He continued to work in the Dusting House until 1804, when he was promoted to a "Working Foreman in the Dusting House" (Supply 5/222) a position he held until sometime between 1814 and 1818, when he became the Foreman of the Glazing Mill (Supply 5/231 and WO54/524). During this period his wage increased from 1/6d per day, peaking at 3/10d per day in 1812 (Supply 5/230). He also progressed from being allowed to watch in turn every 5th night, for which he received 1/-d, to the supervisory post of a Rounder, which gave him an extra 2/- every third night (Supply 5/230). It would seem that he did not sign the Petition on Pay and Conditions at the Mills which was presented to the Board in February 1800 (Supply 5/220). The Return on the Marital Status of the Employees made in 1801, recorded that he was a married man with 3 children, living in Waltham Abbey (Supply 5/221). By 1818, his family had increased in number to 7 (Supply 5/231).

There was a huge explosion on Lower Island on the 27th November 1811, and among the seven men killed was Daniel Goats. His remains were allegedly buried with the other casualties, but his body was not actually discovered until sometime afterwards. A reward was paid to the finder, and by a Board Order dated the 17th January 1812, John Smith received a gratuity of £1 for recovering the body (Winters, *op.cit.* p.153).

Although not proved, the John Smith covered by these notes, was the most likely recipient of the reward.

In 1818, economies were made at the Mills drastically reducing the labour force. A List of Employees dated the 28th August 1818, recorded the names of the people to be retained between the 3rd September and the 31st December of that year (Supply 5/231). John's services were no longer required as the Glazing Mill Foreman, but, with 26 years' service behind him, he was to be retained as a Warder at the main entrance to the Manufactory. The Board's Orders of the 4th September 1818 and the 30th June 1820, confirmed that John was to be retained on a reduced daily pay of 2/-d (subsequently increased to 2/4d) but he was allowed to watch in turn, for which he received, on average, 2/-d per week, giving him annual pay of £41.14.2d. He was also allowed, apparently rent-free, a Board's "cottage as a porter's lodge". The lodge was at the main entrance to the Manufactory adjacent to the Engineers' yard on the west side of Powder Mill Lane, being Plot No. 91 on the Town Map in Appendix 1, and was to remain the family home until the late 1830s (Supply 5/232).

A Return dated the 1st April 1833, recorded that his wife had died, that he then had 6 children and that his pay was reduced to £33.16s.0d per annum because he was no longer allowed to watch (WO54/587). A Return of Domestic Properties owned by the Board dated 28th May 1840 (WO44/133) recorded that John was offered a cottage, one of 5 owned by the Board on the south side of High Bridge Street almost opposite Powder Mill Lane. The entry read, "Refused to be occupied by J. Smith warder, & would have been taken down but (the) roof was connected with no 54." It can only be assumed that he had retired by 1839 and that with his length of service he would have received a pension, but his name was not recorded in the 1841 Census for Waltham Abbey.

John Smith (2) in the 1792-1802 records, started employment with the Ordnance Board at Waltham Abbey on the 11th November 1793, and in August 1794, he was a Labourer working in the Corning House at 1/6d per day (Supply 5/216). The Corning House was his workplace throughout that year (Supply 5/217). During 1795, he was "setting and drawing stoves" and still paid 1/6d per day (Supply 5/217). By September 1798, he was working as a Millman, was a Private in the Volunteer Company and it was also confirmed that his starting date with the Board was the 11th November 1793 (also Supply 5/217).

On the 7th May 1796, No.15 Upper Head Mill blew up for a second time (apparently it had blown up the previous February) and, "John Smith, the Millman, threw himself down, by which he escaped injury" (Winters, *op.cit.* p. 52). The same Mill blew up again on the 13th February 1798, but without causing injuries (Winters, *op.cit.* p.54). John would appear to have made a habit of blowing up Mills, since on the 5th December 1798, he, together with Richard Wright, was involved with another Mill explosion which was "caused by a practice of putting too much powder on the beds than was allowed" (Winters, *op.cit.* p.54). The Petition on Pay and Conditions at the Mills presented to the Board in February 1800, recorded that he was still working as a Millman earning 2/-d per day, and that he was illiterate (Supply 5/220). A Return on the Marital Status of the Employees recorded that he was a married man without issue (Supply 5/221). In November 1801, although still employed as a Millman, John was "cleaning and deepening the river, canals and performing sundry necessary work" (Supply 5/221). This entry was the last relating to John Smith (2).

John Smith (3) in the 1792-1802 records, commenced employment as a Labourer in the Dusting House at Waltham Abbey on the 2nd June 1794, earning 1/6d per day (Supply 5/216) before transferring to the Corning House, where he was employed throughout 1794 (Supply 5/217). He enlisted as a Private in the Volunteer Company on the 7th May 1794, and was still serving in September 1798 (Supply 5/219). In June and July 1795, he was "setting and drawing stoves" (Supply 5/217) before returning to the Corning House. The Petition on Pay and Conditions at the Mills presented to the Board in February 1800 showed that he was illiterate (Supply 5/220).

On the 16th June 1801, John was burnt when the Corning House caught fire. A Report to the Board dated the 23rd June (Supply 5/195) stated, "We beg to represent the situation of the poor men who were burnt when the Corning House took fire on the 16th instant while under repair. These men are burnt in a dreadful manner, their pain is very great." It went on to say "our Surgeon has represented the necessity of the men most burnt having immediate assistance in wine, as a considerable suppuration is come to their constitutions. They cannot support it without wine, and we have directed wine to be immediately provided to them, and request your permission for our continuing to supply these poor men with such wine and proper support as their Surgeon may think their respective situations require." The fire was caused "from a blow of a copper hammer on pit wheel" (Winters, *op.cit.* p.59). A letter from the Storekeeper to the Board dated the 29th July 1801, stated that the men who were burnt requested that they be reimbursed for the loss of clothing. The list included John Smith, whose claim amounted to £2.13s.0d in all – for a hat (9/6d) handkerchiefs (5/-d) stockings (3/6d) shirt (7/-d) and sheets (£1.0.0d). The same letter continued that John Smith, amongst others, suffered so much that he wished for death to release him from his torture, and that it was a matter of surprise that he was recovering. The constant attention the men needed meant that their wives could not undertake seasonal work (haymaking) at which they could earn sufficient to pay the rent. It was requested that financial allowances be made (Supply 5/221). A Return of Artificers and Labourers dated the 3rd November

1801, stated that "John Smith (3rd)" and others had been so severely burnt in the Old Corning House that it would be dangerous to expose him with the other men in repairing the river banks at that time, but that instead, he could perform trifling jobs as they occurred (Supply 5/221). This appears to be the last entry for him in the records. It is assumed that he must have made a full recovery, since neither he nor his family were awarded a pension or compensation.

John Smith was an Apprentice to the Master Cooper, Richard Todd, in September 1810. He was paid 6/-d per week, with the Master Cooper receiving the same amount for teaching him the trade (Supply 5/228). He was still serving his time in August 1812 with his pay increased to 6/2d per week, while the Master Cooper received 6/6d extra per week in respect of his Apprentice (Supply 5/229). In this document he was referred to as John Smith (2) to distinguish him from the Dusting House Foreman, the only other John Smith at the Mills at that particular time. However, by 1814, he was no longer employed by the Board.

Most of the youngsters started their Apprenticeships at Waltham Abbey at the age of 12 or 13, so John would have been born circa 1796/1798. The following John Smith started work in the Engineers' Department in 1823 and was born in 1797, so it is possible that they are one and the same person.

John Smith, born circa 1797, joined the Engineers' Department as a Labourer on the 4th October 1823 (WO54/550). In April 1825 he was paid 2/2d per day for 313 days, which gave him an annual income of £33.18.2d (WO54/550). The same Return recorded that he was a 28-year-old married man with one child, and at that time had some 18 months' service. In October 1825, it was noted that he was without issue, which indicates his child had died. However, the Return for April 1826 (WO54/554) showed that he had one child, so it was possible that another child had been born. He continued to work as a Labourer in the Engineers' Department and was still on the same rate of pay in April 1833 (WO54/587) by which time, he had 4 children. A Return of Persons belonging to the Civil Establishment of the Ordnance at the Gunpowder and Small Arms Manufactories at Waltham Abbey, Faversham and Enfield dated October 1830, recorded that John was one of 15 Labourers to be employed at Waltham Abbey Powder Mills and the Enfield Small Arms Manufactory, and that they were "to undertake different services as labourers in the manufactories where steadiness and sobriety are required." (WO54/570).

John Smith, born circa 1784, started employment as an occasional Labourer in the Engineers' Department on the 10th July 1815, and was paid 2/8d per day. In February 1816, he was a 31-year-old bachelor living in Waltham Abbey (WO54/512). However, he no longer worked for the Engineers in February 1817 (WO54/520).

Richard Smith was working as a Labourer in various parts of the manufactory on the 18th June 1807, "setting and drawing stoves, loading and unloading barges etc." for which he was paid 2/-d per day (Supply 5/226). In January 1810, he was a Marker of Barrels, for which he received 2/6d per day (Supply 5/228). He was still in the same trade in August 1812, but his wage had then risen to 3/3d per day and, in addition, he received 2/-d every 3rd night as a Rounder (Supply 5/229).

Thomas Smith was employed as a labourer, "dusting and glazing powder" in late 1792 or early 1793, earning 1/6d per day. However, he had ceased to be employed at the Mills by September 1793 (Supply 5/216).

William Smith was working at the Mills in September 1798 as a Labourer "setting & drawing stoves and clearing willow plantation", for which he was paid 1/6d per day (Supply 5/219). He joined the Volunteer Company as a Private (Supply 5/219) and a Petition on Pay and Conditions at the Mills presented to the Board on the 2nd February 1800, showed that he was illiterate (Supply 5/220). A Return on the Marital Status of the Employees dated the 8th May 1801, recorded that he was a married man with 4 children, and that he was working as a Labourer refining Saltpetre at 1/6d per day (Supply 5/221). In October 1801, Robert Coleman recorded in his Minute Book that 24 men were required to work at the Royal Powder Mills at Faversham or be discharged, and Smith agreed to go (Winters, *op.cit.* p. 60). However, his name did not appear in the Faversham records, neither did it appear again in the Waltham Abbey records until 1812. Therefore, it can only be assumed that he was discharged. A William Smith was recorded as working as an occasional Labourer in the Engineers' Department in September 1812, earning 2/8d per day for a six-day week (WO54/512) and a List of Employees dated the 13th February 1814, noted that a William Smith was employed as a Saltpetre Refiner at 2/8d per day and, when not working extra, was allowed to watch in turn (Supply 5/230). There are no other references to William Smith.

John Smithe was employed as a Barrel Marker in August 1808, paid 2/-d per day and allowed to watch in turn (Supply 5/227). He was still performing the same task in September 1810, but was then entered in the records as John Smith. His pay had been increased to 2/3d per day and he was allowed to watch in turn, for which he received 1/6d per night (Supply 5/228).

George Sole was an occasional Labourer in the Engineers' Department on the 16th May 1814, earning 2/8d per day. In February 1816, he was a 50-year-old bachelor living in Waltham Abbey (WO54/516).

James Somerville was a Labourer refining Saltpetre in April 1789 (Winters, *op.cit.* p.33).

William Sorrell was employed as a Labourer "drawing and setting stoves and in the Willow plantation" in August 1812. He was paid 2/8d per day and, in addition to his wage, he was allowed to watch in turn (Supply 5/229). In February 1814 he was a Corning House Man, then paid 3/3d per day, and 1/6d per night when it was his turn to watch (Supply 5/230).

Edward Speller (1), born circa 1768, was a Bricklayer who was paid £1.9.9d for work carried out by the Engineers' Department within the Manufactory between the 15th and 21st July 1809 (Supply 5/228). He was still employed as a casual Bricklayer in February 1816, and then paid 4/7d per day (WO54/516). At that date he was a 38-year-old widower living in Waltham Abbey with 3 unmarried children, and the Engineers had first employed him on the 23rd July 1806. He was still employed as a Bricklayer in February 1817, but by then his daily wage had been reduced to 4/1d (WO54/520).

Edward Speller (2), born circa 1773, started his employment as a Labourer in the Engineers' Department on the 21st May 1804; in December 1821, he was a 49-year-old married man living in Waltham Abbey with 5 children (WO54/536). In April 1823, he was paid 4/1d per day as a Carpenter, which for 313 days in the year gave him an annual income of £63.18.1d (WO54/542). Edward was still employed as a Carpenter in April 1830, at the same wage (WO54/570).

Edward Speller (3), born circa 1798, was working as a Cooper in June 1818, earning 3/6d per day (Supply 5/231). The same document noted that he was then a 20-year-old bachelor living in Waltham Abbey.

Edward Speller (4), born circa 1801, was working as a Cooper in June 1818, earning 3/6d per day, and was a 17-year-old bachelor living in Waltham Abbey (Supply 5/230).

Francis Speller, born circa 1812, was engaged as a general Labourer on the 2nd October 1833, replacing James Speller, who had died. He was paid £33.9.6d per annum, which included an allowance to watch (WO54/593). He was still in the same position in October 1834, and this record noted that he was a bachelor. He could possibly have been the son of James Speller below.

James Speller, born circa 1782, started a life-long employment with the Ordnance Board at Waltham Abbey on the 24th January 1800 (Supply 5/232) and initially worked as a Labourer (Supply 5/220). The Petition on Pay and Conditions at the Mills presented to the Board in February 1800 showed that he was literate (Supply 5/220) while a Return on the Marital Status of the Employees in May 1801, recorded that he was single (Supply 5/221).

Robert Coleman, the Clerk of the Cheque, recorded in his Minute Book on the 23rd October 1801 that 24 men were required to work at Faversham or be discharged, and James was one of those who agreed to go (Winters, op.cit. 60). However, the Faversham records did not record his name nor did the Waltham Abbey records show a break in his service, so it must be assumed that James continued his employment as a Labourer. In May 1804, he was working in the Corning Houses as a Labourer earning 2/1d per day, with an additional 1/-d when it was his turn to watch – on average every 5th night (Supply 5/222). By January 1806, he was employed as a Millman and paid 2/3d per day (Supply 5/224) but he had transferred to the Dusting House by June 1807, with his daily wage cut to 2/1d, although he earned an additional 1/- a night when on watch (Supply 5/226).

James had returned to the trade of Millman by August 1808 with his pay reinstated at 2/3d per day, and he was "allowed 6d per night when on duty" (Supply 5/227). He was still a Millman in August 1812, but was then paid 3/-d per day (Supply 5/229) as he was in February 1814 (Supply 5/230). Following the end of the Napoleonic War, gunpowder production at the Royal Mills was reduced and James was demoted. In June 1818, he was working as a Labourer "setting and drawing stoves", for which he received 2/-d per day (Supply 5/231). The same document recorded that he was then a 37-year-old married man living in Waltham Abbey with 4 children. The Establishment was reduced in numbers in September 1818, but James was retained as a Labourer refining Saltpetre with his pay unchanged (Supply 5/231). In May 1819, he was refining Brimstone and then paid 2/4d per day with 1/-d extra when it was his turn to watch (Supply 5/231). The same document noted that he then had 5 children. He had returned to the Saltpetre Refinery by April 1821 (Supply 5/232).

When the Establishment was reduced yet again in March 1822 and set to produce only 100 to 200 barrels of gunpowder and regenerate another 2000 barrels annually, James was retained. However, he was reclassified as a Millman, with his pay and allowance to watch in turn set at £44.4.0d per annum (Supply 5/232). He continued to work as a Millman with the same pay and allowances until his death in July 1833, and on the 2nd August, Francis Speller filled his position (WO54/593).

John Speller, born circa 1771, started work at the Mills on the 29th November 1791, "mixing composition" at 1/6d per day (Supply 5/215). Between July and September 1792, he was "dusting and glazing powder" (Supply 5/216). In March 1793, he replaced William Goodhew as a Millman, "grinding Saltpetre and charcoal (Supply 5/217). He also enlisted as a Private in the Volunteer Company on the 7th May 1794 (Winters, op. cit. p.42).

He signed the Petition on Pay and Conditions at the Mills which was presented to the Board in February 1800 (Supply 5/220). The Return on the Marital Status of the Employees in May 1801, recorded that he was then married with 3 children (Supply 5/221) and by 1822, he and his wife, Sarah, had a family of 5 children (Supply 5/232). John continued to be employed as a Millman for the rest of his working life and his wages gradually increased, peaking at 3/-d per day in 1812 (Supply 5/229). In April 1832, his annual wage amounted to £46.16.0d, which included an allowance to watch in turn (WO54/581).

On the 16th April 1834, two Mills exploded when not at work, and John was called before Lt. Col. Moody as a witness (Winters, *op.cit.* p.103). Soon after this John died, and his wife, Sarah, was awarded a pension with effect from the 18th November 1836 (Supply 5/237).

John Speller, born circa 1803 and trained as a Cooper, was making cement casks for Harwich at £54.12.0d per annum in October 1825 (WO54/550).

John Speller was working as a Cooper in February 1814, earning 1/9d per day (Supply 5/230. His wage indicated that he was a youth of some 11 to 13 years (see notes on James Slaker/Staker) and he was possibly the John Speller, Cooper, mentioned in the previous note.

William Speller started work with the Ordnance Board as a Labourer in the Corning Houses on the 11th November 1793, earning 1/6d per day (Supply 5/216) and this was to be his occupation until at least 1798 when he became a Saltpetre Refiner (Supply 5/219). In the meantime he had enlisted as a Private in the Volunteer Company on the 7th May 1794 (Supply 5/219). The Petition on Pay and Conditions at the Mills submitted to the Board in February 1800 showed that he was illiterate, while the Return on the Marital Status of the Employees noted that in May 1801, he was a married man with one child (Supply 5/221). Robert Coleman, the Clerk of the Cheque, recorded in his Minute Book on the 23rd October 1801, that 24 men were required to work at Faversham or be discharged, and William was one of those who agreed to go (Winters op.cit. 60). However, the Faversham records did not mention his name, nor did the Waltham Abbey records show a break in his service, so it is assumed he was continued in his employment as a Saltpetre Refiner.

In May 1804, he was still employed as a Saltpetre Refiner at 2/-d per day and was allowed to watch in turn – on average every 5th night - for which he received 1/-d (Supply 5/222). This was also the case in January 1806, when he had 12 years' service with the Board (Supply 5/224).

George Stacey was working in the Corning Houses earning 2/2d per day in January 1806, at which time he had 1 year's service with the Ordnance Board (Supply 5/224). The Corning House continued to be his work place until at least September 1810, when he was being paid 2/6d per day, and, in addition, he was allowed to watch in turn, for which he received 1/6d per night (Supply 5/228).

George Staker, born circa 1801, was 13 years' old when he was employed as a Cooper in February 1814. He was paid 1/9d per day, and in common with all the other Coopers, he was not allowed to watch (Supply 5/230). He was still employed as a Cooper in June 1818, and was then paid 3/6d per day (Supply 5/231). The same document recorded that he was then a 17-year-old single man living in Waltham Abbey. When the Establishment was reduced in numbers in September 1818, George was dismissed (Supply 5/231).

James Stachen was working as a Saltpetre Refiner in June 1807 at 2/-d per day, and when not working extra was allowed to watch in turn (Supply 5/226). This was also the case in August 1808 (Supply 5/227). His name did not appear in the records again until February 1814, when he was employed as a Saltpetre Refiner at 2/8d per day and then allowed to watch in turn (Supply 5/230).

Joseph Stanton started work at the Mills in September 1805, and in January 1806 he was employed as a Saltpetre Refiner, earning 2/-d per day (Supply 5/224). In June 1807, he was a "Labourer in various parts of the Manufactory, setting and drawing stoves and loading and unloading barges, etc." (Supply 5/226). By August 1808 he had returned to the Saltpetre Refinery, was still paid 2/-d per day, and "when not working extra allowed to watch in turn" (Supply 5/227). This was also the case in September 1810 (Supply 5/228) as well as in August 1812, but by then his daily pay had risen to 2/8d (Supply 5/229). By February 1814, he was employed as a Marker of Barrels with his pay increased to 3/3d per day; he was still allowed to watch, for which he received 1/6d per night (Supply 5/230).

Robert Steel first worked for the Engineers' Department as a casual Millwright on the 19th February 1812, earning 5/8d per day; at the time he was a 35-year-old married man, living in Waltham Abbey with 3 unmarried children (WO54/516). Robert was still working for the Engineers' Department in February 1817, but by then, his daily wage had been reduced to 5/2d (WO54/520).

Richard Stevens was set to work by Daniel Cornish in October 1787 at 9/-d per week, possibly renovating the Mills following their purchase by the Government from Mr. Walton (Winters, op.cit. p.28). Thereafter, he was employed as a Millman, "having lately worked for Mr. Walton" (Winters, *op.cit.*p.31). On the 24th

January 1789, Richard was judged to be unfit for service, and a letter dated the 12th September 1789 from James Wright and John Clowdesly to Major Congreve, stated that they had given notice to Richard Stevens, who was not to be employed after the 20th of that month (*WASC* 1392).

Joseph Stevens was working as a Cooper in August 1812 at 1/9d per day (Supply 5/229). He was still in the same trade in February 1814, but was then paid 2/4d daily, and, like all Coopers, was not allowed to watch (Supply 5/230).

William Stevens worked as a Labourer in the Corning Houses in January 1792, earning 1/6d per day (Supply 5/215). However, he may have left the Board's employment, since his name does not appear in the Waltham Abbey records after a January 1792 entry until May 1804, when he was described as a Labourer in the Corning Houses at 2/1d per day. In addition, he was allowed to watch in turn, for which he received 1/-d per night (Supply 5/222). Sometime after this, he was promoted to one of the three working foremen in the Corning Houses, and in January 1806 he was paid 2/6d per day (Supply 5/224). The same document noted that he then had 3 years' service with the Board, indicating that he had returned to the Mills in 1802 or 1803. William continued as a working Foreman, but in June 1807, although still paid 2/6d per day, he was allowed 1/6d every third night as a Rounder, checking on the nightly watch (Supply 5/226). By August 1808, his pay had increased to 3/-d daily and his Rounder's allowance was then set at 2/-d per night, as was the case in 1810 (Supply 5/227).

At 11.15 a.m. on the 27th November 1811 there was a huge explosion at No. 4 Press House; the ensuing fire engulfed the Corning House, together with the Reel House, which also exploded. There was much damage to the town with many windows shattered, and reports in the press stated that the explosion was heard as far away as Hackney, Blackwall and Marylebone (Winters, *op.cit.* p.72). A graphic account of the explosion was reported in the *Cambridge Chronicle* on the 29th November 1811, and reads as follows:

"A Dreadful Accident. A powder mill at Waltham Abbey was blown up on Wednesday last, 8 lives were lost, and seven of those persons left families. The whole town of Waltham was in great danger, as it was thought the magazine would have blown up. A man was, in consequence, sent through the streets of Waltham to caution the inhabitants to leave their houses instantly. No further explosion had, however, taken place at the date of our last account. At Stepney a mirror of plate glass was broken by the shock; at Hackney several panes of glass were forced in; and at Blackwall the windows throughout the whole street were shattered. Near the New-road, Marylebone, several houses were much broken; and the labourers who were excavating in the park felt the earth shake where they were at work. Even ships of the river were shaken. Some of the morning papers mistook it for an earthquake. This seems singular that the shock should be felt so much more in London, while the damage done in the town was but trifling, except that the current of air at that time might have directed the concussion from the town" (Winters, *op. cit.* p.72).

Among those killed was William, Foreman of the Corning House, who left a widow, Elizabeth, a daughter, also Elizabeth, aged 11 years, and a son, John, aged 3 years (Supply 5/229). Elizabeth was granted a pension of 21/-d per week with effect from the 28th November 1811 (Supply 5/231). She was still in receipt of her pension in 1823 (Winters, *op.cit.* p.96) but died in December 1832 (Supply 5/207).

C. Stewart was mixing composition at the Mills in November 1789 (Winters, op.cit. p.32).

Michael Stokes was the Master of the barge *Amherst* working for the Board at Waltham Abbey in 1792. He was also Master of the *Earl of Chatham* in 1805 (Winters, *op. cit.* p.55).

Thomas Story worked in the Corning Houses as a Labourer in May 1805, with pay of 2/1d per day, and, in addition, he was allowed to watch in turn, on average every 5th night, for which he received 1/-d (Supply 5/222).

Benjamin Stroud was a 20-year-old Labourer, who, in 1841, lodged with the Rapley family in High Bridge Street (*1841 Census*).

John Sullivan was a casual Labourer in the Engineers' Department in September 1812, earning 2/8d per day for a six-day week (WO54/512).

Michael Summers, born circa 1782, was first employed by the Board in the autumn of 1805, possibly as a Labourer. On the 30th January 1806 he was appointed as a Millman (Supply 5/22) and at that date was paid 2/3d per day (Supply 5/224). This was also the case in June 1808, but then he was allowed 3d per night extra when on duty (Supply 5/226). Michael was still a Millman in February 1814, with his daily wage increased to 3/-d, with an additional 6d for night work (Supply 5/230). In a letter to the Board dated the 10th December 1817 (Supply 5/201) it was stated that the dwelling house formerly occupied by James Allsup "will be ready to let in two distinct tenements on the 31st instant" and continued "…those tenements should be let at 3/-d per week each to John Braddock, Foreman of Magazines, and Michael Summers, Millman." The property has been identified as one of 5 cottages on the south side of High Bridge Street almost opposite Powder Mill Lane, in the old Tanyard, but there is no actual evidence to show that Michael ever lived there.

Peace in Europe saw a reduction in the manufacture and regeneration of gunpowder, and as a consequence, the Board required the Establishment at the Royal Powder Mills to be cut back and expenditure to be reduced. In June 1818, Summers' daily pay had been cut to 2/8d, although he was still allowed an extra 6d if he worked at night (Supply 5/231 & WO54/524). The same documents recorded that he was then a 45-year-old married man living in Waltham Abbey, with 5 children.

A list sent from Waltham Abbey to the Board on the 28th August 1818, noted the names of the people the Storekeeper proposed to retain between the 3rd September and the 31st December 1818, in order to meet the new production and financial requirements. Michael's name was on that list with his pay and allowance unchanged (Supply 5/231). However, a few days later, a letter from the Mills to the Board stated "We respectfully beg leave to add the names and stations of those people whom it will be necessary to discharge in consequence of this arrangement" and Michael Summers' name was on the list (Supply 5/231). An Order of the Board dated the 4th September 1818 rescinded this second proposal, and Michael continued to be employed as a Millman (Supply 5/232). He was still employed on the same terms in September 1820, and it was also recorded that he then had 6 children (Supply 5/232) but, sadly, it appears that one had died by April 1821 (Supply 5/232). In February 1822, his annual pay as a Millman was £46.18.8d, including an allowance to watch in turn, for which he received 2/-d per night. At that date he had 16 years' service, was 39 years' old lived in Waltham Abbey, was still married and had 5 children (Supply 5/232).

Michael left the Board's employment sometime after April 1825, since his name does not appear in the Return for October 1825. Subsequent records confirmed that he was appointed as a Saltpetre Refiner on the 10th February 1826 (WO54/554) and a similar Return dated the 1st April 1828, recorded that he then had

2 years' service (WO54/562). As a Saltpetre Refiner he was paid a Labourer's wage, his annual income in April 1826, including an allowance to watch in turn being £39.0.0d (WO54/554). At that date he was still living in Waltham Abbey, but by then had 7 children. He continued to refine Saltpetre until the 5th September 1834, when he resumed his original trade as a Millman (WO54/623). By October 1839, his annual remuneration increased to £46.16.0d (WO54/623).

A Return of Properties owned by the Board dated the 20th December 1834 compiled by the Royal Engineers' Office, recorded that Michael Summers had been leasing one their cottages since the 22nd July 1829, at a rental of £5.4.0d per annum or 2/-d per week (Supply 5/237). The same document also stated that the cottage had been vacated by December 1834, and it was proposed to let it to Patrick Hayes, Cylinderman. This located the cottage as on the south side of High Bridge Street, and was formed out of the dwellings in the old Tanyard, being Plot No.55 on the Town Map in Appendix 1. A similar list of properties, again prepared by the Royal Engineers' Office, indicated that he had moved following the death of William Turner to the opposite side of High Bridge Street, living in one of a row of tenements known as Bank Cottages (WO44/133) being part of Plot No. 48 on the Town Map in Appendix 1. The move was confirmed in the *1840 Waltham Abbey Poor Rates* (ERO D/P 75/11/16). Michael was still a Millman in October 1839 and by then, had 8 children (WO54/623). By the time the 1841 Census was taken, he had left Waltham Abbey.

James Sumpter worked as in Cylinderman at Fisher Street in West Sussex between June 1807 and February 1814, producing charcoal for Waltham Abbey (Supply 5/226 & 5/230). During this time, his wages increased from 2/-d per day to 2/8d.

William Sutton, born circa 1743, was appointed as a Master Millwright to the Board on the 24th April 1771. He worked until October 1787 as a Millwright at the Faversham Gunpowder Mills earning 3/-d per day, when he was sent to Waltham Abbey Mills (Supply 5/113). He was allowed to travel to Waltham "...on the inside of the coach..." and while working away from home at Waltham, his pay was to be £2.2.0d per week (Winters, *op.cit.* p.28). At Waltham he was the Acting Overseer of Works under Bartholomew Bennett. However, although he continued to work at the Waltham Mills until November 1788 (Supply 5/114) he had returned to Faversham by 1789, when he reverted to his Faversham rate of pay of 3/-d per day (Winters, *op.cit.* p.32).

William Sweetlove was employed on the 19th December 1812 as a casual Millwright, earning 5/8d per day. He was then a 60-year-old married man, living in Waltham Abbey with 2 unmarried children (WO54/516).

William Sykes, born circa 1776 and originally trained as a "Taylor," was appointed as a Millman on the 1st October 1812 (Supply 5/232). Winters confirmed that he was also a Millman in June 1813, and he was still working in that capacity in February 1814, earning 3/11d per day, in addition to which, he was paid 6d per night when on duty (Supply 5/230). When the Establishment was reduced in numbers in September 1818 William was retained, not as a Millman, but as a Saltpetre Refiner, with his pay reduced to 2/-d per day (Supply 5/231). This was confirmed by an Order of the Board dated the 4th September 1818 (Supply 5/232). For a while in 1819 he worked as a Brimstone Refiner earning 2/4d per day, and, in addition, was allowed to watch in turn, for which he received 1/-d per night (Supply 5/231). The same document recorded that he was then a 42-year-old married man without issue, living in Waltham Abbey. His position as a Saltpetre Refiner was reconfirmed in October 1819 by a second Order of the Board.

In the spring of 1822, the Ordnance Board decided to reduce the production and regeneration of gunpowder at Waltham Abbey still further, and the Establishment was to be trimmed to an even lower level. Accordingly, Empson Middleton and James Wright drew up lists of people to be dismissed and William Sykes was on the list (Supply 5/232). The men were subsequently made redundant on the 1st June, and several Petitions were submitted by the men asking for financial assistance. Many were long service employees in middle age, and they pointed out that they had little hope of finding employment after the corn harvest had been gathered. The Storekeeper was sympathetic and forwarded their Petitions to the Board for consideration. William, although he does not appear to have been one of the Petitioners, was awarded two weeks' pay to ease his financial burden (Supply 5/232).

T

John James Tamkin, son of Thomas and Sarah Tamkin, was baptised at Waltham Abbey on the 16th March 1811. Although trained as a Bricklayer, he was appointed as a Labourer in the Engineers' Department on the 1st January 1833 (WO54/587). He was then a 22-year-old bachelor, and the same document stated that he was paid 2/2d per day, which, for 313 days' work, gave him an annual wage of £33.18.2d. WO54/587 dated the 1st October 1833, indicated that by that date he had married and had one child. He was still with the Engineers' Department on the 1st April 1834 earning the same money (WO54/593) although this was the last mention of him in the Mills' records.

Nevertheless, according to Winters (*op.cit.* p.113) John was still working as a Bricklayer in the Engineers' Department in 1855. The 1841 Census recorded that John was a Bricklayer, and that he and his wife, Rebecca, lived in Malting Yard off High Bridge Street with their children, John (9) Sarah (6) Rebecca (4) and Mary Ann (1). John's mother, Sarah, lived with them, as well as William Clayden, who was a 25-year-old School Teacher.

Thomas Tamkin was born circa 1768. On the 10th October 1789, he was employed as a Bricklayer by a contractor working for the Ordnance Board at the Faversham Gunpowder Mills. He married Sarah Smith, the daughter of John Smith, at Faversham on the 31st July 1791. They had a daughter, Phoebe, baptised at Faversham on the 19th August 1792, and a son, John (see previous entry for John James Tamkin) who was baptised at Waltham Abbey on the 16th March 1811 (*FGPR,* p. 78).

Thomas joined the Engineers' Department at Waltham Abbey as the Foreman Bricklayer on the 16th May 1803, and was taken on the Establishment the same day ((WO54/512). The Department not only undertook works at Waltham Abbey, but also at the

413

Small Arms Factory, Enfield. Thomas was described in most documents as Master Bricklayer, i.e., he had served and completed an Apprenticeship. In 1804 he was paid 4/-d per day, and, in addition, was allowed 6/-d per week to train an Apprentice in his trade (Supply 5/222). He was paid £1.15.0d for work carried out in the Manufactory between the 15th and 21st July 1808 (Supply 5/228) and during the Napoleonic wars his daily wage peaked at 6/4d for a six-day week. In addition, he received one and a half days' pay for working on a Sunday (WO54/512).

Considerable redevelopment work took place within the Manufactory during 1814/1815, which included new houses on Horse Mill Island for William Newton, the Master Worker, and David Wilkie, the Second Clerk, which they occupied in the summer of 1815 (Supply 5/232). On page 82 of his book, Winters quotes from an unknown source dated the 29th August 1815, "Three houses building in Powder Mill Lane out of materials forming the Horse Mills at this place. Tenants are not allowed to have lodgers, that no dilapidations may take place to the premises being of timber, etc." A statement dated the 4th April 1821, "of monies to which the public were entitled to receive credit between the 1st January and the 31st December 1821 shewing the amounts received by the Storekeeper", recorded that Thomas had been living in a Board of Ordnance house, Tenement No. 22, from the 1st September 1815, and that the rent was £1 per annum (Supply 5/232). The same information was repeated the following year (Supply 5/232 and WO54/536). The house and its large garden have been identified as being at the northern end of a terrace of houses located in Powder Mill Lane, and shown as part of Plot No. 64 of the Town Map in Appendix 1.

A Return dated the 28th February 1817, recorded that Thomas, then 48 years of age and married with one unmarried child, was provided with a house. His pay, in common with others at the

414

Mills, had been reduced to 5/10d per day, although his allowance for training an Apprentice had risen to 8/-d per week (WO54/520) and was increased to 9/-d the following year (WO54/524). A memo dated the 14th December 1818, stated that Thomas Tamkin, Master Bricklayer, was to continue to pay the same rent of £1 per annum for the cottage he occupied in Waltham Abbey (5/202). A Return of Employees for 1819 showed that he no longer trained an Apprentice (WO54/528).

From 1819 until he retired in 1833, his pay remained the same at 5/10d per day for 313 working days a year, which gave him an annual income of £91.5.10d. During this period, Thomas and Sarah continued to live in Powder Mill Lane. A Return dated the 31st January 1831 of persons belonging to the Civil Establishment of the Ordnance at the Gunpowder Manufactories at Waltham Abbey, Faversham and Enfield, recorded that Thomas Tamkin was one of 3 Artificers to be employed at Waltham Abbey and Enfield, that he was the Master Bricklayer and that he was to be paid 5/10d per day. His duties were to work with the Artificers and Labourers in the gunpowder manufactories, consequently requiring "great attention, sobriety and steadiness of conduct" (WO54/570).

Under an Order of the Board dated the 15th March 1833, "Thomas Tamkin, Master Bricklayer, to be discharged and granted a pension of £31.10.9d per annum until an opportunity to employ him again should arise" (Supply 5/208). The final record relating to Thomas within the Ordnance is dated the 28th May 1840, when a Return of Domestic Property for 1840 noted that his cottage in Powder Mill Lane was then occupied by Mr Hayward, the Foreman of Works (WO44/133). Thomas died on the 3rd October 1840, and the 1841 Census showed that Sarah, his widow, lived with their son, John, and his family in Malting Yard, off High Bridge Street. Sarah died in 1863 aged 91 years (*FGPR*, p.79).

William Tarry was working as a Labourer in August 1812, "drawing and setting stoves and in the willow plantation" (Supply 5/229). This was also the case in February 1814, and throughout this period, he was paid 2/8d per day and allowed to watch in turn (Supply 5/230).

Thomas Taylor was employed as a casual Labourer in the Engineers' Department on the 6th April 1815 at 2/8d per day. In February 1816, he was a 45-year-old married man living in Cheshunt with 1 child (WO54/516).

William Taylor was working as a Labourer in August 1812, "drawing and setting stoves and in the willow plantation." He was paid 2/8d per day and, in addition, was allowed to watch in turn (Supply 5/229). In April 1833, a William Taylor, together with another employee, Charles Carter, was apprehended by the Thames police for being in possession of Government stores from the Waltham Abbey Powder Mills, although the outcome of the arrests is unknown (Supply 5/208).

George Teeman was employed as a Cylinderman at Fernhurst in West Sussex on the 1st November 1796 at 1/6d per day (Supply 5/219) and a Return on the Marital Status of the Employees in May 1801, noted that he was a bachelor (Supply 5/221). In November 1801, the cylinders were "out of repair" and George was employed stacking timber in the yards, as well as levelling and preparing the ground where the cylinders were to be resited (Supply 5/221). The last Return to mention George Teeman was in June 1807, when he was still a Cylinderman, with his pay increased to 2/-d per day (Supply 5/226).

James Teeman was working as a Cylinder Man in West Sussex in June 1807, earning 2/-d per day (Supply 5/226).

John Teeman was working as a Cylinderman at Fernhurst in June 1807 (Supply 5/226) and continued to be employed in this position until he was discharged in September 1818, when the requirement for charcoal at the Royal Gunpowder Mills was reduced (Supply 5/231). Initially he was paid 2/-d per day, which peaked at 2/8d in 1812 (WO54/512) but had been reduced to 2/4d by the date of his discharge. In June 1818, it was recorded that he was a 48-year-old married man with 5 children who had been provided with an apartment at Fernhurst ((Supply 5/231).

William Teeman worked as a Cylinderman in West Sussex in September 1810, continuing to do so until at least February 1814. During this time his pay rose from 2/-d to 2/8d per day (Supply 5/228 and 5/230).

John Terry worked as a Saltpetre Refiner in August 1812 until February 1814 (Supply 5/229 and Supply 5/230). Throughout this period he was paid 2/8d per day, and, in addition, was allowed to watch in turn, for which he received 1/6d per night.

William Teversham was working as a Puntman in September 1810, and was paid 2/-d per day as well as being allowed to watch in turn (Supply 5/228). By August 1812, he was a Corning House Man who was paid 3/3d per day and was still allowed to watch, for which he received 1/6d per night (Supply 5/229). He was employed in the Corning Houses on the same terms in February 1814 (Supply 5/230).

John Thornton was a Puntman in 1806 at 2/-d per day; at that date he had 1 year's service (Supply 5/224).

John Thorogood was employed as an occasional Labourer in the Engineers' Department on the 2nd October 1815, at 2/8d per day. In February 1816, he was a 44-year-old bachelor living in Waltham Abbey (WO54/516).

S. Thorp worked as a Labourer in the Corning Houses in March 1790, earning 1/6d per day (Supply 5/214).

David Thorpe was appointed Junior Clerk in place of Henry Dugleby in August 1801 (Supply 5/195).

James Tims worked as a Cylinderman at Fisher Street in West Sussex in June 1807, earning 2/-d per day (Supply 5/226). He was still making charcoal in August 1812, but was then paid 2/8d per day (Supply 5/229).

Martin Tims worked as a Cylinderman at Fisher Street in August 1814 earning 2/8d per day (Supply 5/229).

John Todd was born in 1784 and trained as a Cooper (WO54/524). Having commenced work as an Assistant Cooper at Waltham Abbey on the 22nd July 1802 (Supply 5/232) in May 1804 he was described as a Refiner earning 2/-d per day, and, in addition, was allowed to watch in turn, for which he received 1/-d each night (Supply 5/222). In March 1805, he was again working as a Cooper and paid a weekly wage of £1.2.0d (Supply 5/223). In January 1806 he was described as the Foreman of Coopers with his pay increased to 4/-d per day (Supply 5/224). By June 1807, he was listed as the Working Foreman of Coopers, and, entitled to take an Apprentice, he took on Richard Todd, Jnr., son of Richard Todd the Cooper, for which he was paid 9/-d per week (Supply 5/226). John continued as the Foreman Cooper, and a letter from the Board dated the 6th January 1809, recommended4 his pay be increased to 5/-d per day "...in the zeal he has manifested in his duty." (Supply 5/199). It would seem his keenness was recognised, since he was appointed Master Cooper the same day (WO54/232).

John continued as the Master Cooper, and by August 1812, his pay had increased to 6/4d per day. Although still entitled to train an Apprentice, it appeared that he had not done so since Richard Todd, Jnr. had served his time on the 26th July 1809 (Supply 5/229). He is listed as the Master Cooper in 1813 (Winters, *op.cit.* p.75) and was still earning the same money in February 1814, but was then allowed £18.5.0d per annum in lieu of training an Apprentice (Supply 5/230). A Return for June 1818 showed that in common with the rest of the workforce, his pay was reduced at the end of the Napoleonic war to 5/10d per day (Supply 5/231). The same Return recorded that he was a 33-year-old married man with 1 child, living in Cheshunt. When the Establishment was reduced in numbers in September 1818, John was retained with his pay unchanged (Supply 5/231). He was still the Master Cooper in May 1819, but, sadly, his only child had died (Supply 5/231). Proposals were made in March 1822 to form an Establishment to regenerate 2000 barrels of gunpowder as well as to make some 100 or 200 barrels of gunpowder annually, and John was to be retained (Supply 5/232). However, a Return for October 1822 showed that John Todd, Master Cooper, had been discharged by a Board Order dated the 9th August 1822; his pay at that time was £91.15.10 per annum (WO54/542).

Richard Todd, Snr. worked as an "Extra Cooper" at Purfleet from the 1st July 1779 to the 16th July 1783 (Supply 5/216) and came to Waltham Abbey on the 20th July 1792, where he was paid 2/6d per day (Supply 5/217). He joined the Volunteer Company as a Private on the 7th May 1794 (Supply 5/219) and the signed Petition on Pay and Conditions at the Mills presented to the Board in February 1800, showed that he was literate (Supply 5/220). However, he was not listed in the Return on the Marital Status of the Employees at the Mills dated May 1801 (Supply 5/221). In November 1801, he was described as a Master Cooper, and was employed in repairing store barrels and tubs, etc. (Supply 5/221). As a Master Cooper, he would have been entitled to train an Apprentice, and a Richard Todd Junior, presumably his son, started an Apprenticeship on the 22nd July

1802. In May 1804, Richard Todd, Snr. was described as a Cooper, but he was paid 3/1d per day, which would indicate that he was still a Master Cooper (Supply 5/222). This was the last record found relating to Richard Snr; he may well have died, since Richard Todd, Jnr. completed his Apprenticeship under John Todd, Foreman of Coopers and Master Cooper in his own right.

Richard Todd, Jnr. was appointed as an Apprentice Cooper on the 22nd July 1802 with a daily wage of 1/4d, and "one day extra allowed for week agreeable to the Board's Order dated the 12th March 1801" (Supply 5/222). Initially he served under his father, Richard Todd Senior, and then under John Todd, the Foreman of Coopers (Supply 5/199). He was still paid the same wage in 1808 (Supply 5/227) and when he collected 2 months' pay on the 30th September that year, he signed for it with "a bold and firm hand" (Supply 5/227). A letter dated the 26th July 1809 confirmed that he had completed his Apprenticeship, and that he was to be appointed as a Cooper at 2/6d per day (Supply 5/199). He was still employed as a Cooper in September 1810 (Supply 5/228) but by August 1812, he was described as a Labourer earning 2/8d per day, "drawing and setting stoves and in the willow plantation" (Supply 5/229). This was the last record for Richard Todd, Jnr.

Philip Tongue was working as a Corning House Man in August 1812 (Supply 5/229). This was also the case in February 1814, and during this time he was paid 3/3d per day, as well as being allowed to watch in turn, for which he received 1/-6d per night (Supply 5/230).

Alexander Toppin (Topin) was "drawing and setting stoves" in January 1806 earning 2/-d per day, and at that date he had some 6 months' service with the Board (Supply 5/224). In June 1807, he was employed as a Sieve Puncher and Proof House Man, still at 2/-d per day (Supply 5/226). This was also the case in August

1808, according to Supply 5/227. In September 1810, he was working as a Puntman at the same rate of pay, but was then allowed to watch (Supply 5/228). By 1812, he had returned to the Proof House with an increase in pay to 2/8d daily (Supply 5/229), and this was also the case in February 1814 (Supply 5/230).

William Toynbee was grinding Saltpetre and Charcoal, etc. in March 1790 (Supply 5/214). In August of that year he was marking barrels, and by December 1790, he was employed in the Stores (Supply 5/215).

John Tribe was employed as a Cylinderman in West Sussex on the 1st June 1797 (Supply 5/219). A Return on the Marital Status of the Employees dated the 8th May 1801, recorded that he was a married man with 1 child (Supply 5/221). In November 1801, the cylinders were "out of repair" and he was employed stacking timber in the yards, as well as levelling and preparing the ground where the cylinders were to be resited (Supply 5/221). John continued to work as a Cylinderman and in September 1807, was being paid 2/-d per day (Supply 5/226). In August 1808, he was employed as a Saltpetre Refiner earning 2/-d per day, and, in addition, when not working extra was allowed to watch in turn (Supply 5/227). This was also the case in September 1810 (Supply 5/228), but since refining Saltpetre was not undertaken in West Sussex, it can only be assumed that John had moved to Waltham Abbey.

James Tufnell was a single man of 21 who was employed by the Engineers' Department in June 1825 for 4 months on a temporary basis at 2/2d per day, and was to be discharged thereafter (WO54/550).

William Tufnell was working as a Millman in February 1814 at 3/-d per day, and paid an additional 6d per night when on duty (Supply 5/230).

A. J. Tulloh, Capt. (Royal Artillery) was appointed Assistant Superintendent at Waltham Abbey on the 29th November 1839 (Winters, *op.cit.* p.105), and remained in that position until 1845 when he was promoted to Superintendent (W. H. Simmons, M.B.E., F.R.I.C., 1963: *A Short History of the R.G.P. at Waltham Abbey:* Officers in Charge of the R.G.P.F.).

John Turley, born circa 1767, worked as a Labourer in April 1789 "cutting and planting willow trees, cutting of the new canal at the new Corning House, removing earth to the Store, unloading barge of coal and charring wood" (Supply 5/213). In August of that year he was "mixing composition" and paid 1/6d per day (Supply 5/214).

Isaac Turner, born circa 1754, was a Labourer at Faversham in November 1787 (Supply 5/219) and was to be transferred to Waltham Abbey as a Labourer glazing gunpowder (Supply 5/213). He was "entered for transfer" and finally started work at Waltham Abbey on the 1st February 1788 cutting Alderwood, earning 1/6d per day (Supply 5/213). In April 1788, in common with the rest of the workforce, he was "cutting and planting willow trees, cutting of the new canal at the new Corning House, removing earth to the Store, unloading barge of coal and charring wood" (Supply 5/213). In September 1789, he was employed as a Collier, the term then commonly used to describe a Charcoal Burner (Supply 5/214).

For the next 5 years, Isaac spent the summer months working in the country cutting Alder wood - which was considered the best wood to make charcoal - returning to the Mills in the winter either charring (making charcoal) or undertaking various labouring tasks within the Manufactory (Supply 5/214–5/216) and during this period, was paid 1/6d per day. Isaac's summer/winter routine ended when the new charcoal works were set up in West Sussex. In June 1795, he was "setting and drawing stoves etc." still at 1/6d per day (Supply 5/217) and he was still "attending the stoves" in September 1798 (Supply 5/219). The Petition on Pay and Conditions at the Mills submitted to the Board in February 1800 showed that he was literate (Supply 5/220).

Samuel Turner was working as a Corning House Man In August 1812 earning 3/3d per day, and, in addition, allowed to watch in turn, for which he received 1/ 6d a night (Supply 5/229).

Charles Turnham, the only son of William and Ann Turnham, was baptised at Waltham Abbey on the 31st August 1787 (WASC 2180, p.117). He was employed as a Labourer, and in the autumn of 1805 he was "drawing and setting stoves, loading and unloading barges etc." for which he was paid 2/-d per day (Supply 5/224). From 1808 until at least 1810, he continued as a Labourer, performing the same tasks as before, as well as working in the willow plantations. Although on the same rate of pay, he was then allowed to watch in turn, for which he received 1/6d per night (Supply 5/227 and Supply 5/228). In August 1812, he was employed as a Punt man with his pay increased to 2/8d per day, and was still allowed to watch in turn (Supply 5/229). By February 1814 he had progressed from the punts to working in the Corning House, where he was paid 3/3d per day and was still entitled to watch (Supply 5/230). Following the end of the Napoleonic wars the need for gunpowder was severely reduced, and Charles was not retained at the Mills.

Edward Turnham, the fourth son of John and Sarah Turnham, was baptised at Waltham Abbey on the 10th October 1802 (WASC 2180, p.118). He started an Apprenticeship under Hugh Jones, the Master Mixer of Composition (Gunpowder Maker) on the 14th August 1815 (Supply 5/232). Initially, his pay was 6/-d per week (Supply 5/231) which rose to 7/-d weekly in the final stages of his Apprenticeship in 1822 (Supply 5/232). A Return for October 1822 (Supply 5/233) recorded that Edward Turnham, Apprentice, having completed his Apprenticeship with the Master Mixer, was to be discharged by the Board's Order of the 22nd May 1822. However, luck was with Edward. Anthony Lambert, who had been engaged as an Apprentice Cooper, had discharged himself, possibly in September 1822. Undeterred by his treatment, Edward told the Board that he was prepared to train as a Cooper and to accept the same rates of pay granted to Lambert if he could fill his position, namely, 1/9d per day in the first year, 2/-d in the second, and when he could complete 6 powder barrels in a day, his pay would be increased to 3/6d per day. The Board agreed to this and confirmed his appointment from the 1st October 1822 (Supply 5/204). Edward progressed rapidly, and by October 1825 was clearly producing 6 barrels daily, since he was then being paid £54.12.0d annually (WO54/550).

Edward had married by October 1827 (WO54/558) and had a child by April 1830 (WO54/570). In October 1830, his annual pay was £45.12.6d (WO54/587) By October 1839, it had been restored to its former level (WO54/632). The same document stated that he then had 3 children, and Edward and his young family moved into a cottage owned by the Board sometime in 1839 or 1840, which had previously been occupied by John Simpson Jnr. (WO44/133). The cottage was one in a row known as Bank Cottages (see notes on William Turnham). The 1841 Census recorded that Edward and his wife, Charlotte, together with their children, Mary, Edward and John, lived on the north side of High Bridge Street, and that all of the occupants were born in the county. Further information on Edward and his family after 1841 can be found in WASC 2180 by Peter Huggins.

James Turnham, Snr. married Ann Robinson at Waltham Abbey on the 27th March 1759 (WASC 2180, p.117). On the 21st September 1787, by a direction of the Duke of Richmond, Daniel Cornish was asked by Major Congreve "to hire the best of the millmen and labourers who lately worked at Mr Walton's Powder Mills. They will be paid nine shillings per week for a month certain." It went on to say that should the Government purchase the Mills, they [the men] would be given every opportunity to remain employed there (Winters, *op.cit.* p.27). James was engaged as a Labourer renovating the Mills in October 1787, and retained. In November 1788, he was the Warder at the Refinery House (Winters, *op.cit.* p.32) and confirmation that he was a Warder at 1/6d per day was given in a Return dated the 21st March 1789 (Supply 5/212). Another Return for September 1789, recorded that he was "Warding at the Refining House" and that he was 76 years of age (Supply 5/215). He was still working in July 1795, and died in 1797, being buried at Waltham Abbey on the 11th June 1797 at the reputed age of 83 years. James and Ann had 4 sons, 3 of whom were to work for the Ordnance Board at Waltham Abbey.

James Turnham, Jnr., the second son of James and Ann, was baptised at Waltham Abbey on the 15th August 1764. Like his father, he was recruited as a Labourer by Daniel Cornish in October 1787, and paid 9/-d per week (Winters, *op.cit* p.27). He remained at the Mills and in March 1789, was "cutting alder wood", for which he was paid 1/6d a day (Supply 5/212). This was the last entry found for James, Jnr.

John Turnham, the eldest son of James and Ann, was baptised at Waltham Abbey on the 11th October 1761 (WASC 2180, p.117). He started work with the Ordnance Board in the barges on the 12th April 1791, earning 1/6d per day (Supply 5/215) and was to spend his working life either in the punts operating within the Mills, or on the barges transporting stores and gunpowder. From January to March 1792, he was "setting and drawing stoves and working in the punts" (Supply 5/215). A Return for September 1792, noted that he worked "in the punts & likewise drawing and setting stoves, landing and shipping gunpowder etc." (Supply 5/216).

By February 1793 he had replaced Edward Heddy as a Bargeman (Supply 5/216) and was taking materials to London by barge with John Cook and William Fuller. He was apparently afraid of being "seized by the Press Gangs" because the Rex Officers at Waltham Abbey wrote to the Duke of Richmond stating that Cook, Fuller and Turnham were Gunpowder Makers and Bargemen, and were apprehensive of the Impress Officers on the River Thames. They requested, "you be pleased to grant them protection" (WASC 0475). John continued to work as a Bargeman, and in July 1795, was still earning 9/-d per week (Supply 5/217).

A Petition presented to the Board in February 1800 relating to Pay and Conditions at the Mills, showed that John was literate (Supply 5/220) and a Return of the Marital Status of the Employees at Waltham Abbey taken on the 8th May 1801, recorded that he was married with 6 children (Supply 5/221).

Another Return made in November 1801 confirmed that he was still employed as a Bargeman, but that when the barges were not in use, he, together with other men, were engaged in "cleaning and deepening the river, canals, ditches and other work necessary to be performed" (Supply 5/221). It was recognised by the Board that transporting gunpowder was hazardous, and an Order dated the 8th May 1804 authorised, "while transporting gunpowder to Picketts Field, Bargemen are allowed double pay" (Supply 5/222).

By the 28th March 1805, John was described as a Master Bargeman, with his pay doubled to 3/-d per day (5/222). Together with John Cook, he was in charge of 19 men "shipping gunpowder, landing stores, drawing stoves, transporting gunpowder and in the willow plantation" (Supply 5/223). John continued working as a Master Bargeman, with his wage peaking at 5/2d per day in 1812 (Supply 5/229). On the 2nd March 1816, the Rex Officers at Waltham recommended that John Turnham, then 57 years with 26 years' service, should receive a daily superannuation of 3/-d "because of the hurts they [Turnham and others] have received in this dangerous manufactory." It also stated that Mr. Turnham had been "much injured by falls and bruises in the performance of his duty, the nature of which, and constant exposure to wet, damp and night work, has confirmed the rheumatism and other complaints so firmly upon him as to render him totally unable to continue the performance of his duty" (Supply 5/230). He was granted a pension of 21/-d per week commencing the 1st April 1816 (Supply 5/200) and continued to receive this pension for the rest of his life, recorded as £54.12.0d in later documents (Supply 5/232). The 1841 Census noted that John and his wife, Sarah, were living in Blackboy Alley, together with the Shaddock family. John was buried at Waltham Abbey on the 13th September 1842, and Sarah, his wife, was buried at Waltham on the 31st March 1844, aged 84 (WASC 2180, p.117).

John Turnham was working as a Cooper at the Waltham Abbey Mills on the 1st September 1810 at 2/6d per day, but in common with others of his trade, he was not allowed to watch (Supply 5/228). This rate of pay indicated that he had limited experience as a Cooper, but by August 1812 his wage had risen to 4/6d per day, signifying that he was then fully qualified (Supply 5/229). He was still in the Board's employment as a Cooper in February 1814 (Supply 5/230). John would have been about 20 years of age in 1812 when he had achieved the maxim pay for a Cooper, and could, therefore, be John Isaac Turnham born in 1793, the eldest son of John Turnham, the Master Bargeman (WASC 2180, p118).

Samuel Turnham was a Labourer employed in February 1814 in "drawing and setting stoves and in the willow plantation." He was paid 2/8d per day and also allowed to watch in turn (Supply 5/230). However, he was not retained after the end of the Napoleonic war.

Samuel Turnham, born circa 1796, started work as a general Labourer at the Mills on the 24th February 1827, with a basic annual income of £33.16.0d. He was also allowed to watch in turn, which increased his annual pay to £39.0.0d (WO54/558). The same Return recorded that he was a 30-year-old bachelor. A Return for April 1828, however, stated that he was married and had one child (WO54/562), A footnote to a List of Employees dated the 1st October 1830, recorded that Frederick Simpson had been appointed as a "Labourer in the room of Samuel Turnham on the 12th May 1830", i.e., Samuel's services had been terminated and he had been replaced by Frederick Simpson (WO54/570).

William Turnham, the third son of James and Ann, was baptised at Waltham Abbey on the 24th October 1766 (WASC 2180, p.117). He had originally trained as a Wool Comber (Supply 5/232} before starting work at the Waltham Abbey Powder Mills on the 18th February 1790 (Supply 5/214). He worked at Waltham Abbey as a Labourer "in the punts & sett & draw stoves" for which he received 1/6d per day (Supply 5/215). By December of that year, he was "grinding salt petre etc." i.e., he was a Millman (Supply 5/215). In April 1791, William was correctly described as a Millman (Supply 5/216) and continued in this capacity until sometime in 1804 (Supply 5/222). During his period as a Millman, his daily rate of pay rose from 2/-d to 2/3d, with an extra 3d if he worked at night (Supply 5/217 and 5/222). William joined the Volunteer Company as a Private on the 7th May 1794 (Supply 5/219). He signed the Petition relating to the Pay and Conditions at the Mills presented to the Board in

February 1800 (Supply 5/220) and a Return on the Marital Status of the Board Employees in May 1801 noted that he was married and had 7 children (Supply 5/221).

Another change in William's occupation took place in 1805 when he was described as a Saltpetre Refiner, with a reduction in his pay to 2/-d per day, but, "when not working extra, allowed to watch in turn" (Supply 5/224). He continued to refine Saltpetre until sometime in 1818, with his pay peaking at 2/8d per day in 1812, and an additional 1/-d a night when it was his turn to watch (Supply 5/229). However, by 1818, his rate of pay had been reduced to 2/4d per day (Supply 5/231).

When the Establishment at Waltham Abbey was reduced in 1818, it was proposed that William be retained on the same pay but not allowed to watch (Supply 5/231) and this was confirmed by a Board Order dated the 4th September 1818 (Supply 5/232). A List of Employees dated the 19th May 1819, showed that he was the working as a Brimstone Refiner, still paid 2/4d per day and then allowed to watch in turn, for which he earned 1/-d (Supply 5/231). The same document noted that he was living in Waltham Abbey and still had 7 children. On the 4th October 1819, the Board issued an Order appointing William as a Saltpetre Refiner, a trade in which he was to continue for the rest of his working life (Supply 5/232).

A statement "of monies to which the public were entitled to receive credit between the 1st January and the 31st December 1821 shewing the amounts received by the Storekeeper" recorded that on the 4th May 1821 William was living in a cottage purchased by the Ordnance Board (Supply 5/232) and paying the Board £8.9.0d per annum rent (Supply 5/232). The tenement has been identified as being at the eastern end of a row of cottages known as Bank Cottages on the north side of High Bridge Street, to the west of Powder Mill Lane, a stone's throw away from the

Saltpetre Refinery, Plot No. 48 on the Town Map in Appendix 1. In 1822 the Establishment was reviewed again, and William was retained as a Saltpetre Refiner at £41.14.4d annually, which included an allowance for watching in turn (Supply 5/232). By a Board order dated the 18th January 1823, his total annual pay was reduced to £39.0.0d (WO54/542) and remained so until he died in 1834, having worked at the Powder Mills for some 44 years (WO54/593). His cottage was subsequently occupied by Michael Summers (Supply 5/237).

William Twinham was working as a Saltpetre Refiner in August 1812 at 2/8d per day, and, in addition, when not working extra, he was allowed to watch in turn (Supply 5/229).

John Tyler, born circa 1787, commenced work as a Labourer at the Powder Mills on the 25th January 1810 at 2/-d per day (WO54/554). In August 1812, he was working as a Corning House Man earning 3/3d per day and, in addition, he was allowed to watch in turn, for which he received 1/6d (Supply 5/229). He was still employed in the Corning Houses in February 1814 (Supply 5/230).

John joined the Engineers' Department as an occasional Labourer on the 14th May 1818, and In May 1819, was paid 2/4d per day; he was then a 32-year-old married man without issue, living in Waltham Abbey (WO54/532). By April 1823, he was on the Establishment, since he was paid 2/2d per day for 313 days in the year, which totalled £33.18.2d per annum (WO54/542). He received the same wage in October 1839, and the same document (WO54/623) confirmed that he and his wife were still childless.

William Tyler was a Master Mason by trade who was set to work by Daniel Cornish in October 1787, renovating the Mills following their purchase from Mr. Walton. He was not retained after the work was completed (Winters, *op.cit* p. 28).

William Tyser was a Carpenter by trade, who in October 1787 was set to work by Daniel Cornish, renovating the Mills following their purchase from Mr. Walton. He was not retained after the work was completed (Winters *op.cit* p. 28).

U

Robert Upton, born circa 1793, started work as an Apprentice in the Engineers' Department under the Master Carpenter on the 8th November 1806, and was paid 6/8d per week (WO54/512). In May 1819, he was employed within the Engineers' Department as a Millwright, "occasionally as the service requires" and paid 5/2d per day. At that date he was a married man of 26 with 3 children, living in Waltham Abbey (WO54/528). Robert was still a casual Millwright earning the same money in September 1820. At that date he had 4 children (WO54/532) as was also the case in 1821 according to WO54/536). In April 1832, he was employed as a Carpenter earning 4/1d per day, which, for 313 days' work, gave him an annual income of £63.18.1d. By April 1832 he had 5 children and was still living in Waltham Abbey. In addition, it would appear that he been appointed to the Establishment as a Carpenter on the 8th March 1822 (WO54/542).

W

John Wackett, born circa 1790, began work as a casual Labourer in the Engineers' Department on the 12th September 1815, earning 2/8d per day. He was then a 25-year-old bachelor living in Cheshunt, and was possibly the son of Richard Wackett below (WO54/516).

Richard Wackett was born circa 1761 and employed on the 16th May 1807 as a common or casual Labourer within the Engineers' Department (WO54/516). Between the 15th and 21st July 1809, he was paid 11/-d for work carried out by the Engineers' Department within the Manufactory (Supply 5/228). In February 1816, he was classified as a casual Labourer earning 2/4d per day in the Engineers' Department, and was then a 55-year-old man living in Cheshunt with 2 married and 4 unmarried children (WO54/516). Richard continued to be employed as a Labourer "occasionally as required" and in April 1818 he was living in Waltham Abbey (WO54/524). However, he had returned to Cheshunt by September 1820, when it was noted that he still had 6 children (WO54/532). It was recorded that he had returned to the Abbey by April 1821 (WO54/536) and during this period his pay remained at 2/4d per day. It would appear, however, that one of his children died between April and December 1821, because in WO54/536 it was recorded that he then only had 5. By April 1823 (possibly in March 1822) Richard had been appointed to the Establishment and was then paid 2/2 per day, which for 313 days, gave him an annual income of £33.18.2d (WO54/542). He was still in the Engineers' employment in April 1828 earning the same money, at which date he had some 20 years' service, and was still living in Waltham Abbey (WO54/562).

Stephen Wackett was working as a casual Labourer in the Engineers' Department in September 1812, earning 2/8d per day for a six-day week (WO54/512).

William Wackett (1) was born circa 1787 and started his employment as a casual Labourer in the Engineers' Department on the 9th August 1814, earning 2/8d per day. He was then a 29-year-old bachelor living in Waltham Abbey (WO54/516).

William Wackett (2) was born circa 1787 and started his employment as a casual Labourer in the Engineers' Department on the 29th April 1815, earning 2/8d per day. He was then a 26-year-old married man with one child, living in Enfield (WO54/516).

William Wackford was working as a Millman in August 1812. He earned 3/-d per day, and, in addition, was allowed 6d per night when on duty (Supply 5/229).

Henry Wakeland was working as Millman in January 1806 earning 2/3d per day, and at that time had been employed at the Mills for some six months (Supply 5/224). He was still a Millman in June 1807, but then, in addition to his pay, he was allowed an extra 3d when working at night (Supply 5/226). In August 1808 he was working as a Labourer, "setting and drawing stoves and in the willow plantations etc." with his pay reduced to 2/-d per day, although then allowed to watch in turn (Supply 5/227). At 11.15 a.m. on the 27th November 1811, there was a huge explosion at No. 4 Press House, and the ensuing fire engulfed the Corning House and the Reel House, which also exploded. There was much damage in the town with many windows shattered, and reports in the press recorded that the explosion was heard as far away as Hackney, Blackwall and Marylebone (Winters, op.cit. p.72). Among those killed was Henry, who left a widow, Ann, and a daughter, Harriet, aged 18 months (Supply 5/229). Ann received a pension of 17/6d per week (Supply 5/229) which she was still paid in 1826 (Winters, *op.cit.* p.96).

Robert Wakeland was earning 2/-d per day in January 1806 as a Labourer, drawing and setting stoves etc., and at that date had been employed at the Mills for some 3 months (Supply 5/224). By August 1808 he was employed in the Corning House, where he continued to work until at least February 1814 (Supply 5/227 and Supply 5/230). During this period his daily rate of pay increased from 2/6d to 3/3d, and, in addition, he was allowed to watch in turn for which he received 1/6d per night.

Samuel Wakeland was earning 2/-d per day in January 1806 as a Stoveman, drawing and setting stoves etc., and at that date had been employed at the Mills for some 9 months (Supply 5/224). He was still working as a Stoveman in June 1807 at the same rate of pay, but was then allowed to watch in turn, for which he received 1/-d per night (Supply 5/226).

Benjamin Wall, Snr. was born circa 1748 (Supply 5/214) and commenced work as a general Labourer at the Mills on the 1st April 1789 (Supply 5/213). Initially he was employed in "cutting and planting willow trees, cutting of the new canal at the Corning House, removing earth to the store, unloading barge of coals and charring wood" for which he was paid 1/6d per day (Supply 5/213). In September of that year he was "dusting and glazing powder" but by March 1790, he had transferred to the Corning House (Supply 5/214) and this was to remain his workstation until he retired in 1816.

Benjamin enlisted as a Private in the Volunteer Company when it was formed at the Mills on the 7th May 1794 (Winters, *op.cit.* p.42), and another Return listing the Volunteers dated September 1798, noted that he was then a Foreman at the Corning House and also a Rounder (Supply 5/219). The signed Petition on Pay and Conditions at the Mills presented to the Board in February 1800 showed that he was illiterate, confirming also that he was the Foreman of the Corning House and, in addition, still a Rounder at 1/6d per day (Supply 5/220).

On the 16th June 1801, Benjamin, with others, was repairing the Corning House when it caught fire following an explosion. The fire was caused "from a blow of a copper hammer on a pit wheel" (Winters, *op.cit.* p.59). The Storekeeper sent a letter to the Board on the 23rd June, listing the names of the men who had suffered terrible burns and seeking permission to support the casualties. The letter went on to say that Benjamin Wall and two others were "Burnt so as to prevent them working, but they may soon be well." In addition, it stated, "Our surgeon has represented the necessity of the men most burnt having immediate assistance in wine, as a considerable suppuration is come on their constitutions. They cannot support it without wine, and we have directed wine to be immediately provided to them; we request your permission for our continuing to support these poor men with such wine or other proper support as their surgeon may think their respective situations require" (Supply 5/195). It would appear that the Board responded immediately because, replying the same day, the writer said he had "the Board's commands to transmit to you on the other side hereof a list of the men who have been burnt and otherwise hurt by the fire which lately destroyed the Corning House at Waltham Abbey; and I am to desire the Storekeeper will pay the men all their pay until they are recovered" (Supply 5/195).

Benjamin recovered from his burns since a Return of Articifers and Labourers dated the 3rd November 1801 recorded that he was employed "cleaning and deepening the river and canals, and performing sundry other necessary works" (Supply 5/221). In May 1804, as a Foreman in the Corning Houses, he was paid 2/4d per day, and every third night he was allowed 1/6d as a Rounder (Supply 5/223). Over the ensuing years his daily rate of pay peaked at 4/-d per day in 1812, and his Rounder's allowance had then increased to 2/-d (Supply 5/229). On the 2nd March 1816, the Storekeeper recommended to the Board that Mr. Wall, the Foreman of the Corning House with a length of service of 28 years, should be one of several superannuated because "of the hurts they have received in this dangerous Manufactory." The letter went on to say, "Mr. Wall was a very trustworthy servant" and that he had been "much burnt in a Corning House fire in the year 1801." In addition, it said that he had been "with the Merchants before [the] Government purchased the Powder Mills" i.e., that he had worked for Mr. Walton prior to 1787. The Storekeeper recommended a daily pension of 4/-d, but in their reply dated the 6th March, the Board awarded Benjamin Wall a pension of only 3/-d per day for six days in the week, commencing on the 1st April 1816 (Supply 5/200) which he was still receiving in 1826 (Winters, *op.cit.* p. 96).

Benjamin Wall Junior was employed as a Labourer in the Corning House on the 11th April 1789, and was paid 1/6d per day (Supply 5/214). Robert Coleman, Clerk of the Cheque, recorded in his Minute book on the 4th November 1793, "B. Wall, jun., Ch. Davie and Wm. Dunn, labourers, being taken up on a suspicion of stealing iron from a farmer's gate. Discharged them" (Winters, *op.cit.* p.40). Having been described as Ben Wall Junior, it is almost certain that he was the son of Benjamin Wall, Snr. It is possible that he returned to work in the Engineers' Department on the 16th September 1815 as an occasional Labourer at 2/8d per day, and at that date, he was a 47-year-old bachelor living in Waltham Abbey (WO54/516).

John Wall started an Apprenticeship under the Master Worker on the 11th April 1797 and served as a Private in the Volunteer Company (Supply 5/219). In May 1804, he was working in the Corning House as a Labourer with pay of 2/-d per day and, in addition, allowed to watch in turn, on average every 5th night, for which he received 1/-d (Supply 5/222). A Return for January

1806 noted that he then had 5 years' service, which would suggest that he had not completed his Apprenticeship and had possibly left the Mills for a short period. The same document recorded that he was then paid 2/2d per day (Supply 5/224). Sometime between June 1807 and August 1808, John transferred to the Saltpetre Refining House as a Labourer with his pay reduced to 2/-d per day, although he was still allowed to watch (Supply 5/227). John died sometime after this since his widow, Susan, "In consequence of her distressed circumstances" was awarded a donation of £2.2.0d by the Board (Winters, *op.cit.* p.75).

William Wallace, born circa 1776, commenced his employment at the Mills on the 13th October 1795. In September 1798 he was working in the Mixing House, and had enrolled as a Private in the Volunteer Company (Supply 5/219). This document recorded the names of the Volunteers in 1798, and since his name was struck through, it would appear that he had left the Gunpowder Mills soon afterwards.

A William Wallace was engaged as a Millman on the 26th April 1810 (Supply 5/232) and paid 2/3d per day, with an extra 6d per night when on duty (Supply 5/228); he was still a Millman in August 1812, but by then his pay had been increased to 3/-d per day (Supply 5/229). By February 1814, he had transferred to the Corning House, where he was paid 3/3d per day and allowed to watch in turn, for which he received 1/6d per night (Supply 5/230).

With peace in Europe, the manufacture and regeneration of gunpowder were reduced and, as a consequence, the Establishment and the men's wages were cut back. By June 1818, William's daily pay had been reduced to 2/11d, although he was still allowed to watch and was paid 1/-d per night when performing this task (Supply 5/231). At the time he was a 42-

year-old with 5 children, living in Waltham Abbey with 2 of the children (WO5//524). A list of names of the people the Storekeeper proposed to dismiss from the Establishment on the 4th September 1818 to meet the new production and cost requirements, was sent to the Board on the 28th August (Supply 5/231). Although William's name was on the list, he continued to be employed as a Corning House man earning 2/11d per day, and was still allowed to watch, for which he then received 1/-d (Supply 5/231). In 1820, it was recorded that he then had only 4 children (Supply 5/232). He continued in this position earning the same wage and allowance, until 1822.

A List of Employees dated the 6th February 1822 recorded that his position as a Corning House Man had been reconfirmed on the 4th October 1819 with annual pay of £50.16.11d, which included an allowance to watch (Supply 5/232). In the spring of 1822 the Ordnance Board decided to reduce the production and regeneration of gunpowder still further, and the Establishment at Waltham was cut again. On the 21st March 1822, Empsom Middleton and James Wright drew up a list of people who were to be retained or dismissed (Supply 5/232). William was included in the list of those to be dismissed on the 1st June 1822, after some 31 years' service (Supply 5/232). The men asking for financial assistance submitted several petitions; many were long service-employees in their middle-age, and they pointed out that they had little hope of finding employment after the hay and corn harvest had been gathered. The Storekeeper was sympathetic and forwarded their petitions to the Board for consideration. William, along with four others, signed (with a cross) a separate petition on the 12th July, saying that he had been away unsuccessfully looking for work and he, together with the others, was awarded two weeks' pay to ease his financial burden (Supply 5/203).

John Wallen was employed as a Labourer in February 1814, "drawing and setting stoves and in the willow plantation" at 2/8d per day, as well as being allowed to watch in turn (Supply 5/230).

William Wallis joined the Engineers' Department as an occasional Labourer on the 8th October 1815, being paid 2/8d per day. He was then an 18-year-old bachelor living in Waltham Abbey (WO54/516). Sometime after this it is possible that he may have transferred to the Storekeeper's Department and worked within the Manufactory, since a William Wallis, Corning House man, was to be discharged in September 1818 when the number of employees on the Establishment was reduced. (Supply 5/231).

William Wandstall was a Carpenter's Assistant in the Engineers' Department who was paid £1.3.3d for work carried out by the Department within the Manufactory between the 15th and 21st July 1809 (Supply 5/228).

John Want was a single man of 27 who had been employed on a temporary basis as a Labourer for 4 months at 2/2d per day, and was discharged at the end of October 1825 (WO54/550).
Richard Want (1) was working as a Millman in August 1812 earning 3/-d per day, and, in addition, he was allowed 6d per night when on duty (Supply 5/229).

Richard Want (2) was working as a casual Labourer in the Engineers' Department, and was paid 2/8d per day for a six-day-week in September 1812 (WO54/512)

Thomas Want (1) was working as a Millman in February 1814 earning 3/-d per day, together with an additional 6d if he was on duty at night (Supply 5/230).

Thomas Want (2) started work as a Labourer in the Engineers' Department on the 15th April 1815, earning 2/8d per day; in February 1816, he was a 21-year-old bachelor living in Waltham Abbey (WO54/516).

William Want was engaged as an occasional Labourer by the Engineers' Department on the 30th July 1811 at 2/8d per day; in February 1816, he was a 60-year-old bachelor living in Waltham Abbey (WO54/516).

James Warby (1) was born circa 1772 and trained as a Brickmaker, starting his employment as a Labourer at the Gunpowder Mills on the 16th May 1805 (WO54/554). On the 14th November 1805, he became a Saltpetre Refiner (Supply 5/232) and according to Supply 5/224 was paid 2/-d per day. The Refinery was to remain his workplace until at least February 1814, and he was then paid 2/8d per day, in addition to which, he was allowed to watch in turn if he was not "working extra" (Supply 5/230). In June 1818, he was working as a Labourer setting and drawing stoves with his wage reduced to 2/4d per day, although he was still allowed to watch, for which he received 1/-d per night. He was then a 45-year-old married man with 6 children, living in Waltham Abbey (Supply 5/231). With peace in Europe, the manufacture and regeneration of gunpowder were reduced and, as a consequence, the Establishment and wages were cut back. On the 28th August, the Storekeeper drew up a list of people to be retained between the 3rd September and 31st December 1818, and Warby's name was on the list. However, a letter to the Board a few days later amended the list and stated, "We respectfully beg leave to add to the names and stations of those persons whom it will be necessary to discharge in consequence of this arrangement." and included James Warby (Supply 5/231). The Board did not appear to have enforced this second list, since James was retained on the Establishment as a Saltpetre Refiner by Board Orders dated the 4th September 1818 and 4th October 1819 (Supply 5/232). Moreover, he still received the same rate of pay and watch allowance, which gave him an annual income of £41.14.4d (Supply 5/232).

James was still a Saltpetre Refiner in January 1822, but was recorded as having joined the Engineers' Department as a Labourer on the 18th July 1822 (WO54/542). There he was paid 2/2d per day for 313 days in the year, which gave him an annual income of £33.18.2d. A Return of Persons belonging to the Civil Establishment of the Ordnance at the Gunpowder and Small Arms Manufactories at Waltham Abbey, Faversham and Enfield, showing in detail several points of information called for by the Master General and Board's Order dated the 31st January 1831, recorded that James Warby was one of 15 Labourers to be employed at Waltham Abbey and Enfield. He was to be was to be paid 2/2d per day and employed to undertake different services as a Labourer in the Manufactories, where steadiness and sobriety were particularly required (WO54/575). He was still employed on the same terms in October 1831 (WO54/575).

James Warby (2) was employed as a Corning House Man. In February 1814, he was earning 3/3d per day and allowed to watch in turn, for which he received 1/6d per night (Supply 5/230).

Joseph Warby was working as a Labourer in August 1812, "drawing and setting stoves and in the willow plantation" earning 2/8d per day, as well as being allowed to watch in turn (Supply 5/229).

Joseph Ward was working in the Corning House at 2/2d per day in January 1806 earning 2/2d per day, at which time, he had 6 months' service (Supply 5/224).

Thomas Ward was a married man with one child in May 1801, and employed in the Engineers' Department as a Labourer at 1/6d per day (Supply 5/221). The Clerk of the Cheque, Robert Coleman, recorded in his Minute Book on the 21St October 1801 that 24 men were required to work at Faversham or be discharged (Winters, *op. cit.* p. 60). Ward agreed to go, but since his name did not appear in the Faversham documents or subsequent records for Waltham Abbey, it can only be assumed that his services were terminated.

William Warner worked as a Labourer in the "Engineers' Dept. Established" in May 1804, earning 1/6d per day, with "one day extra allowed per week agreeable to the Board's Order dated 12th March 1801" (Supply 5/222).

John Warwick was a common Labourer who was paid 17/-d for work carried out by the Engineers' Department in the Manufactory between the 15th and 21St July 1809 (Supply 5/228).

John Watson started work at the Mills as a Labourer in the Corning House on the 15th July 1793 where he earned 1/6d per day (Supply 5/216) while in January 1794, he was "grinding "salt petre and brimstone." On the 4th May 1794, he enlisted as a Private in the Volunteer Company (Winters, *op. cit.* p. 42). By August 1794, he was working "on the barges and punts" as he was in December 1794 (Supply 5/216 and 5/217). In June 1795 John was described as a Bargeman (Supply 5/217). The next reference to a John Watson was found in August 1812, when a man of that name was employed as a Saltpetre Refiner earning 2/8d per day, and, in addition, when not working extra, was allowed to watch in turn (Supply 5/229). This was also the case in February 1814 (Supply 5/230).

William Watson (1) was a casual Labourer in the Engineers' Department in September 1812, earning 2/8d per day for a six-day-week (WO54/512).

William Watson (2), born circa 1801, was engaged as a Labourer within the Engineers' Department on the 1st June 1826. He was paid 2/2d per day, which gave him an annual income of £33.18.2d. He was a 25-year-old married man without issue (WO54/554).

Benjamin Watts, born circa 1775, was engaged as an occasional Labourer within the Engineers' Department on the 20th April 1815 at 2/8d per day. He was then a 40-year-old married man without children, living in Waltham Abbey (WO54/516). He was still working as a Labourer in February 1817, but was then only paid 2/4d per day (WO54/520). The 1841 Census showed that a Benjamin Watts, of a similar age and described as a Labourer, was living in High Bridge Street.

John Wayman was engaged as a Labourer in the Refining House on the 10th October 1794 at 1/6d per day (Supply 5/217). He enrolled as a Private in the Volunteer Company (Supply 5/219) and the Petition on Pay and Conditions at the Mills presented to the Board in February 1800, showed that he was still a Refiner and was literate (Supply 5/220). A Return dated May 1801 on the Marital Status of the Employees, recorded that he was a married man with a child (Supply 5/221).

In November 1801, there was a "considerable depot of saltpetre etc." and he was directed by the Comptroller to "take care of the Refinery and Saltpetre Stores" (Supply 5/221). John continued to work as a Refiner, and by May 1804, his wage had been increased to 2/-d per day. Like all the Refiners, he received an additional 1/-d per night when it was his turn to watch – on average every 5th night (Supply 5/222). By August 1812 he was employed as a Warder, retaining his daily rate of pay of 2/-d (Supply 5/229) while a Return for February 1814, noted that his pay was then 2/8d per day and that he was also a Rounder every 3rd night, for which he received 2/-d (Supply 5/230).

Letters to the Board dated the 29th November and 3rd December 1814, recorded that John Wayman had died on the 5th November 1814 of a rupture brought about by the various hurts he had received over the 20 years he had worked for the Mills, and his wife Mary, aged 61, had petitioned the Board because she had been left destitute. In her Petition of the 29th November she stated that she was "very infirm" and she "therefore humbly prays that your honours in your wisdom will be pleased in consideration of the deceased being 20 years in your service, think of her and admit her partake of that bounty which has so often been extended to dry the tears of distress." A letter to the Storekeeper from the Office of Ordnance dated the 9th December 1814, said, "in consequence of the services of her late husband and her advanced age rendering her incapable of earning a livelihood" she was to be placed on the Charity list at 3/6d per week from the date of her husband's death (Supply 5/200). Mary was still in receipt of an annual pension of £9.2.0d in 1822 (Winters, *op. cit.* p.96).

Henry Webb was working as a Puntman in August 1812 earning 2/8d per day; he was also allowed to watch in turn (Supply 5/229). A John Webb was recorded as a Puntman in February 1814, although the name John could possibly have been a clerical copying error (Supply 5/230).

Isaac Webb (1), born circa 1757, commenced his employment as a Labourer at the Mills on the 27th March 1800 (WO54/558). A Return on the Marital Status of the Employees made on the 8th May 1801, recorded that Isaac was a married man with 2 children (Supply 5/221). In November 1801, in common with the majority of the workforce, he was "cleaning and deepening the river and canals", and performing "sundry other necessary works" (Supply 5/221). In May 1804, he was described as a Refiner with pay of 2/-d per day and, in addition to his pay, he was allowed to watch in turn – on average every 5th night – for which he received 1/-d

(Supply 5/222). By January 1806, he was a Millman earning 2/3d per day (Supply 5/224) but in June 1807, his workplace was the Corning House with pay reduced to 2/2d per day, although he was then allowed to watch, for which he received 1/-d (Supply 5/226). Isaac remained a Corning House Man until at least February 1814, when he was earning 3/3d per day and his allowance to watch was 1/6d per night (Supply 5/230).

In June 1818 he had returned to the Refinery with his wage reduced to 2/4d per day but he was still allowed to watch, for which he received 1/-d per night. He was then a 60-year-old married man who lived in Waltham Abbey who had 2 children. (Supply 5/231). With peace in Europe, the manufacture and regeneration of gunpowder were reduced, and, as a consequence, the Establishment and wages were cut back. On the 28th August, the Storekeeper drew up a list of people to be retained between the 3rd September and 31st December 1818 with Webb's name included. His position as a Saltpetre Refiner at 2/4d per day, was confirmed by Orders of the Board dated the 4th September 1818 and 4th October 1819, and in addition to his daily pay, Isaac was still allowed to watch for 1/- per night (Supply 5/232). He continued to refine Saltpetre, (Brimstone) in May 1819 and by February 1822 he was earning £41.14.4d per annum, which included his watch money, then set at 2/-d per night (Supply 5/232).

In the spring of 1822 the Ordnance Board decided to reduce the production and regeneration of gunpowder still further, and the Establishment at Waltham was cut again. On the 21st March 1822, Empsom Middleton and James Wright drew up a list of people who were to be retained or dismissed (Supply 5/232). Isaac was included in the list of those to be dismissed on the 1st June 1822 after some 22 years' service (Supply 5/232). However, under an Order of the Board dated the 22nd May, his services were retained as a general Labourer, and he was required to carry out any type of work needed within the Manufactory. His annual income was set at £39.0.0d per annum (Supply 5/233). His pay was then reduced by £2.10.0d per annum by Orders of the Board dated the 27th December 1822 and 15th January 1823 (WO54/542) but by October 1824, had been restored to their former level (WO54/546). On the 24th October 1827, Isaac was classified as a Stoveman with his pay and watch money increased £44.4.0d per annum (WO54/558). He was still working as a Stoveman in October 1830, then aged 70, with over 30 years' service (WO54/570).

Isaac Webb (2) worked in the Corning House as a Labourer earning 2/2d per day in January 1806, at which time he had 9 months' service (Supply 5/224). By June 1807, he was employed as a Stoveman with his pay reduced to 2/-d per day, but he was then allowed to watch in turn, for which he received 1/-d (Supply 5/226). He continued to be employed as a Stoveman, i.e. at the Gloom Stoves drying gunpowder, until at least February 1814, when he was paid 2/8d per day but no longer allowed to watch (Supply 5/230).

James Webb was a common Labourer who was paid 17/-d for work carried out by the Engineers' Department in the Manufactory between the 15th and 21st July 1809 (Supply 5/228).

John Webb (1) worked as a Millman in August 1812 earning 3/-d per day and, in addition, he was allowed 6d per night when on duty (Supply 5/229).

John Webb (2) worked as a casual Labourer in the Engineers' Department in September 1812, earning 2/8d per day for a six-day week (WO54/512).

Samuel Webb was working in the Corning House in June 1807. He was paid 2/2d per day and, in addition, Corning House Men were allowed to watch in turn, for which they received 1/-d (Supply 5/226).

William Webb applied for work at the Mills on the 30th November 1787, having previously worked as a Cooper for Mr. Walton (Winters, *op.cit.* p.28). In May 1804, he was working as a Labourer in the "Engineers' Dept. Established" earning 1/6d per day, with "one day extra allowed per week agreeable to the Board's Order dated 12th March 1801" (Supply 5/222). In August 1808, a William Webb was employed as a Labourer in the Storekeeper's Department "setting and drawing stoves and in the willow plantations" earning 2/-d per day (Supply 5/227).

James Welch was working as a casual Labourer in the Engineers' Department in September 1812, earning 2/8d per day for a six-day-week (WO54/512).

William Welch worked as a casual Labourer in the Engineers' Department in September 1812, earning 2/8d per day for a six-day-week (WO54/512). He was still labouring on a casual basis in February 1814, and was then a 19-year-old bachelor living in Waltham Abbey (WO54/516).

Samuel Wells worked as a casual Labourer in the Engineers' Department in September 1812 earning 2/8d per day for a six-day-week (WO54/512).
Thomas Wells was working as an extra Bargeman in February 1814, earning 3/10d per day (Supply 5/230).

Thomas West was engaged as a Labourer on the 5th March 1797, and also enlisted as a Private in the Volunteer Company (Supply 5/219).

William West, son of Thomas West, worked in the New Corning House earning 1/6d per day. On the 18th April 1801, this building blew up with a tremendous explosion. Nine men were in the building, including William, and all were killed, together with four horses (Supply 5/220). A Report on the circumstances of the widows and children of those killed prepared and sent to the Board by the Storekeeper, stated that Mary West was William's mother and was aged 46. Her husband was a Day Labourer and she had 4 children, receiving part of her subsistence for the labours of her son. She was awarded a pension of 2/-d per week (Supply 5/220) which commenced on the 19th May 1801 (Supply 5/231). There was considerable confusion over William's mother's name, but it was clarified in a letter to the Board dated the 5th January 1802, in which it was stated that she had been married to one West several years before, but was then known as Mary Edwards, and had been incorrectly reported by the Mills as West. She lived in Cheshunt (Supply 5/231) and was still in receipt of her weekly pension of 2/-d in 1837 (Supply 5/237).

George Wheatley was engaged on the 7th December 1812, as an occasional Labourer by the Engineers' Department and paid 2/8d per day. In February 1816, he was a 60-year-old married man with 2 married and 2 unmarried children, living in Waltham Abbey (WO54/516).

John Wheatley was working as a Saltpetre Refiner in June 1807, as he was in September 1810. During this period he was paid 2/-d per day and when "not working [extra] allowed to watch" (Supply 5/226 and 5/228).

Edwin Wheble was appointed Surgeon at the Mills in 1839, replacing Robert Hilton (Winters, *op.cit.* p.122). The 1841 Census recorded Edwin as a Surgeon-Apothecary living with his family in Romelands.

James White was employed as the Foreman of Labourers in the Engineers' Department earning 2/-d per day. Between August and September 1790, he worked within the Manufactory with his wages submitted by William Spry, Colonel commanding the Royal Engineers, and paid by the Storekeeper, James Wright. He signed for his pay "with a firm hand" (WASC 1382). His name appeared on an anonymous letter to "His Majesties Hon. Board of Ordnance" and recorded, "men whose work is very dangerous were frequently found in public houses neglecting his Majesties duty and whose names ought to be reported." A note dated the 7th February 1792, asked that the matter be referred to Major Congreve and that he to "cause an enquiry to be made and report the result to the Board." Major Congreve held his enquiry and the third and last name in the Report was White's when he was described as "very troublesome & scorns to use those well which are placed under him a general murmur reigns throughout the yard" (Supply 5/190). Winters also referred to these incidents in his *Centenary Memorial* (pp.34/35) and recorded that complaints were made without foundation, while White was described as the "Foreman of Labouring Hands." A Report on the Marital Status of the Employees made on the 8th May 1801, recorded that he was working as one of the Foreman at 2/-d per day, and that he was married without issue (Supply 5/221). He was still employed as a Foreman of Labour in the "Engineers' Dept. Established" in 1807, earning 2/6d per day (Supply 5/222). A letter dated the 16th July 1806, recommended, "Mr. White, Foreman of Labourers, should retire from the situation upon 6/- per week, which would be borne upon the Charity List in consideration of his service." The letter went on, "the vacancy in the appointment of Foreman of Labourers... is not to be filled up for the present" (Supply 5/197).

Daniel Wicks was a Carpenter 2nd class, and was paid £1.8.4d for work carried out by the Engineers' Department in the Manufactory between the 15th and 21st July 1809 (Supply 5/228).

Charles Wiggs worked in June 1807 as "a Labourer in various parts of the Manufactory, setting and drawing stoves, loading and unloading barges etc.", for which he was paid 2/-d per day (Supply 5/226). This was also the case in August 1808, when he was also allowed to watch in turn (Supply 5/227). A letter dated the 26th July 1819 recorded an increase in Wiggs' pay as a Cooper from 2/-d to 2/6d per day (Supply 5/199). This rate of pay would indicate that he was under training and had yet to achieve the outputs expected of a trained artisan. He was still working as a Cooper on the same rate of pay in September 1810, and like all Coopers, he was not allowed to watch (Supply 5/228). In August 1812 he was being paid 4/6d per day, the rate of pay for a trained Cooper (Supply 5/230). Charles was still a Cooper in June 1818 but, in common with the majority of the workforce, his wage had been cut and was then only 4/-d per day (Supply 5/231). At that date he was a 24-year-old bachelor living in Waltham Abbey.

Thomas Wiggs was an Apprentice in September 1812 to the Master Millwright at 6/8d per week (WO54/512).

John Wilday was born circa 1762 and had trained as a Baker before being engaged as a Labourer at the Faversham Gunpowder Mills on the 26th January 1789. In August of that year he worked "at the Stoves at Night time" (Supply 5/114). He continued to work as a Stoveman, but by 1796, he was a Labourer in the Dusting and Reeling Houses (Supply 5/72). He was still at Faversham in 1825 when he was stopped 1/[d for medical attendance between the 1st July and the 31st December, at which time he was a Stoveman (Supply 5/116) He was still a Stoveman in April 1828, when he was paid 2/4d per day (Supply 5/116f). Soon after this he was classified as a Charcoal Burner and was transferred to the Mills at Waltham Abbey on the 19th November 1832. At Waltham he worked as a Labourer in the Cylinder House making charcoal, and was paid 2/2d per day as well as being allowed to watch in turn, which gave him an annual income of £39.0.0d (WO54/587). When he came to Waltham he was a married man with 5 children. He continued to work as a Cylinderman, but by April 1834, his annual income had been cut to £28.5.6d as opposed to his previous earnings of £39.0.0d (WO54/593). On the 11th April 1834 he moved into a small cottage at the junction of High Bridge Street and Powder Mill Lane, previously occupied by George Miller (Supply 5/237) for which he paid rent of 2/-d, and this has been identified as part of Plot No. 61 on the Town Map in Appendix 1. John and his wife did not live in their cottage for long, since a Return of Properties owned by the Board dated December 1834 and prepared by the Engineers' Office, recorded that John had been superannuated and his cottage was to be let to J Wraight, Cylinder House Man (Supply 5/237). When he retired he was some 72 years' old and had served the Board for 45 years. His name did not appear in the 1841 Census for Waltham Abbey.

David Wilkie, born circa 1788 in Ireland (Winters, *op. cit.* p. 150), was appointed as a Clerk at Keyham Point on the 7th March 1806 before being transferred to the Royal Gunpowder Mills as the Second Clerk on the 28th July 1806. At Waltham he was paid £80.0.0d per annum and, in addition, allowances of £12.0.0d and £8.0.0d per annum for lodgings and coal and candles respectively (Supply 5/226). On the 25th July 1812, he joined the Royal Artillery as a Lieutenant and served until the 19th May 1813, when he rejoined the Mills and was reappointed as the Second Clerk (Supply 5/230). He served as the Second Clerk in June 1818, and his basic salary was still £80.0.0d per annum, but with a gratuity of £35.0.0d, in addition to which, he was then entitled to a house, coupled with £8.0.0d per annum for heat and light (Supply 5/231).

A Statement dated the 4th April 1821 of "monies to which the public were entitled to receive credit between the 1st January and the 31[St] December 1820 shewing the amounts received by the

Storekeeper", recorded that David Wilkie, Second Clerk, had been living rent-free in a Board of Ordnance house since the 14th April 1815, and that the dwelling was within the Manufactory on Horse Mill Island (Supply 5/232). The house in question is Plot No. 97 on the Town Map in Appendix 1. Wilkie occupied the position of Second Clerk until 1839 and during this period his salary, gratuity and allowance for heat and light gradually increased to £145.0.0d per annum. He also remained a bachelor, living on Horse Mill Island (WO54/623). Following the death of Thomas Littler, Wilkie was appointed as the First Clerk on the 19th August 1839, but his salary remained unchanged. The 1841 Census recorded that he was still living on Horse Mill Island (known as Wall Marsh in the Census) with John and Elizabeth Tyler as his servants.

William Wilkinson was appointed as a Plantation Labourer on the 30th November 1840 at 2/6d per day (Supply 5/238). In the 1841 Census he and his wife, Eleanor, and their 2 children were living on Lower Island.

Charles Wilks was born circa 1760 and was the son of Edward Wilks, who, at one time, was the Storekeeper at Faversham (*FGPR*, p.87). Charles was to serve the Ordnance Board for some 64 years. He started his career with the Board on the 1st October 1780 as the Overseer of Works at Chatham, and was promoted as the Clerk of the Works there on the 25th August 1783. On the 1st December 1794, he was transferred to the gunpowder mills at Faversham as the Clerk of the Works, before occupying the same position at Waltham Abbey on the 26th February 1800. Charles continued at Waltham Abbey, and, in September 1804, he was described as the Clerk of the Works for "the Powder Mills in general." On the 9th March 1805, he was appointed as the Superintendent at the Gunpowder Mills at Ballincollig in County Cork, Ireland, following their purchase by the Board from a private owner. Charles continued as the Storekeeper in Ireland until Government production ceased there in 1815. In 1808 he was appointed as a magistrate and elected a Freeman of Cork in 1814 (*FGPR* p.87).

While he was in charge at Ballincollig, he submitted plans to Matthew Boulton, the Birmingham steam engine pioneer concerning "A scheme for the valves of large pumps" (8th October 1811) and they included pen and wash drawings and plans, and sections of his designs. He also published the works, *Observations on the Height of Carriage Wheels, The Comparative Advantage of employing one or two Horses with one Carriage,* and *Repairing Roads* (1814). As Superintendent of the Ballincollig Factory, it was he, therefore, who began the overhaul of the site, improving access from the Kilkenny Road, re-building the Inniscarra Bridge. He also expanded the barracks, mills and administrative buildings and offices, and built cavalry barracks and canals on the site. It is speculated that he married his wife, Elizabeth, in Ireland. Elizabeth died on the 11th May 1831 at the age of 73, and is buried in the Church of the Holy Cross, Waltham Abbey.

Wilks returned to Waltham Abbey as the Storekeeper on the 15th January 1825, where his annual salary was £600.0.0d, plus an allowance of £25.0.0d for coals and candles and £27.7.6d in lieu of "attendance in Labour." He was also provided with a house in Powder Mill Lane. He was then a 64-year-old married man with one child (WO54/554). On the 22nd October 1827 he went to London, and Winters in his in his Centenary Memorial (p.98) quoted an interesting entry from the imprest book which read "Chase hire from Waltham to London and back for Charles Wilks for imprest, £2. One day's extra expenses £2." The extra expenses were equivalent to three weeks' wages for a Labourer. By the Board's Order No. 609 dated the 28th October 1831, Charles Wilks was made redundant that day. It also stated that the post of Storekeeper was to be abolished, thereby saving

£652.7.6d per annum (WO54/581). Nevertheless, by 1832, Wilks had filled one of the 4 most important government-appointed posts in the Board of Ordnance as Storekeeper of the Purfleet Gunpowder Magazine on the north bank of the Thames, following the death of the incumbent there, Mr. Godfrey (Winters, *op cit*, p.93). The Purfleet site consisted of 5 huge storage depots, where all gunpowder was received and stored, prior to distribution. Only one of the Magazines survives as a listed building.

Charles died on 17th November 1847. His tomb in Swanscombe churchyard bears the inscription:

Charles Wilks Esq.
formerly of Purfleet Essex
and late of Greenhithe
Died 17 November 1847
aged 87 years, 64 of which he served in
Her Majesty's Navy and Ordnance

(*Charles Wilks Esq.* (1760-1847) by R. Venn)

Further information on the Wilks' family can be found in the *Faversham Gunpowder Personnel Register, 1573-1840.*

G Williams was engaged as a Labourer on the 8th July 1796. In September 1798, he was working in the Dusting House and had enrolled in the Volunteer Company as a Private (Supply 5/219).

Joseph Williams was engaged as an occasional Labourer by the Engineers' Department on the 7th March 1815, and was paid 2/8d per day. In February 1816, he was a 23-year-old married man with 2 children living in Waltham Abbey (WO54/516).

Samuel Williams was working as a Saltpetre Refiner in August 1812 (Supply 5/229) as he was in February 1814 (Supply 5/230). During this period he was paid 2/8d per day, and in addition, when not working extra, he was allowed to watch in turn.

Thomas Williams was working as a Millman in January 1806 earning 2/6d per day (Supply 5/224). A Thomas Williams was a Puntman in June 1807 at 2/-d per day (Supply 5/226).

William Williams (1) was born circa 1755, and was engaged as a Bricklayer's Labourer in the Engineers' Department on the 14th December 1811 (WO54/516). In September 1812 he was paid 2/8d per day for a six-day-week (WO54/512). He was still working as a Labourer for the Engineers' Department in February 1814 earning the same money. At that date he was a 60-year-old married man with 5 children living in Waltham Abbey (WO54/516).

William Williams (2) was working as a Saltpetre Refiner in August 1812 (Supply 5/229) as he was in February 1814 (Supply 5/230). During this period he was paid 2/8d per day, and, in addition, when not working extra, he was allowed to watch in turn.

William Wilson was working as a Labourer "setting and drawing stoves and in the willow plantations" in September 1810 at 2/-d per day, and allowed to watch in turn (Supply 5/228). In August 1812, he was employed as a Millman earning 3/-d per day, and, in addition, he was allowed 6d per night when on duty (Supply 5/229).

John Wilson was working as a Labourer "setting and drawing stoves and in the willow plantations" in August 1812. He was paid 2/8d per day and allowed to watch in turn (Supply 5/229).

William Wiltshaw was engaged as an occasional Labourer by the Engineers' Department on the 11th November 1815 and paid 2/8d per day. In February 1816, he was a 20-year-old bachelor living in Waltham Abbey (WO54/516). His age indicated that he was possibly the son of Thomas and Elizabeth in the following entry.

Thomas Wiltshire (also Wiltshaw and Willsher) was working as a Corning House Man in January 1806 earning 2/2d per day, and at that date had been employed by the Ordnance for some 12 months (Supply 5/224). He continued to work in the Corning House, and by August 1808 was earning 2/6d per day. In addition to his pay, he was allowed to watch in turn, for which he received one shilling (Supply 5/227).

At 11.15 a.m. on the 27th November 1811, there was a huge explosion at No. 4 Press House, and the ensuing fire engulfed the Corning House and the Reel House which also exploded. There was much damage in the town with many windows shattered, and reports in the press recorded that the explosion was heard as far away as Hackney, Blackwall and Marylebone (Winters, *op.cit.* p.72). Thomas Wiltshire, by now the Foreman of the Reeling House, was the only survivor, but was severely injured. It was agreed by the Board that his wife, Elizabeth, should continue to receive his pay of 2/10d per day, and that the surgeon, Robert Hilton, should be allowed to receive payment for "extra to effect Wiltshire's recovery" (Supply 5/199). However, Wiltshire died on the 13th December, leaving Elizabeth, who was pregnant, and 7 children, William (16) and James (13) – who were both in service together – Mary (11) Thomas (9) John (7) Sarah (5) and Ann (3). The Board agreed to pay the funeral expenses (Supply 5/229) and Elizabeth was awarded a pension of 19/10d per week with effect from the 14th December 1811 (Winters, *op.cit.* p.87). She continued to receive her pension under the name Wiltshaw over the years, usually quoted in most documents as £51.11.4d per annum (Supply 5/237). The 1825 Rateable Valuation for Waltham Abbey (D/DHfB29) showed that Widow 'Wilsher' was living with her family in High Bank cottages on the north side of High Bridge Street, being part of Plot No. 48 on the Town Map in Appendix 1, and the 1841 Census recorded that she lived in Meeting House Row with her son, John.

William Wines, born circa 1777, started his Apprenticeship in the general manufacture of gunpowder on the 16th February 1789; he was then aged 12 and was paid 1/-d per day (Supply 5/213). He was recorded as having completed his general Apprenticeship at the end of January 1793, and on the 1st February of that year was grinding Saltpetre and Charcoal (Supply 5/216). He continued as a Millman throughout 1793 and 1794, and .his rate of pay for the whole of this period was 1/6d per day (Supply 5/216 & 5/217).

Robert Coleman, Clerk of the Cheque, recorded in his Minute Book that on the 13th/14th May 1793, William had gone away from his watch without leave and was ordered off his watch (Winters, *op.cit.* p.39). Winters also stated that William lived in the Market Place where Mr. H. I. James lived in 1881. He enlisted as a Private in the Volunteer Company on the 7th May 1794 (Supply 5/219). Coleman also recorded in his Minute Book that on the 9th March 1795, the Rounder had found W. Wines, watchman, asleep on duty and he was chequered (Winters, *op.cit.* p.45). William was still a Brimstone Millman in June 1795, as he was in 1798 when he was still serving with the Volunteer Company (Supply 5/219).

George Winter was set to work as a Labourer by Daniel Cornish in October 1787 at 9/-d per week, possibly renovating the Mills following their purchase by the Government from Mr. Walton (Winters, op.cit. p.29).

George Wiseman was working as a Saltpetre Refiner earning 2/-d per day in January 1806. He was also allowed to watch in turn when not working extra, and at that date, he had some 3 months' service (Supply 5/224). He was still a Refiner in February 1814, but was then paid 2/8d per day and still allowed to watch (Supply 5/230).

David Witaker was engaged as an occasional Labourer by the Engineers' Department on the 31st July 1814 at 2/8d per day. He was a 31-year-old married man with 3 children living in Cheshunt in February 1816 (WO54/516).

Elias Wolstenholme was employed on the 11th June 1825 as a temporary Labourer for 4 months, and was to be discharged at the end of October. At the time, he was a 25-year-old bachelor living in Waltham Abbey (WO54/550). However, he was retained as a Labourer within the Engineers Department earning 2/2d per day, which was equivalent to £33.18.2d per annum (WO54/558). This was also the case in April 1828 (WO54/562).

William Wolstenholme, a trained Carpenter, started at his trade in the Engineers' Department on the 14th April 1826. In April 1827, he was paid 4/1d per day, and at that date he was a 57-year-old widower with 7 children, living in Waltham Abbey (WO54/558). He was still in employment with the Board in October 1827 (WO54/558).

James Wood, born circa 1765, was first employed as an occasional Labourer in the Engineers' Department on the 7th May 1812. In September 1816, as an occasional or casual Labourer, he was paid 2/4d per day; he was then a 47-year-old widower without children (WO54/516). James continued to work for the Engineers' Department "occasionally as required" for the same rate of pay until April 1823, when he was described as a Labourer and paid 2/2d per day for 313 days, giving him an annual income of £33.18.2d (WO54/542). This would indicate that he had been appointed to the Establishment as others had been appointed in the Engineers' Department, probably on the 8th March 1822.

A Return of Persons belonging to the Civil Establishment of the Ordnance at the Gunpowder and Small Arms Manufactories at Waltham Abbey, Faversham and Enfield, showing in detail several points of information called for by the Master General and Board's Order dated the 31st January 1831, recorded that James Wood was one of 15 Labourers to be employed at Waltham Abbey and Enfield. He was to be paid 2/2d per day, and employed to undertake different services as a Labourer in the Manufactories where steadiness and sobriety were particularly required (WO54/575). He was still employed on the same terms in October 1831. He was then 65 years' old and still a widower (WO54/575).

George Woodbridge was a Carpenter 2nd class in the Engineers' Department, who was paid £1.8.4d for work carried out by them in the Manufactory between the 15th and 21st July 1809 (Supply 5/228). By September 1810, he had been appointed as a Cooper and was paid 2/6d per day but was not allowed to watch (Supply 5/228). In August 1812, he was a achieving the outputs expected of a fully trained Cooper, since he was then paid 4/6d per (Supply 5/229). This also applied in February 1814 (Supply 5/230).

James Woodbridge was working as a Millman earning 2/3d per day in January 1806 (Supply 5/224). This was also the case in June 1807, but, in addition, he was allowed an extra 3d if he worked at night (Supply 5/226). He was described as a Charcoal Millman in August 1812, then earning 3/-d per day and, in addition, he was allowed to watch in turn, for which he was paid 1/6d per night (Supply 5/229). In February 1814, James was employed in the Dusting House with his pay and allowance unchanged (Supply 5/230).

Thomas Woodbridge, born circa 1798, was working as a Cooper in August 1812 earning 2/4d per day and, in common with all Coopers, he was not allowed to watch (Supply 5/229). This was also the case in February 1814 (Supply 5/230) and his rate of pay would indicate that he was under training and had yet to achieve the outputs expected of a trained artisan. Thomas was still a Cooper in June 1818, but his wage had risen to 3/6-d per day (Supply 5/231). At that date he was a 20-year-old bachelor living in Waltham Abbey. However, when the Establishment was reduced in numbers in September 1818, Thomas was not retained (Supply 5/231).

William Woodbridge, a Carpenter by trade, was set to work by Daniel Cornish in October 1787, possibly renovating the Mills following their purchase by the Government from Mr. Walton (Winters, *op.cit.* p.28).

Thomas Woodhouse was working as a Millman in January 1806 earning 2/3d per day (Supply 5/224) and continued to be employed as such with his pay unchanged until at least September 1810 (Supply 5/228).

James Wraight/Wreight, born in 1801, was engaged as a Saltpetre Refiner at Faversham before being appointed as a Charcoal Burner there on the 26th April 1824, for which he was paid 2/4d per day. He was then a 22-year-old bachelor. In December 1826, he was stopped one shilling for medical attendance between the 1st July and the 31st December (Supply 5/116). He continued to be a Charcoal Burner in the Kent Mills until he was transferred to Waltham Abbey in November 1832 (Supply 5/207) where he worked as a Labourer in the Cylinder House, making charcoal by the new process recently installed

461

there. He was paid 2/2d per day and allowed to watch in turn, which gave him an annual income of £39.0.0d (WO54/587). In common with the majority of the workforce his wages had been reduced by April 1833, and his income was then £33.9.6d, on which he had to support his wife and 3 children (WO54/593). However, by 1839, his wages had been restored to £39 per annum (WO54/623).

On the 16th April 1834, two mills exploded "when shut up" and James, who was on watch, was called before Lt. Col. Moody as a witness (Winters, op.cit. p.103). Late in 1834 or early 1835, James moved into a cottage owned by the Board at the junction of High Bridge Street and Powder Mill Lane, which had been vacated by John Wilday who had retired, and his rental was 2/-d per week (Supply 5/237). The tenement has been identified as part of Plot No. 61 on the Town Map in Appendix 1. The 1841 Census confirmed that he was still living in the same cottage with his wife Lucy and children, Sarah (10) George (8) Helen (6) Winford? (4) Mary (2) and Eliza (4 months) together with two youths, Edward Findlay and James Bell, both aged 15, who may have been Apprentices at the Mills.

Several of the Wraight family subsequently worked at the Mills, and more information on the family can be found in the *Faversham Gunpowder Register 1573 –1840*.

Frederick Wright, born circa 1815, was the son of James Wright, Jnr. A Return dated the 1st April 1831 recorded, "Frederick Wright, a single lad, aged sixteen and a half, was appointed as Apprentice to the respective officers on the 15th November 1830." He was paid £46.19.0d per annum – a considerably higher wage than other Apprentices (WO54/575). A note for 1834 in Winters' book, *Centenary Memorial* (p.103) recorded, "Fred. Wright, an apprentice to the Rex Officers, and Hugh Jones, master worker paid, viz., Fred Wright, 79 days at 3s,

£11.17.0d; Hugh Jones for instructing Fred. Wright, 79 days at 6d, £1.19.6d." On the 4th July 1837, Frederick Wright made an application to be appointed as Assistant Master Mixer, with an increase of 1/-d per day. On the 9th November that year, he was sent to Faversham "for the improvement in manufacturing gunpowder" (Winters, *op.cit.* p.104). He returned from Faversham in October 1838 and was appointed to serve Hugh Jones, the Master Worker. A note dated the 22nd October stated that his salary was to be £100.0.0d per annum (Winters, *op.cit.* p.102). There seems to have been a major upheaval when Frederick returned from Faversham, for on the 22nd October, Hugh Jones retired taking his pension, Thomas Sadd was appointed as the Master Worker (WO54/626) and Frederick Wright resigned (WO54/602).

Wright went to the U.S.A. where he became a School Teacher. Chip Bragg, an American researching the manufacture of gunpowder during the American Civil War, discovered that Frederick Wright was the only man in the South who had seen powder made by the incorporation process, so Wright was recruited and employed as the Chief Powdermaker, initially in the fall of 1861 at the Manchester, Tennessee, Powder Mills, and then at the Augusta Mills in 1862. He subsequently worked in nitre mines until captured by Federal forces on the 28th December 1863. He remained in the munitions industry after the war, and died in the 1870's. His brother, James, also lived in Tennessee.

Henry Wright (1) was the son of James Wright Jnr., the Deputy Store Keeper at the Mills in 1822. He wrote three long letters to Winters recalling his memories of the Waltham Abbey Powder Mills, the workforce and townspeople, which appear in his book *Centenary Memorial,* published in 1887. Henry was born circa 1807 and appointed as an Apprentice in the London District on the 28th January 1828 ((WO54/593). His mentor in London was his uncle Joseph, who had been the Clerk of Works at Faversham until 1823 when he was appointed the Principal Clerk of the Works at the Tower of London. In his own words, Henry was appointed as a "superior apprentice under his uncle and received pay of 3/6d per day. His drillings were that I was to become a Clerk of Works" (Winters, *op.cit.* p.145). He was time-served in 1833, and appointed as a temporary Foreman of the Works on the 11th December 1833 in the Eastern District, being stationed at Ipswich. On the 11th July 1834 he was appointed as a Clerk of Works, 4th Class with a salary of £109.10.0d per annum and entitled to a house. At the time, he was a 27-year-old bachelor (WO54/593).

He returned to Waltham Abbey in 1835 as a temporary Clerk of Works and the successor to William Drayson (Supply 5/237) who was his godfather. Although he was entitled to a house, he lived with his father in Powder Mill Lane. His sojourn at Waltham was brief and he was soon posted to the Dover District, before sailing to Canada with his small family on the 25th August 1839. He returned to England in 1846 and continued to supervise public works throughout the country until he retired to Finchley, circa 1868 where he died on the 26th December 1885 (Winters, *op. cit.* pp.141/151).

Henry Wright (2) trained as a Butcher but joined the Engineers' Department as a casual Labourer on the 7th May 1814. In February 1817, he was being paid 2/4d per day as a Labourer and was then a 22-year-old bachelor living in Waltham Abbey (WO54/520).

James Wright, Snr. was appointed to the Ordnance service at Woolwich on the 1st July 1758 by Lt. General, His Grace, the Duke of Richmond. He was employed as an Extra Clerk at Woolwich on the 13th May 1760 and the Clerk of the Stores in Portugal on the 30th April 1762. On returning to England, he was appointed the Clerk of the Cheque at Priddy's Hard, a major

Navy Armaments department, on the 27th January 1777. On the 1st November 1787, he was posted to Waltham Abbey as the Storekeeper of the newly acquired Gunpowder Mills, with an annual salary of £150.0.0d and an additional £25.0.0d for accommodation (Supply 5/216). In July 1795 he was the Captain commanding the Volunteer Company (Supply 5/217). By May 1804, his salary had increased to £300.0.0d per annum, plus £25.0.0d per annum for house rent and a further allowance of £25.0.0d for coal and candles (Supply 5/222). While at Waltham, Wright carried out a series of experiments on the manufacture of charcoal using the cylinder method which the mills operated at Fernhurst and Fisher Street in Sussex for Major Congreve, the Comptroller of the Royal Laboratory at Woolwich.

In December 1804 it was recorded, "the Storekeeper's accounts are shamefully behind and renders the office liable to all censure which the Board intimate." In his defence Wright replied, "I am employed every day (Sundays included) from 9 o'clock in the morning until 6 or 7 at night (one and a half hours excepted for dinner-time) in the duty of my office, and ever was my wish to discharge my business with care and faithfulness" (Winters, op.cit. p.62). Winters also noted, "on the 15th January Wright received a remonstration" [from the Board] and on the 6th March that year, there was an entry in the accounts which read "Paid James Wright, late storekeeper, allowed by order of the Board, £11.14s.4d for travelling 148 miles [chase hire and turnpike] 1s 7d per mile, viz. travelling into Sussex to pay bills and take a general survey and remain at the Cylinder Works, from Waltham Abbey to Fisher Street 60 miles, to Fernhurst and back 16 miles; to Petworth and back, 12 miles; to Waltham Abbey, 60 miles – 148miles" (Winters, op.cit. p.63). Whether Wright was discharged or resigned is not known.

More information on the Wright family can be found in the *Faversham Gunpowder Personnel Register 1573-1840.*

James Wright, Jnr., born circa 1778, was the son of James Wright, Snr., and was appointed as a Junior Clerk at Faversham on the 17th April 1801 (Supply 5/232) before transferring to Waltham Abbey in the same position on the 1st September 1801. At Waltham he was paid £70.0.0d per annum, together with annual allowances for lodging, coals and candles of £20.16.0d and £12.10.0d respectively (Supply 5/222). James married and he and his wife, Lucy, baptised their first child, also Lucy, on the 3rd March 1805 (Winters, *Our Parish Registers*). He was promoted to First Clerk on the 20th March 1805 with an increased salary of £80.0.0d per annum, but his allowances remained unchanged Supply 5/226). The Board purchased the Corn Mill house and its buildings in June 1809. The dwelling house, in Romelands, was, "to be appointed to the first clerk," and was to be "provided with an iron safe to preserve the documents of the Board in" (Winters, *op.cit.* p. 66). No firm evidence has been found to prove when James, as the First Clerk, moved into this property, or indeed, when he vacated it. Winters in his book, *Centenary Memorial* (p. 67) recorded, "This house was occupied in 1818 by Mr. James Wright, storekeeper, and in which James Wright of Moorsburg, Tennessee, America, was born in that year." This statement is incorrect on two counts because in 1818, James was the Clerk of the Cheque and in that year he was living in Powder Mill Lane.

James was appointed Clerk of the Cheque on the 26th February 1812 at a salary of £150.0.0d per annum, with £12.10.0d per annum for coals and candles, a £20.0.0d gratuity, and a house provided. He was also placed "upon the Establishment" (Supply 5/229). On the same date, Thomas Littler was promoted in his place as the First Clerk. A Statement dated the 4th April 1821 of "monies to which the public were entitled to receive credit between the 1st January and the 31St December 1820 shewing the amounts received by the Storekeeper" recorded that James Wright, Clerk of the Cheque, by an Order of the Board dated the 12th September 1814, was entitled to live rent-free in a tenement owned by the Board (Supply 5/232). A Return of Properties owned by the Board prepared by the Royal Engineer's Office in December 1834, recorded that James Wright had occupied a house with garden on the west side of the River Lea since the 8th September 1814 (Supply 5/237) while a similar Return prepared by the same office in 1840 noted that Wright was the first occupant, i.e., it was newly built, and comprised of Plots 93 and 94 on the Town Map in Appendix 1. The building still stands. The Return of April 1821 also recorded that James was renting some 14 acres of Lammas - or half-year land - at £1.1.0d per acre, with effect from the 1st May 1820 (Supply 5/232).

Continuing with his career at the Mills, James remained the Clerk of the Cheque until March 1822. During the period from 1812 to 1822, his basic salary remained at £150.0.0d per annum but by 1822 his service gratuity was also £150.0.0d per annum, and he also received the same allowance of £12.10.0d for coals and candles (Supply 5/232). It was also the custom for senior members of the staff to be provided with "attendant labour," possibly to act as gardeners, but this 'perk' was withdrawn on the 30th June 1821, and a monetary grant of £13.16.0d paid in lieu (Supply 5/232). James was appointed Deputy Storekeeper on the 20th March 1822 with a salary of £300.0.0d per annum, provided with a rent free house and allowances amounting to £39.17.6d per annum. He was then 47 years' old, had just over 21 years' service and had 9 children (WO54/546). To save money, the Board abolished the position of Storekeeper on the 28th October 1831, and Lt. Col. Moody, R.E. was appointed to have the general superintendence of the Establishment at Waltham Abbey. Mr. Wright was to have charge of the Store Department (Winters, op.cit. p.102) with the same salary and allowances (WO54/587). In April 1833, he was severely reprimanded by the Board for allowing two employees to remove Government stores from the Mills at Waltham Abbey, and the two were apprehended by the Metropolitan Police (Supply 5/208).

The 1841 Census recorded that James, described as an Ordnance Storekeeper, his wife Lucy, together with their daughters Lucy (35) and Eliza (25) were living in Powder Mill Lane with their servant, Mary Dowsett. Winters, in his publication, *Our Parish Registers*, recorded that a tomb in the churchyard, raised slab (near north wall) read "Sacred memory of Mrs. Lucy Wright, wife of James Wright, died 19th September 1845, aged 62."

John Wright (1) was working as a Labourer in the "Engineers' Dept. Established" in May 1804, earning 1/6d per day with "one day extra per week agreeable to the Board's Order dated the 12th March 1801 (Supply 5/222). In February 1814, a John Wright was recorded as being a Puntman earning 2/8d per day (Supply 5/230).

John Wright (2) was appointed as a Saltpetre Refiner at Faversham on the 1st July 1821 and as a Cylinderman there on the 19th November 1832. He transferred to Waltham Abbey and was appointed to the same trade on the 2nd June 1833. In October 1833, he was paid £33.16.0d per annum and, in addition, he was allowed to watch in turn, which increased his annual income to £39.0.0d. He was then a 33-year-old married man with 3 children (WO54/587).

Joseph Wright was employed as an occasional Labourer in the Engineers' Department on the 11th June 1814 at 2/8d per day. He was still in the same position in February 1814, and at that date, was a 23-year-old bachelor living in Waltham Abbey (WO54/516).

Richard Wright replaced William Dunn (1) as a Labourer in the Dusting House in 1793 and was paid 1/6d per day (Supply 5/216). In January 1794, he was working in the Corning House (Supply 5/216) and on the 7th May of that year he enlisted as a Private in the Volunteer Company (Supply 5/219). Richard was employed as a Millman in August 1784, then paid 2/-d per day, and allowed an extra 3d per night when on duty (Supply 5/217). On the 5th December 1798, Wright, together with John Smith, was involved in a Mill explosion which was caused by putting too much powder on the beds than was allowed (Winters, *op.cit.* p.54).

Thomas Wright was set to work as a Labourer by Daniel Cornish in October 1787 at 9/-d per week, possibly renovating the Mills after their purchase from Mr. Walton (Winters, *op.cit.* p.28) and had previously worked as a Millman for Mr. Walton (Winters, *op.cit.* p.31). On the 24th January 1789, Thomas was judged to be unfit for service (Supply 5/212) and a letter from James Wright and J. Clowdesly to Major Congreve dated the 12th September 1789, stated that they had given notice to Thomas Wright, who was not to be employed after the 20th September (WASC 1392).

John Wrighter was working in the Corning House as a general Labourer in February 1793, earning 1/6d per day (Supply 5/216).

Henry Wybrow was working in the Mixing House in February 1814 earning 3/-d per day, in addition to which, he was allowed to watch in turn, for which he received 1/-d per night (Supply 5/230).

Y

William Yaxley was working as a Corning House Man in January 1806 earning 2/2d per day, and at that date, he had been employed with the Ordnance for 1 year (Supply 5/224). He was in the same position with the same wage in June 1807, but was then allowed to watch in turn, for which he received 1/-d per night (Supply 5/226).

Domestic Properties
at the Royal Gunpowder Mills

The first recorded house purchased by the Ordnance Board at Waltham Abbey was in 1805 when it bought the Chequer or Turnpike Inn from the executors of Mr. Ellis Were, who died that year. However, there was a "fine" outstanding to the Wake family, and since Charles Wake was a minor, the transaction was not completed until 1815 when he became of age (WO44/681a). William Newton occupied turnpike house until 1815 at which time it was falling into disrepair. Another 19 properties were purchased in 1808, which were either on the north side of West (High Bridge) Street or in Powder Mill Lane (WO44/681a). A document in this series gives the date of purchase, and, in some cases, who the sitting tenants were. Most of these were, or had been, employed by the Board, and several, such as Samuel Britten, Daniel Cornish, William Turnham, John Pittendrigh and then his son George, Thomas Pallet and then his son William, were still in the same cottages in the 1820s.

A single tenement was purchased the following year; this was either in High Bridge Street or Powder Mill Lane, and was followed by the Pin Factory and its pair of cottages in Romeland on the 9th March 1811 (WO44/681a). The Board redeveloped Horse Mill Island in 1815, and built three more cottages in Powder Mill Lane with materials salvaged from the old buildings demolished on the island. The Board also purchased the Cornmill in Romeland in 1815, and it was suggested that it was used as quarters for the Master Worker, but it was finally decided that it should remain as a mill ((WO44/679). It was possibly in 1815 that the building occupied by James Allsup, the Post Master, was purchased from the Jessop family. This was on the south side of High Bridge Street opposite Powder Mill Lane, and was subsequently divided into two dwellings. Around this time the

Engineers' Department was constructing houses for the senior staff, such as the Storekeeper. In 1816 Newell Cannopp agreed to sell the single dwelling, together with its outbuildings and old barn, to the Board for £600, all of which had formed an old Tanyard on the south side of High Bridge Street. The dwelling was then let to a Mr. Clayson who sub-let it to vagabonds. The dwelling backed onto the extended cooperage and was considered a fire risk. Clayson had no objection to the sale and the dwelling was divided into three tenements; the old barn was demolished and a wooden building was converted into wood sheds-cum privies for two of the tenements (WO44/679).

In 1833 William Drayson surveyed the lands, manufacturing facilities, houses and tenements belonging to the Ordnance Board at Waltham Abbey. Every building on the map he produced was given a reference number, which the Royal Engineers' Office used in the schedules of domestic dwellings they produced in subsequent years. These schedules gave the location of the building, the names of the present occupiers and when they were admitted, the names of the previous occupiers and, if the property was then vacant, who the next tenant was to be. The following tables are based on the schedules produced by the Engineers' Department in 1834 and 1840, the 1825 valuation of Waltham Abbey and a list of properties owned by the Board in 1821, coupled with information listed in various Labour Returns noted within the main text.

Using Drayson's reference system, the majority of the tenements are shown below on a modified form of Crawter's map of Waltham Abbey for 1826 (WAMP 900/172).

William Drayson Ref. No.	Location	Description	1821	1825	1834	1840
16	Lower Island	Cottage	Henry Myers, Warder.	-	John Nigh	William Nottage
21	High Bridge Street south	Cottage in the Storehouse yard.	-	-	Benjamin Archer	Charles Clayton
39	High Bridge Street north	Master Saltpetre Refiner's House	John Johnson	John Braddock	Samuel Knowler Junior	-do-
44	High Bridge Street north	House	Samuel Britton	Samuel Britton	James O'Brien	-do-
48	High Bridge Street north	5 Cottages known as High Bank	Daniel Allsup Jeremiah Aylin John Cook James Boswell Wm. Turnham	-do- -do- -do- Widow Wiltshaw Wm. Turnham	Thomas Baldock James Boswell then J Simpson Jnr. Edward Essex John Simpson Wm. Turnham	-do- Ed. Turnham Ed. Essex Patrick Hayes M Summers
49	2 Cottages High Bridge Street north	House divided into two dwellings in 1817.	James Allsup (Post Master) Daniel Cornish	James Allsup Daniel Cornish	Mrs Allsup Daniel Cornish	Mrs Allsup Benjamin Cornish
50	High Bridge Street south	House	Joseph Mitchell	-do-	-do-	-do-
51	House in High Bridge Street north	Let to Officers of the Small Arms Factory	William Breeze Clerk of the Survey	G Lovell	G Lovell	Griffith
52	Cottage in High Bridge Street south	One of three tenements formed from a dwellings in the Tanyard	Benjamin Guinn	Benjamin Guinn	B Guinn (deceased), then William Adams	William. Adams

473

53	-do-	-do-	R Hudson	Widow Hudson	Widow Hudson	Widow Hudson
54	-do-	-do-	-	William Dyer	W Bunce (deceased) J Lording	J Davey of the R. Es Dept. Then Jeremiah Betts
55	-do-	Tenement occupied by James Allsup, divided into two in 1817	M Summers	J Clark	M Summers then P Hayes	Unoccupied
56	-do-	-do-	John Braddock	J Braddock moved to No. 39, then Thomas Sadd.	Thomas Sadd, then let to Lt. Col. Moody as an office	Lt. Col Moody
57	High Bridge Street south	House and gardens	Empson Middleton Storekeeper	Empson Middleton Storekeeper	Lt. Col. Moody Royal Engineers	-do-
60	High Bridge Street north	Four cottages	Robert Perkis James Dunn John Archer William Sayer Baker	Robert Perkis W Bunce. Thomas Adams. William Sayer.	Robert Perkis. Unoccupied. - William Sayer	Unoccupied. Unoccupied. John Nigh and then his Widow. William Sayer.
61	Junction of High Bridge Street north and Powder Mill Lane	Two Cottages	James Rowland, carpenter. George Miller.	-do- . -do-	-do- . John Wilday	W Ellison then James Frere – Royal Small Arms Factory. James Wraight.
62	Powder Mill Lane	Three cottages let to senior artisans	John Simpson. George Pittendrigh. William Pallet	John Simpson died 1826, followed by widow, then Thomas Freeman followed by widow. G Pittendrigh. William Pallet.	B Guinn. G Ridpath. Henry Coreham. Richard Higgins.	B Guinn & then William Allsup. John Gibbs. R Higgins.

63	Powder Mill Lane	Three cottages let to senior artisans	John Lockyer William Davies James Pallet	-do- -do- -do-	J O'Brien H Brown Widow Pallet	G Bloomfield -do- Mrs E Pallet
64	Powder Mill Lane	Three houses built with salvaged material from Horse Mill Island and let to senior foremen.	Hugh Jones. Samuel Knower Senior. Thomas Tamkin.	-do-	-do-	Thomas Sadd and then Robert Walker. Robert Slimes. Thomas Hayward.
65	Romeland near church	House & garden	Thomas Austen	Thomas Austen	Thomas Austen	Thomas Austen
70	Romeland	House & garden	Thomas Littler	Thomas Littler	Thomas Littler	–
71	Romeland	Two Cottages	–	Thomas Clayton then Charles Clayton	Frederick Simpson.	Frederick Simpson. John Fleming
73	Powder Mill Lane	House connected to the Engineers Office	William Drayson, Clerk of Works	William Drayson, Clerk of Works	Henry Wright Clerk of Works	John W Baker Clerk of Works
91	Powder Mill Lane	Warder's Lodge at main entrance to Mills.	John Smith	John Smith	John Smith	Sergeant Major Livesy, Warder
92	Powder Mill Lane	Cottage at the entrance to the Mills in Powder Mill Lane built in 1814 for £249 as a surgery, then used as a house for the Office Keeper.	Joseph Brown	Joseph Brown	Joseph Brown	Joseph Brown
93 & 94	Powder Mill Lane	House, stables (93) and garden for senior staff.	James Wright Clerk of the Cheque.	James Wright Deputy Storekeeper.	James Wright Deputy Storekeeper.	James Wright Deputy Storekeeper.

96	Horse Mill Island	A stable converted to a house for the Master Worker	William Newton	Charles Newton, his son. Divided into two in 1826, and then occupied by Jeremiah Betts, Office Keeper for the Royal Engineer's Department and John Simpson, Foreman Millman who probably died before he could move there.	Jeremiah Betts.	J Betts. Reverted to one tenement in 1840 as the accommodation for the Master Worker, then Thomas Sadd. Betts moved to High Bridge Street South into one of the cottages in the old Tanyard.
97	Horse Mill Island	Cottage for the second Clerk	David Wilkie	David Wilkie	David Wilkie	David Wilkie
98	Horse Mill Island	Cottage	Timothy Bates	Timothy Bates	Timothy Bates	Timothy Bates, Warder.
160	Aqueduct Lock	Two cottages which were rent free to the occupiers whose wives were required to ensure that bargemen passing through the lock took no more water than was necessary.	John Brown. Benjamin Poulter.	John Brown. John Goats.	John Brown, John Goats	John Brown.

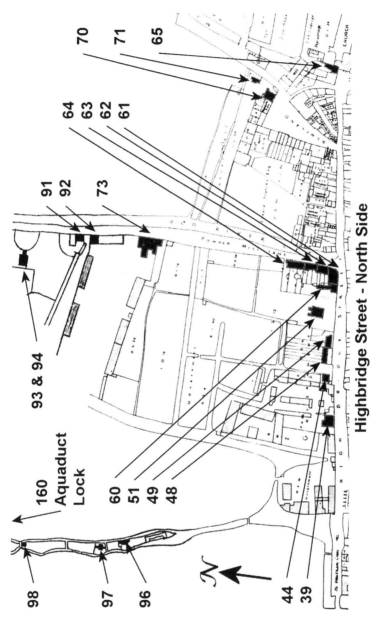

Domestic Properties identified on map of Waltham Abbey surveyed by H. Crawter & Sons, 1826. (WAMP-900-172).

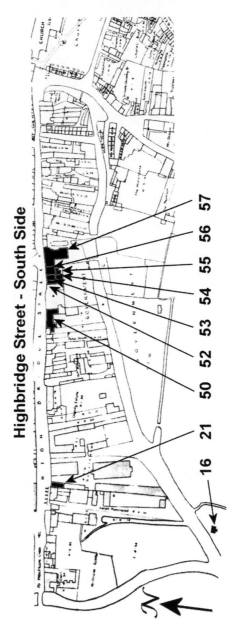

Domestic Properties identified on map of Waltham Abbey surveyed by H. Crawter & Sons, 1826. (WAMP-900-172).

References

National Archives WO Series

WO44/133   Waltham Abbey, houses, cottages, dwellings and buildings attached to the Gunpowder Mills 1840

WO44/679   Purchase of premises from Mr. N Cannop in High Bridge Street with sketch

WO44/681a   Houses purchased by the Ordnance in 1808, 1809, 1811 and 1816

WO54/512   List of Officers and other persons in the employ and pay of the Ordnance at Waltham Abbey in the Manufactory and Engineering Departments in August and September 1812

WO54/516   -do- in the Manufactory in February 1816

WO54/520   -do- in February 1817

WO54/524   -do- in Manufactory & Engineers' Departments in April & June 1818

WO54/528   -do- in May 1819

WO54/532   -do- in September 1820

WO54/536   -do- in April 1821

WO54/536   -do- in Manufactory February 1822

WO54/542   -do- in Manufactory & Engineers' Departments in April 1823

WO54/546   -do- in Manufactory in October 1824

WO54/550   -do- in Manufactory & Engineers' Departments in April & October 1825

WO54/554   -do- in Manufactory & Engineers' Departments in April & October 1826

WO54/558   -do- in Manufactory & Engineers' Departments in April & October 1827

WO54/562   -do- in Manufactory & Engineers' Departments in April & October 1828

WO54/566   -do- in Manufactory & Engineers' Departments in April & October 1829

WO54/570 -do- in Manufactory & Engineers' Departments in April & October 1830

WO54/575 -do- in Manufactory & Engineers' Departments in April & October 1831

WO54/581 -do- in Manufactory & Engineers' Departments in April & October 1832

WO54/587 -do- in Manufactory & Engineers' Departments in April & October 1833

WO54/593 -do- in Manufactory & Engineers' Departments in April 1834

WO54/623 -do- in Manufactory & Engineers' Departments in April 1839

National Archives Supply Series

Supp 5/189 RGF Waltham Abbey Entry Book of Letters, Vol.1, 10th March – 26th September 1789

Supp 5/194 -do- Vol. 7, 2nd January – 11th June 1801

Supp 5/195 -do- Vol. 8, 12th June 1801 – 30th December 1803

Supp 5/196 -do- Vol. 9, 2nd January 1804 - 7th June 1805

Supp 5/197 -do- Vol. 10, 8th June 1805 – 31st December 1806

Supp 5/198 -do- Vol. 11, 1st January 1807 – 21st December 1808

Supp 5/199 -do- Vol. 12, 1st January 1809 – 29th December 1811

Supp 5/200 -do- Vol. 13, 6th January 1812 – 27th December 1816

Supp 5/203 -do- Vol. 16, 21st September 1819 -22nd July 1822

Supp 5/204 -do- Vol. 17, 8th July 1822 – 30th July 1825

Supp -do- Vol. 18, 8th June 1825 – 28th November 1828

5/205
Supp   -do- Vol. 21, 15th November 1830 – 28th December
5/207   1832
Supp   -do- Vol. 22, 2nd January 1833 – 16th June 1838
5/208
Supp   -do- Vol. 2, 22nd August 1788 – 24th March 1789,
5/212   Waltham Abbey Entry Book of Letters
Supp   -do- Vol. 3, 12th March 1789 – 1st September 1789
5/213
Supp   -do- Vol. 4, 2nd September 1789 – 1st April 1790
5/214
Supp   -do- Vol. 5, 2nd April 1790 – 28th March 1792
5/215
Supp   -do- Vol. 6, 3rd April 1792 – 5th September 1794
5/216
Supp   -do- Vol. 7, 6th September 1794 – 31st December
5/217   1795
Supp   -do- Vol. 8, 1st January 1796 – 31st December 1797
5/218
Supp   -do- Vol. 9, 1st January 1798 – 26th July 1799
5/219
Supp   -do- Vol. 10, 30th June 1799 – 2nd May 1801
5/220
Supp   -do- Vol. 11, 8th May 1801 – 31st December 1802
5/221
Supp   -do- Vol. 12, 3rd January 1803 – 12th October 1804
5/222
Supp   -do- Vol. 13, 13th October 1804 – 22nd June 1805
5/223
Supp   -do- Vol. 14, 23rd June 1805 – 29th September 1806
5/224
Supp   -do- Vol. 15, 15th October 1806 – 2nd July 1808
5/226
Supp   -do- Vol. 16, 13th June 1808 – 2nd April 1809
5/227

Supp 5/228 -do- Vol. 17, 1st April 1809 – 18th November 1810

Supp 5/229 -do- Vol. 18, 1st December 1810 – 31st August 1813

Supp 5/230 -do- Vol. 19, 1st September 1813 – 16th December 1817

Supp 5/231 -do- Vol. 20, 1st January 1818 – 24th December 1819

Supp 5/232 -do- Vol. 21, 3rd January 1820 – 10th June 1822

Supp 5/233 -do- Vol. 22, 10th June 1822 – 28th July 1825

Supp 5/234 -do- Vol. 23, 2nd August 1825 – 11th July 1829

Supp 5/235 -do- Vol. 24, 9th July 1829 – 2nd November 1831

Supp 5/236 -do- Vol. 25, 8th November 1831 – 30th December 1834

Supp 5/237 -do- Vol. 26, 3rd January 1835 – 23rd December 1839

Bibliography

PH2005 Huggins, P. J. - *The Wright Family 2005*

WASC 2180 Huggins, P. J. - Waltham Abbey Historical Society, *Waltham Abbey Gunpowder People*

WASC 0158 Simmons, W. H., M.B.E., F.R.I.C. - *A Short History of the Royal Gunpowder Factory at Waltham Abbey*

WASC 2221 Venn, Richard - *Papers on Charles Wilkes*

WASC 0011 Winters, William - *Centenary Memorial of the Royal Gunpowder Factory*, Waltham Abbey, 1887

WASC 0368 Winters, William - *Our Parish Registers*

FGPR The Faversham Society: *Faversham Gunpowder Personnel Register 1573 – 1840*

WAAC   *Waltham Abbey Accident Register* - List of names of injured or killed in accidents at Waltham Abbey

WAI   *Waltham Abbey Images* - An extensive collection of images reflecting 200 years of the production of gunpowder and explosives at Waltham Abbey for the Crown

WAMP   *Waltham Abbey Maps & Plans Collection* - An extensive collection of maps and plans reflecting 200 years of the production of gunpowder and explosives at Waltham Abbey for the Crown

WASC   *Waltham Abbey Special Collection* - An extensive collection of documents reflecting 200 years of the production of gunpowder and explosives at Waltham Abbey for the Crown

WASC 0475   Extracts from Letter Books, Reports, etc, 1787-1805

WASC 1382   Accounts for 1790

WASC 1392   Letter dated 12th February 1789 regarding explosion

WASC 2229   Harding, D. F. – *Small Arms of the East India Company: 1600-1856*, Vol.III Ammunition & Performance
Murphy, Sylvia C.M., 20 November 2011 – *John Braddock - Powder Master*

About the Authors

Derek Armes spent his working life in the construction industry running civil engineering projects in the United Kingdom and Overseas.

He came into historical research by way of family history, and on his retirement joined Ware Museum as a volunteer, accessioning items in the Museum's collection. During his time at Ware Museum he researched and wrote two books relating to Ware in WW1 and WW11.

Following an enforced break from the museum due to a family illness, Derek joined The Royal Gunpowder Mills as a volunteer in their Archive. He researched the documents held at the Mills and at the National Archives at Kew, after which, he wrote this publication with Sandra Taylor.

Sandra Taylor was born in London and has had a life-long passion for its history, as well as that of U.K and European history in general. On retiring from her job as Assistant to the Beadle and part-time Archivist at one of the Great Twelve Livery Companies in London's City, she attended Middlesex University, graduating in 2002 with a B.A. (Hons) degree in English Literary Studies with History.

Thereafter, she joined the Waltham Abbey Historical Society, and is a volunteer at the Epping Forest District Museum in Waltham Abbey where she has digitised all of the museum's photographic collection, and gives support to the Collections' Officer with accessioning. In addition, again as a volunteer, she has researched into the Royal Gunpowder Mills' Archive, producing with Derek this snap-shot social history of the personnel who worked at the Mills from 1787 to 1841.

Printed in Great Britain
by Amazon.co.uk, Ltd.,
Marston Gate.